AMERICAN BOOK DESIGN
AND WILLIAM MORRIS

AMERICAN
BOOK DESIGN
AND
WILLIAM MORRIS

SUSAN OTIS THOMPSON

1977

R.R.BOWKER COMPANY

NEW YORK & LONDON

Published by R. R. Bowker Company
1180 Avenue of the Americas, New York, N.Y. 10036
Copyright © 1977 by Susan Otis Thompson
Printed and Bound in the United States of America

Library of Congress Cataloging in Publication Data

Thompson, Susan Otis.
American book design and William Morris.

Bibliography: p.
Includes index.
1. Book design.   2. Book industries and trade—
United States—History.   3. Morris, William, 1834–
1896.   I. Title.
Z116.A3T47   686.2'24   77-8783
          ISBN 0-8352-0984-9

To Mother, Jack, Louise, Keeler, and Peter

Contents

Illustrations

Preface

LATE IN THE NINETEENTH CENTURY American book design suddenly underwent a dramatic change. This revolution itself was brief but its effect was lasting. Ideas of bookmaking had been controlled until this time by two opposing forces. From one side there was the pressure of mechanical industry for quantity regardless of quality—books in their multitude were often cheap in appearance as well as in price. From the other side, the anxious aspirations of the time for culture included a rather diffuse longing for fine books. It required only the one right intervention to direct these sentiments into a concerted movement for the book as an art object and away from the mass blights of industrial manufacture. It has commonly been agreed that the Englishman William Morris, with his Kelmscott Press which formed part of the larger Arts and Crafts Movement, provided such a catalyst from 1891 until the early years of the twentieth century. This book examines that crucial decade and a half in three basic ways.

First, I describe the real extent of Morris' influence on America. The extraordinary impact of his work spread with a rapidity that has never been properly appreciated. Printers in the remotest sections of the United States broke up their old formes for new layouts and strange fonts. The great commercial houses of Boston, Chicago, and New York adapted themselves to the new practices. But the greatest accomplishment of this revolution was that it engendered and fostered its own offspring. All of those brilliant young men of the nineties who were to become the leaders of twentieth-century bookmaking first took up their tools in the excitement of the movement whose name now suggests to many people a kind of harmless pottering—Arts and Crafts. But to them it was an ideal charged with a transforming energy and one that they could put into immediate practice. This was the heroic generation that raised American typography for the first time into a position of world prominence: Updike, Rogers, Goudy, Bradley, Cleland, Dwiggins, Ransom, Nash, Rollins.

Their own words and words of those who knew them claim the inspiration of Morris for these men; most of all, their work does. They began by copying Morris' style; they went on to their own styles. On the way, however, they did not forget Morris' teachings about the nature of typography; he gave them conceptual as well as visual inspiration. In a general but real sense, early twentieth-century American printing has Morris as its progenitor.

Secondly, the Arts and Crafts style itself has to be delineated very precisely to show its particular influence in what has seemed to be a mingled stream of forms. The literature of book design is surprisingly lacking in such exact descriptions of book styles in any period. While generalizations are commonly made about incunabular, Renaissance, Baroque, Rococo, Neo-Classical, and Romantic bookmaking, few attempts have been made to set up limits separating one style from another. The exact constituents of the Arts and Crafts style show clearly which American books belong to it and which do not.

Thirdly, there is a crucial distinction to be made between Arts and Crafts and the other prominent format for fine books in the late nineteenth century. These two styles are generally confused with their contemporary, Art Nouveau, which was a decorative system without effect on the format itself. The style I call Aesthetic is distinct from both Arts and Crafts and Art Nouveau, although closely associated with them. Thus there were in fact three related yet individual new kinds of design at work in those great years of American bookmaking.

Acknowledgments

THIS BOOK has been written while I have been teaching at the Columbia University School of Library Service, and I wish to thank both deans under whom I have worked, Jack Dalton and Richard Darling. Professor Allen Hazen has given invaluable assistance, supplemented by helpful suggestions from two other readers of the original manuscript, Professors Phyllis Dain and Oliver Lilley. Other colleagues whom I would especially like to thank for their encouragement and interest in my subject are Alice Bryan, Frances Henne, Maurice Tauber, Terry Belanger, James Ramer, and the late John Waddell. Professor Ray Trautman gave not only encouragement, but also access to his fine history of printing collection.

First among those I would like to thank for helping me gain access to books are Kenneth Lohf and his staff in the Rare Books and Manuscripts Section of the Columbia University Libraries. Evelyn Kraus, her successor, Ann Wilkinson, and the staff in the School of Library Service and Graphic Arts Collections at Columbia have also been of great assistance. Maud Cole in the Rare Book Room at the New York Public Library has been most helpful, as has Robert Nikirk at the Grolier Club. James Wells of the Newberry Library welcomed me in Chicago. Staff at Princeton University Libraries and at the City University of New York (City College) have been a source of encouragement. The private collector Victor Borsodi shared his reminiscences about his friend Bruce Rogers and gave me access to an unpublished Rogers autobiographical manuscript. Joseph Dunlap not only lent me many hard-to-find books, but also gave me the initial inspiration and much advice, based on his own profound knowledge of Morris. I am especially grateful to him and his wife, Barbara.

For their advice and reminiscences, I am also indebted to typographers Robert Leslie, Joseph Blumenthal, Max Stein, Eugene Ettenberg, the late James Hendrickson, Milton Glick, and Melvin Loos. Colin Franklin, the British private press expert, gave useful comment in the early stages of my work, and conversations with James Mosley of the St. Bride Printing Library and with John Dreyfus were most fruitful. The William Morris Society has also been most helpful.

Philip Grushkin took many photographs for me, under less than ideal circumstances. Virginia Wageman at the Princeton Art Museum and Hubbard Ballou of the Columbia University Photographic Services furnished other pictures. Joseph Dunlap, Robert Judson Clark, Eleanor McDowell Thompson, Thomas Sloan, Sandra Markham, Princeton

University Library, City University of New York (City College) Library, and Columbia University Libraries all lent books for photographing. (A list of specific credits follows the index.)

Finally, I would like to thank Alice Koeth, who designed the book, and staff members of the R. R. Bowker Company: Jean Peters, Bowker librarian; Chandler Grannis, former editor-in-chief of *Publishers Weekly;* Desmond Reaney, manager of the Book Editorial Department; Judy Garodnick, acquisitions editor; and Sylvia Archer, Filomena Simora, and Helen Einhorn.

Epigraphs

MANY OF US REMEMBER how in the early nineties of the last century a few books arrived from time to time in America which startled us by the novelty and quality and virility of their typography. The style of them was entirely novel to us, because few, if any, printers had any knowledge of the masterpieces of early typography or the earlier manuscript books, and, therefore, we believed that William Morris was creating a new school of typography, instead of re-creating the earliest.

Henry Lewis Bullen, "William Morris, Regenerator of the
Typographic Art," *Inland Printer* LXIX (June 1922): 369.

There was so much difference between the anemic type and presswork of the eighties and the Kelmscott style that Morris's work came like a breath of northwest wind into a murky and humid atmosphere.

Carl Purington Rollins, "Morris's Typographical Adventure,"
Printing and Graphic Arts VI (June 1958): 30.

. . . in the short quarter century from 1890 to 1914 the spirit of adventure seized the printers . . .

. . . in no similar length of time was so much interesting and stimulating work issued from the American press.

Carl Purington Rollins, "The Golden Age of American Printing,"
New Colophon II (September 1949): 299–300.

I

The Ordinary Book
of the Nineteenth Century

THE TERM often used for Kelmscott influence, "The Revival of Fine Printing," is appropriate for the European part of the movement, where fine printing had traditions going back to the origins of the craft itself. But in America the utilitarian aspects of printing tended to be uppermost. From the days of pioneer settlement to the growth of modern business the dissemination of news and advertising has been one of the primary concerns of American printing, so that periodical publishing has been of central importance. Despite notable attempts at fine bookmaking, such as Joel Barlow's *Columbiad* of 1807,[1] late nineteenth-century concern with artistic typography was, in the United States, more of a revolution than a revival.

The Industrial Revolution changed the United States from a relatively poor agrarian society to a relatively wealthy industrialized one, with the Civil War years marking the watershed. Much of the new wealth went into the pockets of the tycoons, but it also helped to create a rapidly expanding urban middle class, which, in the best American tradition, hoped to better itself still further. The mid-nineteenth century saw the establishment not only of factories but also of many new elementary and secondary schools (with an inevitable rise in the rate of literacy), of institutions of higher learning with their Germanic emphasis on original research, of museums, of public libraries, of Mechanics Institutes. All of these promoted the use of books in one way or another, as did indeed the Industrial Revolution itself, with its emphasis on applied science. R. H. Shove has described how before the 1830s, American publishers ignored any market but the well-to-do, who were the only regular purchasers of books.[2] After the Civil War, the new popular demand meant that many publishers rushed to provide cheap books, flooding the market with shoddily produced editions. Such enterprises as George Munro's Seaside Library or Donnelley and Lloyd's Lakeside Library reprinted standard fiction in ten-cent quartos, some without covers, some with paper covers.[3] Even large, established publishers such as Harper's put out cheap series.

Cheap-book publishers were aided in lowering their prices by the lack of international copyright agreement in this country, which meant that foreign authors did not have to be

1

paid royalties. An 1884 letter in *Publishers Weekly* described the matter rather piquantly:

> The absence of international literary copyright, and the license every book-puddler [*sic*] has taken to himself in making books, are no doubt factors in producing the demoralization of the trade that exists to-day. In the rage for cheapness we have sacrificed everything for slop, and a dainty bit of bookmaking is like a jewel in the swine's snout.[4]

This anomalous situation was, however, corrected in 1891 by the passage of an International Copyright Act, and the cheap-book publishers were soon out of business. Their profits had already fallen off in the eighties, partly because of public reaction to the physical offensiveness of their wares. Thus the entrepreneurs' eagerness to exploit a situation peculiar to the United States placed the American public—and printing industry—in an unusually receptive frame of mind for the appreciation of fine typography.

But there were still larger forces stemming from the Industrial Revolution that affected bookmaking quality. The most conspicuous of these was the mechanization of every book process. The United States played an important role in this internationally shared movement, especially after the Civil War.[5] In the urge toward speed, the new iron printing presses were powered by steam, then by electricity. Curves triumphed over plane surfaces; after the impression and inking cylinders came the cylinder for the printing surface, thus achieving the high-speed rotary press. Paper-making machines turned out huge rolls of paper for these presses. Stereotyping and electrotyping were further aids to large editions. The pantograph machine accelerated the production of punches and matrices. Typecasting was separately mechanized, but eventually combined with automatic typesetting when the Linotype and Monotype machines appeared with their "distribution by the melting pot" and subsequent re-casting as the type was set. The different steps in bookbinding were mechanized. The new art of photography revolutionized illustration before the century was over for it could be adapted to all three generic types of printing: relief, intaglio, and planographic.

A less obvious result of the Industrial Revolution in bookmaking was the substitution of new and inferior materials. From the 1820s, publishers began to issue books in cloth bindings, which meant that they would not usually be re-bound in leather. Aniline colors, by-products of coal tar developed during the nineteenth century, were widely used in ink-making although they were not permanent coloring agents. An early twentieth-century expert on ink pointed to "a continuing retrogression in ink manufacture and a consequent deterioration of necessary ink qualities."[6] New knowledge in chemistry also led to the deterioration of paper. Since rags had always been an expensive raw material, a search had been going on for some time for other cellulose sources. During the nineteenth century the most plentiful material of all—wood—was successfully pulverized by first mechanical, then chemical methods. Paper became cheaper, but because of shorter wood fibers and the chemicals used in its manufacture it was doomed to a relatively short life.

Another concomitant of industrialization was inflation. Although the new source of paper kept it at pre-Civil War prices, Shove estimated that by 1875 "the other expenses of publishing, as labor, rent, advertising, and distributing, had increased from fifty to two hundred percent. . . ."[7] Publishers, in an attempt to keep book prices from rising also, cut back on production details. Hasty or careless presswork can be seen in imperfect register or uneven inking. Illegibly small type was used to save space.

All of these factors in nineteenth-century book production—a demand for more and cheaper books, mechanization, changes in materials, rising prices—adversely affected the appearance of the book, which also reflected contemporary taste.

The same high degree of elaboration and eclecticism of style which characterized the reign of Queen Victoria in England marked the America of the Gilded Age. The ability of the new machines to produce ornamental detail cheaply and lavishly led to the manufacture of objects with decoration rivaling in amount and intricacy the most sumptuous products of handicraft. Moreover, the middle class was able to buy these objects in quantities heretofore possible only for the upper class. The Victorian parlor was often a heterogeneous assemblage of superfluous objects. Clarence Cook's *The House Beautiful*, first published in 1878, gave a contemporary estimate:

> There needs to-day to be a protest made by some one against the mechanical character of our decoration, for, with unexampled demand . . . there has come an unexampled supply. . . . And all these things . . . are so cheap, that everybody gets them, and, of the smaller decorative things, gets so many that our homes are overrun with things, encumbered with useless ugliness, and made to look more like museums or warerooms than like homes of thinking people and people of taste.[8]

The Victorian book did not escape these trends. There was as yet no profession of book designer, while the practicing printer was more noteworthy for his technical than his artistic knowledge. The illustrations might be by several different hands, reproduced by several different processes. In any case, no one saw the advisability of relating the lines of the type to those of the drawings or imposing any kind of unity on the decoration of the book. The covers were, in John T. Winterich's vivid words, "prettied up with filigree, scrollwork, curlicues, scrimshaw, doodads . . . drowned in gilt, or attired, like Joseph, in coats of many colors."[9]

The exuberant eccentricity of Victorian display types can be attributed in part to the rise of advertising, with its need for eye-catching letters. The more exotic of these were little used in books but the habit of combining a variety of types within one piece of printing marred many title pages. From the English viewpoint of Halliday Sparling, America and Germany were particular villains, but British printers shared the guilt.

> Those printers who . . . in Great Britain or . . . America, resisted or did not feel the temptation to crowd their title-pages and sometimes their pages, with a mixture of heteroclite signs and faces, often adding to the effect with rococo or fretsaw "ornaments," might be numbered on the fingers of one hand.[10]

A much-simplified outline of the generic styles of type will make this typographic confusion more understandable. Nonroman types include Gothic (also known as black letter), which is based on the prevalent book hands of the late Middle Ages, and faces derived from other scripts, such as italic or uncial. The roman style of letter goes back, via the hands of the humanists, to the inscriptional capitals of the ancient Romans for the upper case and to the minuscule of the Carolingian Renaissance for the lower case. In the fifteenth century Italy produced the largest number and highest quality of roman types. Venice, in particular, was the location of two highly influential printers using this style: Nicholas Jenson and Aldus Manutius. The former's type is distinguished by such details as a slanting crossbar on the lower case "e" and serifs that extend in both directions on the upper case "M." Although Jenson's fonts have been revered as the most beautiful of the early romans, it was the Aldine that became the standard Western roman, via the great French type designers of the sixteenth century and the Dutch houses of the seventeenth. In 1722 the Englishman William Caslon designed one of the most famous examples of this style. All of these faces are known generically as old-style.

In the middle of the eighteenth century John Baskerville devised a transitional type. This new kind of type, eventually to be called modern-style and brought to the peak of cold brilliance by the Italian Bodoni, differed from the old-style in three basic ways:

Old-Style	*Modern-Style*
a. Blunt, bracketed, sloping serifs	a. Hair-line, unbracketed, straight serifs
b. Little contrast between thick and thin strokes	b. Much contrast between thick and thin strokes
c. Diagonal stress for the thick strokes	c. Horizontal stress for the thick strokes

These are still the two major divisions of roman type. There are also sans serifs, slab serifs, and decorated types, all loved by the Victorians.

After the triumph of modern-style in the Neo-Classical period, William Pickering and Charles Whittingham revived Caslon in the 1840s, but the general re-use of old-style developed so slowly that only in the nineties did it become conspicuous. It was associated with antiquarian book design, and therefore connected in people's minds with the Kelmscott Revival. A. F. Johnson has tried to correct this misapprehension by pointing out that after 1840 old-style came slowly back into favor on its own, a change that presumably would have taken place without Morris.[11]

But text types in the Victorian period were still largely modern-style. At the turn of the eighteenth to the nineteenth century, the widespread vogue for copper-plate engraving, the Neo-Classical taste for austerity and dignity, and the centuries-old trend toward rationalizing type design instead of basing it on calligraphy had brought about this ascendency. The undistinguished versions of modern-style that filled Victorian compositors' cases gave a gray appearance to text pages, remarkable neither for legibility nor beauty. This was Walter Crane's judgment: "Modern type, obeying, I suppose, a resistless law of evolution, had reached, especially with American printers, the last stage of attenuation."[12]

1. Printed by Fry and Kammerer for C. and A. Conrad and Co., Philadelphia; Conrad Lucas and Co., Baltimore.
2. Raymond H. Shove, *Cheap Book Production in the United States: 1870 to 1891* (Urbana: University of Illinois Library, 1937), p. v.
3. Ibid., p. 5.
4. G. Mercer Adam, Letter to the Editor, dated January 26, 1884, *Publishers Weekly*, XXV (February 2, 1884): 151.
5. For an account of this role, see Hellmut Lehmann-Haupt, *The Book in America* (2d ed.; New York: Bowker, 1952).
6. David N. Carvalho, *Forty Centuries of Ink* (New York: Banks Law Publishing Co., 1904), p. 208.
7. Shove, *Cheap Book Production*, p. 4.
8. Clarence C. Cook, *The House Beautiful* (New York: Scribner's, 1895), pp. 281-283. For a discussion of mid-century taste as affected by machines, see Nikolaus Pevsner, *Pioneers of Modern Design: From William Morris to Walter Gropius* (3d ed.; Baltimore: Penguin Books, 1965).
9. John T. Winterich, *The Works of Geoffrey Chaucer: A Facsimile of the William Morris Kelmscott Chaucer* (Cleveland: World, 1958), p. ix.
10. H. Halliday Sparling, *The Kelmscott Press and William Morris Master-Craftsman* (London: Macmillan, 1924), pp. 28–29.
11. Alfred Forbes Johnson, "Old-Face Types in the Victorian Age," *Monotype Recorder*, XXX (September–December 1931): 5-7.
12. Walter Crane, *Of the Decorative Illustration of Books Old and New* (3d ed. rev.; London: George Bell, 1905), p. 190.

II

Bibliophilic Aspirations

AT THE SAME TIME there was in America a desire, especially on the part of bibliophiles, not only for more books, but for beautiful ones. In the United States the mid-century affluence that had spread book buying through the middle class also swelled the ranks of these bibliophiles. Book-collectors' clubs, a natural result of interest in fine books, were formed in the United States from the 1850s.[1] They survived for varying lengths of time, but most of them managed to issue at least a few finely printed volumes. In early 1884 the most prestigious of all, the Grolier Club of New York, was formed. The constitution expressed its aim as "the literary study and promotion of the arts pertaining to the production of books." A contemporary commentator remarked: "[The limited editions are to be] . . . models of construction, and, in being followed as guides, are intended to be of practical value in the advancement of art."[2]

Amateur publishing, another trend of the times, was more concerned with content than form (which distinguishes it from "artistic" private presses). Small, inexpensive printing presses were available for young people who wished to publish their own choice of literature in a format equally personal. The movement, begun as early as 1812 when Thomas G. Cundie, Jr., published the *Juvenile Portfolio* in Philadelphia, arrived at large-scale organization in 1876 when the National Amateur Press Association was formed in the same city, and reached a climax in 1891 with the publication of *A Cyclopedia of the Literature of Amateur Journalism* in Hartford, Connecticut, by Truman J. Spencer.[3]

Another result of late nineteenth-century concern with printing was the production of entire books by fine artists, the tacit assumption being that books could be true works of art, reflecting an individual artist's personality. There have always been one-man books: William Blake made the greatest ones, but he was not the first or the last. In the eighteenth century entire books, text and ornaments, were engraved on copper plates. Handwriting manuals from the sixteenth century on had been cut in their entirety on either wood or copper, although not always by the calligrapher himself. In some of the blockbooks of the fifteenth century, the same hand may have cut both pictures and text.

5

But these earlier cases of unity derived as much from the restrictions of available technology as from artistic intention. After the invention of lithography at the end of the eighteenth century, it became simpler than with wood or copper to combine writing and drawing by the same hand. Artists usually confined themselves to illustrations, but by the 1880s at least, there were signs of a new feeling for the unity of a book in reaction to Victorian eclecticism.

The professional book designer who began work in the nineties was foreshadowed in the eighties by artists who assumed total, or almost total, responsibility for the design of lavish editions. They arranged type layout or sometimes lettered the texts themselves. On the whole they were not rebelling against the new mechanical methods but trying to live with them, not always with brilliant results. For example, Elizabeth Barrett Browning's *Sonnets from the Portuguese* was published in a large, oblong format by Ticknor, with an 1886 copyright. The artist, Ludvig Sandöe Ipsen, supplied a decorated title page and frames for each sonnet. Each of these bordered pages is preceded by an introductory page with a medallion. The text is entirely in capitals of a highly eccentric design (Plate 1). The work was hand lettered, reduced by photography, then placed on stone for lithographic printing. Keats' *Odes and Sonnets*, published by Lippincott in 1888, is again a very large book on thick, coated paper. Will H. Low drew the illustrations, reproduced photomechanically, and designed all the book's ornamentation, including the binding.[4] Among other American artists who were contributing more than illustrations to book design in the eighties, Elihu Vedder, Edwin Abbey, and Howard Pyle were outstanding.

There was also an English artist who made a significant contribution to the American book scene in the eighties. W. J. Linton, the well-known wood engraver, established in Hamden, Connecticut, the most noteworthy private press in America prior to the nineties. The Appledore Private Press published forty-one items between 1875 and 1897.[5] In 1882 Linton brought out in 225 copies *Golden Apples of Hesperus: Poems Not in the Collections*. It is a letterpress book of 187 pages with small, charming cuts scattered throughout. Linton wrote:

> For anything unusual or unsatisfactory in the production of the book I ask consideration: the whole of it,—drawing, engraving, composition, and printing (the printing my first attempt), being the work of my own hands, at odd times, with long intervals, and many hindrances.[6]

Linton's delicate books do not foreshadow those of Morris, as C. P. Rollins noted when he described Linton's faint ink and resultant illegibility.[7]

The late nineteenth-century connection of art with printing is also seen in the pages of periodicals. There were journals dedicated entirely to bibliophily, as well as ones intended for professional printers. Arthur B. Turnure's *Art Age*, printed at the Gilliss Press in New York City, was one of the latter. Walter Gilliss later wrote H. L. Bullen of the American Type Founders Company, "I remember when we were printing the *Art Age* nearly 40 years ago and our lament was that Printers never bought or read anything."[8] The *Art Age* was intended to change that situation.

Generally disregarded since its demise, this important journal needs description. In the first issue, April 1883, Turnure set the tone by stating that the *Art Age* would appeal to those who realized the importance of artistic bookmaking. He then pointed out the novelty of a journal concerned with fine printing and binding although he believed there was a growing audience for such a publication. He found the bookmaking trade in an unsatisfactory condition:

> As yet, it may be said fairly, a very few firms have done much to advance the higher arts of book-making, or to keep pace with the growing demand for tasteful bindings, beautiful title-pages, perfection of impression, and suitable paper. . . . There is a great need and opportunity for improvement in typographic art, and those who buy bound books, as well as those who realize that they should be represented by well-executed printing in their business dealings, will hereafter have at least one journal in which their interests are regarded.[9]

Turnure wrote for the *Art Age* an amazing series of prophetic articles—unsigned, but surely by the editor. "Book Titles" criticized early nineteenth-century title pages with their ornamental types and called for still more simplicity than in the ones currently being produced.[10] "A Cluny for Bookmakers" described the lack of historical models for American printers, such as he supposed the Parisians could find in the Cluny Museum, and looked forward to the day when that lack would be supplied.[11] "Future American Bookmaking" stated that general interest in bookmaking had spread within the last year

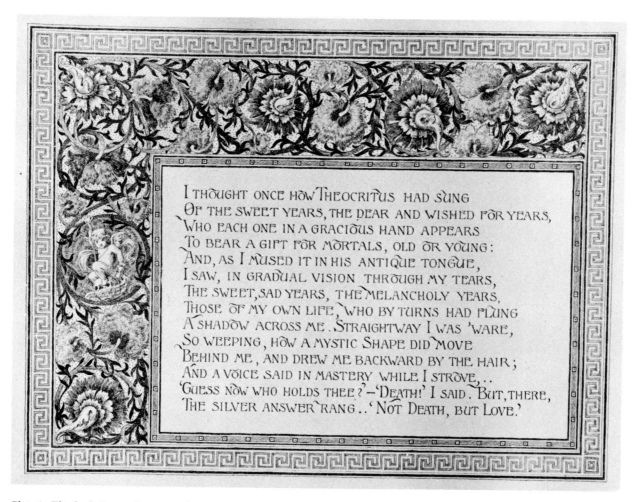

Plate 1. Elizabeth Barrett Browning, *Sonnets from the Portuguese*. Boston: Ticknor, 1886.

and went on to comment on the inventiveness of American typography and its "readiness to adopt and adapt what is good. We imitate with extraordinary facility and we are quick to accept good ideas." The article ended with the prophecy: "Bookmaking as an art in the United States will develop with surprising rapidity in the near future. . . ."[12] But it was in describing the current fad for *éditions de luxe* that Turnure most succinctly characterized the typographic situation of the eighties. In 1883 he wrote:

> Deliberately making a rarity of a new book certainly is laughable and would find no extenuation if there were not a serious motive that influenced publishers to print limited editions. This motive is found in the converse of the marvellous advances made in cheapening the cost of standard publications, which, while they give good literature at a very low price to the consumer, also have the effect of driving out of market typographically worthy books. . . . The benefit to typographic art, therefore, is a sufficient excuse for the modern limited editions; and on this plea, if no other, their publication deserves encouragement. The quantity of wretched printing that is issued annually is something incredible. The average pressman has rapidity in producing copies as his first ambition, and painstaking is apt to be his last thought.[13]

Concerns similar to those of Turnure can also be traced in the pages of the *American Bookmaker*, a periodical for professional printers, published from 1885 in New York by Howard Lockwood and Company. Its issues were filled with articles about historical and contemporary fine printing. George Wharton Edwards, an artist whose work was often Gothic in inspiration, showed a very early (1887) awareness of the coming importance of the designer's role. His article is also evidence that American printers had some opportunity to be aware of Morris' work before the establishment of the Kelmscott Press.

> Here is a field [books] that has been too much neglected by the artists of our country and generation. It has been too much the fashion for unthinking ones to sneer at the designer . . . [Now the] designer is upon his proper footing, is recognized and honored. This has been brought about within a few years and by the efforts of William Morris and Walter Crane.[14]

In 1890 the name of the man who inspired Morris to set up his press was mentioned in the context of printing art:

> The delivery of "Lectures on the Art of Printing" is a step in the right direction. Emery Walker has just given such a lecture in the City of London College. . . . Let us have such lectures in the United States.[15]

That same year Morris was again brought to the attention of American printers:

> . . . the teachings of William Morris are brought to mind—an artist in the truest sense, whose example and precepts have contributed in such great measure to the advancement of the industrial arts in America as well as in his native land.[16]

In 1891, not long before the publication of the first Kelmscott book, a case was made for the improvement of public taste:

Public taste has been educated and improved to such an extent that a simple declaration on the part of the maker of a book that it is of superior workmanship does not in itself by any means carry conviction to the average buyer.... In fact it would seem that within the past twenty years a revolution of no slight importance to the art of bookmaking has occurred and is yet in progress. Briefly stated, by this is meant that poorly made books nowadays owe their existence to the manufacturers and not to the public.[17]

Thus, according to the *American Bookmaker*, bibliophily had reached the public, preparing the way for a typographic revolution.

1. Review of *American Book Clubs* by A. Growoll, *Nation*, LXVI (March 3, 1898): 173.
2. "The Grolier Club" reprinted from the *Critic and Good Literature* of March 15, 1884, in *Publishers Weekly*, XXV (March 22, 1884): 352.
3. William Dunlop, "Product of a Mimic Press," *American Book-Lore*, I (September 1898): 37–38.
4. The above examples were suggested by Frank Weitenkampf's catalogue of the 1919 New York Public Library exhibition, *Illustrated Books of the Past Four Centuries* (New York: New York Public Library, 1920).
5. See R. Malcolm Sills, "W. J. Linton at Yale: The Appledore Private Press," *Yale University Library Gazette*, XII (January 1938): 43–52.
6. [William James Linton] *Golden Apples of Hesperus: Poems Not in the Collections* (Hamden: Appledore Private Press, 1882), p. vi.
7. Carl Purington Rollins, *Souvenirs of My Inky Past* (New York: New York Public Library, 1950), p. 5.
8. Walter Gilliss to Henry Lewis Bullen, September 10, 1921, Typographic Library Manuscripts Collection, Columbia University Libraries.
9. [Arthur B. Turnure] "Preface," *Art Age*, I (April 1883): 1–2.
10. [Arthur B. Turnure] "Book Titles," *Art Age*, I (October 1883): 17–18.
11. [Arthur B. Turnure] "A Cluny for Bookmakers," *Art Age*, I (January 1884): 57–58.
12. [Arthur B. Turnure] "Future American Bookmaking," *Art Age*, I (April 1884): 97–98.
13. [Arthur B. Turnure] "Limited Editions," *Art Age*, I (May 1883): 9–10.
14. "George Wharton Edwards," *American Bookmaker*, IV (May 1887): 137.
15. Henry G. Bishop, "English Notes for American Printers," *American Bookmaker*, X (March 1890): 67.
16. "Art Designing," *American Bookmaker*, X (June 1890): 153.
17. "Bookmaking: Good and Bad," *American Bookmaker*, XII (January 1891): 4.

III

Classic & Romantic Book Styles

NINETEENTH-CENTURY styles of bookmaking fall into the two main lines of classicism (Neo-Classical and Aesthetic) and romanticism (Romantic, Gothic Revival, Antique, Artistic, Arts and Crafts, and Art Nouveau). Although they mingle, overlap, and are often confused each style has its own characteristics.

The earliest was the Neo-Classical, which had already begun in the eighteenth century. Its characteristics include modern-style type, wove paper, a tendency to large format, wide leading (i.e., space between lines) and margins, centered title pages, and little ornamentation. If there is decoration, it is likely to be engraved and with Classical/Renaissance motifs. Barlow's *Columbiad* (1807), mentioned earlier, is an example.

The Aesthetic style was partially an outgrowth of the Neo-Classical and resembles it in its emphasis on white space on the page and Renaissance ornament used in a restrained fashion. It is in contrast to the Neo-Classical, however, by its use of small formats and, in the later part of the century, by old-style or italic type on laid paper. An English printing house, the Chiswick Press, provided early prototypes of such books—for example, the *Aldine Poets*, made for the publisher William Pickering. These were neatly printed, sober volumes worthy of the scholar-printer for whom they were named. Some Chiswick books had Renaissance headpieces and initials, which, along with the small format and neat printing, remind one of sixteenth-century French books. These are the volumes that seem to have provided the model for Aesthetic bookmaking. I call this the Aesthetic style because it often appears in connection with the writers and artists forming the movement of that name—Pater, Whistler, Wilde, Ricketts, et al., many of whom were involved with Arts and Crafts as well. The Aesthetic style of bookmaking has, in fact, not been clearly recognized, although writers have sensed its presence without formulating a description or actually naming it. The most notable instance is the article by A. J. A. Symons in the *Fleuron* of 1930, which, in attempting to justify the importance of Aesthetic books (although he does not use that term), claimed that "press books" (part of the Arts and Crafts Movement) "were not merely accidental to the period but express an essentially contrary spirit."[1] Symons was sensitive to the differences of the two styles. Today we can see that each expressed the period in different ways.

At other times writers seem less concerned with the dichotomy they are describing. In his book on Elkin Mathews and John Lane, the influential London publishers of Aesthetic books, James G. Nelson said that the Bodley Head book was "generally in accord with the principles of the Arts and Crafts Movement so far as book design was concerned...."[2]

John Russell Taylor, in *The Art Nouveau Book in Britain*, was well aware of the distinction between Arts and Crafts and Art Nouveau, as well as being aware of Whistler's very different influence.[3] These threads remain to be sorted out.

Aestheticism, or Art-for-Art's-Sake, began in the 1860s and by the 1880s embraced all art forms in Great Britain and the United States.[4] As with Arts and Crafts, from which Aestheticism in its early stages cannot always be separated, John Ruskin's call for honest craftsmanship and the revolt in applied art against superfluous ornament were formative influences. From abroad, the French influence was always strong, but a more dramatic influence was the discovery of Japanese art, when wares from the newly opened East came to Europe wrapped in woodcut prints. Their simplicity of line, asymmetrical composition, solid blocks of color, and two-dimensionalism profoundly moved a whole generation of artists. The most important of these for bookmaking was an American expatriate, James McNeill Whistler, who from 1878 designed his own books and catalogues. These are distinguished by asymmetric title pages in italic Caslon capitals and text pages in small type with wide margins.

By the early eighties trade publishers began to issue books that combined the small Renaissance format of the Chiswick Press with the Japanese love of asymmetry. An American example from 1881 is Houghton Mifflin's edition of W. D. Howells' *A Day's Pleasure and Other Sketches* in the Modern Classics series. The asymmetric binding has Japanesque decoration, but the internal ornament is Renaissance.

Whistler's friend, Oscar Wilde, came to the United States in 1882 for his famous lecture tour in connection with the American production of Gilbert and Sullivan's *Patience*. He brought not only the ideas of Art-for-Art's-Sake but also a book of poems by another friend, Rennell Rodd, *Rose Leaf and Apple Leaf*, published in a luxury edition by J. M. Stoddart and Company of Philadelphia (the American publishers of Gilbert and Sullivan) in 1882. Its vellum binding, asymmetric title page (Plate 2), Japanesque decorations, brownish ink, parchment paper printed on one side only and interleaved with green tissue, show the Aesthetic book raised to preciosity.[5] Wilde suggested the artist Francis Lathrop to design the cover.[6]

The introduction by Wilde to this book gives a statement of his philosophy that shows his break from the Pre-Raphaelite predecessors of Arts and Crafts and their mentor, John Ruskin:

> ... the ultimate expression of our artistic movement in painting has been, not in the spiritual visions of the pre-Raphaelites ... but in the work of such men as Whistler....
>
> ... this love of art for art's sake, is the point in which we of the younger school have made a departure from the teaching of Mr. Ruskin....
>
> ... to us the rule of art is not the rule of morals....[7]

11

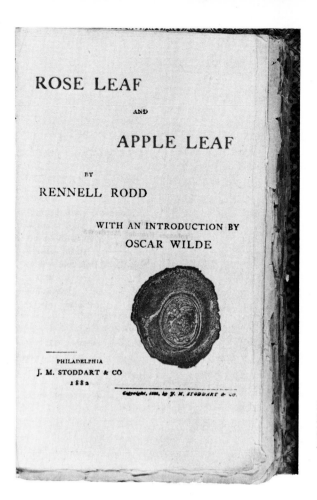

ROSE LEAF

AND

APPLE LEAF

BY

RENNELL RODD

WITH AN INTRODUCTION BY
OSCAR WILDE

PHILADELPHIA
J. M. STODDART & CO
1882

Copyright, 1882, by J. M. STODDART & CO.

Plate 2. Rennell Rodd,
Rose Leaf and Apple Leaf.
Philadelphia:
J. M. Stoddart, 1882.

It is, indeed, this lack of interest in morality, this emphasis on the form of the work of art itself rather than on the minds of the artists, that set off Art-for-Art's-Sake from the contemporary movement of Arts and Crafts. By the nineties, Aestheticism had evolved into *fin-de-siècle* decadence. The Wilde scandal in 1895 put an end to some of the more publicized manifestations of the style, when, for example, Aubrey Beardsley was fired as art editor of the *Yellow Book*. However, after playing its important role in the nineties, the influence on book design lingered into the twentieth century.

The characteristics of Aesthetic book design may be summarized as follows:

1. A small, pocketable format, sometimes with tall, slim proportions.
2. A relatively simple binding with a repetition of the title page or with decoration.
3. A centered or asymmetric title page with little or no ornament except for the frequent use of printers' marks and a great deal of white space.
4. Small, light type, usually old-style, placed high on the text pages, with wide margins; italic often used for running heads, title pages, other preliminaries, and sometimes for texts.
5. Rag paper, often handmade laid, with deckle edges.
6. Sparing use of ornament in the text; if present, usually Renaissance headpieces and initials.
7. Sparing use of color, usually pastel, or red on the title page.
8. Commercial rather than private publication.
9. Use of mechanical rather than hand methods.

This is not to say that all of these characteristics are necessary for a book to have an Aesthetic appearance. Only a few of them, in proper balance, can achieve that—for example, Theodore Child's *The Desire of Beauty* (Plate 3). The Aesthetic aura is one of simplicity, restraint, understatement, even when the book is as fancy as Rodd's. The style, in fact, is, in its elements and its total effect, a reaction to the heavily charged books of Romanticism, the other major influence on nineteenth-century bookmaking.

The elaboration and exuberance of ornament made possible by the new industrialism had been emotionally justified by the sentimental extravagance of the Romantic period. The severe undecorated pages of the Neo-Classical books were joined during the nineteenth century by highly decorated pages in which vignettes intruded on the text, in which children and animals were prominent figures, or in which were featured rustic borders of intertwining branches, all reproduced from wood engravings and usually combined with modern-style type.

An example of mid-century American book design in the Romantic mode is Washington Irving's *Sketch Book* in the Artist's Edition published by Putnam in 1864. It is in small, neat, modern type with wide margins. There are 120 wood engravings by various artists, mostly within the text although some are irregularly shaped, requiring special type arrangements. Besides the typographic title page, there is a decorated one with a wood engraving within an ivy frame of Irving's home at Tarrytown. The decorated section headings have ornamental lettering and curlicues.

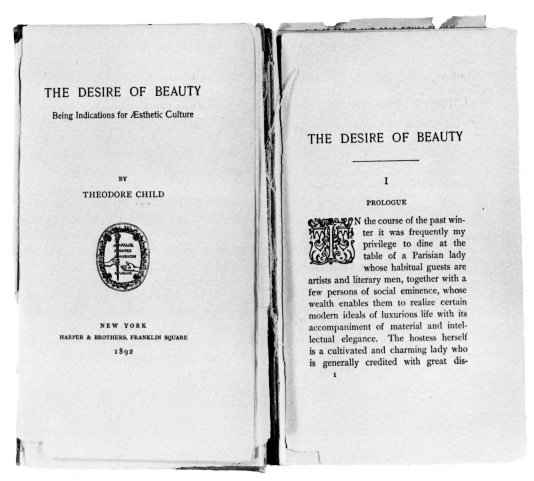

Plate 3. Theodore Child, *The Desire of Beauty: Being Indications for Aesthetic Culture.* New York: Harper, 1892.

The black and white austerity of the Neo-Classical book also gave way to the use of color. The great illustrated books of the early part of the century were colored by hand, but experiments in color printing were proving successful.[8] The new art of lithography, invented by Senefelder at the turn of the century, proved especially adaptable to color, and gift books with chromolithographed decorations flooded the Victorian market.[9]

Chromolithography was also prominent in Gothic Revival books, an important sub-category of Romantic books which emphasized the simulation of medieval illumination. Gothic motifs were gilt stamped on cloth covers or blind stamped on calf and used for internal decoration. Other medievalistic details included clasps, goffered edges, and the like. A modest example in book design is *Patient Waiting No Loss* by Cousin Alice (Alice B. Neal),[10] which has a pointed, cusped arch stamped on the covers and chromolitho-graphed on the added title page.

Vivian Ridler has described another late nineteenth-century approach to design based on historical models which he has dubbed Old-Style or Antique.[11] Using motifs from the Gothic period through the seventeenth century, it often became a crowded, overly decor-ated style for jobbing work, with a development parallel to and sometimes overlapping the Artistic. Ridler gave credit to the Caslon Revival for spawning it, but the Gothic Revival was obviously responsible as well. The major practitioner of this style was Andrew White Tuer of the Leadenhall Press, one of whose notable productions was Joseph Crawhall's *Chap-Book Chaplets* (1883). This put into artistic form the older and cruder chap-book style with its heavy type and woodcuts.[12] In a similar vein one of the Arts and Crafts groups, the Century Guild, published a periodical in the eighties called the *Hobby Horse*, the design of which was influential in commercial publishing and in Kelmscott work itself.

Artistic printing, a combination of Romantic and Aesthetic elements, was a widespread development of the seventies and eighties, especially in jobbing work but with some ef-fects on bookmaking. Vivian Ridler has described its creation by American commercial printers and its enthusiastic reception in England.[13] Artistic work emphasized an abundance of ornament, often Japanesque in deference to the current interest in Japanese art, but also including other historical styles. The eccentric types, in their irregularity, look some-times like harbingers of Art Nouveau. There is much use of color, printed in close register, and an emphasis on asymmetry. But geometrical forms, including paneled arrangements, are also important. A particularly prominent component of the style is the use of brass rules bent, with the help of a new machine, into almost any shape. George Joyner, in his book, which is itself an example of Artistic printing, described the Grouping Style as another important element, i.e., the filling out of uneven lines by ornaments.[14] This was also done in medieval manuscripts and became a part of Arts and Crafts. The demise of Artistic printing as a result of Arts and Crafts has been described by H. L. Bullen, who also implied American leadership:

> In the eighties and nineties of the last century much attention was given to what we called commercial art printing. . . . Our job types and our job printing were anything but commonplace, and they were admired and copied in England and in Europe. We know now that our pretty and our startling effects, however well executed, were meretricious to the last degree. Morris opened our eyes.[15]

The affinity of Art Nouveau to Artistic printing has already been suggested; in a large sense, it is also part of the Romantic line. Many strains within Art Nouveau have been pointed out by art historians: William Blake, the Pre-Raphaelites, Japanese and other Oriental art, the Gothic Revival, Neo-Rococo, Neo-Baroque, the Celtic Revival, the Arts and Crafts Movement.[16] Art Nouveau was evolving in the eighties, as the title page of Arthur H. Mackmurdo's 1883 *Wren's City Churches* (also designed by him) so vividly indicates,[17] but in the nineties became the overwhelming art movement. Despite its evolution from the historical styles its most important attribute is its break from historicism, its claim to being the first truly original, modern style. As such, despite its ornateness, it is the parent of the Bauhaus and the whole Modern Movement of the twentieth century.

Art Nouveau, as a style, was applied to all handicrafts, from the locks on doors to the buildings themselves. Some items, such as glassware, could have their very shapes changed to fit the new style. The conservative and utilitarian art of bookmaking resisted such total change. In fact, Art Nouveau books exhibited no special alterations of format; they can be classified as such only by the Art Nouveau ornament they display. The Aesthetic format and the Arts and Crafts format are major strains in the bookmaking of the nineties, sometimes with Art Nouveau ornament, sometimes without. The three flow into each other, intermingle, and still remain at least partially distinguishable. For example, the books of the "literary publishers" often have Aesthetic formats with Art Nouveau covers and/or title pages, while those of the private presses combine Art Nouveau with Arts and Crafts.

The Art Nouveau ornament itself is of two varieties that sometimes overlap: the curving, sinuous, whiplash line especially associated with continental Art Nouveau, usually asymmetrical, dependent upon floral and foliate forms, upon water and hair and the female body; and the rectilinear style originating in Great Britain, especially in the Glasgow School, with its attenuated forms, geometrical ornaments, and greater tendency to symmetry. Some of Ricketts' binding designs are perhaps the most brilliant examples of the latter in the book arts. It is this version of Art Nouveau that links up with the Art Deco of the 1920s and 1930s.

1. A. J. A. Symons, "An Unacknowledged Movement in Fine Printing: The Typography of the Eighteen-Nineties," *Fleuron*, VII (1930): 116.
2. James G. Nelson, *The Early Nineties: A View from the Bodley Head* (Cambridge: Harvard University Press, 1971), p. 76.
3. John Russell Taylor, *The Art Nouveau Book in Britain* (London: Methuen, 1966).
4. Elizabeth Aslin, *The Aesthetic Movement: Prelude to Art Nouveau* (New York: Praeger, 1969), p. 13.
5. For further comment, see *The Turn of a Century 1885–1910* (Cambridge: Department of Printing and Graphic Arts, Houghton Library, Harvard University, 1970), p. 4.
6. Rupert Hart-Davis, ed., *The Letters of Oscar Wilde* (New York: Harcourt, Brace and World, 1962), p. 96.
7. In Rennell Rodd, *Rose Leaf and Apple Leaf* (Philadelphia: J. M. Stoddart, 1882), pp. 12, 14.
8. See Ruari McLean, *Victorian Book Design and Colour Printing* (2d ed., Berkeley and Los Angeles: University of California Press, 1972).
9. For example: *The Iris: An Illuminated Souvenir for MDCCCLII.* Edited by John S. Hart, LL.D.

Philadelphia: Lippincott, 1852), which has letterpress text (modern-style type) and colored plates.
10. (New York: Appleton, 1853.)
11. Vivian Ridler, "Artistic Printing: A Search for Principles," *Alphabet and Image*, No. 6 (January 1948): 9.
12. See Paul McPharlin, "Crawhall's Chap-Book Chaplets, 1883," *Publishers Weekly*, CXLII (November 7, 1942): 1965–1970.
13. Ridler, "Artistic Printing: A Search for Principles," p. 4.
14. George Joyner, *Fine Printing: Its Inception, Development, and Practice* (London: Cooper and Budd, 1895), pp. 40ff.
15. Henry Lewis Bullen, "William Morris: Regenerator of the Typographic Art," *Inland Printer*, LXIX (June 1922): 372.
16. Tschudi Madsen, *Art Nouveau* (New York: McGraw-Hill, 1967), Chapter 5.
17. Illustrated in Peter Selz, and Mildred Constantine, eds., *Art Nouveau: Art and Design at the Turn of the Century* (New York: Museum of Modern Art, 1959), p. 27, and in many other books on Art Nouveau.

IV

The Arts & Crafts Movement

THE CLASSIC SIMPLICITY of the Aesthetic format kept it from having a dramatic public impact. By 1890 many people were concerned with the possibilities of the Book Beautiful, but they had as yet no inspirational model despite the experiments of the artists. It was then that a man, already well known in other realms, appeared in the domain of books.

The life of William Morris has been recounted many times.[1] Born at Walthamstow in 1834, he was the son of a well-to-do businessman who left him a substantial income. He went up to Oxford in 1853 with High-Church sentiments and the dream of taking orders. After making friends with the future painter, Edward Burne-Jones and his Birmingham circle, reading Ruskin's *Stones of Venice* (with its crucial chapter, "The Nature of Gothic"), visiting the cathedrals of Belgium and France, and becoming disillusioned with Oxford education, Morris decided to abandon the idea of becoming a clergyman and turn instead to architecture. At this time he was also beginning his long and successful career as a poet. His first book, *The Defense of Guenevere*, published in 1858, was based on tales of the Middle Ages. On finishing at the university in 1855 Morris remained in Oxford, in the office of G. E. Street, a Gothic Revival architect. This new career did not last long, however; in 1856 Morris came under the influence of the Pre-Raphaelite painter and poet, Dante Gabriel Rossetti, decided to become a painter, and moved to London in rooms with Burne-Jones at Red Lion Square. Upon finding no furniture to suit him, Morris, who had always been adept with his hands, decided to make his own.

In 1859 he married Jane Burden of Oxford, commissioning his architect friend, Philip Webb, to build a house for them at Upton, Kent. In 1860 they moved into Red House, as it was called, again resorting to the talents of Morris and his friends for the furniture and decorations. In 1861 a group of these friends, including Morris, Burne-Jones, Rossetti, Webb, the painter Ford Madox Brown, the mathematician C. J. Faulkner, and P. P. Marshall, a surveyor and sanitary engineer, formed Morris, Marshall, Faulkner & Co., "Fine Art Workmen in Painting, Carving, Furniture and the Metals."[2] The painter Arthur Hughes

16

was also listed but was never actually a member of the firm. In 1875 the firm was reorganized as Morris & Co., with Morris as its only manager. The company had enjoyed success from the start, winning two gold medals at the Great Exhibition of 1862. As the century wore on it became one of the leading decorating firms of England, with an international clientele. Morris himself designed fabrics, wallpapers, tapestries, embroideries, carpets, stained glass, and tiles, working from a sure knowledge of all the handicrafts involved.

A commonly held assumption is that Morris & Co. revolutionized the late-Victorian interior. Since Pevsner's *Pioneers of Modern Design: From William Morris to Walter Gropius* (first published as *Pioneers of the Modern Movement* in 1936), Morris has been seen as the fountainhead of modernism because of his emphasis on fitness to purpose, on understanding materials and techniques, on unity rather than eclecticism, and especially because of his attempt to combine utility and beauty. Yet one must remember that although Victorian rooms *were* less cluttered and more unified after Morris his designs do not look modern today. They were based on historical styles of the past and are transitional between historicism and the Modern Movement, as Pevsner points out, rather than being the first examples of modern art.[3] Their overwhelming success lies in the fact that during a period of shoddy machine production Morris & Co. showed how beautiful handcrafted things could be and how they could be assembled with taste.

It was from the building and decoration of Red House, followed by the activities of the firm, that the whole Arts and Crafts Movement grew. Unlike Aestheticism, Arts and Crafts did have a wider-reaching moral basis than Art-for-Art's-Sake; Art-for-Life's-Sake might well be the opposing term.[4] John Ruskin, the writer on art and morality whom Morris had read at Oxford, was even more the ideational mover of Arts and Crafts than he had been of Aestheticism. He saw Gothic art in quite another way from the eighteenth-century Revivalists, Horace Walpole and William Beckford. It was not picturesqueness that he valued but the fact that Gothic was a freer, less rule-ridden art than the Classical style. With its abundance of detail it allowed scope for the individual workmen to express their own creativity. In this possibility for self-expression in handicraft, Ruskin saw the only chance to save men's souls from the brutalizing effects of the new factories that were turning them into automated cogs of an assembly line.

There were other nineteenth-century thinkers who turned backwards for relief from the unlovely realities of the Industrial Revolution. Thomas Carlyle, who had looked on the Middle Ages as a favorable contrast to nineteenth-century disorder in *Past and Present* (1843), influenced Ruskin. A. W. N. Pugin, the Gothic Revival architect, also wrote important books, notably *Contrasts* (1836) and *The True Principles of Pointed or Christian Architecture* (1841), that upheld the Gothic style and its emphasis on handicrafts as the true national style of England.

It was in this tradition that Red House was decorated with heavy, dark furniture, painted with scenes from *Le Morte d'Arthur*, and that Morris & Co. emphasized stained glass and tapestries as among its finest products. The numerous fabrics and wallpapers designed by Morris went well with the company's other products, while their two-dimensionalism, floral motifs, and harmonies of color made them also possible for the Aesthetes and, later, devotees of Art Nouveau.

Morris was as much given to verbal expression as to handicrafts. He once said: "If a chap can't compose an epic poem while he's weaving tapestry, he had better shut up, he'll never do any good at all."[5] In 1876 he began to be involved in politics, becoming treasurer

17

of the Eastern Question Association, a body devoted to keeping England out of war against Russia on behalf of the Turks. In the early eighties he broke with the Liberal party and became an active Socialist, trying to bring into realization his ideas about the nobility of the individual working man and his labor. The connection between a properly organized society and its art is the great theme of the many public lectures he gave, beginning with "The Decorative Arts" in 1877. Thus, Morris' ideas, as well as the artifacts of Morris & Co., were well known in England.[6]

During the 1880s other people with similar ideas began to organize themselves. A. H. Mackmurdo and Selwyn Image founded the Century Guild in 1882, W. R. Lethaby and Walter Crane the Art Workers' Guild in 1884, and C. R. Ashbee the Guild of Handicraft in 1888. This new Arts and Crafts Movement was described by Walter Crane as: "The demand for the acknowledgment of the personality of each responsible craftsman in a co-operative work. . . . [and] The principle . . . of regarding the material, object, method, and purpose of a work as essential conditions of its artistic expression. . . ."[7]

In America there were movements parallel to the English Gothic Revival and Arts and Crafts. Before and after the Civil War, churches and public buildings often took pseudomedieval shapes. Scott's novels were the first great best sellers in this country.[8] And the Pre-Raphaelite Brotherhood had American followers.[9]

That there was still, at the end of the century, a pervasive mood of sentimental Romantic medievalism may be seen by turning to literature—even to Frank Norris, who, before becoming one of the leaders in the movement toward naturalism, wrote a poem called *Yvernelle: A Legend of Feudal France* (1892). Literary historians attribute the persistence of a Romantic mood to nostalgia for the long ago and far away that gripped the American people in their search for identity and escape during the post-Civil War days of industrialization, expanding wealth, and rapid social change. James D. Hart has pointed to the establishment of the Daughters of the American Revolution, the phenomenon of American heiresses marrying European titles, the popularity of the Grand Tour, as factors, along with the immense success of the romantic novel, that indicate the American's desire to find roots in European culture and to flee from his own current problems.[10]

The great national business boom, even between its panic subsidences, did not elevate all Americans. "The disillusion rising out of deferred hopes led to the idealization of the past . . . ,"[11] especially as seen in regional literature, the voice of the nonurban population. Indiana, for example, produced several successful novelists, such as Charles Major (*When Knighthood Was in Flower*, 1898), Booth Tarkington (*The Gentleman from Indiana*, 1899), Maurice Thompson (*Alice of Old Vincennes*, 1900), and George Barr McCutcheon (*Graustark*, 1901), who wrote idealized romances that showed up unintentionally the emptiness of the very culture they seemed to be extolling; e.g., the "democratic" hero often turned out to be an aristocrat in disguise. "Romance at the century's end applied a patch to the mortal wound inflicted on the rural ideal by industrial America."[12]

There was still another aspect of Romanticism that emphasized the new rather than the old—a *fin-de-siècle* mood, the feeling that change was necessary and inevitable as the century came to an end. The rapid and unsettling events of the Industrial Revolution, the profound shifts in thought caused by the growth of scholarship and science gave people of the nineteenth century a particularly poignant feeling of leaving one era and entering another. Toward the end of the century the adjective "new" was ubiquitous: the New Hedonism, the New Woman. This interest in change accounts in part for the *épate le bourgeois* side of the Aesthetic Movement and for the tremendous success of Art Nouveau in the 1890s. As one observer of the period has said: "The Eighteen Nineties were so tolerant of novelty in art and ideas that it would seem as though the declining century wished to make amends for several decades of intellectual and artistic monotony."[13] The desire for novelty, combined with the lasting love of the Middle Ages, set the stage for Arts and Crafts' reinterpretation of the Gothic, although the older Gothic Revival style in book-making persisted, especially in certain elaborate productions.

An example is Richard de Bury's *Philobiblon* in three volumes, printed by De Vinne in 1889 for the Grolier Club, in an edition of 297 on handmade paper and 3 on vellum. The first volume is the Latin version of the text in Gothic type (Plate 4), the second volume an English version in modern-style roman type with Renaissance arabesque ornament, and the third volume, also in roman, has notes by Andrew Fleming West. The ornaments by James West, Charles M. Jenckes, and George Wharton Edwards include a vellum binding; red, black, and gold end papers; a block-set title page with a gilt "P"; line fillers, fleurons, decorated initials, and headpieces throughout the text. The marginal notes of the first volume are in roman and italic, an unpleasant contrast to the Gothic text. The whole is intensely pseudo-Gothic but not artistically successful because of the inharmonious

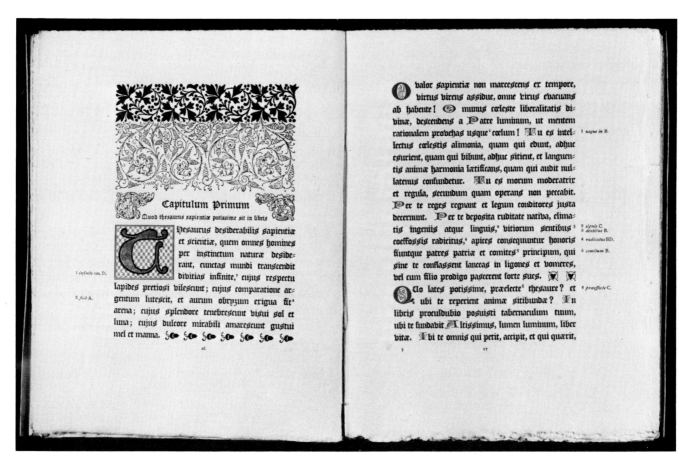

Plate 4. Richard de Bury, *Philobiblon*. New York: Grolier Club, 1889.

design. The books from this earlier Gothic Revival style tend to exhibit in their type and art work more pointed, angular lines than the blunt, rounded lines of Arts and Crafts.

As early as 1881 there was a Morris & Co. showroom in New York[14] (by the turn of the century there were others in Boston and Chicago as well), laying the foundation for an American Arts and Crafts Movement. In 1891 Walter Crane visited the United States, bringing the ideas and ideals of the English movement as Oscar Wilde had done for Aestheticism in 1882. Specific artists, such as John La Farge and Louis Tiffany, were inspired by English examples.[15] The same regionalism that fostered Romantic literature may have encouraged Arts and Crafts by its "more or less handmade habitat,"[16] i.e., a tradition of handicraft and artisanship. There was also a strong anticapitalist movement seen in such writers as Henry George (*Progress and Poverty*, 1879) and Edward Bellamy (*Looking Backward*, 1888) who were, however, without the Arts and Crafts antipathy for machine production. In general, the Ruskinian combination of art with morality and his emphasis on Truth to Nature were profoundly attractive to Americans.[17] Dickason has pointed out two mid-century periodicals inspired by Ruskin: W. J. Stillman's *Crayon* of the 1850s and the *New Path* put out by the Society for the Advancement of Truth in Art, founded in 1863.[18]

The major periodical of American Arts and Crafts was the *Craftsman*, published by the United Crafts at Eastwood, New York, from 1901 to 1916, under the direction of Gustav Stickley. The first issue (October 1901) was entirely devoted to "William Morris: Some Thoughts upon His Life, Work and Influence," which gave Morris the whole credit for the journal's inspiration. The second issue was devoted to Ruskin, the third to "The Gilds of the Middle Ages," the fourth to "Textiles Old and New," the fifth to "Robert Owen and Factory Reform," and the sixth to "The Gothic Revival," giving a fair picture of their spectrum of interests.

The first American Society of Arts and Crafts was founded in Boston in 1897 with Charles Eliot Norton, Ruskin's friend, as president. The Guild of Arts and Crafts of New York was founded by four young women in January 1900.[19] There were also Morris Societies, such as the one founded in Chicago in May 1903 with Oscar L. Triggs as secretary. Their *Bulletin* (November 1903 to February 1905) gives indications of rather widespread interest in Morris. There were seventy-five charter members, most of them from Chicago but a few from other parts of the country. The second issue mentions new Morris circles or possibilities of them in Columbus, Ohio, Toledo, Ohio, and Billings, Montana. Talks on Morris were given in Pittsburgh, Nashville, and Chicago, and an entire course on him was offered at the University of Chicago. In 1902 Triggs published a book on Arts and Crafts in which he wrote: "I count 1860 as the approximate year of its beginning, when William Morris built his famous Red House on the outskirts of London."[20]

Back in England, still another body, the Arts and Crafts Exhibition Society, had been formed in 1888. At the time of its first exhibition, William Morris realized that none of his books, as a physical object, was worthy of inclusion. His friend, the typographer Emery Walker, gave a lecture on printing in which he presented lantern slides of enlarged type specimens from the fifteenth century. This lecture was a momentous occasion for it opened Morris' eyes to the creative possibilities within type itself.

1. The first biography is still the standard one: John William Mackail, *The Life of William Morris* (London: Longmans, Green, 1899), 2 vols.
2. From the title of their first prospectus, April 1861.

3. Nikolaus Pevsner, *Pioneers of Modern Design* (3d ed.; Baltimore: Penguin Books, 1965), p. 107. For a rebuttal of Pevsner, see Herwin Schaefer, *Nineteenth Century Modern: The Functional Tradition in Victorian Design* (New York: Praeger, 1970), which points out the continuing line of undecorated simplicity in functional and vernacular objects.

4. Used by Peter A. Wick in Introduction to *The Turn of a Century 1885-1910* (Cambridge: Department of Printing and Graphic Arts, Houghton Library, Harvard University, 1970), p. 1.

5. Quoted in Mackail, *William Morris*, vol. 1, p. 186.

6. Lionel Trilling has pointed to Morris' great personal force: "The peculiar power and charm of William Morris are suggested by the deep admiration in which he was held by two great writers of the generation after his own, William Butler Yeats and George Bernard Shaw. The dissimilarity of these men is legendary. . . . Antithetical as they were in their hopes for life, both men acknowledged Morris as master." ("Aggression and Utopia: A Note on William Morris' 'News from Nowhere,'" *Psychoanalytic Quarterly*, XLII (April 1973): 214-215.

7. Walter Crane, "Arts and Crafts," *Encyclopaedia Britannica* vol. II (11th ed., 1911), p. 701.

8. David A. Randall, "Waverley in America," *Colophon*, N.S., I (Summer 1935): 39.

9. See David H. Dickason, *The Daring Young Men: The Story of the American Pre-Raphaelites* (Bloomington: Indiana University Press, 1953).

10. James D. Hart, *The Popular Book* (New York: Oxford University Press, 1950), pp. 181-186.

11. Jay Martin, *Harvests of Change* (Englewood Cliffs, N.J.: Prentice-Hall, 1967), p. 217.

12. Larzer Ziff, *The American 1890's* (New York: Viking, 1966), p. 92.

13. Holbrook Jackson, *The Eighteen Nineties* (New York: Knopf, n.d.), pp. 17-18.

14. Elizabeth Aslin, *The Aesthetic Movement: Prelude to Art Nouveau* (New York: Praeger, 1969), p. 129.

15. For a thorough discussion of American Arts and Crafts, see Dickason, *The Daring Young Men* and Robert Judson Clark, ed., *The Arts and Crafts Movement in America 1876-1916* (Princeton: Princeton Art Museum, 1972).

16. Quoted in Warner Berthoff, *The Ferment of Realism* (New York: Free Press, 1965), p. 28.

17. For a discussion from the viewpoint of the history of ideas, see Roger B. Stein, *John Ruskin and Aesthetic Thought in America: 1840-1900* (Cambridge: Harvard University Press, 1967).

18. Dickason, *The Daring Young Men*, p. 5.

19. "Exhibition of the Gild of Arts and Crafts of New York," *Craftsman*, II (May 1902): 99.

20. Oscar Lovell Triggs, *Chapters in the History of the Arts and Crafts Movement* (Chicago: The Bohemia Guild of the Industrial Art League, 1902), p. 1.

21

V

The Arts & Crafts Book Model

MORRIS' INTEREST in the physical book reached much farther back than 1888. In 1866 he and his friend from Oxford days, Edward Burne-Jones, had planned a fine edition of Morris' *The Earthly Paradise*. Burne-Jones drew many illustrations, some of which Morris cut on wood blocks himself. Specimen pages were set up at the Chiswick Press, but the book was never issued.[1] Around 1872 more trial pages were set up for a fine edition of Morris' *Love Is Enough*, with decorations by himself and Burne-Jones, but the book was issued in another format. At various times, especially during the early seventies, Morris wrote out and illuminated such manuscript books as the 1874 *Odes of Horace* which was displayed at the first Arts and Crafts Exhibition. (Along with typography and book collecting, Morris' illumination was the subject for an exhibition at the Morgan Library in the fall of 1976.)

The next two books published by Morris after the Exhibition of 1888 were designed by himself and printed at the Chiswick Press in the so-called Basel type, modeled on a face of about 1500. They are *The House of the Wolfings* (1889) and *The Roots of the Mountains* (1890), each actually issued late in the preceding year. The page layouts were designed to present a unified double opening. Composition of the title pages was closely supervised by Morris to the extent of inserting another word to improve the spacing and to writing a poem especially to fill up empty space. The former book was issued in a large paper as well as an ordinary edition, but Morris was becoming aware that such a practice ruined the marginal proportions. Consequently, the latter was issued in a fine paper (Whatman) edition rather than large paper.

In 1890 Morris was setting up his own press. Before examining its work it may be well to glance at Morris' expressed views on bookmaking since they are said to contradict his practices. For example, it is frequently remarked that not only are the Kelmscott books strangely luxurious in view of Morris' socialist ideas, but that they are also more elaborate than Morris' own pronouncements on book design would lead one to expect. One of the reasons for this belief is that the highly decorated opening pages are the ones most often reproduced, leading to the idea that these pages are typical, whereas, in fact, the more numerous text pages are much simpler.

The appendix gives a list of Morris' statements on the physical book and excerpts therefrom. These excerpts are summarized below, in categories arranged in descending order of importance, according to the amount of space given them by Morris.

Type

The form of the type is of the first importance to Morris, so much so that undecorated books can seem beautiful to him. He sees a need for some irregularity in the form but wishes to avoid eccentricity. At one time, long primer seems to him the smallest advisable size for a text type, at another, small pica. He is anxious to avoid grayness or compression so he calls for bold type, drawn wide, each letter sharply differentiated.

For roman letters, those of Jenson appeal to him more than any others, including Aldus and Caslon; he loathes the modern faces of Bodoni and Didot. His own copy of Jenson is blacker than the original, however, In fact, he prefers Gothic type, especially for lower case, and in a rounder, less spiky form, without contractions or ligatures.

Composition

Morris is for close spacing, making a solid page, and says so many times. The spaces should be as nearly equal as possible, and rivers should be avoided at all costs. Double columns are better for Gothic than roman type. Leading between the lines should also be avoided and the type should have as small a body as possible.

Placement on the page—in other words, the margins—is of paramount importance. For this, the two facing pages should be regarded as one unit. The margins should increase in the following order: binder edge (i.e., gutter), head, fore, tail. Large paper copies are not advisable since the margins must be wrong in either the large or ordinary paper issue.

Paper

It is very important to have first-quality paper, which means handmade entirely of linen, well sized, and laid rather than wove. Cheap paper should not pretend to be better than it is. Small books should be printed on thin paper; big books are better since they lie open more easily.

Decoration

Both types of decoration—ornament and illustration—are good, but they should form an integral part of the page in harmony with the type. The precision and beauty of the line is important in book decoration. Commercial ornaments are worthless. Medieval art is admirable; Renaissance art deplorable.

Unity

Each craftsman who works on the book must be an artist able to work harmoniously with the others. The overall harmony is of supreme importance.

Architectural Analogy

The construction of a book is as important as that of a building. A beautifully decorated book is surpassed as a work of art only by a comparable building.

Craftsmanship

Utility and art may go hand in hand if the designers know the materials and methods of the craft, and the craftsmen understand the artistry of the design.

As for Morris' own press, the name Kelmscott originally belonged to his country house, Kelmscott Manor. He later named his home in town at Hammersmith, Kelmscott House, and the press was set up nearby.

In the fashion he had learned from Walker, Morris had photographs of fifteenth-century type enlarged and based his own designs on them. The punches were cut by Edward P. Prince and the types cast under the direction of Talbot Baines Reed. The first face, based on the type used in Leonard of Arezzo's *History of Florence* (Venice, Jacobus Rubeus, 1476) and in Pliny's *Natural History* (Venice, Nicholas Jenson, 1476), was called Golden because it was intended for first use in *The Golden Legend*. That book was delayed, however, and the first book from the press in May 1891 was Morris' own *The Story of the Glittering Plain*. There has been some debate about whether the Rubeus or Jenson type is closer to the Golden.[2] The Rubeus is heavier than Jenson but less heavy than the Golden. Jenson's work has the lightness of the Renaissance while Morris' pages look darker and more Gothic. For his next type Morris was inspired by the fonts of the incunabula printers Peter Schoeffer, Johann Mentelin, and Gunther Zainer. The result was a Gothic face called Troy from Raoul Lefevre's *The Recuyell of the Historyes of Troye*, printed at Kelmscott in 1892. The Chaucer type, used most notably in the 1896 *Works of Chaucer*, was a smaller version of Troy.

Morris did not do the actual printing himself but was able to find workmen for his Albion handpresses who achieved excellent presswork. Joseph Batchelor, Little Chart, Kent, made special paper for him. Vellum for superior copies, being unattainable in Rome because of the Vatican monopoly, was also from an English source. Ink, however, was imported from Germany.

The fifty-three titles printed at the Kelmscott Press have wood-engraved initials, borders, and other decorations designed by Morris in styles reminiscent of Erhard Ratdolt and other fifteenth-century printers. Some have illustrations by Walter Crane, C. M. Gere, and Burne-Jones. Simple typographic half titles are often supplemented by elaborate double spreads within borders and by colophons that give the production information, followed by printer's devices. Many of them are printed in both black and red with blue added in two cases. The type is closely set, without leading, and with a general avoidance of white space so that short lines are often filled out with fleurons. The margins increase in width in the prescribed Morrisian fashion. The books were bound by J. & J. Leighton in either gray paper boards or vellum with ties. A special pigskin binding for some copies of the *Chaucer* was designed by Morris and executed by T. J. Cobden-Sanderson. Formats include sextodecimo, octavo, quarto, and folio. A good proportion of the titles are medieval or medievalistic, including Morris' own writings. After Morris' death in 1896, the press was carried on through books already planned until 1898.

These were the books then that were models for the Revival of Fine Printing. Obviously, not all the books that were so inspired did copy them exactly. It is now time to codify the general characteristics of the books following in the wake of the Kelmscott Press that are sufficiently reminiscent of Morris' style to enable one to point out the resemblance and which constitute the Arts and Crafts style. As with the Aesthetic style, no given book need have every one of these characteristics in order to have an Arts and Crafts appearance. Nor is each one necessarily found in the Kelmscott books; they may be adaptations.

MATERIALS

Binding

    a. Paper boards with cloth backstrip; title printed on boards or printed paper label pasted on.

    b. Vellum, limp or stiff, often with silk ties and gilt-stamped title on spine or front cover.

    c. Blind-stamped leather with raised bands, sometimes with clasps.

Paper

    a. Very white, thickish, handmade, laid paper, with watermarks. (Machine-made paper with chain lines is also referred to as laid.)

    b. Plain end papers.

    c. Deckle edges. (Although most Kelmscott books had trimmed edges, the earlier ones did not, and deckle edges were already associated with fine printing.)

Ink

    a. Very black, in striking contrast to the white paper.

    b. Frequent use of red as a second color, especially for title pages, large initials, and shoulder notes. Sometimes another color, such as blue or green, in place of the red or along with the black and the red.

DESIGN

Typeface

    a. Often modeled after Jenson's, via Morris.

    b. Some other old style: Caslon or a heavier face.

    c. Gothic often used for display purposes and sometimes for texts.

    d. Avoidance of italic or modern-style type.

Title Page

    a. Often double opening regarded as one unit.

    b. Woodcut borders, initials, and ornaments.

    c. Gothic lettering, sometimes with background of arabesque or foliate tracery.

    d. All, or mostly all, capital letters.

    e. Block arrangement of words, flush left and right, often with fleuron line fillers.

    f. Symmetrical rather than asymmetrical orientation of page or opening.

    g. Sometimes title page relegated to frontispiece treatment opposite incipit page or abbreviated to a label title telling only the subject of the book.

Other Preliminaries

    a. Half title in caps, flush left, in upper left corner of page.

    b. Table of contents, etc., in caps and block arrangement.

Text Layout

    a. Lines closely spaced without leading between them; no rivers of white space, including around initials.
    b. Fleurons instead of indentations for new paragraphs and fleuron line fillers.
    c. Two pages of an opening regarded as one unit.
    d. Margins in order of increasing width: gutter, head, fore, tail.
    e. Running titles not as headlines but as shoulder notes.
    f. Pagination numerals close to text block.
    g. Decorated initials at beginning of sections with adjacent text lines in caps.
    h. Woodcut, black and white illustrations, usually within borders, often full page.
    i. Sometimes woodcut borders used on text pages.

Colophon

    a. Full information (more than on title page) as to facts of production, including names of artists and craftsmen, sometimes in archaic language.
    b. All caps, block arrangement.
    c. Woodcut printer's device and/or fleurons.

PRESSWORK

    a. Heavy inking.
    b. Heavy impression.

FORMAT

    a. Often large: folio or quarto.
    b. Also full range of sizes and shapes.

PRODUCTION

    a. Small, limited editions with numbered, signed copies.
    b. Hand methods.

SUBJECT MATTER

    a. Medievalistic.
    b. Literary classics.
    c. Bibliophily.
    d. Unpublished *belles lettres*.

The basic opposition between Arts and Crafts and Aestheticism is that between manuscript and printed models. Many of the incunabula of the fifteenth century copied Gothic manuscripts as closely as possible; Arts and Crafts, in returning to these incunabula for inspiration also produced dark, compact books that recall the handwritten books of the Middle Ages. On the other hand, the Aesthetic books were based on the first format to emerge in response to the new technology of printing, the light, open pages of the sixteenth-century Renaissance.

It is not surprising, therefore, that the Renaissance Aesthetic style, less ornamented and more legible, has carried over into our own century, or that since World War I American printers have largely turned away from Arts and Crafts. But in the nineties what seems to have been wanted was precisely an inspirational jolt so strong that people would look at books with new eyes; nothing less than a return to the standards and ideals of the earliest Western printed books which tried to look like manuscripts. What provided the rejuvenating shock to American typography were medievalistic books, shaped for the connoisseur and priced for the well-to-do, in a utilitarian democracy that had never known the Middle Ages.

1. See Joseph R. Dunlap, *The Book That Never Was* (New York: Oriole Editions, 1971).

2. See André Tschan, *William Morris* (Berne: Monotype Corporation, 1962).

VI

Contemporary Comment

THE VERY FIRST references to Kelmscott books appeared, of course, in English journals. According to Morris' son-in-law, Morris was annoyed when public notice was given in England of his printing activities.[1] An item about *The Glittering Plain* in the *Athenaeum* of February 21, 1891,[2] brought in so many requests for publicly available copies of his first book that Morris changed his plans to include the production of such copies, the demand for which further increased after another note in the *Athenaeum* on April 4, 1891.[3]

But even before these notices mentioned by Sparling, there had been a description in the *Athenaeum* for September 13, 1890, of a new edition of *The Golden Legend* to be published by Quaritch and Ellis.[4] "In place of the black letter, to the use of which there are manifold objections, a fount of types newly designed by Mr. Morris after the fashion of those employed by Nicholas Jenson will be substituted." There was no mention of the new press, and the piece concluded: "As the impression will be a limited one, subscribers would do well to send their names to the publisher forthwith." This shows that from an early stage the public had been invited.

The February 21 notice in a general, and very widely read, periodical was followed quickly by a notice in a trade journal. The *Printing World*, edited by John Bassatt in London, said on February 25, 1891, that "Mr. William Morris, author of 'The Earthly Paradise,' has for some time past been preparing a new fount of type modelled upon that of an early Italian work, which struck him as being suitable for one of his forthcoming books."[5] This bare mention was followed later in the year by a more skeptical item to the effect that:

> Mr. William Morris, the poet and author, is having a cottage fitted up, near his pretty house overlooking the Thames, with all the necessary requirements for printing books, and intends to show the world at large what beautiful work he is capable of turning out, not only in a literary way, but also as an artist-printer. As a literary man he is a success, as an art-printer—well, we shall see.[6]

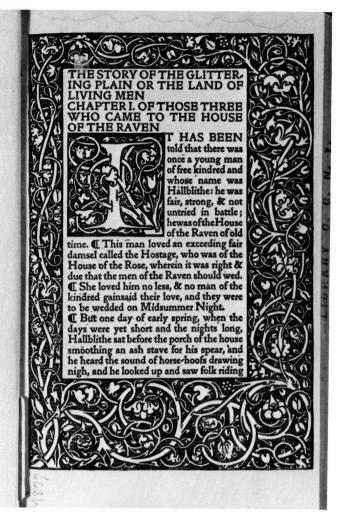

THE STORY OF THE GLITTERING PLAIN OR THE LAND OF LIVING MEN CHAPTER I. OF THOSE THREE WHO CAME TO THE HOUSE OF THE RAVEN

IT HAS BEEN told that there was once a young man of free kindred and whose name was Hallblithe: he was fair, strong, & not untried in battle; he was of the House of the Raven of old time. ⁋ This man loved an exceeding fair damsel called the Hostage, who was of the House of the Rose, wherein it was right & due that the men of the Raven should wed. ⁋ She loved him no less, & no man of the kindred gainsaid their love, and they were to be wedded on Midsummer Night. ⁋ But one day of early spring, when the days were yet short and the nights long, Hallblithe sat before the porch of the house smoothing an ash stave for his spear, and he heard the sound of horse-hoofs drawing nigh, and he looked up and saw folk riding

Plate 5. William Morris, *The Story of the Glittering Plain*. Boston: Roberts Brothers, 1891.

The editor could already have seen, for by this time Morris' first book had been published.

The *Printing World* was a new publication, but its scope was international, with reports on American, French, and other foreign journals, and this coverage may well have been matched by a comparable readership abroad. A longer established journal, the *British Printer*, did not pick up the news until later but in doing so sounded a new note of enthusiasm: "Considerable interest has recently been excited in the author of the 'Earthly Paradise' by reason of his establishing a private press of his own in which to print his works. . . ."[7]

The American trade journals were not so quick in picking up the news although a general periodical, the *Critic* of New York, did so rather early. On February 28, 1891, only a week after the *Athenaeum* notice of February 21, it reported that:

William Morris, the poet and house decorator, intends in future, it is said, to be his own printer, and has established a press in a cottage near his Hammersmith residence. He has long been preparing a new font of type modelled upon that of an early Italian work which has caught his fancy.[8]

The *Critic*, however, did not take special notice of the first book from the press at the time of its issuance. It was not until the second one that further notice appeared on November 21, 1891.[9]

It was an American publisher, not printer, who first brought the Kelmscott style to the eyes of Americans. Roberts Brothers of Boston, the regular American publishers of Morris, were evidently so struck by the format of *The Story of the Glittering Plain*, the Kelmscott version of which was a first edition of this romance by Morris and also the first book from the press, that they issued a photographic facsimile of it (Plate 5) in a limited edition of 500 copies at $2.50, a high price for fiction. The Roberts Brothers advertisement in the Fall Announcements number of *Publishers Weekly*[10] and another advertisement in the November 7, 1891, *Publishers Weekly*[11] gave brief, factual information. The book had actually appeared the week of October 24, 1891, as announced in the "Weekly Record" of *Publishers Weekly*.[12] A descriptive note by the magazine's editors began with the following sentence: "Gotten up in imitation of an old missal with peculiarly cut type and artistic initial letters, the work of the author also."[13] The *Critic* noted on March 19, 1892, that "*The Glittering Plain* reappears now in conventional type."[14] This second Roberts Brothers edition was priced at $1.50.

The American reviews of the new book by Morris did not fail to make note of its format but were not wildly enthusiastic. The *Critic* was the first to review it and the most favorable: "It is a handsome book, and it contains a beautiful story."[15] The Chicago *Dial*, in its review of "Recent Books of Fiction," simply mentioned without comment that the Roberts Brothers editon was a facsimile of the Kelmscott format.[16]

The *Nation*, on the other hand, was obviously glad to criticize both content and format, the acidulous style of the criticism being maintained in subsequent comments on the Kelmscott Press published in this journal. "In default of any other *raison d'être*, we imagine that this artistic combination of imitation vellum, parchment, and antique lettering may be intended to take a place with other bric à brac on a drawing-room table."[17]

In April 1892 Henry Lewis Johnson's *Engraver and Printer* (Boston) was one of the first American professional printing periodicals to make note of the new press.[18] "Editorial Notes" in July 1892 made reference to Kelmscott publication of *The Golden Legend* at $48.[19]

W. Irving Way, a bibliophile who was to be an important figure in the book world of the nineties, wrote often on fine books for the *Inland Printer* of Chicago. His article describing Eugene and Roswell M. Field's *Echoes from the Sabine Farm*, published by Francis Wilson in 100 copies, is interesting in that he mentioned quite a few other recent finely printed books without referring to the Kelmscott editions.[20] One has the impression that he was not yet familiar with them. However, by July, later in 1892, his regular feature, "Books, Authors, and Kindred Subjects," signed "Irving," had the following paragraph: "Mr. William Morris' Kelmscott Press Books are so eagerly sought by collectors that the editions are sold out long in advance of issue and the prices double, treble, and even quadruple within a few months."[21]

The *American Bookmaker*, the other leading printers' journal of the time, was slow to take notice of Morris. The knowledgeable and famous printer Theodore De Vinne seems to have been the first to mention him in these pages. "Masculine Printing" from the proceedings of the United Typothetae was a plea for bolder typefaces along the lines of Morris' "Basle" and "Jensen."[22]

Morris was now being interviewed by the British press about printing. The *Engraver and Printer* reported on such an interview that had appeared in the *Daily Chronicle*, in which Morris said English printing was "far ahead of other countries" and American printing "abominable."[23]

In the face of Morris' disapproval of American printers, this same month saw American printers beginning to shower him with superlatives. The most enthusiastic words about the Kelmscott books that had yet been seen in America appeared in the March 1893 *Inland Printer*.

> William Morris . . . showed to a few friends, a short time since, an advance copy of his reprint of Caxton's "Recueil of the Historyes of Troye." On looking through it, Dr. Furnival said enthusiastically, "It's the most beautiful book I ever saw; it's the most beautiful book ever printed!" and the same opinion was expressed by the art editor of the *English Illustrated Magazine*. . . . The volume is, indeed, a credit to English craftsmanship, and assuredly stands at the head of all specimens of book typography hitherto produced. . . . A new era has dawned in English printing. . . .[24]

On the other hand, the same month also saw the beginning of the virulent criticism which was to counterbalance the adulation of Kelmscott books and this in a journal read not just by printers but by the general public. The *Nation* published on March 16, 1893, an article dated from London on February 25, 1893, and signed "N.N." The periodical indexes identify the author as Elizabeth Robins Pennell, the wife of Joseph Pennell, the illustrator. The Pennells were American expatriates living in London, intimate friends of Whistler and authors of his biography. Elizabeth Pennell was a persistent critic of the Kelmscott Press, sometimes stooping to rather surprising accusations as in the present piece where she goes into detail about Morris' supposed penny-pinching.[25]

W. Irving Way, writing a few months later in the *Inland Printer*, had obviously read both the *Daily Chronicle* interview, with its criticism of American printing, and Mrs. Pennell's piece. He was ready to find faults with Morris' books, but his increasing admiration was also apparent. He began by referring to the British publisher Kegan Paul's 1883 *Fortnightly Review* essay in which he called for William Morris to design type. He then described Morris' *The Glittering Plain*, the first Kelmscott book "printed from type designed by him, and on a fine handmade paper which is said to have been made at his own mill. . . . It is claimed that he did the composition and presswork with his own hand, if he did not actually make the vellum in which the book is bound." (Morris did not, of course, own the Batchelor paper mill, nor did he do the composition and presswork entirely by himself, any more than he made the vellum.) Way found that the Golden type's "superiority to the types in general use today . . . cannot be questioned," but he found a lack of variety in the decorations. His other criticisms were that the register is "occasionally defective," the paper of uneven weight, and the title borders of the smaller works "too heavy and allow[ing] too little margin."[26]

A second installment of the article, appearing in the July 1893 *Inland Printer*, began with criticism of the heavy Kelmscott type impression, at the same time stating that Morris was ready to profit from constructive suggestions. This brought Way immediately to a more positive turn of mind: " . . . the 'golden type' possesses certain beauties which recommend it instantly to the 'man of feeling.' And when the eye becomes a little accustomed to a page of Mr. Morris' type, a page of ordinary typography pales into artistic insignificance."[27] The printers of America may well have been impressed by the awe that showed through Way's attempts to be critical, especially since the articles were illustrated with pages from Kelmscott books, which do look startlingly different in this context.

The *American Bookmaker*, without a regular contributor as up to date as Way, had been a little slower to appraise Kelmscott work. In November 1893, however, it published a piece by L. H. Woods.[28] Woods felt that hope for English printing had appeared in the form of the group led by William Morris. He then praised Beardsley's *Le Morte d'Arthur* and stated that publishers were beginning to realize their need for artists "for the general design and decoration of the printed page," not just for illustrations.

A month later, the *American Bookmaker* was virulent against Morris:

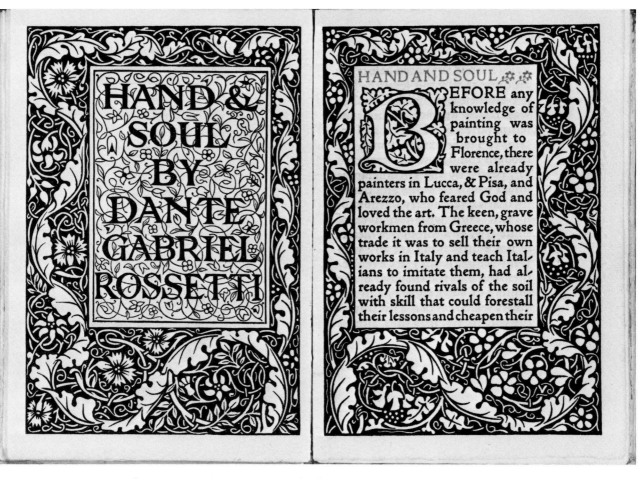

Plate 6. Dante Gabriel Rossetti, *Hand and Soul*. Hammersmith: Kelmscott, 1895.

What is flamboyantly claimed to be one of the gems of recent aesthetic (?) English typography is an edition of Tennyson's "Maud," printed at the Kelmscott Press with gold ink on vellum leaves. William Morris rushes from one experiment to another in his peculiarly insane crusade against plain black and white page text from modern fonts of light faced letters, artistic in design, sharply engraved and far more beautiful and effective than any of his resurrected monstrosities used in futile imitations of antique bookmaking.[29]

The "gold ink" must be a garbling of Golden type.

People were beginning to notice Kelmscott influence. The *Engraver and Printer* for Midsummer 1894, in an editorial about an interview of De Vinne that had appeared in the *Daily Chronicle*, said that De Vinne gave the credit for the bolder type now being used (the kind he had called for in "Masculine Printing") to the effect of printing dry and to the example of William Morris.[30]

The *Inland Printer* at the same time was not giving Morris much credit. Irving Way

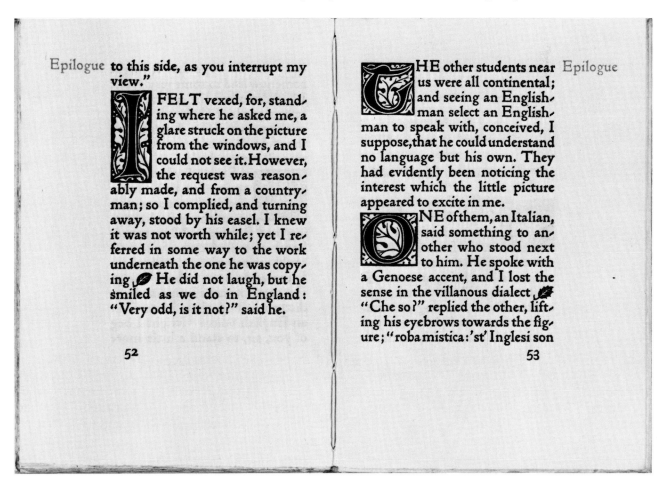

Plate 7. Dante Gabriel Rossetti, *Hand and Soul*. Hammersmith: Kelmscott, 1895.

was still feeling skeptical. In "Books, Authors, and Kindred Subjects" he offered the following: "'A miss is as good as a mile,' is a proverb one will hunt Bartlett in vain for: We give the origin of the proverb in the accompanying cuts from a late Kelmscott Press book. . . ."[31] The cuts were from the title page and opening text page of Morris' *Amis and Amile.*

A few months later the *American Bookmaker* was also regarding Morris with suspicion. Albert Henry, in a piece called "Classical Printing," after characterizing Kelmscott types and presswork as "affecting the antique," told the following story:

> An instance of the mental attitude of some employing printers in this country toward Mr. Morris' "beautiful books" came to my attention some time ago. A well-known printer of St. Louis was approached by a noted "booklover," who, handing him with dainty care a packet, said: "Look at that—*that* is what *I* call printing!" It was one of Mr. Morris' "creations." Our St. Louis friend, with the irreverence of one whose income is derived from railroad tariffs and general job work, thumbed the book over, noting with a professional eye the many little affectations and departures from established style, the uneven presswork and peculiar allowances for margin, and then returning the volume to the happy owner, he replied: "Well, *that* is what I call a *bum* job!"[32]

This antagonism on the part of contributors to the two largest professional typographic journals, both on the side of printing management, may have stemmed from more than resentment at Morris' socialism and his criticisms of American printing. It is conceivable that managers and owners might be resistant to stylistic changes that would add costs without increasing profits—part of the well-known conservatism of printers. Of course, once a style is established profits *are* increased by adopting it.

Way, however, became in the very next year, a personal disciple of Morris. In the spring of 1895 he made a trip to London, after which he established his own publishing house, Way & Williams. In an article in *Modern Art*, itself one of the earliest periodicals to adopt the Arts and Crafts format, Way described part of his trip.[33] On April 29, 1895, Way went to see the Kelmscott Press. He mentioned to Sydney Cockerell, the secretary of the Press, his "new departure in a business way" for which he had come to England to establish connections. "My first thought was that Mr. Morris would consent to print a book for us, something that could be issued at a modest price." He then went to see Morris at Kelmscott House, who welcomed him and told him how he had "wanted to make some nice books, but had no thought of developing such a business as has come to the Press." Way then described their arrangement for the joint book, which was to be Rossetti's *Hand and Soul* (Plates 6 & 7). (It was indeed published by Way & Williams in December 1895, the only book Morris printed for the American public.) Ellis and Elvey waived the copyright. The book was to be in Golden type, black and red, bound in full vellum, with a special title drawn by Morris. A price would be "submitted for consideration on my return to America." By the time of this article it was clear that Way had left the Pennell camp and was ready to join in defending the other side.

> There was never any question about the price. Do I think Mr. Morris made any money by the transaction? I know he barely covered expenses. The Kelmscott Press is not a money-making venture. Consider the care with which every detail is pro-

duced. Mr. Morris does all the designing—the paper is specially made, and costly, the inks are the best that money can buy in a country where vicious chemicals are unknown, [Did he know Morris had to go to Germany for his ink?] the type is set by hand, the sheets are dampened with the greatest care, the type is inked by a hand roller, not "dabbed," but thoroughly inked, and the presswork, all by hand, is as carefully done as if each impression were from an engraved or etched plate. . . . I do not see how Mr. Morris can hope to make a dollar out of this publication.

Mr. G. W. Smalley, in one of his letters to the "Tribune," in December, 1894, referred to the productions of the Kelmscott Press as possessing . . . "a dearness which I am almost inclined to call impudent. The profits of one book are said to approach $50,000." Hyperbole and "are saids" too often, alas, characterize the public utterances of Mr. Smalley.[34]

The truth about the financial circumstances may have been somewhere in between these two estimates. Jeannette L. Gilder (identified by the *19th Century Reader's Guide*) in the *Critic* wrote of a morning at Hammersmith in the summer of 1894:

I asked Mr. Morris to tell me, if it was not an impertinent question, whether it paid him in pounds, shillings and pence to print such handsome books. He answered that it did; but his secretary, who had just entered the room, begged leave to contradict this statement. "You have not," said he, "counted your work and your time, Mr. Morris. You are thinking only of the mechanical part; but if you put in your time and your skill, at what you would be paid for them by another person, you could hardly say that your publications made money." Mr. Morris smiled but said no more on the subject. The profit did not seem to interest him very much: it was the artistic results which he accomplished that pleased him.[35]

By March 1896 the Kelmscott style was prevalent enough for American printers to be concerned with a reaction to the Morris influence. J. S. Cushing of the Norwood Press wrote "Notes on Morrisania" for the *Engraver and Printer*, the first page of which has typography in imitation of Morris.[36] The gist of the article was, however, that this style was good for collectors, not readers, a charge reiterated to this day. After criticizing its legibility and practicality in detail and chiding "young publishers who have sprung up since the advent of Morris as a book-maker" (presumably Way & Williams among them) for agreeing with Morris, he decided that this fad, like others, would pass away. Cushing even disapproved of Caslon type. His summation, however, tried to be fair and anticipated, before Morris' death, hundreds of other critical opinions of his influence expressed in later years:

Mr. William Morris deserves all credit for the success he has attained in reproducing the handmade books of past ages, and for re-awakening thereby an increased interest in book-making as an art.

But his books, owing to their great cost, are not for the people. They are for the rich few only.[37]

Another persistent school of thought that wished to give Morris the credit for improving the appearance of books whether costly or cheap was also in evidence at this time. *Modern Art* reported on a paper read by Carl Edelheim before the Philobiblon Club of Philadelphia on January 29, 1896.[38] Edelheim had written Bernard Quaritch, the London bookseller, a friend of Morris: " . . . almost by return of mail I received, not only a lot of printed matter relating to the Kelmscott Press and its publications, but also a lengthy paper by Mr. Morris himself, in which he sets forth his aims and his methods." He then read the paper later printed as the last book of the Kelmscott Press, *A Note by William Morris on His Aims in Founding the Kelmscott Press . . .* (1898).

At the end of the talk, he stated his belief in the influence of the Grolier Club.

I have not found anywhere, either in short paragraphs or in long articles treating of the Kelmscott Press and kindred subjects, so much as an allusion to the Grolier Club. And still, from what I have been told in England, there is no doubt in my mind that the same has largely influenced, if not the methods of Mr. Morris, his determination to add his share in resuscitating and improving an art which stood so sorely in need of it.[39]

His conclusion was that, because of Grolier and Kelmscott "efforts and results":

Wherever we look today, in this country or in Europe, a perfect race in the production of the best possible type and the most beautiful appearance of books has begun, which happily extends from the costliest to the cheapest. That it has extended to the latter, I consider the most promising and the most important feature. Improve the taste and the understanding of the beautiful in the masses, and you create the groundwork for future improvement in every direction.[40]

What is remarkable in all this is the vehemence provoked by the Kelmscott books, whether pro or con. This extreme emotion on the part of American critics, after the initial noncommittal notices of Morris' printing, can be discerned at least by early 1893, less than two years after the appearance of his first book. The acceptance of the Kelmscott style was not immediate, as a survey of contemporary comment shows; however, in the context of the evolution of printing styles, it was amazingly rapid.

1. H. Halliday Sparling, *The Kelmscott Press and William Morris Master-Craftsman* (London: Macmillan, 1924), p. 76.
2. "Literary Gossip," *Athenaeum*, No. 3304 (February 21, 1891): 252.
3. "Literary Gossip," *Athenaeum*, No. 3310 (April 4, 1891): 442.
4. "Literary Gossip," *Athenaeum*, No. 3281 (September 13, 1890): 355.
5. ["Note"] *Printing World*, I (February 25, 1891): 59.
6. "Trade News and Notes," *Printing World*, I (October 25, 1891): 322.
7. "The Poet, William Morris," *British Printer*, IV (Nov./Dec. 1891): 48.
8. "Notes," *Critic*, XVIII (N.S. XV) (February 28, 1891): 117.
9. "Notes," *Critic*, XIX (N.S. XVI) (November 21, 1891): 290.
10. "Fall Announcements—Roberts Brothers," *Publishers Weekly*, XL (September 26, 1891): 451.
11. "Some Recent Publications," *Publishers Weekly*, XL (November 7, 1891): 686.
12. "Weekly Record," *Publishers Weekly*, XL (October 24, 1891): 627.
13. Identifying the incunabular style with liturgy was not unique on the part of *Publishers Weekly*, for the files of Roberts Brothers correspondence in the Special Collections of Columbia University contain a letter from J. & R. Lamb, 50 Carmine Street, New York, Ecclesiastical Art Workers, established 1859, dated November 13, 1891, requesting a copy of *The Glittering Plain*.
14. ["Note"] *Critic*, XX (N.S. XVII) (March 19, 1892): 168.
15. "Morris' *Story of the Glittering Plain*," *Critic*, XIX (N.S. XVI) (November 29, 1891): 298.
16. "Recent Books of Fiction," *Dial*, XII (December 1891): 275.
17. "Recent Fiction," *Nation*, LII (December 17, 1891): 472.

18. "General Notes," *Engraver and Printer*, II (April 1892): 86.
19. "Editorial Notes," *Engraver and Printer*, III (July 1892): 23-24.
20. W. Irving Way, "Eugene Field-Francis Wilson-R. M. Field," *Inland Printer*, IX (April 1892): 581-584.
21. "Irving" [i.e., W. Irving Way] "Books, Authors, and Kindred Subjects," *Inland Printer*, IX (July 1892): 871.
22. Theodore Low De Vinne, "Masculine Printing," *American Bookmaker*, XV (November 1892): 143.
23. "Editorial Notes," *Engraver and Printer*, III (March 1893): 87-88. This anti-American bias of Morris was not just a passing fancy. In respect to bookmaking, it can be documented as follows: Joseph Pennell in *The Graphic Arts: Modern Men and Modern Methods* (Chicago: University of Chicago Press, 1921) said (p. 92) that Howard Pyle's *Robin Hood*, designed entirely by himself and photoengraved, "made an enormous sensation when it came out here [i.e., England], and even impressed greatly the very conservative William Morris, who thought up to that time, 1883, nothing good artistically could come out of America."

In Morris' article on printing, written with Emery Walker, and published in *Arts and Crafts Essays* (London: Rivington, Percival, 1893), page 123 states that: "America has produced a good many showy books, the typography, paper, and illustrations of which are, however, all wrong, oddity rather than rational beauty and meaning being apparently the thing sought for both in the letters and the illustrations."

In a letter to his daughter Jenny, November 17, 1888, Morris described Emery Walker's famous lecture on printing: "There was a ridiculous Yankee there who was vey much 'risen' by Walker's attacks on the ugly American printing; who after the lecture came blustering up to Walker to tell him he was wrong; so I went for him and gave him some candid speech on the subject of the said American periodicals. He was not a nice-looking man: no chin little forehead: in short a mere nose with whiskers (sandy)." (Philip Henderson, ed., *The Letters of William Morris to His Family and Friends* [London: Longmans, Green, 1950], p. 303.) Could this possibly have been, by the way, S. S. McClure, the American syndicate tycoon who sold material to American periodicals and later founded *McClure's Magazine*, the famous muckraking journal? McClure was in London in late 1888 and he had sandy whiskers. He was not chinless,

however, but Morris' wrath may have lent hyperbole to his account.

In 1895, Benjamin Tucker, editor of *Liberty*, New York, an anarchist periodical, asked Bernard Shaw to write a reply to Max Nordau's *Degeneration* (1893), in which he had criticized, among others, William Morris. Shaw's open letter was published in *Liberty*, reprinted in *Modern Art* in 1895, and issued as a book. The following sentence appeared: "William Morris objected to the abominable ugliness of early Victorian decoration and furniture . . . and . . . to the shiny commercial gentility of typography according to the American ideal, which was being spread through England by Harper's Magazine and The Century, and which had not, like your abolition of 'justification' in Liberty, the advantage of saving trouble." (George Bernard Shaw, *The Sanity of Art* [New York: Boni & Liveright, 1907 ed.], pp. 107-108.)
24. "A New Era in English Printing," *Inland Printer*, X (March 1893): 518.
25. "N.N." [i.e., Elizabeth Robins Pennell], "The Kelmscott Press," *Nation*, LVI (March 16, 1893): 196-197.
26. W. Irving Way, "William Morris and the Kelmscott Press," *Inland Printer*, XI (June 1893): 213-215.
27. W. Irving Way, "William Morris and the Kelmscott Press," *Inland Printer*, XI (July 1893): 301-303.
28. L. H. Woods, "Prospects of Printing as a Fine Art," *American Bookmaker*, XVII (November 1893): 139-140.
29. "Editorial Comment," *American Bookmaker*, XVII (December 1893), 165.
30. "Editorial," *Engraver and Printer*, VI (Midsummer 1894): 18.
31. "Irving," [i.e., W. Irving Way] "Books, Authors, and Kindred Subjects," *Inland Printer*, XIII (July 1894): 332.
32. Albert Henry, "Classical Printing," *American Bookmaker*, XIX (October 1894): 95.
33. W. Irving Way, "A Visit to William Morris," *Modern Art*, IV (July 1, 1896): 78-81.
34. Way, *Modern Art*, IV (July 1, 1896): 78-81.
35. [Jeannette L. Gilder] [Morning with William Morris], *Critic*, XXIX [N.S. XXVI] (October 10, 1896): 214.
36. J. S. Cushing, "Notes on Morrisania," *Engraver and Printer*, IX (March 1896): 150-152.
37. Ibid.
38. "The Kelmscott Press," *Modern Art*, IV (April 1896): 36-39.
39. Ibid.
40. Ibid.

VII

Boston & Its "Literary Publishers"

WHEN THE FORMAT of a book is chosen, the decision can depend on a number of people who have different functions in book production. There are those, primarily publishers, who decide what to print, but may or may not have their own printing plants. Then there are those, primarily printers, who, according to how much of the publishing responsibility is also theirs, fall in a range from commercial jobbing presses at the command of others to noncommercial private presses at the command only of the owner. Thus, the three major groups responsible for format are trade publishers, commercial presses, and private presses.

It was in Boston, the American city traditionally the closest to the mother country, that the English Arts and Crafts Movement exercised the earliest and the greatest influence on American bookmaking. The reason for this is not far to seek—Boston was already an important center of both publishing and printing, and at the same time a focal point for education and literature. It was the intellectual capital of America, with its roots in Great Britain.

Among the trade publishers, it was the small "literary publishers," especially Copeland & Day, that most reflected new developments. On the other hand, Bruce Rogers, at Houghton Mifflin's Riverside Press, was the most important designer of the time. In commercial printing, the Heintzemann Press was a small but influential house, and the University Press reflected current trends; but it was D. B. Updike, with his highly personal Merrymount Press, who was to lead twentieth-century American typography. In private presses, Boston had little activity directly reflecting Arts and Crafts.

There was a well-developed spirit of bibliophily among Boston's men of letters. The Club of Odd Volumes, founded in 1887, was one of the nation's leading bibliophile societies. There were also literary societies, especially the Visionists, with members from the young Harvard men, who were interested in the Aesthetic *fin-de-siècle* movement, and whose book ideas were best expressed by the literary publishers, those houses run by amateur bookmen to publish advanced literature in well-designed formats. The

38

A·QVARTER·YEARLY
REVIEW·OF·THE·LIB-
ERAL·ARTS·CALLED
THE·KNIGHT·ERRANT
BEING·A·MAGAZINE
OF·APPRECIATION

PRINTED·FOR·THE·PROPRIE-
TORS·AT·THE·ELZEVIR·PRESS
BOSTON··A·D·MDCCCXCII···

VOLVME·FIRST·   NVMBER·ONE·

Plate 8. *Knight Errant*. Boston: Elzevir Press, 1892.

Arts and Crafts Movement was represented by an exhibition in 1897, followed by the formation of a society that laid heavy emphasis on bookmaking. The Craftsman's Guild, formed in 1900, was a result of that emphasis. It was not until 1905 that the Society of Printers was formed, carrying Arts and Crafts into the twentieth century.

The role of printing periodicals was important. New York had the *American Printer* (known also as the *Printer and Bookmaker*) and Chicago the *Inland Printer*, the two leading American typographic journals. Boston had in the nineties the *Engraver and Printer*, and then in 1903 the *Printing Art*. But it was a magazine with a broader scope than typography that most effectively carried the Arts and Crafts philosophy to book-making and paved the way both for the *Printing Art* and the Society of Printers. This was Joseph M. Bowles' *Modern Art*, first published in Indianapolis from 1893 to 1895, then moved to Boston where it ended in 1897. It has been known chiefly as the proving ground for Bruce Rogers, but Bowles' interpretation of Arts and Crafts in his editing and his own writing was highly symptomatic of the times, although it has attracted little notice.

There is a still earlier Boston publication that was equally significant in American Arts and Crafts printing. With such avant-garde literary and artistic groups as the Pewter Mug Associates, the Procrastinatorium, and the Visionists, some Harvard men and their cronies created an atmosphere in Cambridge in the early nineties out of which came the journal entitled the *Knight Errant*. It had been preceded by another magazine from the Harvard group, called the *Mahogany Tree* (January to December 1892) the format of which was conventional. The *Knight Errant*, on the other hand, physically resembled the two English periodicals, the *Hobby Horse*, put out by the Century Guild, an Arts and Crafts body, and the *Dial* of Charles Ricketts. The *Knight Errant* (Plate 8), which ran for four quarterly numbers dated from April 1892 to January 1893, was printed by Francis Watts Lee in five hundred copies at the Elzevir Press in Boston, and edited by Bertram Grosvenor Goodhue and Ralph Adams Cram. Frederick Holland Day and Herbert Copeland were among the contributors, with Day, for example, writing three out of the four sections on bookmaking. Physically it is a large quarto in heavy old-style type on handmade paper with wide margins and a striking medieval cover by Good-hue, dated 1891. Goodhue also did initials and tailpieces. Cram, who became a fashionable architect specializing in Gothic Revival, has described how his group, who were really monarchists, called themselves socialists because socialism was avant-garde and "We were William Morris enough to hate industrialism. . . ."[1]

> I like to think that they are right who say that the ambitious and short-lived *Knight Errant* was one of the earliest and most potent of these factors in the re-creation of the bookmaker's art.
>
> What we aimed to do was to take the English *Hobby Horse* and, in a manner of speaking, go it one better. It was to be not only an expression of the most advanced thought of the time . . . but, as well, a model of perfect typography and the printer's art. We had special hand-made paper prepared for us, and a new and beautiful fount of type, while Goodhue designed a most decorative and symbolical cover. . . . Fred Day determined the nature of the pagination and the general make-up, Frank Lee looked to the printing, and altogether we produced, I think, a very notable piece of work.[2]

Cram took a paternal pride in the *Knight Errant*, but outside observers came to similar conclusions, including one at the heart of the Arts and Crafts Movement, Walter Crane, who, in discussing his 1891–1892 trip to the United States, mentioned the magazine and its founders approvingly.[3]

The first number of the *Knight Errant* (April 1892) contained a very favorable notice by Lee on the Kelmscott Press *Poems by the Way* and Blunt's *Love Lyrics*. The second number (July 1892) had a whole article by Lee, entitled "Some Thoughts upon Beauty in Typography Suggested by the Work of Mr. William Morris at the Kelmscott Press," with several Kelmscott page facsimiles. He referred to Kegan Paul's 1883 piece and the hope expressed in it that an artist like Morris would design type. Lee thought the Golden type of Morris even better than Jenson's fifteenth-century face.[4] In the fourth number (January 1893), Goodhue, in "The Final Flowering of Age-End Art," brought in both the *Hobby Horse* and Morris:

> . . . there are the "Hobby-Horse" men: [Horne, Image, MackMurdo], and several others who have for years been writing and drawing for the few who could and would see and hear. . . . Since Mr. Morris established the Kelmscott press, those who once drew but one sort of pleasure from the reading of books, now obtain many.[5]

At the same time that the *Knight Errant* was running its course, Frederick Holland Day was setting up his publishing firm of Copeland & Day. Herbert Copeland was not entirely a silent partner, but it was certainly Day who was the prime moving force and who had the most to do with typography.[6] He was born in 1864 in what is now Norwood, Massachusetts, son of a well-to-do leather merchant. From 1884 to 1889 Day was secretary to the Boston branch of the A. S. Barnes Company. An outstanding, early artistic photographer, he also traveled widely, corresponded with literary men, studied New England local history and genealogy, and collected the Pre-Raphaelites and Keats. Day was responsible for the American Memorial to Keats set up at Hampstead in 1894. Invitations to 750 guests for the opening ceremony were printed at the Kelmscott Press. After the firm of Copeland & Day was dissolved in 1899, Day went back to Europe for a while, then home to Norwood where he lived as a virtual recluse until his death in 1933. He was always an eccentric, noted for his exotic clothes, long hair and beard, and pince-nez, very much the literary Bohemian. Copeland was a Bostonian who went to Harvard in 1887 from the Boston Latin School. After his graduation he was on the editorial staff of the *Youth's Companion* during the time that his own publishing firm was active, and he was able to draw on its editors and contributors for Copeland & Day. After the demise of Copeland & Day he was associate editor, with Bliss Carman, of the *Literary World* from 1903 to 1905. He continued doing desultory literary work until his death in 1923.

Bertram Grosvenor Goodhue, the major designer for Copeland & Day, was born in 1869 in Pomfret, Connecticut. C. H. Whitaker, his biographer, has said: "Certain it is . . . that Goodhue inherited much direct from the Pre-Raphaelite group, whether or no the knowledge of their doings and sayings came across to the little town of Pomfret."[7] Goodhue trained as an architect with Renwick, Aspinwall, and Russell in New York, before going to work with Ralph Adams Cram and Charles Wentworth in Boston. Cram has described his connection with bookmaking:

> To the new publishing firm of Copeland & Day, Goodhue was a godsend, helping with drawings and advice to make their earlier books works of unique distinction.

With Frank Lee he gave the short-lived "Knight Errant" its noble format, making it in fact the first example of the Morris sort of printing in America.[8]

Goodhue went on to do many other book decorations and pieces of graphic art, as well as becoming a leading architect, before his death in 1924. It is unfortunate that he is best known today for the Merrymount and Cheltenham typefaces because his woodcut decorations are greater achievements. Ingalls Kimball has described the intrinsic dichotomy of his style. Although unbound by tradition, "Goodhue loved medievalism. He delighted in black letter and in all the quirks of Latin abbreviations. He loved the crafts and yet was the most modern of the moderns."[9] His Gothic decorations, although certainly within the Arts and Crafts style as a whole, show a detailed knowledge of the historical Gothic style and the use of pointed lines more than do many Arts and Crafts practitioners. At the same time, he was never merely a traditionalist.

Day's feelings about the need for native American talent in bookmaking can be seen in the third number of the *Knight Errant*: "The utter lack of originality in the forms of ornamental bindings and title-pages brought out in this country is one of the chief misfortunes to be deplored in the progress of our bookmaking."[10] Copeland & Day made up a major portion of their own list from John Lane imports, without letting that fact interfere with commissioning bold, creative designs by American artists for other titles, most notably by Goodhue. Their further attachment to Europe (and limited editions) can be seen in *A List of Books Published by Copeland and Day . . .* (1895), which also offered for sale books from "Famous Modern Presses": three Daniels, fifteen Kelmscotts,

THE DECADENT.

I.

THE 3.20 train from Boston slowed up as it drew into a way station, and Malcolm McCann, grim and sullen from his weary ride in the dirt and cinders, the coal-smoke and the fœtid air, the fretting babies and hot, worrying men, that characterise a railway journey in August, hurried out with a grunt of relief.

It was not a pretty station where he found himself, and he glared ill-naturedly around with restless, agressive eyes. The brick walls, the cheaply grained doors bearing their tarnished legends, "Gents," "Ladies," "Refreshment Saloon," the rough raftered roof over the tracks, — everything was black and grimy with years of smoke, belching even now from the big locomotive, and gathering like an ill-conditioned thundercloud over the mob of scurrying, pushing men and women, a mob that swelled and scattered constantly in fretful confusion. A hustling business-man with a fat, pink face and long sandy whiskers, his silk hat cocked on one side in grotesque assumption of jauntiness, tripped over the clay-covered pick of a surly labourer, red of face and sweaty, blue of overalls and mud-coloured of shirt, and as he stumbled over the

1 a annoying

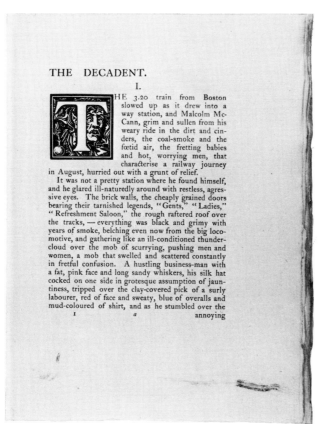

Plate 9. Ralph Adams Cram, *The Decadent: Being the Gospel of Inaction.* Boston: Copeland & Day, 1893.

Plate 10. Dante Gabriel Rossetti, *The House of Life*. Boston: Copeland & Day, 1894.

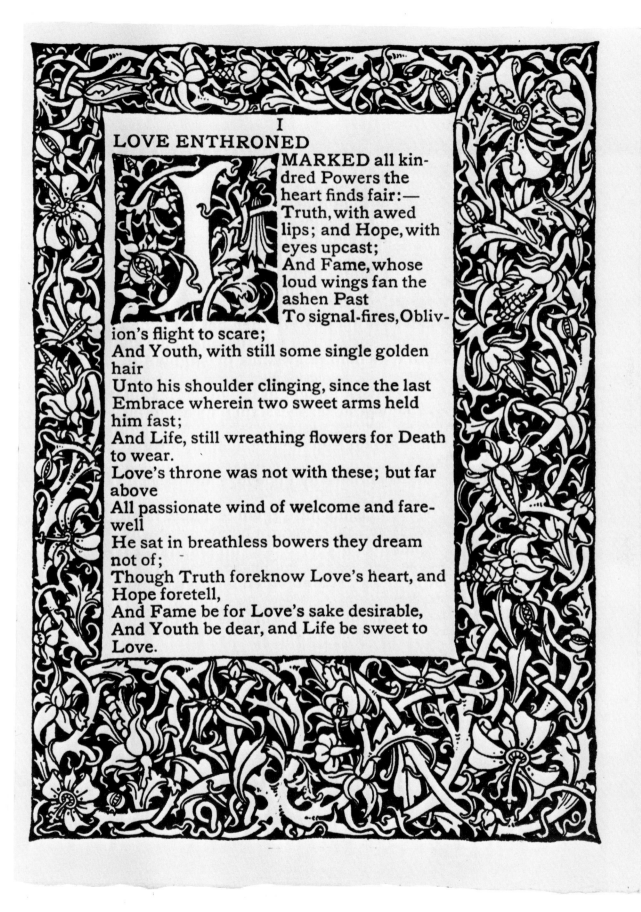

I
LOVE ENTHRONED

I MARKED all kindred Powers the
heart finds fair:—
Truth, with awed lips; and Hope, with
eyes upcast;
And Fame, whose loud wings fan the
ashen Past
To signal-fires, Oblivion's flight to scare;
And Youth, with still some single golden
hair
Unto his shoulder clinging, since the last
Embrace wherein two sweet arms held
him fast;
And Life, still wreathing flowers for Death
to wear.
Love's throne was not with these; but far
above
All passionate wind of welcome and fare-
well
He sat in breathless bowers they dream
not of;
Though Truth foreknow Love's heart, and
Hope foretell,
And Fame be for Love's sake desirable,
And Youth be dear, and Life be sweet to
Love.

five designed by Ricketts, and one Appledore. The 1896 catalogue added two more Daniels, one more Kelmscott, and one Eragny.

Publishers Weekly gave a favorable send-off to the new firm, announcing that Copeland & Day intended to publish only "fine limited editions."[11] The books listed include the *Tempest* with Walter Crane designs, "a fine edition" of the *Hobby Horse*, Rossetti's *House of Life*, Francis Thompson's *Poems* with designs by Laurence Housman, Wilde's and Beardsley's *Salome*, Richard Garnett's *Poems*, and a "revolutionary essay" privately printed "for the author," *The Decadent: Being the Gospel of Inaction*. Three months later, *Publishers Weekly* ran a sort of corrective notice, obviously at the publishers' own instigation, stating that Copeland & Day hoped for large, not limited, editions.[12]

The first book actually issued in 1893 was nevertheless a limited edition of very esoteric appeal, the privately printed essay referred to above. The secret author was none other than Ralph Adams Cram. The colophon tells us that 110 copies were printed by the University Press on "thick yellow French handmade paper" and 15 on "thin Lalanne paper." The frontispiece and initials were designed by Goodhue and cut on wood by John Sample, Jr. The binding for the copies on Lalanne paper is limp vellum with green silk ties, gold lettering on the spine, and a gold Art Nouveau floral ornament in the upper left corner of the front cover. The pictorial frontispiece is in red. The title page is in black with the publisher's device in the middle. The text pages, in Caslon, have wide margins and catchwords (Plate 9). There are three large initials in white on dark pictorial backgrounds, and the overall feeling of the book is decidedly Arts and Crafts.

Even more in the Arts and Crafts line is the first Copeland & Day title for publication and the first of the English Love Sonnet series: Rossetti's *The House of Life*. It was printed between July and December of 1893 by the University Press in 500 copies on French handmade paper and 50 on Michallet paper with rubricated initials. The title page, like *The Decadent*, has the title paragraph in caps above the Copeland & Day device, then the date in roman numerals. Goodhue designed the three borders at the beginnings of the parts and the fourteen floriated initials for the poems (Plate 10). Each sonnet, in Bookman type, has its own page, with the layout flush left, and with wide margins. Copeland & Day's 1894–1895 catalogue said: "The form in which the book is presented is one quite new in American bookmaking, whose beauty is in no small degree due to Mr. Goodhue's charming designs." This is quite literally true in both its statements. Closer to Kelmscott books than *The Decadent*, it is perhaps the next American book, after the Riverside Press *A Day at Laguerre's*, to approximate Kelmscott typography. At the same time Goodhue's designs are not only charming but rather original. Taking Kelmscott bookmaking as a point of departure, this American version is a fresh creation, thanks not only to Day's plan for the layout but also to the creativity of Goodhue. The bookmaking department of the *Knight Errant* in the fourth and last number (January 1893—issued in 1894) did not fail to praise the new book:

The [designs of Goodhue's] strongly suggest Mr. Morris' work in their general appearance; more probably from the fact that he is practically the only man who has heretofore done anything in this style, than on account of any great similarity which really exists between the two. There is much in these drawings of which we feel Mr. Morris would not approve, certainly much that he has never done; and while Mr. Goodhue's style would hardly have been possible without Mr. Morris', it cannot be justly said that he has copied him. The borders, in feeling with the poems, are exceedingly good, and are much better drawn than many of those from the Kelmscott press.[13]

Kraus has pointed out two interesting facts concerning *The House of Life*. First, proof sheets for it have been found at Harvard dated December 1892 although the public announcement was a year later.[14] This implies that Goodhue was at work on his designs not much more than a year after the appearance of the first Kelmscott book. Second, Day's papers, then (1941) owned by Goodspeed's Book Shop, show that the Visionists had planned to publish books, namely, *House of Life, Sonnets from the Portuguese*, Wilde's *Fisherman and His Soul*, and Keats' *Sonnets*. They made a prospectus with sketches of the title and text pages. Copeland & Day issued the first two of these in formats resembling the earlier sketches.[15] These formats are the ones based on Kelmscott, so again the genesis of the planning is taken back to an early stage.

W. D. Orcutt has left an account of his first encounter at the University Press with a Copeland & Day book. Although he does not make it clear whether it was *The Decadent* or *The House of Life*, it may have been the latter since he emphasizes the direct Kelmscott derivation.

> Fred Day came to John Wilson for cooperation, but he received a discouraging reception. No better mechanical printer than John Wilson ever lived, but to him Fred Day was just another good man gone wrong. He received him with intended courtesy, but showed by every gesture his complete antagonism to the layout called for in the sample pages for which Day asked.
>
> It so happened that this slight little man, with Vandyke beard and broad black hat, appealed to my youthful imagination. His exaggerated reserve made it difficult to approach him, but there was a subtle twinkle in his eye that discounted his apparent chagrin at finding Mr. Wilson so unsympathetic. I had not lost a word of that first conversation between them, and after Day left the office I found myself eagerly awaiting the instructions for the sample pages to be turned over to me for execution.
>
> "Here, William," John Wilson said impatiently, "take this and see if you can make anything out of it."
>
> It was the day following before I carried out his orders. In the meantime I went to the Harvard Library, with Fred Day's notes in my hand, and studied with infinite care the few examples of Morris volumes they had there. It was a turning point for me, for through Fred Day I came to understand William Morris, and through William Morris to understand why the printing of the 1890's contained so little that appealed to me. When I returned to the Press I even succeeded in imparting my enthusiasm to the compositor who set the page under my supervision.
>
> From the moment that first sample page was placed in Fred Day's hands, John Wilson left the manufacture of the Copeland and Day books to me. I am sure he thought me as crazy as he did Fred Day, and by that token lost faith in my future adaptability as a maker of books. But I had discovered that there was a creative side to the manufacturing of books after all. One of the earliest volumes in my autographed collection is a copy of "Esther," inscribed to me in Fred Day's handwriting, "whose aid has been not inconsiderable in producing so perfect an example." It was too high praise, for it was all his and Goodhue's, but I have never received an acknowledgment that pleased me more.[16]

DEDICATION: TO THE BEST-BELOVED

NIGHT on our lives, ah me,
how surely has it fallen!
Be they who can deceived,
I dare not look before.
See, sad years, to your
own. Your little wealth
long hoarded,
How sore it was to win!
how soon it perished all!
Beauty, the one face loved, the pure eyes mine
so worshipped,
So true, so touching once, so tender in their dreams!
Find me that hour again, I yield the rest uncounted,
Urns for the dust of time, divine in her sole tears,
Unseen one! Unforgotten! oh, if your eyes be-
hold it,
By chance, this page revealed, which trembling
holds your name
Marged in the ultimate wreck of fame and
meaner joys,
Co-partner be with me in this my soul's last
sorrow,—
Pearl of my hidden life,—this grief that not again
Unspoiled love's rose shall blow, the dear love
which was ours.

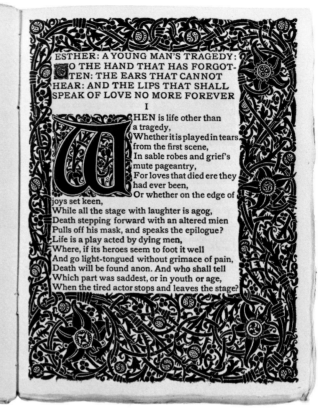

ESTHER: A YOUNG MAN'S TRAGEDY:
TO THE HAND THAT HAS FORGOT-
TEN: THE EARS THAT CANNOT
HEAR: AND THE LIPS THAT SHALL
SPEAK OF LOVE NO MORE FOREVER
I

WHEN is life other than
a tragedy,
Whether it is played in tears
from the first scene,
In sable robes and grief's
mute pageantry,
For loves that died ere they
had ever been,
Or whether on the edge of
joys set keen,
While all the stage with laughter is agog,
Death stepping forward with an altered mien
Pulls off his mask, and speaks the epilogue?
Life is a play acted by dying men,
Where, if its heroes seem to foot it well
And go light-tongued without grimace of pain,
Death will be found anon. And who shall tell
Which part was saddest, or in youth or age,
When the tired actor stops and leaves the stage?

Plate 11. Wilfrid Scawen Blunt, *Esther: A Young Man's Tragedy,*
together with The Love Sonnets of Proteus. Boston: Copeland & Day, 1895.

II

WHEN forty winters shall
besiege thy brow,
And dig deep trenches in
thy beauty's field,
Thy youth's proud liv-
ery, so gaz'd on now,
Will be a tatter'd weed,
of small worth held;
Then being ask'd where
all thy beauty lies,
Where all the treasure of thy lusty days,
To say, within thine own deep-sunken eyes,
Were an all-eating shame and thriftless praise.
How much more praise deserv'd thy beauty's use,
If thou couldst answer "This fair child of mine
Shall sum my count and make my old excuse,"
Proving his beauty by succession thine!
This were to be new made when thou art old,
And see thy blood warm when thou feel'st it cold.

III

LOOK in thy glass, and
tell the face thou viewest
Now is the time that face
should form another;
Whose fresh repair if
now thou not renewest,
Thou dost beguile the world,
unbless some mother.
For where is she so fair
whose unear'd womb
Disdains the tillage of thy husbandry?
Or who is he so fond will be the tomb
Of his self-love, to stop posterity?
Thou art thy mother's glass, and she in thee
Calls back the lovely April of her prime;
So thou through windows of thine age shalt see,
Despite of wrinkles, this thy golden time.
But if thou live, remember'd not to be,
Die single, and thine image dies with thee.

12 13

Plate 12. *Shakespeare's Sonnets.* Boston: Copeland & Day, 1897.

The rest of the English Love Sonnet series continued the Kelmscott resemblance and Goodhue's brilliant designs. The second one, issued in 1895, was Wilfred Scawen Blunt's *Esther: A Young Man's Tragedy, together with The Love Sonnets of Proteus*. The University Press printed 500 copies on Dutch handmade paper, with a Copeland & Day watermark, and 50 copies described as on English seventeenth-century paper, with rubricated initials. Like the Rossetti, there is one sonnet in Bookman to a page, with an elaborate and very black initial and a full border for the openings of the parts, with the type set very close (Plate 11).

The third in the English Love Sonnet series was Elizabeth Barrett Browning's *Sonnets from the Portuguese* (1896), in the same format with new designs by Goodhue. The fourth and last was *Shakespeare's Sonnets* (1897) produced in the same format, although Goodhue's initials are more modern and less Morrisian (Plate 12). The prices, incidentally, for this luxurious series were as follows, the first one being for the ordinary copies, the second for the deluxe: Rossetti—550 copies at $2.50 and $5.00; Blunt—550 copies at $3.50 and $6.00; Browning—800 copies at $2.00 and $5.00; Shakespeare—800 copies at $2.50 and $5.00. The 1896–1897 Copeland & Day catalogue quoted the *Book Buyer* concerning these volumes: "A series so luxurious in design and typography that it is a pleasure to remember that an American publisher made the books." When the Copeland & Day books were finally sold off, the *List of Publications for Sale en Bloc, 1899* offered none of the Rossetti, not even the plates, but did offer the plates for the other three, 82 bound copies of the Blunt, 185 bound copies of the Browning, and 9 bound copies of the Shakespeare with 500 sheets and cases.

The typical Copeland & Day book resembled those of the other literary publishers, and was in the Aesthetic vein: Caslon or other old-style type, centered running heads in caps, laid deckle-edge paper, wide margins, little decoration except on the cloth binding, centered all-block title page with device, small format.

Aside from books adhering closely to this archetype, there are several items that deserve to be mentioned because they are closer to Arts and Crafts. There were, for example, a few medievalistic titles. *This Is of Aucassin and Nicolette: A Song-Tale of True Lovers* (1897), Englished by M. S. Henry and versified by Edward W. Thomson, was printed by John Wilson & Son. It is on laid paper, in Bookman, with no decorations except for large black initials and the liberal use of fleurons in the text. There is one Morrisian-decorated initial at the text opening with a flush left title in caps. John Wilson & Son also printed in the same format *Our Lady's Tumbler: A Tale of Mediaeval France*, translated into English from the Old French by Isabel Butler (1898). The title page, in flush left caps, is filled out with leaves. There are black and white initials that imitate in form the traditional blue and red rubricated ones (Plate 13).

Goodhue was responsible for the Gothic Revival decorations on still another item printed at the University Press for distribution to friends at Christmas 1895: Louise Imogen Guiney's *Nine Sonnets Written at Oxford*. It is a small pamphlet in blue paper wrappers, solid set in Bookman type, with Kelmscott initials, and an exceedingly spotty use of filler leaves to separate the sonnet lines which are run on. The double-spread opening has brilliant woodcuts utilizing architectural motifs (Plate 14).

Copeland & Day were the publishers of some books in Colonial guise: Charles Knowles Bolton's *On the Wooing of Martha Pitkin: Being a Versified Narrative of the Time of the Regicides in Colonial New England* (1896); Louise Imogen Guiney's *Patrins: To Which Is Added an Inquirendo into the Wit & Other Good Parts of His Late Majesty*

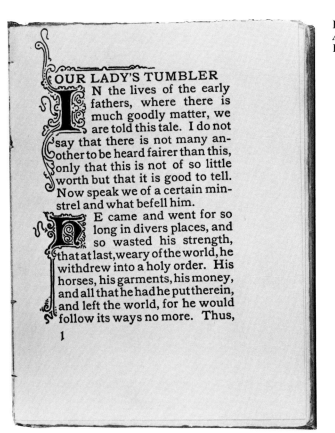

King Charles the Second (1897); Gelett Burgess' *Vivette or The Memoirs of the Romance Association* (1897), designed by himself.

A few of their books incorporated a modern boldness of design. For example, Stephen Crane's *The Black Riders* (1895), was put into a text format as bizarre for its time as the poetry itself, seemingly inspired by Ricketts' work on Wilde's *Sphinx* (1894), which Copeland & Day had published jointly with Mathews and Lane. The title page is in undecorated paragraph arrangement, while the text has the poetry in small caps in green ink printed high on the pages. The deluxe edition of *The Black Riders* consisted of fifty copies on Japan vellum, three of which were bound in real vellum with the title, author, and a lily design stamped in gold on the front and back. The ordinary edition has the same design in black on gray boards (Plate 15).

Also in 1895 Copeland & Day put out jointly with John Lane, Richard Le Gallienne's *Robert Louis Stevenson: An Elegy and Other Poems Mainly Personal.* Five hundred copies on English laid paper and thirty on handmade were printed at the Everett Press, Boston, in an Aesthetic format in small Caslon type. The red and black hand-lettered title page, however, is not Aesthetic and is, in fact, too bold for the text. The roman caps, with the Copeland & Day device in the middle, are flush left and right with no empty space and are surrounded by a solid black border in Morrisian proportions (Plate 16). This unexpectedly effective page is by Will H. Bradley, soon to become a major figure in American book design.

Finally, some Copeland & Day bindings, more or less in the Arts and Crafts pattern,

Plate 15. Stephen Crane, *The Black Riders.* Boston: Copeland & Day, 1895.

Plate 16.
Richard Le Gallienne,
*Robert Louis Stevenson:
An Elegy and Other Poems Mainly Perso*
Boston: Copeland & Day,
1895.

are so modern in appearance and so successful that they may well have influenced later designers. One of the best known of these is on *Songs from Vagabondia* by Bliss Carman and Richard Hovey (1894). The artist was Tom B. Meteyard. On the front of the brown paper boards is a black woodcut of the two authors and the artist. Both sets of endpapers are illustrated with heavy black cuts with inset verses. One has a picture of a port (Plate 17), the other of a forest. The wide popularity of the *Songs* placed this attractive but simple binding before many readers. It was also Copeland & Day's first book by American authors.

After John Lane opened a New York office in 1896, Copeland & Day no longer

Plate 17. Bliss Carman and Richard Hovey, *Songs from Vagabondia*. Boston: Copeland & Day, 1894.

published the *Yellow Book* jointly with him, but by this time they had built up a list of American authors. And in any case other English publishers had cooperated with Copeland & Day. Nevertheless, Day began to lose interest in publishing the next year, in favor of his photography. When Copeland & Day finally came to an end in 1899, they had published two periodicals (the *Hobby Horse* and the *Yellow Book*) and ninety-six books, all but two of which were *belles lettres*.[17] Most of the books went to Small, Maynard.[18]

The Kelmscott-inspired books of Copeland & Day, hailed by *Publishers Weekly* on their demise,[19] were praised again in 1903 by *Printing Art*:

> Many of the initials, from designs by B. G. Goodhue, were largely of a mediaeval character, and the combination with Old Style Antique [Bookman] and other heavy-faced types, formed some of the most characteristic and interesting examples of decorative printing which have been produced in this country.[20]

On the whole, through the years Copeland & Day has been fondly remembered and described as influential in its bookmaking. And it is the Goodhue/Kelmscott designs that are almost certain to be singled out for praise, as in the following quotations from the *Literary Miscellany* and from Ralph Adams Cram:

51

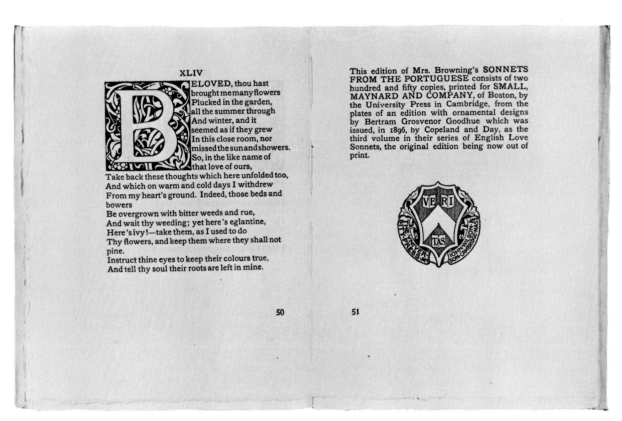

Plate 18. Elizabeth Barrett Browning, *Sonnets from the Portuguese*. Boston: Small, Maynard, 1902.

Among other things new . . . which Mr. Day introduced or helped to establish in everyday usage are the black face types, pictorial end-papers, blind stamped cloth covers and the printer's or publisher's colophon. The *English Love Sonnet* series, in which he first used black faced type, is as successful a creation in its way as are any of the Kelmscott books.[21]

This crusade for the improvement of the craft of bookmaking was a very significant showing of the buoyant temper of the time. Three firms, made up of members of our crowd—Copeland & Day, Small, Maynard & Co., and Stone & Kimball— were the leaders in this, and it is not too much to say that the first of these did a work of regeneration the effects of which were not to be discounted and are still operative. Copeland and Day's books were models of admirable art, and will always be items of high value in the eyes of bibliophiles. For some of these volumes Goodhue made his wonderful initials and decorations based on the art of William Morris.[22]

Small, Maynard & Company was, indeed, "made up of members of our crowd." Herbert Small had been Copeland's freshman roommate at Harvard. He and his partner, Laurens Maynard, began publishing in 1897. In 1899 they bought sixty-odd titles from Copeland & Day, almost doubling their list, which, like the lists of the other literary publishers, was strong in the New Literature, foreign and American. This list was eventually taken over by another Boston house, Lothrop, Lee & Shepard Co. Small, Maynard's

52

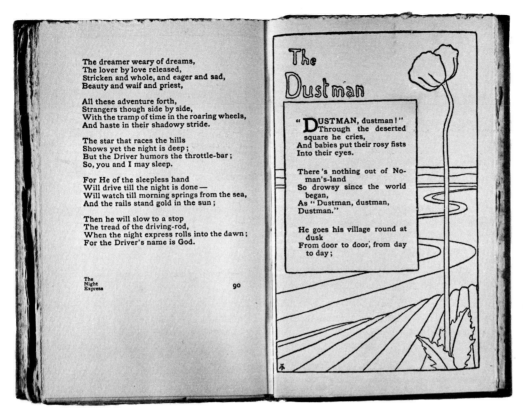

The dreamer weary of dreams,
The lover by love released,
Stricken and whole, and eager and sad,
Beauty and waif and priest,

All these adventure forth,
Strangers though side by side,
With the tramp of time in the roaring wheels,
And haste in their shadowy stride.

The star that races the hills
Shows yet the night is deep;
But the Driver humors the throttle-bar;
So, you and I may sleep.

For He of the sleepless hand
Will drive till the night is done —
Will watch till morning springs from the sea,
And the rails stand gold in the sun;

Then he will slow to a stop
The tread of the driving-rod,
When the night express rolls into the dawn;
For the Driver's name is God.

The
Night
Express   90

The Dustman

"DUSTMAN, dustman!"
Through the deserted
square he cries,
And babies put their rosy fists
Into their eyes.

There's nothing out of No-
man's-land
So drowsy since the world
began,
As "Dustman, dustman,
Dustman."

He goes his village round at
dusk
From door to door, from day
to day;

Plate 19. Bliss Carman, *Behind the Arras: A Book of the Unseen.* Boston: Lamson, Wolffe, 1895.

books were in the same Aesthetic line, but they did re-issue Copeland & Day books in the same format as originally designed, including Arts and Crafts. For example, they published *Sonnets from the Portuguese* (Plate 18) with its Goodhue designs in 1902.

Perhaps the most interesting of all the Small, Maynard books was one with new designs commissioned from Goodhue: José-Maria de Heredia's sonnets, *The Trophies*, translated by Frank Sewall (1900). The University Press printed 750 copies on English handmade laid paper. The binding is brown paper boards with the same design stamped in gold on the front and back. The format closely follows the English Love Sonnet series: centered title page with publisher's device, one sonnet to a page with decorated initial, wide margins, poem titles in centered caps, borders for the opening pages of the different sections in Morrisian proportions, colophon followed by printer's mark. But there are differences as well. The two devices and the borders are in sepia, whereas the Copeland & Day books were all black. The type is not Bookman but a modern-style face giving a sharp contrast between thick and thin strokes with an overall heavy black effect. And the motifs of the decorations are not medievalistic, Kelmscott, or even floral. They are small Renaissance designs that include medallions, vases, temples, ships, fruit, arabesques, chains of beads, leaves, women, hourglasses, balanced scales. There is some correlation with the subjects of the poems as in the border using Egyptian iconography. The overall feeling of this exquisite book is rather rococo; one calls to mind Beardsley's change from very black designs to the dotted lines of *The Rape of the Lock.*

As for Stone & Kimball, they started in Boston but soon moved to Chicago. There was still another Boston publisher, however, not mentioned by Cram, who had "members of our crowd," for W. B. Wolffe of Lamson, Wolffe & Co. was a Harvard man. In fact, he was asked at one point by university authorities "to withdraw either from the firm or the college."[23]

Between 1895 and 1899 Lamson, Wolffe published seventy or so titles, again in the same vein as the other literary publishers, but with more original books being produced too. Bliss Carman's *Behind the Arras: A Book of the Unseen* (1895), has designs by T. B. Meteyard. The Everett Press printed it in Bookman on laid paper with running titles at the bottom outer edge of the type pages and the page numbers on the inner edges. The beginnings of some poems are set within full-page designs (Plate 19). This book elicited a violent reaction from one contemporary critic, Will H. Bradley.

> It is a thousand pities that Lampson [*sic*], Wolffe & Co. should have so poor a notion of what becomes a book of verse, that they should so mistreat . . . Mr. Carman's poems . . . the coarse paper and heavy type . . . are distressing to the eye and touch. Both heavy type and illustrations on such rough paper require the cleanest and sharpest of press-work. Morris uses heavy type and floriated borders in the books brought out at the Kelmscott Press; but he uses very fine and pure white paper and does perfect press-work, producing a book that one can love.[24]

Today, the book seems a charming example of one version of the Arts and Crafts style, besides showing that the avant-garde publishers of Boston in the nineties were leading the way in format as well as in content.

1. Ralph Adams Cram, *My Life in Architecture* (Boston: Little, Brown, 1936), p. 20.
2. Ibid., pp. 85–86.
3. Walter Crane, *An Artist's Reminiscences* (New York: Macmillan, 1907), p. 371.
4. Francis Watts Lee, "Some Thoughts upon Beauty in Typography Suggested by the Work of Mr. William Morris at the Kelmscott Press," *Knight Errant*, I (July 1892): 59.
5. Bertram Grosvenor Goodhue, "The Final Flowering of Age-End Art," *Knight Errant*, I (January 1893): 110.
6. Both men's lives have been described by Joe Walker Kraus, "A History of Copeland & Day 1893–1899" (unpublished M.A.L.S. thesis, University of Illinois, 1941).
7. Charles H. Whitaker, *B. G. Goodhue Architect and Master of Many Arts* (New York: Press of the American Institute of Architects, 1925), p. 16.
8. Ralph Adams Cram, "Partnership," in Whitaker, *B. G. Goodhue*, p. 31.
9. Ingalls Kimball, *Bertram Grosvenor Goodhue: Book Decorations* (New York: Grolier Club, 1931), introduction.
10. [Frederick Holland Day] "Concerning Recent Books and Bookmaking," *Knight Errant*, I (October 1892): 94.
11. "A New Publishing Firm—Copeland & Day," *Publishers Weekly*, XLIV (December 2, 1893): 927.
12. "Literary and Trade Notes," *Publishers Weekly*, XLV (February 17, 1894): 333.
13. G. E. B., "Concerning Recent Books and Bookmaking," *Knight Errant*, I (January 1893): 123–124.
14. Kraus, "Copeland & Day," p. 16.
15. Ibid., pp. 21–22.
16. William Dana Orcutt, "Frederick Holland Day," *Publishers Weekly*, CXXV (January 6, 1934): 52–54.
17. Kraus, "Copeland & Day," p. 135.
18. "Small, Maynard & Co. Acquire Copeland & Day's List," *Publishers Weekly*, LVI (July 15, 1899): 125.
19. "Copeland & Day Retire from the Publishing Business," *Publishers Weekly*, LV (June 3, 1899): 920.
20. "The Use of Decorative Initials," *Printing Art*, I (May 1903): 75.
21. "A Maker of Beautiful Books," *Literary Miscellany*, II (Autumn 1909): 58.
22. Cram, *My Life in Architecture*, p. 85.
23. Hellmut Lehmann-Haupt, *The Book in America* (2d ed.; New York: Bowker, 1952), p. 325.
24. [Will H. Bradley] "Some Book Reviews: A Few Poets," *Bradley: His Book*, I (June 1896), p. 53.

VIII

Bruce Rogers
& J. M. Bowles

WHILE the literary publishers represented the avant-garde of the time, Bruce Rogers worked for the long-established general publisher, Houghton Mifflin, at its Riverside Press. His career had three periods: the early years of Kelmscott inspiration under the influence of J. M. Bowles, the heyday of allusive typography at the Riverside, and the long, later life of still more eclectic but brilliantly successful bookmaking.

Albert Bruce Rogers was born in what is now Lafayette, Indiana, in 1870. He went to college from 1886 to 1890 at Purdue University where he specialized in art under Professor Ernest Knaufft, editor of the *Art Student*, a periodical for which Rogers designed the title page in 1892. Knaufft has described the atmosphere of the time:

> The influence of William Morris in the field of the printed book was still in the future. However, the Arts and Crafts movement was fairly launched and we had just begun to read about William Morris, but only as a worker in textiles, glass, bronze, and other metals. . . .
>
> It must be remembered that fifty years ago there was not among our minor colleges the same degree of cultural information that there is today. No one was then interested in the artistic possibilities of the printed book. There was no recognition of typography as a "fine art."[1]

Rogers himself, however, had begun to appreciate typography, for he has described how:

> As a boy I never had a toy press to play with; and it was not until I was fifteen or sixteen years old that I began to observe books as specimens of the printer's art. There are included here [in an A.I.G.A. exhibit], I think, two books that were the first to attract and hold my attention in that way. One is a copy of a cheap edition of Carlyle's "Heroes and Hero Worship" given me at Christmas, 1889, by a college classmate.

It is commonplace enough in every way, but the first book, so far as I can remember having seen, that had a line of red on the title-page. The other is Stopford Brooke's "English Literature," also with a red and black title-page, but, in addition, printed handsomely on a Dutch hand-made paper, nearly uniform in size and style with the large-paper issues of the Golden Treasury Series. Two of this handsome set, Tennyson's "Lyrical Poems" and "In Memoriam" were, with Brooke, in our LaFayette Public Library, and I frequently took them home to look at and handle.[2]

(The Larremores have amended the above statement. The Carlyle was *Sartor Resartus*, Imperial Edition, New York, White & Allen, n.d. The Brooke was put out by Macmillan of London, 1880. Rogers wrote confirming this on April 3, 1942.[3])

Rogers did some designing while still in college for such publications as the *Purdue Exponent* and *Debris*, the class yearbook. After graduation in 1890, he went to work as an illustrator on the *Indianapolis News*. His biographer, Frederic Warde, has written that at this time Rogers knew nothing of the beginnings of the Kelmscott Press but that he already knew "that illustration was interesting to him only as a means of beautifying books."[4] The hectic newspaper work did not please him so he returned to Lafayette to work at landscape painting. He also worked for a railway in Kansas. But 1893 found him once again in Indianapolis, employed by the Indiana Illustration Company, where he did his first book decorations for John S. Wright's *Botany in Pharmacy*, put out by the Eli Lilly Company.[5] The hand-lettered title and the scrolls for the illustrations have an Art Nouveau quality. The tailpiece is simply two symmetrical leafy arabesques. In the same year (1893), Mary E. Steele's *Impressions* was published by the Portfolio Club with a Rogers title page, this time with Arts and Crafts influence in the layout. The imprint is flush left and right, while the title is an inverted triangle ending in a leaf. The triangular title resembles Updike's *On the Dedications of American Churches* (1891).

Joseph Moore Bowles has told how he met Rogers as early as 1890, probably in the Portfolio Club.[6] Bowles worked in an art store and in 1893 started publishing in Indianapolis a periodical, *Modern Art*, that was to be an important means of spreading the Arts and Crafts gospel. *Modern Art* began in January 1893 in quasi-Arts and Crafts style with wide margins, decorated initials, flush left titles in caps set close to the text, fleuron line fillers, and shoulder notes. But the type was spindly and leaded and the art work looked very mid-nineteenth century. The Spring 1893 number was the first to include Rogers' work but his title page with a budding tree and crocuses is not Arts and Crafts. Summer 1893 had the following mention of Morris: "However Mr. William Morris may achieve success in other directions, there are a few of us who will never envy any of his results more than his Kelmscott Press."[7] In Autumn 1893 Rogers illustrated an article on "Gargoyles." For Spring 1894 he drew a bud, flower, and leaf border for a hand-lettered sonnet on Rossetti by Charles Stuart Pratt. This number also had a white vine on a black background border by Brandt Steele for the first page of text.

The Summer 1894 number had an article by Bowles called "Thoughts on Printing: Practical and Impractical" with an old-fashioned rococo initial by Rogers and, as illustration, two pages from the Gruelle book which Rogers and Bowles were producing. The article itself is perhaps the one best contemporary summary of the attitude in the nineties toward printing on the part of those interested in art and therefore deserves lengthy quotation:

Just as in painting or sculpture, printing, rightly used, is a medium for the expression of art feeling. . . . Many men whose opinions we must respect, because of what they have accomplished in other branches of decorative art, tell us that the practice of printing has fallen so low that considered strictly as an art, it has almost ceased to exist. This may seem a strong statement to make in these days of great and rapid presses, big publishing houses, and the constant outpouring of tons of expensive printing, but these very elements of quantity, rapidity, and the financial success of poor things, are some of the causes of this downfall. Great machines are so absolutely necessary to produce these vast quantities of printed paper that the standard, even in the most costly books, has come to be one of machine finish. . . . A page may be as weak or ugly as it pleases in composition, but it must not bear any mechanical imperfections! . . . There is great lack of interest in the appearance of printed books, and a general impression that a book can not be artistic until it is filled with ornaments or illustrations. . . . This widespread apathy with regard to it is the severest comment that can be passed on the dull ugliness of the ordinary book, each page of which is just like every other, and all of them characterless and uninteresting. Nor are costly books and *editions de luxe* any better as regards the form and composition of the type used in their pale and lifeless pages. There is no doubt about this statement, that artistically the first books printed have never been surpassed. . . . There is no reason in the world

Plate 20. *Modern Art.* Boston: L. Prang & Co., 1896.

Plate 21. *Modern Art.* Boston: L. Prang & Co., 1896.

why, with the improved facilities at our command, we should not do finer printing to-day than was ever done before, but the salvation of modern printing can come in only one way, through a reunion of printers and artists—decorative artists. . . .

Before they can even work intelligently together, the artist must learn enough of the practical side of printing to set type if necessary and the printer must study the laws of decorative art and realize that art printing is only a part of the greater art-life.[8]

Years later, in 1916, Rogers wrote about this indivisible coalition of artist-printer. In a letter to H. L. Bullen he chided him for putting art on a pedestal: "You still, it seems to me, recognize and make a special subject, or class, of so-called 'Art Printing' as done by 'artists,' to be distinguished from 'practical printers.' Now I don't admit that any such distinction exists."[9] Rogers himself had become the most famous example of a new breed of typographer which brought together art and printing: the book designer. D. B. Updike was forming the words of a credo for this budding species at the very time Bowles was publishing his plea for artist-printers.

In Autumn 1894, Bowles, writing for *Modern Art* specifically on "William Morris as a Printer: The Kelmscott Press," with Kelmscott pages reproduced, called Morris "the greatest printer of the age."[10]

Volume three, 1895, marked Bowles' removal to Boston where Louis Prang & Co., the successful lithographers, had agreed to underwrite the publication of *Modern Art*. Winter 1895 was the first issue done in Boston and the first one with a new format, this time totally Arts and Crafts. Bookman type is used; there are block titles, red shoulder notes, pagination, and floriate initials by Rogers that are certainly based on Kelmscott inspiration. This new format did not go unnoticed. In fact Bowles issued an advertising card with a Rogers side border in the Kelmscott style which quoted plaudits from three newspapers. The Spring 1895 number experimented with green ink instead of red, but Summer 1895 went back to red. It also had a very Arts and Crafts title page of Gothic lettering within a border by A. C. Nowell. The next four numbers all had Arts and Crafts title pages, two by Rogers (Plate 20) and one each by Louis Rhead and Gertrude G. Fuller (Plate 21).

Bowles gave a spirited defense in Autumn 1896 of his periodical's format in rebuttal to Theodore Goebel of Stuttgart who found the heavy type of *Modern Art* not leaded widely enough and therefore hard to read. Goebel also did not like the lack of space between the headings of the articles and the text and between the illustrations and the text. In defense Bowles quoted a letter from Harold M. Duncan, editor of *Paper & Press* of Philadelphia, who did not care for the thin, pale, modern type with double leading that made for gray and illegible pages in Goebel's *Die Graphischen Künste der Gegenwart*. Bowles went on to discuss his own Bookman type and to give a rationale of the Arts and Crafts page layout:

This type is not ideal nor what I would wish it to be; it is only the best that could be found, after much research in the type market. It is a trifle ungraceful in drawing, but it is masculine and makes a strong page. The headings are set as they are in order to preserve the *unity of page*. The idea is that the two open pages of white paper are the background. The two pages of type in black or red, properly placed on the paper, form the important fundamental mass of the design, and the initial, border, and other decorations are the flowers which spring from this growth and which *must* be sup-

Plate 22. R. B. Gruelle,
Notes: Critical & Biographical.
Indianapolis: J. M. Bowles, 1895.

ported by it. I claim that the light, hair-line types utterly fail to do this, and are weak, insipid, and characterless both by themselves and in the mass. In nearly every modern book one opens the decorations fairly jump at you, the pages of type are so gray, so delicate that they are powerless to hold them down and back in their proper place; a page and its ornament should be firmly welded together, or better still should appear to be one organic whole. No virile designer can be asked to draw down to the half-dead and microscopic insignificance of line used in ordinary type; in order to keep the two together the type-designer must make the forward step and learn to draw his letters once more with the natural human weight and width of line that the artist employs when he designs a decoration.[11]

Winter 1897 was the last issue published, for Prang & Co. had gone out of business, and Bowles' transfer to Heintzemann was not entirely satisfactory. Except for the title page, Rogers designed the decorations, including some outline vine initials. Bowles again wrote on his favorite subjects, including the first Arts and Crafts exhibition to be held at Copley Hall, April 5–17, 1897.

After the demise of *Modern Art*, Bowles moved to New York and started another periodical called *Art and Life*. Later still, he became a salesman for William Edwin Rudge,

Plate 24. Percy Bysshe Shelley, trans., *The Banquet of Plato*. Chicago: Way & Williams, 1895.

the fine printer who also employed Rogers. He continued to write on the graphic arts, and was the moving spirit of a group of printing enthusiasts called the Stowaways.[12] Elmer Adler stated that without the Stowaways there would have been no Typophiles (a well-known contemporary group which publishes finely printed small books on typographic history) or, for that matter, no American Institute of Graphic Arts.[13] Be that as it may, Bowles had been a moving force in the Printing Revival of the nineties.

At least since Frederic Warde's book on Rogers, Bowles has also been given credit for introducing Rogers to Morris.

> Mr. Bowles had some of the Kelmscott books and showed them to Mr. Rogers, to whom they came as a revelation. He has said that upon seeing Morris's printing, his whole interest in book-production became rationalized and intensified. He abandoned the prevalent idea that a book could be made beautiful through the work of an illustrator alone, and determined instead to use that curiosity he had always felt as to type and paper, toward a study of the physical form of printed books. Naturally anything which could so thoroughly satisfy his eyes as *Poems by the Way* would have an effect, however transitory, on his efforts.[14]

Bowles himself said that he was not sure of the episode:

> I don't remember; I may have done so; I probably did, for I used to buy small Kelmscott volumes, occasionally, direct from Morris by mail, enclosing a money order which cost $1.75; and I would show them to artists and others interested. . . .[15]

He went on to describe the book that Rogers designed and he published: R. B. Gruelle's *Notes: Critical & Biographical* (Plate 22), about the art collection of W. T. Walters:

> During 1894 I got an order to print a book "in the style of 'Modern Art'". . . . I decided to print it in the style of the Kelmscott books and got Mr. Walters' permission to do so. Rogers did the title-page and all headbands and initials, and we worked hard to get the decorations and type page the same "color." At that time the only type we could find that approached the Kelmscott weight was the rather clumsy Old Style Antique [Bookman]. . . . So the book is much more a first step than a masterpiece.[16]

Morris was then brought in even more directly. Bowles sent him proofs of trial pages to see what he thought. ". . . Shortly back they came from Hammersmith, with notations on the margins in Morris' hand (only one or two, I think) such as 'The ink is too pink.' I followed the suggestions, because I saw that they were good. . . ."[17] Carlon and Hollenbeck of Indianapolis printed the book in 975 copies on Michallet paper and 6 on Whatman, the latter rubricated by hand by Rogers. The book was published in April 1895. The red and black title page is in solid-set caps with an outline floral ornament. The headbands and initials are similar and match the type well in the weight of line. Shoulder note running titles and other marginal notes are printed in red. Leaves are used as line fillers for the fly titles.

Another book Rogers worked on in 1894 was A. E.'s [i.e., George Russell] *Homeward Songs by the Way*, published by Thomas B. Mosher of Portland, Maine. Although the colophon dates it March 1895, a month earlier than the Gruelle, Bowles said:

It has always been a toss-up which was the first book with Rogers decorations [although we have seen there were still earlier ones] this [Gruelle] or the "Homeward Songs by the Way". . . . It doesn't matter: anyway, the Walters book is the more important. Also in the little "Homeward Songs" some of the decorations were either drawn in too large a size for the space in which they were to be used, or their reduction was too great, for some reason, for the lines in the designs are crowded. In the Walters book the designs blend better with the type.[18]

Bowles was correct about the Mosher decorations—the book seems clumsy and is actually one of Mosher's less pleasing efforts, although it has some charm. The format is Mosher's usual Aesthetic one; Rogers' designs have Renaissance motifs. (Several sources claim that Rogers lettered title pages for Mosher while still in college,[19] but he graduated in 1890 and Mosher's first book was 1891.)

When Bowles moved to Boston, Rogers soon followed. "In the spring [of 1895] Mr. Prang told me they needed a designer and asked if I knew of one, at fifty cents an hour. I immediately thought of Rogers."[20] The two of them moved in avant-garde circles, such as that of the Pewter Mugs. During 1895, Rogers did free-lance work for the literary publishers who frequented these same circles. For Stone & Kimball he designed two bindings that are reminiscent of Charles Ricketts' work in England: Lilian Bell's *A Little Sister to the Wilderness* and Gilbert Parker's *When Valmond Came to Pontiac* (Plate 23).

For Way & Williams of Chicago Rogers did Art Nouveau designs for Catherine B. Yale's *Nim and Cum*. But with *The Banquet of Plato*, translated by Shelley, he has given another example of Arts and Crafts, despite several writers' assertions that the Gruelle is the only such book he ever worked on. It was printed at the Lakeside Press in Clarendon type on laid paper. There are outline vine initials and tailpieces in Rogers' *Modern Art* manner. The title page is within a woodcut border with a matching publisher's device in the center (Plate 24). This title and the Gruelle book for Bowles are the two most important instances of Rogers' early affinity to Arts and Crafts, although he did several such designs for *Modern Art*.

There also exists an obscure, unrecorded example in the field of books. George Sand's *Fadette*, published by T. Y. Crowell without a date but probably the 1896 Faïence Library edition, has an unsigned Art Nouveau binding with daffodils, reminiscent of Margaret Armstrong. But the title page border is signed "BR," and is one of his outline grapevine designs in Kelmscott proportions (Plate 25). The red and black type within is arranged flush left.

It was 1896 when George Mifflin hired Rogers to work for the Riverside Press. In the four years before he began the famous series of limited editions that brought him worldwide attention, he supervised several books with Arts and Crafts influence.

Friar Jerome's Beautiful Book (1896) by Thomas Bailey Aldrich, with decorations by W. S. Hadaway, is one of the most Gothic productions of the nineties. The binding is brown calf, blind stamped on the front with a picture of Friar Jerome and with green silk ties. Printed in Clarendon on one side only of the paper, it has a simple, undecorated title page with the type in a solid block. The double-spread text opening with a red initial, red rulings under every line, and a red frontispiece, is within a border depicting monks, angels, and books. Except for the last page (Plate 26), the text pages are on rectos only and are within a frame, including, at the top and bottom, scrolls with running titles in Gothic letters. There are large red initials and red rulings.

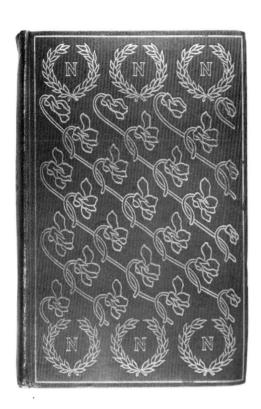

Plate 23. Gilbert Parker,
When Valmond Came to Pontiac.
Chicago: Stone & Kimball, 1895.

Plate 25. George Sand, *Fadette*. New York & Boston: Crowell, n.d.

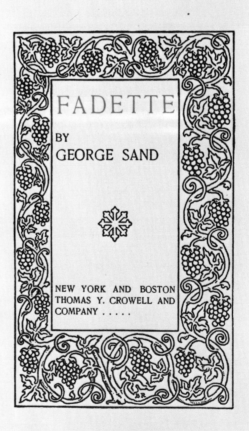

Much more hybrid in its design is *King Arthur and the Table Round*, with notes by William Wells Newell, in two volumes (1897). The title page in centered, black and red Gothic type is within a Renaissance outline pieced border, reminiscent of Geoffroy Tory. Tory himself is noted for having used roman type with such borders, and the opposite effect here is incongruous.

Mifflin finally authorized Rogers to put out a series of bibliophilic volumes, called the Riverside Press Limited Editions. Ellen Ballou, the historian of Houghton Mifflin, has said that it was hoped to capture the spirit of older ages, not to imitate. Mifflin and Rogers admired Morris with reservations and wished to surpass the Grolier Club editions.[21]

The first volume to be published was the *Sonnets and Madrigals of Michelangelo* (1900) in an edition of three hundred. It is a charming Renaissance book, tall and slim but small, with a Renaissance frame on the title page, decorated initials and headband, a dolphin pressmark, and poems set in italic. The series became noted for its variety of styles; Rogers now had a sure hand in allusive typography. Irving Way quoted Rogers on this subject at the time: "'While copying the spirit of the old, I am able with our modern methods to give my work a nicer sense of proportion without laying myself open to the charge of slavish imitation.'"[22] Warde was probably correct in saying that Rogers' historicism was influenced by Updike's brilliant work, and that the popularity of the series was due partly to fatigue with private press sameness, a "succession of vellum-bound quartos in one home-made type. . . ."[23]

The limited editions with Gothic styles may be said, in a general way, to fall within Arts and Crafts, although Rogers himself was working independently from original models, not from any current typographic fashion. Such books include Chaucer's *The Parlement of Foules* (1904), with black Gothic type, red rubrication, and large blue initials with touches of gold; *Oliver and Arthur* (1903); and *The Song of Roland* (1906). Another example is the three volume *Essays* of Montaigne (1902–1904), for which Rogers designed his type called Montaigne, based, like so many others, on Jenson. A few years later Rogers put his admiration of Jenson into words, citing especially the Eusebius of 1470: "I believe it to be at once the most beautiful and the most legible type in the world."[24] Carl Rollins found Montaigne "a very readable type, with many of the characteristics of Morris's 'Golden' type, but with an individuality of its own."[25] Updike has attributed to Rogers himself the following comment:

"... an attempt to meet a want that was felt for a large type-face that should avoid, on the one hand, the extreme blackness of the types which Morris's work had made popular, and, on the other, the somewhat thin effect of the ordinary book-faces when used in the larger sizes."[26]

Despite the high praise of the dozen or so books that he designed in the first two years of the Riverside Limited Editions, Rogers was unhappy because of the working conditions. Instead of quitting, he signed a letter of agreement on July 31, 1903, to plans for a studio of his own. The letter has a definite Morrisian tone:

"It is to me a remarkable and significant step toward what I believe will finally be the result in all lines of work—that the excellence of the product and the happiness of the producer in his work will be the ultimate aim of the manufacturer of any article which has any right to be made artistically.

... this new step marks, I think, a more definite and decided stand than any hitherto taken, in that it is a return to older and less commercial methods, and a reliance upon the men whose personality and skill shall give their product its excellence, rather than upon the exactness and speed and economy of machines, which after all turn out only a machine product."[27]

Plate 26. Thomas Bailey Aldrich, *Friar Jerome's Beautiful Book.* Boston: Houghton Mifflin, 1896.

When the firm was incorporated in 1908, Rogers "hoped to be made a director"[28] but Ferris Greenslet was taken instead. Rogers finally broke off completely from Riverside in 1912 to free-lance. He worked at Carl Rollins' Montague Press where he produced in 1915 Maurice Guerin's *The Centaur*, with Renaissance decorations, the first book to use Rogers' new Centaur type, also modeled on Jenson. It was a refinement of the Montaigne type. As Rogers explained: "It may be that my eye reacted earlier than most from the types made popular in the nineties by the so-called revival of printing; at any rate the Montaigne type soon seemed to me unsatisfactory, and I began to consider means for improving upon it. . . ."[29] Rogers went to England in 1916, then returned to the United States in 1919 and settled down for a period at the printing plant of William Edwin Rudge in Mount Vernon, New York, before going back to free-lancing. He died in 1957.

Critics had been kind to Rogers from the beginning, but it was Alfred W. Pollard of the British Museum who pushed him into international fame with a talk before the Bibliographical Society in 1915 and an essay published by the Carteret Book Club of Newark in 1916, which emphasized his greater affinity with the sixteenth rather than the fifteenth century.[30]

Beatrice Warde, the American-born editor of the London *Monotype Recorder*, essentially agreed with Pollard when she said in 1924:

> The second phase of fine printing opened in America. Owing its inspiration to the Kelmscott example it addressed itself with a competence all its own to the problem of the modern book, and at last we saw printing which was fine but not fantastic, old in style but not archaic. It is not too much to say that but for the experiments of Mr. Bruce Rogers we should still be under the dominion of black type and heavy woodcut decoration.[31]

In 1936 she expressed herself even more vividly: "We owe an immensely greater debt to Mr. Rogers for having managed to steal the Divine Fire which glowed in the Kelmscott Press books, and somehow to be the first to bring it down to earth. . . ."[32]

It has been little disputed that Rogers' prolific mature work constitutes the most brilliant typographic achievement of the twentieth century in America. Like Updike and Cleland, he moved away from the heavy lines of Arts and Crafts and its incunabular models to the lighter lines of Renaissance and post-Renaissance models. Almost from the beginning, Rogers occasionally disparaged the master of Kelmscott.

In a letter to James H. Pershing of Denver, dated June 28, 1900, Rogers wrote from Cambridge:

> Mr. Morris, it seems to me, did not quite hit it with any of his types, although they are very handsome. But the "readability" is lacking in all three faces, and that is the first requisite. His books are, some of them, very beautiful but they are rather curiosities of bookmaking than real books.[33]

In 1912 he came out against the Morris imitators, saying that Kelmscott influence was enormous but not beneficial, except for the emphasis on sound craftsmanship.[34]

In 1929 he wrote to Henry Watson Kent from London that he and his wife, Emery Walker and his daughter Dorothy, and T. E. Lawrence were all going to Kelmscott Manor because Lawrence wanted to meet Morris' daughter May. "*He* is a great admirer of Morris—and I try to keep up the illusion of being—when in that company."[35]

The next year he admitted Morris inspiration while emphasizing its brevity of tenure, although he was mistaken about the Walters [Gruelle] volume being the only example. Edward F. Stevens had written him about Frederic Warde's statement that Morris had determined his career, and Rogers replied:

> . . . the direct influence of Morris's work [on mine] was very transitory, lasting through only one book—"The Walters' Collection" volume. . . . Today, and for many years past, I get almost no thrill out of any of the books of "the '90s'"—except, perhaps, Ricketts' "Hero & Leander" and "The Sphinx."[36]

In 1931 he again mentioned Morris to Kent in a slightly disparaging way: "Consider, in contrast [to my performance], the splendor of Bodoni's . . . or the Whittinghams, or the Didots, or a dozen others—even Morris's, granting his taste."[37]

On the other hand, in 1934 he gave Morris rather grudging credit: " 'Bodoni and Morris, I believe, were about the only printers who broke quite away from current styles of typography and did something different.' "[38] A 1938 letter to Frederic W. Goudy acknowledged both their debts: "And though you started with William Morris, just as I and others did, you have kept closer to the spirit of his example than most of us have done; yet so far as I can recall, without having copied anything that Morris did."[39]

Rogers' ambivalence about Morris does not detract from the importance of his Arts and Crafts beginning. In fact, the stylistic eclecticism of his later work dramatizes the original Morris inspiration. It was not a school that Morris created but a whole new era of printing. Indeed, Rogers is probably the prize showpiece of the Morris Revival, for it is not certain that he would have gone into book design at all without the typographic excitement of the nineties and Bowles' enthusiasm, in particular. Rogers never cared for running a press and was as doubting of his own work as of that of Morris. In 1930 Henry Lewis Bullen wrote John Henry Nash: "Rogers himself has a low opinion of printing and told me shortly before his last exile [to England] that he wished he had applied himself to some other art."[40]

1. Ernest Knaufft, *The Early Art Training of B. R. at Purdue University* (New York: Press of the Woolly Whale, 1935), unpaged.
2. Bruce Rogers, Address in American Institute of Graphic Arts, *The Work of Bruce Rogers: Jack of All Trades, Master of One* (New York: Oxford University Press, 1939), pp. xliii–xliv.
3. Thomas A. Larremore and Amy Hopkins Larremore, *The Marion Press* (Jamaica: Queens Borough Public Library, 1943), p. 220.
4. Frederic Warde, *Bruce Rogers: Designer of Books* (Cambridge: Harvard University Press, 1926), pp. 7–8.
5. David A. Randall, "Bruce Rogers' First Decorated Book," *Papers of the Bibliographical Society of America*, LV (First quarter 1961): 40–41.
6. Joseph M. Bowles, "On the Early Work of Bruce Rogers," *Colophon*, Part Eleven (September 1932), unpaged.
7. Joseph M. Bowles, "Note," *Modern Art*, I (Summer 1893), unpaged.
8. Joseph M. Bowles, "Thoughts on Printing: Practical and Impractical," *Modern Art*, II (Summer 1894), unpaged.
9. Letter, Bruce Rogers to Henry Lewis Bullen, November 4, 1916. Typographic Library Manuscript Collection, Columbia University Libraries.
10. Joseph M. Bowles, "William Morris as a Printer: The Kelmscott Press," *Modern Art*, II (Autumn 1894), unpaged.
11. Joseph M. Bowles, "A German Printer's Criticism of Modern Art," *Modern Art*, IV (Autumn 1896): 135.
12. Note by William Reydel to Deoch Fulton, "The Typophiles," *New Colophon*, II (June 1949): 156.
13. Ibid.
14. Warde, *Bruce Rogers*, pp. 8–9.
15. Bowles, "Early Work."
16. Ibid.
17. Ibid.
18. Ibid.
19. E.g., Warde, *Bruce Rogers*, p. 9.

20. Bowles, "Early Work."
21. Ellen B. Ballou, *The Building of the House: Houghton Mifflin's Formative Years* (Boston: Houghton Mifflin, 1970), pp. 529–531.
22. Quoted in W. Irving Way, "The Riverside Press and Mr. Bruce Rogers," *Inland Printer*, XXVI (November 1900): 12.
23. Warde, *Bruce Rogers*, p. 13.
24. Bruce Rogers, Letter to the Editor of the *Dial*, July 9, 1909, reprinted in Bruce Rogers, *Pi* (Cleveland and New York: World, 1953), p. 12.
25. Carl Purington Rollins, "Modern 'Special Types,'" *Printing Art*, I (March 1903): 16–17.
26. Daniel Berkeley Updike, *Printing Types* (2d ed.; Cambridge: Harvard University Press, 1951), vol. II, pp. 216–217.
27. Quoted in Ballou, *The Building of the House*, p. 536.
28. Ibid., p. 538.
29. Bruce Rogers, "Printer's Note" to A. W. Pollard, *The Trained Printer and the Amateur and the Pleasure of Small Books*, 1929, reprinted in Rogers, *Pi*, p. 54.
30. Alfred W. Pollard, *Modern Fine Printing in England and Mr. Bruce Rogers* (Newark: Carteret Book Club, 1916), pp. 2, 18–19.
31. [Beatrice Warde] "Fine Printing, Mr. Bruce Rogers and the 'Monotype' Machine," *Monotype Recorder*, XXII (January/February 1924): 7.
32. Paul Beaujon [i.e., Beatrice Warde], Review of *The Nonesuch Century* in *Signature*, No. 3 (July 1936): 48.
33. Reprinted in Rogers, *Pi*, pp. 8–9.
34. Bruce Rogers, "Progress of Modern Printing in the United States," *Times* (London), September 10, 1912, reprinted in Rogers, *Pi*, pp. 18–19.
35. Bruce Rogers, Letter dated April 24, 1929, reprinted in James M. Wells, "Letters from Bruce Rogers to Henry Watson Kent," *Printing and Graphic Arts*, III (February 1955): 74.
36. *Three Letters from BR. EW.* (Portland, Maine: Southworth-Anthoenson Press, 1941), p. xiii.
37. Bruce Rogers, Letter dated April 24, 1931, in Wells, "Letters," *Printing and Graphic Arts*, IV (May 1956): 47.
38. Quoted in Paul A. Bennett, *Bruce Rogers of Indiana* (Providence: Doomsday Press, 1936), p. 10, reprinted from *Linotype News*, April 1934.
39. Reprinted in Rogers, *Pi*, p. 95.
40. Letter, Henry Lewis Bullen to John Henry Nash, April 2, 1930, Typographic Library Manuscripts Collection, Columbia University Libraries.

IX

Commercial Printing
in Boston

ONE OF THE MOST important and highly regarded commercial presses in the city
of Boston, much praised in typographic literature, was the Heintzemann Press. Ray
Nash has said: "Heintzemann, another Arts and Crafts enthusiast, surrounded himself
at all times with artists and designers. His press was unofficial headquarters for those who
looked at printing in an artistic light."[1] Carl H. Heintzemann was born in Wildugen, Germany, in 1854, the son of a schoolmaster. Upon coming to America, he became a printer's
apprentice in Boston and in 1879 set up his own press which he ran until his death in 1909.
He was a musician, collector of rare books, and an active member of Boston's social and
professional life, helping to found both the Society of Arts and Crafts and the Society of
Printers.

> . . . there can be no doubt that . . . the work of the Heintzemann Press had its influence
> on the typographic tendencies of the times in this country in the early nineties and
> throughout the years of the Morris Revival.[2]

The above quotation is taken from a 1924 display in the *American Printer* designed, according to the introduction, in Heintzemann's typical typographic style, and it does reflect
turn-of-the-century revivalism. The whole is solid set in Bookman type, with the sub-
heading in capitals with fleuron line fillers. The main heading is in black letter with Gothic
type ornaments and there are two large, decorated initials in the text as well as a side border
of Gothic decoration in orange and black.

The Heintzemann Press did a great deal of simple commercial work, but it was also
connected with Copeland & Day and with private printing. Typical of its work in the midst
of current trends is *Two Lyrics* by the Reverend John B. Tabb, printed in 1900 for the
Craftsman's Guild. There were 375 copies on handmade paper and 50 on Japan vellum,
lettered and decorated by Theodore Brown Hapgood, Jr., with some copies illuminated
by Emilie Martheria Whitten. The vellum binding has green silk ties, the title and author

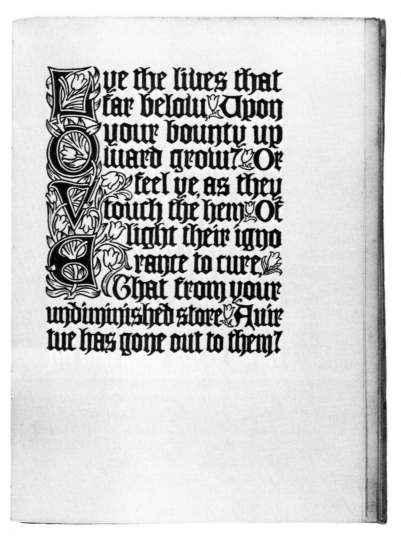

Plate 27. John B. Tabb, *Two Lyrics*. Boston: Craftsman's Guild, 1900.

in Gothic letters, and gold floral motifs in each corner. The title page's Gothic lettering is on top of outline tracery reminiscent of Kelmscott work, and placed above a square floral device filling the rest of the page. The text pages are solid, with Gothic lettering and floral line fillers, set among floral borders extending around some edges (Plate 27). It is an archetypical example of American Arts and Crafts.

The Craftsman's Guild also produced illuminations for printed books such as Copeland & Day's *Sonnets from the Portuguese* and was willing to accept commissions for individual copies. Its beginning was described in *Publishers Weekly* as a group of art workers bending their "efforts toward the revival of the early book and missal illuminating of the monastic period."[3] Edwin Osgood Grover was the moving spirit of the Guild. Grover had been a classmate of Alfred Bartlett, the owner of the Cornhill Press, and edited the *Cornhill Booklet* for him. W. A. Dwiggins also worked for the Guild.

An important contribution of Heintzemann to American typography was his hiring as a compositor Carl Purington Rollins, later to become a leader both in printing and in critical comment. Rollins was born in 1880 in West Newbury, Massachusetts. Like so many other future typographers, he played with type as a child in the local newspaper office. While in high school he published for two years a *Stamp Journal* on a press of his own. At Harvard he printed menus for the student dining halls and became familiar with the ideas of William Morris. The Arts and Crafts philosophy appealed to him deeply.[4] In 1900 he started to work at the Heintzemann Press.

> I have always been devoted to the Kelmscott books. When I was earning $15 a week as a compositor (about 1902) I spent $20 on a Kelmscott edition of Tennyson's *Maud*. At about that time I was spending a good many evenings in the Barton Room in the Boston Public Library reading Morris's own romances in his own printing, and I never found the Kelmscott letters difficult to read, though I did sometimes boggle at Morris's persistent use of archaic English words. When I came to New Haven and found the Kelmscott *Chaucer* used as a doorstop in the Art School library, I rescued it and gradually by successive stages and with the judicious use of sales catalogues, finally got it into the Rare Book Room of the Yale University Library.[5]

After another job on the Georgetown, Massachusetts, *Advocate*, he moved to Montague, Massachusetts, where he joined an experimental socialist group, the New Clairvaux Plantation. He ran their press for over a year before becoming, in 1907, Chief of the Department of Graphic Arts at the Jamestown Exposition in Norfolk, Virginia. In 1909 he moved back to Montague and set up the Montague Press at the Dyke Mill, where Bruce Rogers came to work in 1915. In 1918 Rollins became a designer at Yale University Press and in 1920 Printer to the University. He received an honorary degree of Master of Arts and later that of Doctor of Humane Letters and lectured on the history of typography.

Rollins' writings continued to reflect his interest in and respect for Morris and Arts and Crafts. For example, in 1932 he gave an address at the New School in New York in which not only his socialist sympathies but also his antipathy to machines can be seen. He advocated a small printing shop where superior handwork could be produced, although he acknowledged that machines must be used for things where quantity is more important than quality.[6] He said two years later that "in these days of accelerated machine production, Morris' words are as true as ever, and much more necessary to heed."[7] In a 1934 address at the Yale Library for a centenary celebration of Morris' birth, he spoke of Kelmscott inspiration as being perhaps beyond present-day understanding.[8] Two years later, in an address to the Society of Printers, he again described his own typographic adolescence when he met the leaders of printing in early twentieth-century Boston. The excitement of the Revival period can be glimpsed between the lines:

> The realization that printing was something else or rather something more than merely setting type and impressing it on paper, that there was an aesthetics of printing, that behind the type in the case there was a great and a momentous history, interwoven with the fabric of European and American life for centuries—this realization, which had come to me during my loafing years at Harvard, was brought into focus by two events: my acquaintance with the Society of Printers, and in particular with four or five of its members, and by three formative years with the Heintzemann Press.
>
> . . . Joe Bowles and Henry Lewis Johnson made their appearance as denizens of that

front office; Will Bradley appeared at one time to set type for a series of small books. . . . And then Mr. Heintzemann invited me to make use of his books on the shelves of that fine office which Bertram Goodhue had designed for him. That was a revelation. I do not remember any book in particular, but I do remember that I then began to realize some of the possibilities of type and paper. . . .[9]

That Rollins could himself design in the classic Arts and Crafts style when he so desired is shown by a piece in the *Yale University Library Gazette* a year after the above address. It is in Bookman type with Kelmscott initials, solid set with all display flush left. Rollins appended a note:

The type and format of this issue . . . somewhat unusual today, are those which had some popularity in America when the Kelmscott Press books of William Morris came over to astonish us—whether with delight or disgust. It is not a very handsome type face, but it is readable and reputable. The format is my own, although fitting the type, and similar to the magazine "Modern Art" and some well-printed books of yesteryear.[10]

Finally in 1958, Rollins gave Morris direct responsibility for his own career:

I am sure that I was influenced by Morris to a greater or less degree in everything that I ever did, though, when as a young man I showed some examples of my work to Updike, he said, "If these were imitations of William Morris, I shouldn't be interested." Nevertheless, I think it was probably because of Morris that I became a printer![11]

Rollins was inspired by Morris' idealism more than by his style; he himself did not specialize in Arts and Crafts typography.

But there was a commercial press in the Boston area that did such printing in the nineties: the University Press of Cambridge. It is likely that much of this was due to the presence of William Dana Orcutt, who began work there in 1891 and became its head in 1895. From Orcutt's later voluminous writings on the world of books, we know that he himself was influenced by the Revival, and we know also that his employer, John Wilson, was suspicious of Morris.

According to the printing historian, John Clyde Oswald, the University Press was founded in 1800 by William Hilliard, and was so called because he printed for Harvard.[12] In 1859 the press was acquired by Welch, Bigelow & Company, but it continued to do scholarly work and especially books for the Boston literati. The works of William Morris were printed here for Roberts Brothers, his American publishers. In 1879 Charles E. Wentworth and John Wilson, Jr., son of a famous Scotch American printer, took over as John Wilson & Son; in 1896 this management changed to Herbert White but the old name was retained. From 1898 a Wayside Department added Will H. Bradley influence. In 1903 the *Printing Art* magazine was begun. Both the periodical and the press changed hands again in the twenties.

The University Press had been the favorite press of Eugene Field, and the small literary publishers followed in his wake. The early books of Stone & Kimball and most

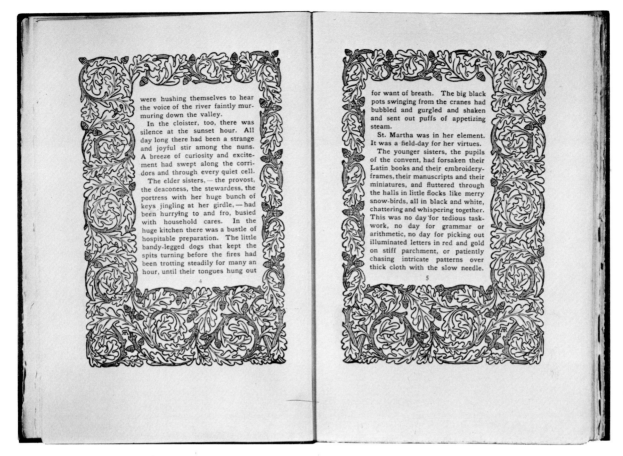

Plate 28. Henry Van Dyke, *The First Christmas Tree: A Story of the Forest.*
New York: Scribner's, 1897.

of the titles of Copeland & Day were printed there. It was therefore well initiated in the Aesthetic style. But it also printed many Arts and Crafts books. For example, the decorated Christmas book was a publishing phenomenon of the times, tending, not surprisingly, toward the Gothic, and University Press did its share of them. Henry Van Dyke's *The First Christmas Tree*, published by Scribner's in 1897, has photogravures from Howard Pyle drawings and designs by Amy Richards. The green cloth binding is stamped in darker green and gold with Gothic letters and a holly design. Holly is the motif on the title page as well, where an outline woodcut border surrounds the title in red, and holly leaves are used as line fillers. The half title, on the other hand, has an oak leaf and acorn border, as do all the text pages (Plate 28). The paper is laid and the type Bookman.

Another Van Dyke book, *The Builders and Other Poems*, was issued by Scribner's in 1900 with Amy Richards' designs. The gold-stamped green cloth cover has a design of tulips; inside, the title-page border has white tulips on a black background while heavy black tulips are used as line fillers among the red lettering of the title (Plate 29). There is no other decoration, but the art work has been subtly and effectively unified. The swirling lines of the cover are repeated in the title-page border. The heavy black of the latter's background is continued by the heavy text type. Even the bold white of the border's design finds a counterpart in the very ample margins of the text pages. The book is on laid paper, in Bookman type, with Jenson used for the individual poem titles.

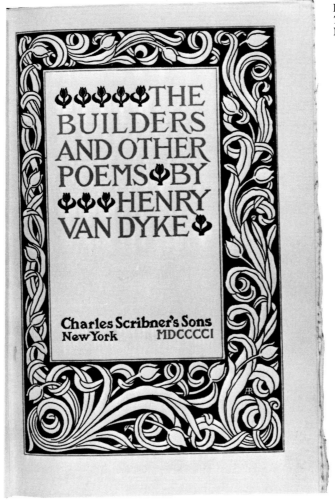

Plate 29. Henry Van Dyke,
The Builders and Other Poems.
New York: Scribner's, 1900.

The fact that the University Press was the American printer of Morris' writings prob-ably did not have anything to do with its Arts and Crafts tendency, but the Morris books themselves show an interesting progression in typographic style. A poem from *The Earthly Paradise*, "The Lovers of Gudrun," (Roberts Brothers, 1870), is not only an unprepossess-ing example of mid-nineteenth century typography but also sheets or plates have been taken from an earlier complete *Earthly Paradise* without even bothering to change the pagina-tion: 245 to 382. *Atalanta's Race*, (Ticknor & Co., 1888), a school edition with wood en-gravings, has spindly type and bad margins. It looks very old-fashioned, as does *The Life and Death of Jason* (Roberts Brothers, 1886) in the Author's Edition. *The Earthly Paradise*, Parts I and II (1893), in the same edition, retain the same appearance despite the existence of the Kelmscott Press. The title page has several different styles and sizes of spindly type in a symmetrical arrangement. The text pages are gray, with small margins, italic headlines, and centered section titles. However in 1895, for Roberts, the University Press printed

The Wood Beyond the World in a totally Arts and Crafts format. The edition is limited to five hundred copies and there is a colophon in Morrisian wording. The green cloth binding is stamped in darker green and gold with a Kelmscott border and Gothic lettering on the front cover. The bordered frontispiece is by Burne-Jones, while the title page has the title and author set flush left. The presswork is gray by Kelmscott standards but not especially so for a trade book.

Whether or not Orcutt was behind this shift in format, his own best-known piece of bookmaking is in the incunabular tradition but more that of the Doves Press than of Kelmscott. *The Triumphs of Francesco Petrarch* was printed for Little, Brown, by the University Press in 1906, in one hundred copies for America and one hundred for England. It is in black and blue Humanistic type designed by Orcutt, a very calligraphic face, based on a manuscript Virgil in the Laurentian Library. It is a large book on laid paper with a University Press watermark. There are wood-engraved full-page illustrations, as well as raised gold initials.

In the 1920s and later, Orcutt wrote a series of books about books. *In Quest of the Perfect Book*, published in 1926, told of Morris' inspiration: "The Kelmscott books awoke in me an overwhelming desire to put myself into the volumes I produced."[13] But in *The Kingdom of Books* the next year, Orcutt gave Cobden-Sanderson an even higher tribute: "... the *Doves Bible* ... has inspired me as no piece of printing I have ever seen."[14] After *Master Makers of the Book* (1928) and *The Magic of the Book* (1930), Orcutt, in *From My Library Walls*, gave Morris the credit for keeping him in bookmaking at a time when he found printing uncongenial.[15] In summary, Orcutt moved from Kelmscott models to Doves without losing his original Morrisian inspiration. Updike and Rogers followed approximately the same course.

As for the long-range importance of the Kelmscott Press, Orcutt had essentially one message to deliver: the belief that the principles of the Revival of Printing could be applied to low-cost, trade volumes, and that his own work at the University Press had initiated such an application in America. His earliest and fullest account is found in *In Quest of the Perfect Book*.[16]

The University Press under Orcutt was an important link in the chain that led to the artistically designed and unified books of Knopf in the twenties. Another link was a press run on still more personal lines, the Merrymount of Daniel Berkeley Updike.

1. Ray Nash, *Printing as an Art* (Cambridge: Harvard University Press, 1955), p. 35.
2. "Carl H. Heintzemann," *American Printer*, LXXIX (August 5, 1924), No. 38 of Craftsman Exhibit.
3. "The Craftsman's Guild," *Publishers Weekly*, LVIII (September 8, 1900): 485.
4. Malcolm W. Davis, "Carl Purington Rollins," *Publishers Weekly*, CXIX (June 6, 1931): 2708.
5. Carl Purington Rollins, "Morris's Typographical Adventure," *Printing and Graphic Arts*, VI (June 1958): 30-31.
6. Carl Purington Rollins, "Harmony of Hand and Machine," in *Off the Dead Bank* (New York: Typophiles, 1949), pp. 15-37.
7. Carl Purington Rollins, "A New Morris Item," in "The Compleat Collector," *Saturday Review of Literature*, XI (September 29, 1934): 151.
8. Carl Purington Rollins, "The Ordeal of William Morris," in *Off the Dead Bank*, pp. 47-48.
9. Carl Purington Rollins, "Whither Now, Typographer?," in *Off the Dead Bank*, pp. 49-52.
10. "The Henderson Memorial Collection of Shaw," *Yale University Library Gazette*, XII (October 1937): 42.
11. Rollins, "Morris's Typographical Adventure," p. 30.
12. John Clyde Oswald, *Printing in the Americas* (New York, Chicago: Gregg, 1937), p. 87.
13. William Dana Orcutt, *In Quest of the Perfect Book* (Boston: Little, Brown, 1926), p. 7.
14. William Dana Orcutt, *The Kingdom of Books* (Boston: Little, Brown, 1927), p. 68.
15. William Dana Orcutt, *From My Library Walls* (London: John Murray, 1946), pp. 164-166.
16. Orcutt, *In Quest*, pp. 54-57.

X

The Arts & Crafts Years
of Daniel Berkeley Updike

UPDIKE WAS BORN in 1860 in Providence, Rhode Island, of an old Yankee family. His father's early death meant that instead of the formal education for which he was so well suited he had to earn a living. In 1880 he took a job in Boston with Houghton Mifflin & Company and was transferred in 1891 to its Riverside Press in Cambridge. He left to set up his own establishment, the Merrymount Press, in 1893, which eventually grew into the most respected printing house in America. Before his death in 1941, Updike had become, with his 1922 *Printing Types*, the foremost American typographic historian and scholar, as well as a recognized book designer of impeccable taste, in a restrained traditional manner. His beginnings were, however, like the others of his generation, part of the Arts and Crafts Movement and therefore, on the whole, more elaborate in style than his later work. This has been common knowledge; what has not been realized is the extent of Updike's involvement in Arts and Crafts.

The early days of the Riverside Press have been thoroughly documented in a history of Houghton Mifflin by Ellen B. Ballou, who quotes Henry E. Houghton from 1871 on quality bookmaking: books should be simple "with a type clear and round, on paper thin, but opaque, of an utterly neutral tint, with close margins, & ink of a neat brown or ebony color, & with a binding . . . plain & simple. . . ."[1] Nevertheless, Houghton's company published many elaborate and costly subscription books and limited editions. The 1883 *Works of Longfellow* had six hundred illustrations by thirty-seven artists, costing $60,000. There were fifty thousand subscribers at prices from $30 to $80, depending on the binding, and it was hailed at the time as the best example of American bookmaking ever produced. These costly editions were in the nineteenth-century tradition of emphasis on illustrations and binding, often done in a very extraneous way, rather than on unity of book design. In the less ambitious books, the Chiswick manner was well established at Riverside.

In 1886 Updike had had a chance to move from the publishing office to the press and had turned it down; in 1891 another chance came and he took it. Ellen Ballou be-

Ad maiorem Regis Sanctorum gloriam

Charitate tua, Lector, ora pro bono statu eorum qui
in confectione huius libri vel scientes vel inscientes
laboraverunt, ut omnes, sive in hoc sæculo adhuc
vivunt in carne, sive deposito carnis onere ex-
pectant sæculum venturum, per Nomen
illud quod est super omne nomen vitam æternam
consequantur

Plate 30. *On the Dedications of American Churches.*
Cambridge: Riverside Press, 1891.

lieves that "his supercilious, critical presence in the Boston office was causing trouble."[2]
(How difficult that presence could be, even in his own office, can be glimpsed in the
memoir by the son of Updike's long-time partner at the Merrymount Press, where he
described, among other things, Updike's Monday morning irascibility.[3])

At this same time Updike and an old friend, Harold Brown, were collaborating on
a book in a field close to their hearts—the ecclesiastical. In 1891 the well-to-do Brown

77

financed its printing at the Riverside Press: *On the Dedications of American Churches: An Enquiry into the Naming of Churches in the United States, Some Account of English Dedications, and Suggestions for Future Dedications in the American Church. Compiled by Two Laymen of the Diocese of Rhode Island.* This is the first book known to have been designed by Updike. The title, partly in Gothic, is in inverted triangle arrangement with a woodcut which is repeated as a tailpiece with the very medievalistic Latin colophon: "Charitate tua, Lector . . ." (Plate 30). The text is in Franklin old-style type with running titles in Gothic. This is a book, sober in content and design, destined, one would think, to obscurity—not so, for Francis Watts Lee in the first number of the *Knight Errant* gave its design an enthusiastic notice, urging readers to get hold of a copy despite its private distribution.[4] George L. Harding has said: "This little book was probably the first product of the modern renaissance of printing in this country."[5] Whether it directly influenced Rogers or not, as Updike's first effort it is an important volume.

How many of the Houghton Mifflin books Updike was actually allowed to design during his two years at the Riverside Press is not known, although Ray Nash has written a speculative article in which he names several possibilities.[6] That he was responsible for the catalogues and some books can be proved from the following contemporary comment, which also shows that Updike received early praise: "The various classes of decorative printing seen in the catalogues, posters, "Atlantic" advertising pages, and many of the books are instances of Mr. Updike's artistic work."[7]

Updike himself named one book he designed at the Riverside Press: F. Hopkinson Smith's *A Day at Laguerre's and Other Days: Being Nine Sketches* (1892). It is interesting that he chose to name this one (in his 1893 circular) for it is an Arts and Crafts book. The binding is tan cloth with the title in caps and a floriated initial, printed in black in a block arrangement. The title page is in red caps with a leaf and a decorated initial. Both the title and imprint are in solid blocks with the date in roman numerals, all within a white on black floral border (Plate 31). The contents page is also block set, flush left and right (Plate 32). There are floriated initials at the beginnings of the stories and a bold leaf is used as a section divider. The text is in old-style type with italic shoulder note running titles. The ending is an inverted triangle, a motif favored by Updike. There is no colophon but there is a publisher's device at the end. It is obvious that Updike must have seen the Kelmscott Press *Story of the Glittering Plain* in order to have designed this, so that this 1892 title may well be the first American book to show such influence. As Harding has said: "It was in tune with the times and was gratefully received by American book buyers whose interest in typographical design was being stimulated by current events in England."[8] The irony is that it came from one of the large trade publishers rather than from a private press or even a literary publisher. A further irony is that Copeland & Day may have been working on their *House of Life* at the same time, as the December 1892 proof sheets would indicate, but in the more leisurely context of their work delayed a year in getting it out. At Houghton Mifflin such delays would have been avoided.

While *The House of Life* was being printed at the University Press, another Goodhue/Kelmscott landmark was being printed by De Vinne in New York: the limited edition of *The Book of Common Prayer*, for the Episcopal Church, finished, according to the colophon, on November 22, 1893. The Standard Prayer Book itself, and the official copies, were printed with plain margins but it was felt that the complimentary and subscription copies should have foliated borders. Updike was hired to provide these and he chose Goodhue, who added Morrisian borders to a text in modern type (Plate 33).

A DAY AT LAGUERRE'S AND OTHER DAYS BEING NINE SKETCHES BY F. HOPKINSON SMITH

BOSTON AND NEW YORK HOUGHTON MIFFLIN AND COMPANY THE RIVERSIDE PRESS CAMBRIDGE MDCCCXCII

Plate 31. F. Hopkinson Smith, *A Day at Laguerre's and Other Days: Being Nine Sketches.* Boston: Houghton Mifflin, 1892.

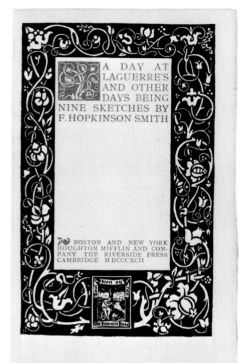

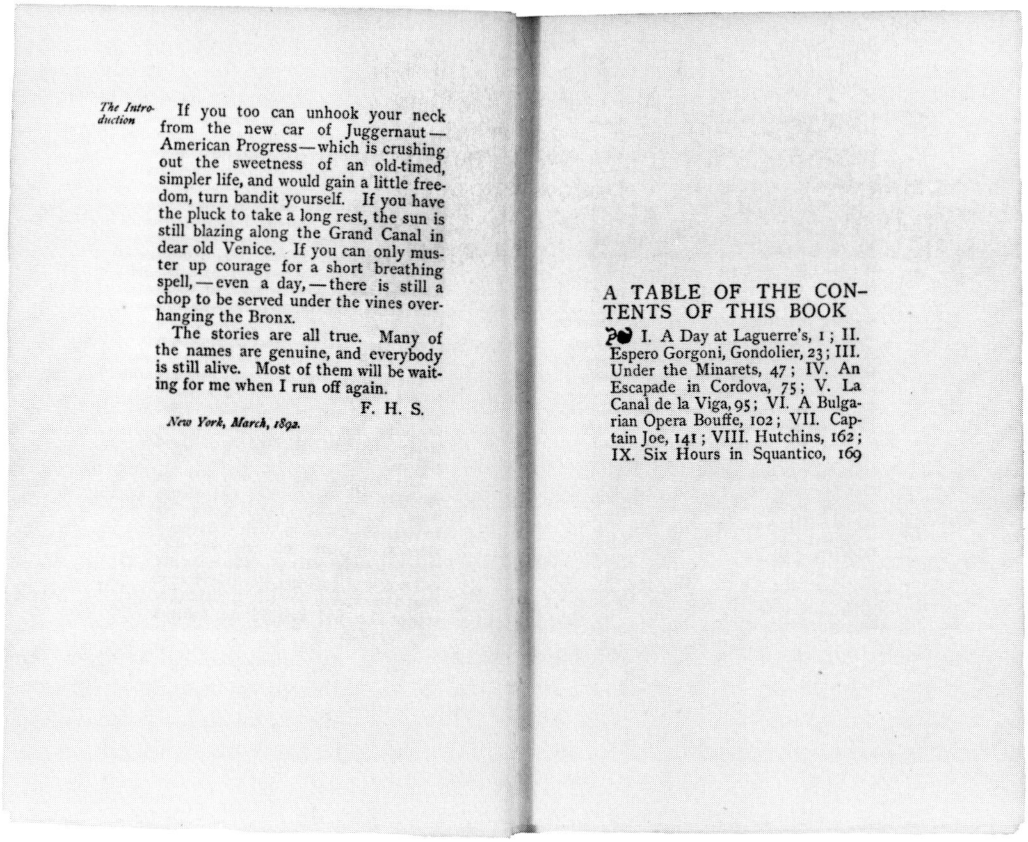

The Introduction

If you too can unhook your neck from the new car of Juggernaut—American Progress—which is crushing out the sweetness of an old-timed, simpler life, and would gain a little freedom, turn bandit yourself. If you have the pluck to take a long rest, the sun is still blazing along the Grand Canal in dear old Venice. If you can only muster up courage for a short breathing spell,—even a day,—there is still a chop to be served under the vines overhanging the Bronx.

The stories are all true. Many of the names are genuine, and everybody is still alive. Most of them will be waiting for me when I run off again.

F. H. S.

New York, March, 1892.

A TABLE OF THE CONTENTS OF THIS BOOK

Plate 32. F. Hopkinson Smith, *A Day at Laguerre's and Other Days: Being Nine Sketches.* Boston: Houghton Mifflin, 1892.

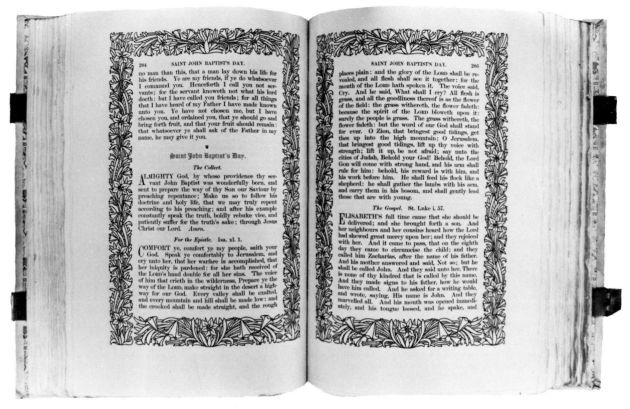

Plate 33. *The Book of Common Prayer*. New York: De Vinne Press, 1893.

Updike was well aware of the incongruity and mentioned it several times.

> In these decorations Goodhue's line was very far from De Vinne's typography, and I fancy it was a painful task for the latter to reprint his uninspired but dignified book with the *appliqués* so continuously, unremittingly (and sometimes unwillingly), supplied by Goodhue and myself.[9]

He also wrote an apologetic leaflet, pointing out the discrepancy between borders and type. No decorated initials, gold, colors, or much variety were possible, therefore "simply treated, flat, decorative borders in black and white of about thirty trees, flowers and plants. . . ."[10] were resorted to. Updike pointed out that medieval craftsmen also used more natural forms than religious symbolism. The book has a very medievalistic binding by Goodhue.

In 1893 Updike issued the first announcement for his own office in Boston, a four-page folder, *To the Trade*. It too is in Kelmscott format, with a pomegranate border and matching initial on the first page, signed "H" and probably by J. E. Hill, who did much of Updike's early designing. The text stressed the eclectic nature of his capabilities and particularly his historical knowledge, including the "modern English style set by Morris."[11] The types of work that he proposed to undertake were listed as: Holiday Books, Privately

80

Printed Books, Ecclesiastical Printing, Decorations for Books, "Practical" Book-Covers, Minor Decorative Printing.

His next circular, dated October 15, 1894, was entitled: *A Few Words About Printing, Book-Making, and Their Allied Arts: Being a Short Description of Some of the Work Done by Mr. Berkeley Updike, at Number Six Beacon Street, Boston, Massachusetts.* It has decorated initials and shoulder notes and is composed in the new Jenson of the American Type Founders Company, based on Morris' Golden (Plate 34). Jenson was not released to the rest of the trade until 1895 by the Dickinson Type Foundry. Ray Nash has explained how this came about:

> Updike had been carrying on experiments with the manager of the foundry, Joseph Warren Phinney, toward reproducing Morris' Golden type for use in the Altar Book. The type was to have been Updike's exclusive property but, on a visit to Wilson's University Press, he saw proofs of it and learned that some of the type had been supplied them—even before he had finally approved the face and in spite of the understanding for its proprietary use. He had this one circular set up in it and printed by Wilson and never made use of it again.[12]

The content of the folder was as up to date as its type. In an Arts and Crafts format Updike stated the new credo of the professional book designer who is not a printer. (Paul A. Bennett once interviewed Updike about the craft of printing and found that the proprietor of Merrymount did not like to set type and could not run presses. "'I am not in love with the smell of ink, type and that sort of thing—I much prefer direction to execution.'"[13])

> . . . there are arising on every side, workers whose place is not that of the man by whom a printer's work is used, nor of the printer himself, but of one, who, by a knowledge of the requirements of clients on the one hand, and the abilities of the printer on the other, is able to produce a better result than either could do alone.[14]

Irving Way found this circular worthy of comment in his column in the *Inland Printer*: "Mr. Updike has lately issued a circular . . . which . . . is printed in a type and manner highly complimentary to himself and to Mr. William Morris and the Kelmscott Press. It is a treat to look upon."[15]

At the same time Updike was soliciting business in Kelmscott style, he was advocating in his writing typographic simplicity. His article, "The Black Art: A Homily" (reprinted by Frederic W. Goudy at his Camelot Press in Chicago, in February 1895), appeared first in the January 1894 *Engraver and Printer*. The text reads in part:

> To-day queer little half-titles in the corner of the page, and title-pages which look as if we were opening into the middle of a book, mystify the reader . . . because some people have managed to impress the public for a moment by very large type and very black borders, and very odd and often very bad arrangements of title-pages, it is supposed that by larger type, uglier borders, and odder effects we may get ahead. . . .
>
> In other words, a great deal of the so-called decorative printing is not decorative, and what modern printing of all kinds needs is simplicity and harmony.[16]

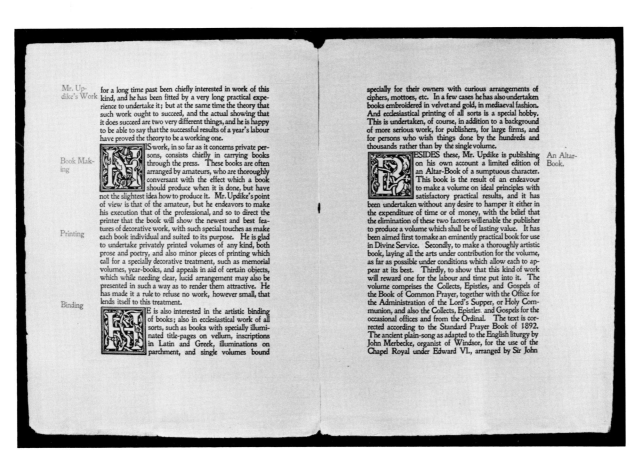

Plate 34. Daniel Berkeley Updike, *A Few Words about Printing,
Bookmaking, and Their Allied Arts*. Boston: Updike, 1894.

The next circular was dated 1894–1895 and addressed *To the Clergy and Laity of
the Episcopal Church and to All Others Who Are Interested in Ecclesiastical Printing*
(Plate 35). It is a straightforward advertising pitch for competency in this field.

An example of the sort of work Updike was doing in this period before the actual
establishment of Merrymount is *Bill Pratt: The Saw-Buck Philosopher* by John Sheridan
Zelie and Carroll Perry, "Printed under the supervision of D. B. Updike" (1895). There
are Arts and Crafts touches here, as in the use of line-filler leaves in the printed spine
label, the black foliage border for the block set title page (Plate 36), the solid block table
of contents, the chapter endings as inverted triangles with leaf tailpieces, and the flush
left chapter titles, the first one filled in with leaves. The type is Caslon and the paper laid.

On November 25, 1895, Updike issued another circular, with a wooduct of a maypole
by Mary J. Newill, and the announcement of the Merrymount Press. From now on he
would not be dependent on using other printers.[17]

During this period, Updike was the American distributor for an English Arts and
Crafts periodical. The *Quest* was printed and published from 1894 to 1896 by the Birmingham Guild of Handicraft, with Updike's name appearing as publisher for the first
time in Number 4, November 1895, the same issue containing the first printing of William

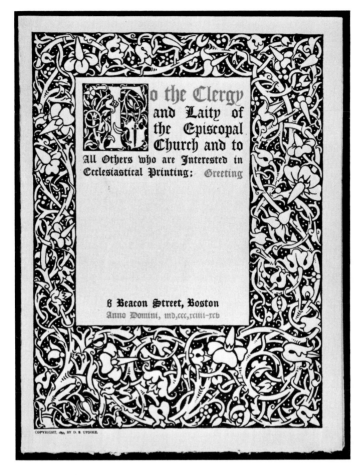

Morris' *Gossip about an Old House on the Upper Thames.* The *Quest* was decorated with Kelmscott initials and borders, the whole layout reminiscent of the *Hobby Horse,* the periodical published by Copeland & Day.

Updike's principal production in the Kelmscott manner, the celebrated *Altar Book,* was published in 1896. Three hundred fifty copies were set at Merrymount (Updike had been working on it since 1893 with backing by Harold Brown, which had enabled him to leave the Riverside Press), printed by De Vinne in New York, and offered for sale at $75. "The presswork was placed with De Vinne, who turned out a magnificent piece of work, although he was frankly out of sympathy with the style of the volume."[18] It is a large book on laid deckle-edge paper, in a blind-stamped brown pigskin binding with raised bands, a red silk marker, and three metal clasps. There are wood-engraved illustrations by Robert Anning Bell, the British artist. Goodhue designed the Kelmscott-style borders and initials, as well as the type, commissioned by Updike and christened Merrymount. It is not as spiky as the ATF Jenson but is even blacker and is similarly modeled on Morris' Golden. There are shoulder note running titles in red, and much other rubrication. Each section begins with a double spread within borders, an illustration on the verso and the text on the recto (Plate 37). The effect is much more unified than the earlier Prayer Book and is very much like an actual Kelmscott production.

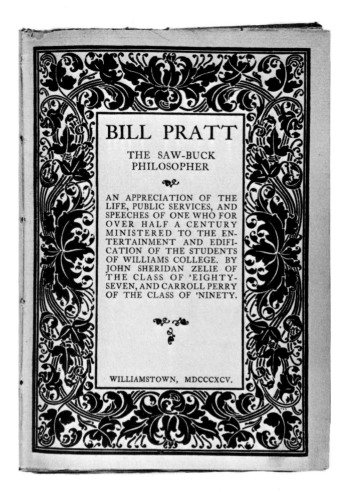

Plate 36. John Sheridan Zelie
and Carroll Perry, *Bill Pratt:
The Saw-Buck Philosopher*.
Williamstown: Privately printed,
1895.

Updike in later years did not retain his affection for the *Altar Book* and regretted its derivative Gothicism. The Larremores have transmitted his answer, dated February 18, 1940, when they asked him to inscribe a copy: "I can scarcely congratulate you on securing the worn-out Altar Book which, in its best estate, I am not, now-a-days very fond of—it is too reminiscent of a particular period. So I don't think I want to autograph it."[19]

At the time of the book's creation, however, his pride could be seen in the announcement he made in his 1894 circular:

> . . . Mr. Updike is publishing on his own account a limited edition of an Altar-Book of a sumptuous character. This book is the result of an endeavour to make a volume on ideal principles with satisfactory practical results, and it has been undertaken without any desire to hamper it either in the expenditure of time or of money, with the belief that the elimination of these two factors will enable the publisher to produce a volume which shall be of lasting value.[20]

Contemporary critics found it rewarding, indeed. Seldom has a modern printed book received such extravagant praise. Joseph M. Bowles, of *Modern Art*, was rather moderate in tone:

. . . to me the most interesting piece of bookmaking yet produced in this country. The renaissance of printing as in itself a fine art has found no more sincere and devoted follower than Mr. Updike. . . . Mr. Goodhue's type . . . must be ranked at once with that of William Morris. . . .[21]

The brochure put out by the press to advertise the book (Plate 38) quoted extravagant comments from two newspapers:

Never has a book issued from the hands of an American or an English publisher in nobler guise than this. . . . The perfect book is here. (New York *Tribune*)

For sharp, clean, perfect printing, it utterly out-distances the Kelmscott Press. . . . Mr. Morris himself has been improved upon. (Joseph Pennell in the London *Chronicle*)[22]

Carl Purington Rollins, a few years later in 1903, referred to the latter statement: " . . . while we may not all of us be willing to go the length which Mr. Joseph Pennell does . . . yet for dignified typography no modern book has come nearer perfection."[23] As for

Plate 37. *The Altar Book: Containing the Order for the Celebration of the Holy Eucharist According to the Use of the American Church.* Boston: Merrymount Press, 1896.

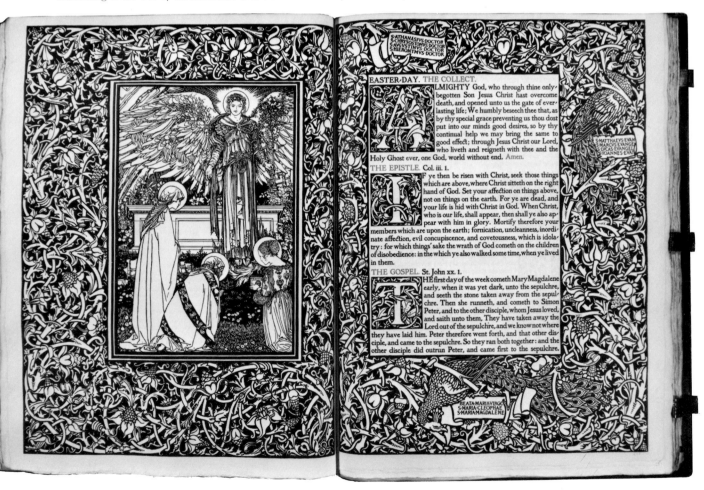

Copyright, 1896 by D. B. Updike.

PLATE FACING THE GOSPEL FOR EASTER-DAY [REDUCED IN SIZE], DRAWN BY R. ANNING BELL FOR THE ALTAR BOOK

Plate 38. Advertisement for *The Altar Book.*

the new Merrymount type, which Updike never used very much, he wrote of it critically in *Printing Types* that he and Goodhue had been seduced by Kelmscott blackness into a face too dark for any but large pages.[24]

The first book actually printed at the new Merrymount Press was George R. R. Rivers' *The Governor's Garden* (1896), published by the Joseph Knight Company. Updike had the idea for the silhouettes used to illustrate the book, but his associate, John Bianchi, has been given credit for arranging the fleuron head and tailpieces.[25] This in itself is interesting, for the usual assumption has been that Bianchi took care of the mechanical and bookkeeping side while Updike did the designing. That Bianchi had far more of a hand in the latter than people have realized has been pointed out by his son.[26] *The Governor's Garden* is in eighteenth-century style, cleverly done. It has a paneled title page with a flower basket cut, the proper names in italic and the imprint worded in archaic fashion (Plate 39). The text is in Caslon with catchwords and ruled running heads. "'The 'period business,'" Mr. Updike now thinks, "is perhaps a bit overdone for the reader's comfort, but its format attracted considerable attention when the book came out in 1896.'"[27]

From this same year a book privately printed at the Merrymount Press is in a neo-

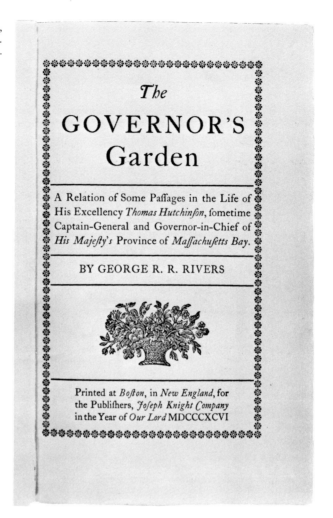

Gothic style that is close to the *Altar Book* but less Kelmscott derived. *Thanksgivings after the Communion of the Body and Blood of Christ* . . . with an introduction by the Reverend George McClellan Fiske, D.D., is a small book in Clarendon type on laid paper, with sparing use of red. The title page is set in a solid block arrangement. There are three double-spread openings with borders although the text pages are undecorated.

Updike developed for the books of one trade publisher, Thomas Y. Crowell & Co., a distinctive style that is based on Arts and Crafts. The type used is Clarendon, which strongly resembles Bookman, found in so many Arts and Crafts books. Other touches are the use of red ink, decorated initials, woodcut title page ornaments, often half titles in the upper left corner, and Gothic type for display. They tend to be small books, probably meant to be bought as gifts. Anna Robertson Brown's *What Is Worth While?* (1897) is the first of these (Plate 40). Updike said in 1934 that it "showed the influence of Mr. Morris' ideas upon commercial work, and the long series of similar 16mo volumes . . . followed the general style of the first one. . . ."[28] It is in gray blue paper boards with a floral panel by Goodhue. The title page is very solid set, with an ornament by Goodhue that is close to one of Goudy's designs. There are shoulder note running titles in red. A large black

Ships and Havens

II. WHITHER BOUND?

I want to talk with you about this question in this little book, as a writer may talk with a reader across the unknown intervals of time and space. The book that does not really speak to you is not worth much. And unless you really hear something, and make some kind of an answer to it, you do not truly read.

There is a disadvantage, of course, in the fact that you and I do not know each other and speak face to face. Who you are, into whose hands this book has come, I cannot tell. And to you, I am nothing but a name. Where you may be, while you turn these pages, I cannot guess. Perhaps you are sitting in your own quiet room after a hard day's work; perhaps you are reading aloud in some circle of friends around the open fire; perhaps you are in the quiet woods, or out in the pleasant orchard under your favorite tree; perhaps you are actually on the deck of a ship travelling across the waters. It is strange and wonderful to think of the many different places into which the words that I am now writing in this lonely, book-lined study may come, and of the many different eyes that may read them.

But wherever you are, and whoever you may be, there is one thing in which you and I are just alike, at this moment, and in all the moments of our existence. We are not at rest;

8

Whither Bound?

we are on a journey. Our life is not a mere fact; it is a movement, a tendency, a steady, ceaseless progress towards an unseen goal. We are gaining something, or losing something, every day. Even when our position and our character seem to remain precisely the same, they are changing. For the mere advance of time is a change. It is not the same thing to have a bare field in January and in July. The season makes the difference. The limitations that are childlike in the child are childish in the man.

Everything that we do is a step in one direction or another. Even the failure to do something is in itself a deed. It sets us forward or backward. The action of the negative pole of a magnetic needle is just as real as the action of the positive pole. To decline is to accept—the other alternative.

Are you richer to-day than you were yesterday? No? Then you are a little poorer. Are you better to-day than you were yesterday? No? Then you are a little worse. Are you nearer to your port to-day than you were yesterday? Yes,—you must be a little nearer to some port or other; for since your ship was first launched upon the sea of life, you have never been still for a single moment; the sea is too deep, you could not find an anchorage if you would; there can be no pause until you come into port.

But what is it, then, the haven towards which

9

leaf is used as a tailpiece. William Rader's *The Elegy of Faith* (1902) has the same Goodhue ornament.

A more elaborate example is Henry Van Dyke's *Ships and Havens* (copyright 1897 and 1898). The beige cloth binding has an overall design by Goodhue of repeated Viking ships in brown with the title and author in red caps in the upper left corner. The title page has a red woodcut of a ship in the middle. The table of contents is set solid; the line fillers are red fleurs-de-lis and black five-pointed snowflakes. At the text opening the chapter title is filled out with fleurs-de-lis and fishes (Plate 41). There are red running heads in Gothic caps. Unaware of this Merrymount/Crowell style, T. M. Cleland has said that this book's "highly rubricated ecclesiastical aspect appears to have no other warrant than that its author was a clergyman!"[29]

Other examples include Henry Van Dyke's *The Poetry of the Psalms* (1900), which has a decorated binding and initials with Celtic interlaced strapwork. The title page is set in a solid block with red fleurs-de-lis line fillers. *Tannhäuser: A Dramatic Poem by Richard Wagner Freely Translated in Poetic Narrative by Oliver Huckel* (1906) has a centered title page, red Gothic shoulder notes, a blue cloth binding decorated in green, gold, and white, and a halftone frontispiece that clashes with the title page. Wagner's *Parsifal* retold by Huckel (1910) is similar except that it has a wood-engraved frontispiece and illustrations by F. Stassen (Plate 42). The simple binding in red cloth has gilt lettering and blind stamping. It is a more pleasing book. Woodrow Wilson's *The Free Life* (1908) is a plain version of this style with a centered title page in Gothic type.

Updike's books that retained more antique flavor than these were usually his privately printed ones. *A Description of the Pastoral Staff Belonging to the Diocese of Albany, New York* is a very large book with paper as thick as cardboard. The double-spread opening has a frontispiece of the Albany Cathedral; both it and the text within have red Gothic architectural borders by Goodhue. The text is solid set in Caslon black letter type with both decorated and red initials (Plate 43).

Another very large book is the 1904 *Agricola* of Tacitus. This is an impeccably printed work in Merrymount type in the undecorated Venetian style favored by the Doves Press. The title page and colophon are in Latin as is the solid set text (Plate 44). It does manage to convey the incunabular spirit but more austerely than the decorated books that follow Morris. The significance of the Doves style in Updike's development was to become apparent from his writings as well.

As late as 1928 Updike put out eight hundred copies of a totally Morrisian book, appropriately enough, Marsden J. Perry's *A Chronological List of the Books Printed at the Kelmscott Press*, presented to members of the Grolier Club. It is in Poliphilus type, on laid paper, with a Kelmscott initial and leaf fleurons. There were still other Updike items with Arts and Crafts touches, but these were representative.

Updike's professed aim, "to do common work well," was characteristically expressed in terms of suitability. "An economy of means and a sort of disciplined sobriety mark [the Merrymount] product; and this comes about, probably, through aiming at suitability— a quality which involves discarding whatever does not organically belong to the particular work in hand."[30] This sense of suitability stemmed, in Updike's case, both from awareness of historical typography and from innate taste. His knowledge of earlier books has led to Updike's being credited with the invention of allusive typography (Rogers has been so credited as well), to which Updike demurred, calling it "simple appropriateness" that printers have adopted throughout the history of typography.[31] Updike's own taste, when he was not being allusive, was clearly in the classical line of the eighteenth century and of Pickering, as revealed by later Merrymount books.

But Updike remained true as well to Morris, despite his later aversion to his own copies of that style. In his 1896 travels to England, he had visited Kelmscott House and Sidney Cockerell and seen the London Society of Arts and Crafts exhibit of Kelmscott books. Just before his death, his library contained a framed page from the *Chaucer*, a gift from Douglas Cockerell, Sidney's son. There was also a portrait of Morris, a gift from Emery Walker, and a portrait of Walker himself.[32] And he defended Morris' work:

> While to my mind the Italian books of the Renaissance possess the highest qualities of style that the world has seen, I believe it possible to attain much of the same quality in almost any manner that a man may choose to adopt. In this connection one should mention William Morris's work, which possessed great distinction and style. . . . He understood the style in which he worked, its capabilities and its disabilities. He made use even of its disabilities in a way that was decorative.[33]

In his monumental 1922 work, *Printing Types*, Updike summed up what he considered to be Morris' contribution to printing, giving one of the most judicious estimates to be found at any date.[34] He pointed out that American printers knew little typographic

Plate 42. Oliver Huckel, *Parsifal: A Mystical Drama by Richard Wagner Retold in the Spirit of the Bayreuth Interpretation.* New York: Crowell, 1910.

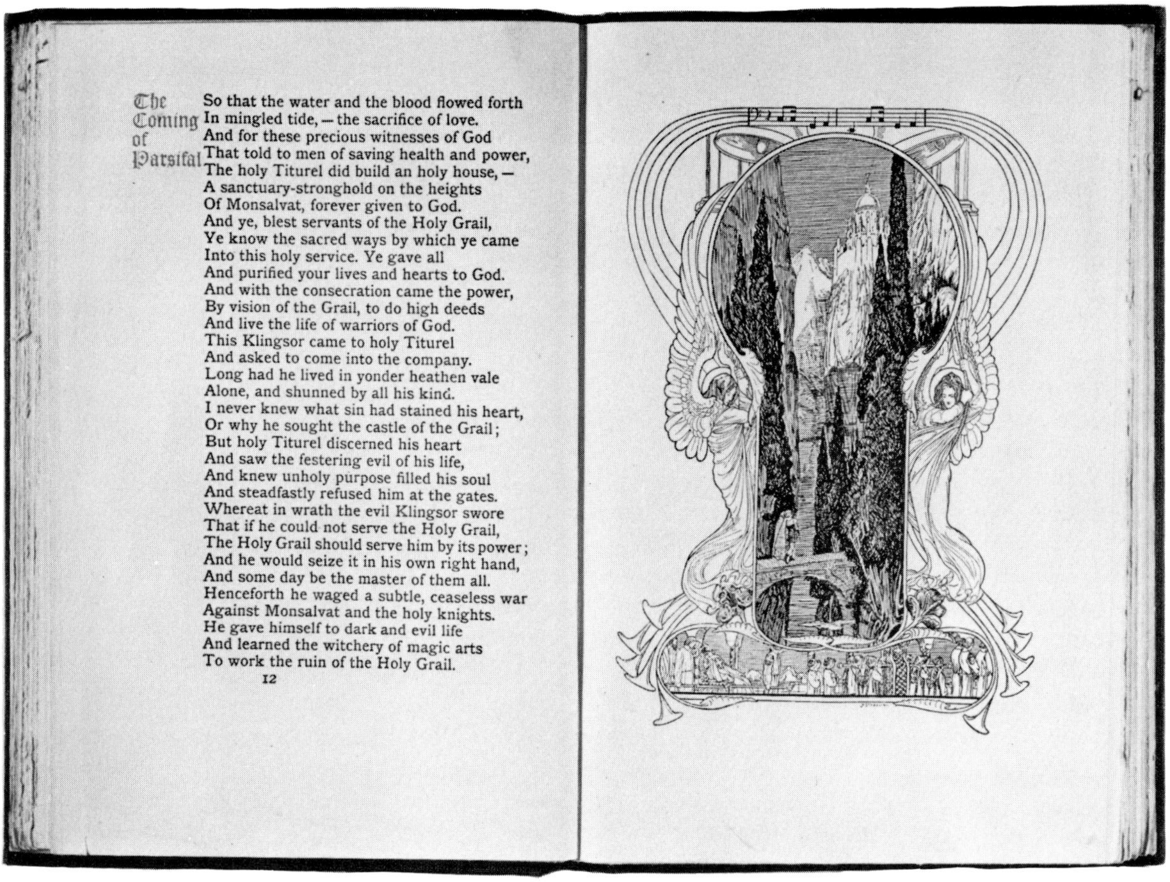
The Coming of Parsifal

So that the water and the blood flowed forth
In mingled tide, — the sacrifice of love.
And for these precious witnesses of God
That told to men of saving health and power,
The holy Titurel did build an holy house, —
A sanctuary-stronghold on the heights
Of Monsalvat, forever given to God.
And ye, blest servants of the Holy Grail,
Ye know the sacred ways by which ye came
Into this holy service. Ye gave all
And purified your lives and hearts to God.
And with the consecration came the power,
By vision of the Grail, to do high deeds
And live the life of warriors of God.
This Klingsor came to holy Titurel
And asked to come into the company.
Long had he lived in yonder heathen vale
Alone, and shunned by all his kind.
I never knew what sin had stained his heart,
Or why he sought the castle of the Grail;
But holy Titurel discerned his heart
And saw the festering evil of his life,
And knew unholy purpose filled his soul
And steadfastly refused him at the gates.
Whereat in wrath the evil Klingsor swore
That if he could not serve the Holy Grail,
The Holy Grail should serve him by its power;
And he would seize it in his own right hand,
And some day be the master of them all.
Henceforth he waged a subtle, ceaseless war
Against Monsalvat and the holy knights.
He gave himself to dark and evil life
And learned the witchery of magic arts
To work the ruin of the Holy Grail.

12

history so that the Kelmscott books appeared "to have fallen from the sky." Some found them wonderful, others freakish. In the long run, Morris' "over-statement" impressed many with the possibilities in strong type and decorations, and his lesson in "unity of effect" remained a permanent reform in American printing.

The inspiration he received from Morris was passed on by Updike; his own work and opinions have always been influential. By 1905, when the Society of Printers was formed in Boston, Updike's reputation among fellow printers was of the highest. W. A. Dwiggins has described the situation from firsthand knowledge:

> To the circle that was beginning to interest itself in the revival of printing as an art he stood as the foremost exponent of the craft in America.
>
> Note, for a moment, this circle. Its judgement was a body of opinion by no means to be ignored. It carried no weight, to be sure, with the rank and file of the printing trade. It was in a sense a camp in opposition. It was, nevertheless, exerting a vigorous influence upon printing, the effect of which was already to be seen in the books of certain publishing firms and in the product of several commercial presses. It was recruited from outside the craft, from the ranks of students of design, from architects, artists and amateurs of printing.
>
> To this group of campaigners the Merrymount Press stood as an emblem of en-

Plate 43. *A Description of the Pastoral Staff Belonging to the Diocese of Albany, New York.* Boston: Merrymount Press, 1900.

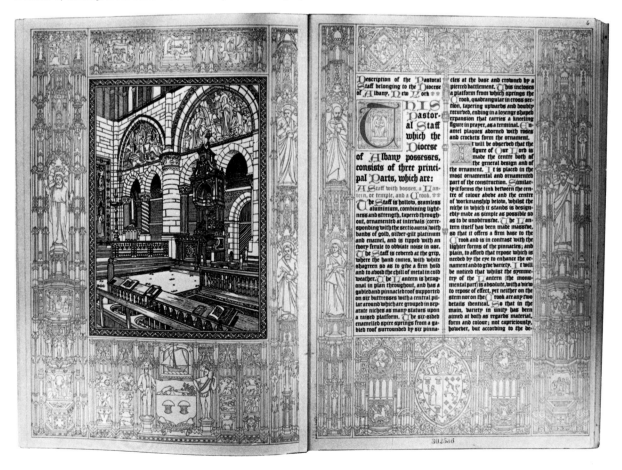

couragement. It was a demonstration of the things that might be hoped to be achieved in commercial printing under a more enlightened dispensation.[35]

In his famous talk of October 18, 1915, to the Bibliographical Society about Rogers' work, A. W. Pollard praised Updike as well.[36] Updike's fame went on steadily increasing until he was on a pinnacle surpassing that of De Vinne in the previous generation. The most illustrious of his colleagues, Bruce Rogers, wrote Henry Lewis Bullen in 1919:

> I like Updike, personally, as little as anyone I know—but this fact doesn't in the least blind me to the equal fact that no other printer on earth today equals, or at all approaches, him in versatility, style, and general excellence of workmanship.[37]

The work kept pouring in, although the press remained small. In 1936 Paul Standard claimed that Merrymount had done more than 15,000 pieces of job printing and 800 books, 66 of which had been included among the American Institute of Graphic Arts Fifty Books of the Year during the past thirteen years, more than any other printer had chosen.[38]

Moreover, he had achieved his success with restricted means, using not more than fifteen typefaces. Forty percent of his books were in Caslon.[39] His other faces included Scotch, Oxford, Bell, Clarendon, French, Bodoni, Poliphilus, Lutetia, and the two cut especially for him, Merrymount by Goodhue and Montallegro by Herbert Horne. This type of restraint is not at all foreign to the spirit of Arts and Crafts. Although Updike's own style was certainly more of the Age of Enlightenment than the late Middle Ages, it is nonsense to say, as Rudolph Ruzicka has, that he sympathized not at all with Arts and Crafts.[40] Many of Updike's first typographic sallies were inspired by Morris, and he never ceased to pay him respect.

Both Updike and Bruce Rogers played leading roles when the Society of Printers was formed in 1905 with William Dana Orcutt as the first president. For the Society's 1906 exhibition in honor of the bicentenary of Franklin's birth, entitled "The Development of Printing as an Art," Rogers and Updike constituted the Committee for "Modern Book-Printing c. 1800–1905." Their long overlooked introduction to this section of the catalogue showed their mutual reassessment of Morris' standing and implied that their own moves toward lighter models may have been influenced more than has been realized by the Doves Press, and behind that, Jenson, not as Morris interpreted him, but in the spirit of the fifteenth-century Renaissance.

> In 1891 a marked influence was felt from the books which William Morris began to print at The Kelmscott Press. . . . At the time of his death considered the leading printer of the period, a retrospect of ten years has placed him rather with those great decorators who have turned their attention to the printed book . . . during the last few years the somewhat Gothic feeling of the Kelmscott Press books has been slowly abandoned for the lighter and more classical styles of type founded on Italian models of the fifteenth century,—a movement in which The Doves Press, London, has been chiefly instrumental . . .[41]

The Commercial Printing section of this same catalogue stated that Caslon was the most used type, while Old Style Antique (Bookman) was another popular face, as was

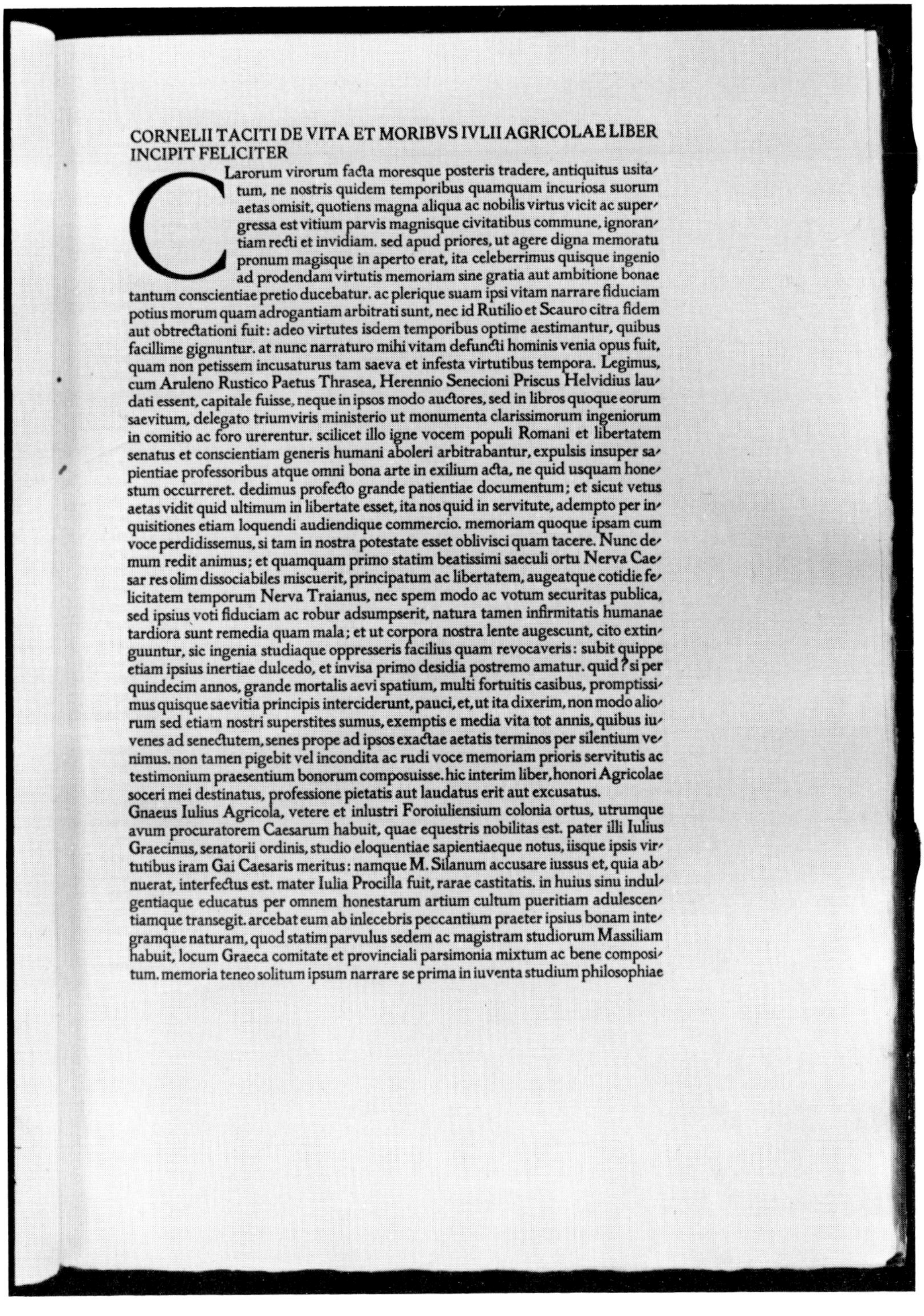

CORNELII TACITI DE VITA ET MORIBVS IVLII AGRICOLAE LIBER INCIPIT FELICITER

Clarorum virorum facta moresque posteris tradere, antiquitus usitatum, ne nostris quidem temporibus quamquam incuriosa suorum aetas omisit, quotiens magna aliqua ac nobilis virtus vicit ac supergressa est vitium parvis magnisque civitatibus commune, ignorantiam recti et invidiam. sed apud priores, ut agere digna memoratu pronum magisque in aperto erat, ita celeberrimus quisque ingenio ad prodendam virtutis memoriam sine gratia aut ambitione bonae tantum conscientiae pretio ducebatur. ac plerique suam ipsi vitam narrare fiduciam potius morum quam adrogantiam arbitrati sunt, nec id Rutilio et Scauro citra fidem aut obtrectationi fuit: adeo virtutes isdem temporibus optime aestimantur, quibus facillime gignuntur. at nunc narraturo mihi vitam defuncti hominis venia opus fuit, quam non petissem incusaturus tam saeva et infesta virtutibus tempora. Legimus, cum Aruleno Rustico Paetus Thrasea, Herennio Senecioni Priscus Helvidius laudati essent, capitale fuisse, neque in ipsos modo auctores, sed in libros quoque eorum saevitum, delegato triumviris ministerio ut monumenta clarissimorum ingeniorum in comitio ac foro urerentur. scilicet illo igne vocem populi Romani et libertatem senatus et conscientiam generis humani aboleri arbitrabantur, expulsis insuper sapientiae professoribus atque omni bona arte in exilium acta, ne quid usquam honestum occurreret. dedimus profecto grande patientiae documentum; et sicut vetus aetas vidit quid ultimum in libertate esset, ita nos quid in servitute, adempto per inquisitiones etiam loquendi audiendique commercio. memoriam quoque ipsam cum voce perdidissemus, si tam in nostra potestate esset oblivisci quam tacere. Nunc demum redit animus; et quamquam primo statim beatissimi saeculi ortu Nerva Caesar res olim dissociabiles miscuerit, principatum ac libertatem, augeatque cotidie felicitatem temporum Nerva Traianus, nec spem modo ac votum securitas publica, sed ipsius voti fiduciam ac robur adsumpserit, natura tamen infirmitatis humanae tardiora sunt remedia quam mala; et ut corpora nostra lente augescunt, cito extinguuntur, sic ingenia studiaque oppresseris facilius quam revocaveris: subit quippe etiam ipsius inertiae dulcedo, et invisa primo desidia postremo amatur. quid? si per quindecim annos, grande mortalis aevi spatium, multi fortuitis casibus, promptissimus quisque saevitia principis interciderunt, pauci, et, ut ita dixerim, non modo aliorum sed etiam nostri superstites sumus, exemptis e media vita tot annis, quibus iuvenes ad senectutem, senes prope ad ipsos exactae aetatis terminos per silentium venimus. non tamen pigebit vel incondita ac rudi voce memoriam prioris servitutis ac testimonium praesentium bonorum composuisse. hic interim liber, honori Agricolae soceri mei destinatus, professione pietatis aut laudatus erit aut excusatus.

Gnaeus Iulius Agricola, vetere et inlustri Foroiuliensium colonia ortus, utrumque avum procuratorem Caesarum habuit, quae equestris nobilitas est. pater illi Iulius Graecinus, senatorii ordinis, studio eloquentiae sapientiaeque notus, iisque ipsis virtutibus iram Gai Caesaris meritus: namque M. Silanum accusare iussus et, quia abnuerat, interfectus est. mater Iulia Procilla fuit, rarae castitatis. in huius sinu indulgentiaque educatus per omnem honestarum artium cultum pueritiam adulescentiamque transegit. arcebat eum ab inlecebris peccantium praeter ipsius bonam integramque naturam, quod statim parvulus sedem ac magistram studiorum Massiliam habuit, locum Graeca comitate et provinciali parsimonia mixtum ac bene compositum. memoria teneo solitum ipsum narrare se prima in iuventa studium philosophiae

Plate 44. Tacitus, *Agricola*. Boston: Merrymount Press, 1904.

black letter for display.[42] In this field the move away from Morris was pointed out:

> The revival of borders and decorative initials was greatly stimulated by the work of William Morris and by the product of other private presses under similar influences. There has been a reaction from heavy borders and profuse rubrication, preference being given now to lettering having plain Roman characteristics, supplemented by simple decorative treatments, avoiding mediaeval effects.[43]

The Society of Printers was, in a sense, the Boston culmination of a series of moves toward printing as an art, in which the work of one man recurred as a *leit-motif*—Henry Lewis Johnson. Born in Limington, Maine, in 1867, he encountered printing through work on a Boston high school paper. In 1891, with his editorship of the *Engraver and Printer*, an early periodical in the printing art movement, he began his long and unlucrative career as an idealistic typographer. He was director of the advisory board of the First Exhibition of Arts and Crafts held in April 1897. This was so successful that a permanent Society of Arts and Crafts was set up with Johnson as a charter member. In 1903 he persuaded the University Press to publish the *Printing Art* under his editorship and this became a major voice in the post-Kelmscott period. As Ray Nash, the chronicler of this Boston movement, has said:

> The Kelmscott approach was architectonic under all its decoration. Previously the designer with respect to printing had been one who added illustration or ornamental features to it. Now, in the new light of the "revival," the designer could find a place to stand in the printing field analogous to that occupied by the architect in building. Over and over again this was the burden of *The Printing Art*.[44]

Then in 1905 came the Society of Printers, of which Johnson was the first secretary. After nine years of the *Printing Art*, he began another periodical, the *Graphic Arts* in 1911, which carried the torch until 1915. Before his poverty-stricken death in 1937, he had lived to edit still another journal, the *New England Printer*.

Thus, Johnson was a factor in making Boston a leader in all four phases of the Kelmscott Revival in America: avant-garde emulation in the early nineties, absorption of the style by commercial publishing in the mid-nineties and early twentieth century, abandonment of it for Doves after 1906, and general improvement of printing during the ensuing years of the twentieth century.

1. Quoted in Ellen B. Ballou, *The Building of the House: Houghton Mifflin's Formative Years* (Boston: Houghton Mifflin, 1970), p. 55.
2. Ibid., p. 325.
3. Daniel B. Bianchi, *D. B. Updike & John Bianchi: A Note on Their Association* (Boston: Society of Printers, 1965).
4. Francis Watts Lee, "Regarding Recent Books and Bookmaking," *Knight Errant*, I (April 1892): 32.
5. George L. Harding, *D. B. Updike and the Merrymount Press* (San Francisco: Roxburghe Club, 1943), p. 10.
6. Ray Nash, "Notes on the Riverside Press and D. B.

Updike," *Gutenberg-Jahrbuch*, XXXV (1960): 329–333.
7. "Current Illustrations," *Engraver and Printer*, IV (May 1893): 13.
8. Harding, *D. B. Updike*, p. 10.
9. Daniel Berkeley Updike, *Notes on the Merrymount Press and Its Work* (Cambridge: Harvard University Press, 1934), p. 10.
10. Daniel Berkeley Updike, *On the Decorations of the Limited Edition of the Standard Prayer Book of MDCCCXCII* (New York: De Vinne Press, 1893), unpaged.
11. Daniel Berkeley Updike, *To the Trade* (Boston:

Updike, 1893), unpaged.

12. Ray Nash, *Printing as an Art* (Cambridge: Harvard University Press, 1955), pp. 30-31.

13. Paul A. Bennett, "Mr. D. B. Updike: The Merrymount Press, Boston," *Linotype News*, XIV (July 1935): 5.

14. Daniel Berkeley Updike, *A Few Words about Printing . . .* (Boston: Updike, 1894), unpaged.

15. "Irving" [i.e., W. Irving Way], "Books, Authors, and Kindred Subjects," *Inland Printer*, XIV (January 1895): 345.

16. Daniel Berkeley Updike, "The Black Art: A Homily," *Engraver and Printer*, V (January 1894): 1-4.

17. Daniel Berkeley Updike, *Merrymount* (Boston: Merrymount, 1895), unpaged.

18. Updike, *Notes*, p. 15.

19. Thomas A. Larremore, and Amy Hopkins Larremore, *The Marion Press* (Jamaica: Queens Borough Public Library, 1943), p. 171.

20. Updike, *A Few Words about Printing*, unpaged.

21. Joseph M. Bowles, "Mr. Updike's Altar Book," *Modern Art*, IV (Autumn 1896): 124-125.

22. *The Altar Book* (Boston: Merrymount, n.d.), unpaged.

23. Carl Purington Rollins, "Modern 'Special Types.'" *Printing Art*, I (March 1903): 16.

24. Daniel Berkeley Updike, *Printing Types* (2d ed.; Cambridge: Harvard University Press, 1951), vol. II, pp. 217-218.

25. Updike, *Notes*, p. 66.

26. Bianchi, *D. B. Updike*.

27. Quoted in Zoltan Haraszti, "Mr. Updike and the Merrymount Press," *More Books*, X (May 1935): 165.

28. Updike, *Notes*, p. 18.

29. Thomas M. Cleland, "A Tribute to Daniel Berkeley Updike," in *Updike: American Printer and His Merrymount Press* (New York: American Institute of Graphic Arts, 1947), p. 82.

30. *The Merrymount Press, Boston: Its Aims, Works, and Equipment* (Boston: Merrymount Press, n.d.), p. 4.

31. Daniel Berkeley Updike, *Some Aspects of Printing Old and New* (New Haven: W. E. Rudge, 1941), p. 27.

32. Paul Standard, "The Libraries Men Live By. I. A. Printer's Library," *Dolphin*, IV (Fall 1940): 46.

33. Daniel Berkeley Updike, *In the Day's Work* (Cambridge: Harvard University Press, 1924), pp. 44-45.

34. Updike, *Printing Types*, vol. II, pp. 204-209.

35. William A. Dwiggins, "D. B. Updike and the Merrymount Press," *Fleuron*, III (1924): 1-2.

36. Alfred W. Pollard, "The Work of Bruce Rogers, Printer," *Transactions of the Bibliographical Society*, XIV (1919): 11.

37. Letter, Bruce Rogers to Henry Lewis Bullen, March 28, 1919, Typographic Library Manuscript Collection, Columbia University Libraries.

38. Paul Standard, "D. B. Updike: The Merrymount Press," *Penrose Annual*, XXXVIII (1936): 17.

39. David T. Pottinger, Grolier Club address in *Daniel Berkeley Updike and the Merrymount Press* (New York: American Institute of Graphic Arts, 1940), pp. 25-26.

40. Stanley Morison and Rudolph Ruzicka, *Recollections of Daniel Berkeley Updike* (Boston: Club of Odd Volumes, 1943), pp. 25-26.

41. *The Development of Printing as an Art* (Boston: Society of Printers, 1906), p. 20.

42. Ibid., pp. 55-56.

43. Ibid., pp. 56-57.

44. Nash, *Printing as an Art*, p. 53.

XI

Chicago & Its "Literary Publishers"

AFTER BOSTON Chicago was the American city most affected by the Morris Revival. It was not as much a publishing center as the large cities of the Eastern seaboard, but it became the home of two of the "literary publishers," Stone & Kimball, the most famous of them all, and Way & Williams, the one most closely connected with Morris. In commercial printing, the Lakeside Press was one of the country's finest, but it played no special role in the Revival of Printing. Chicago also had several private presses. Finally, two future leaders of American typography—Bradley and Goudy—began work in Chicago, both in the footsteps of Morris.

Not only was there a literary renaissance during the nineties in Chicago, there was also a great deal of bibliophile interest. Irving Way estimated in 1892 that the ranks of Chicago bibliophiles had increased from 10 in 1875 to 150 at the time he was writing.[1] The best-known Chicago book club was the Caxton Club, organized in 1895. Herbert Stone and Irving Way, the two leading literary publishers, were among the charter members, as was George M. Millard, head of the rare book department of McClurg's Bookstore where the famous Saints and Sinners Corner, chronicled by Eugene Field, did much to stimulate Chicago interest in fine books. The influential house of Stone & Kimball also provided a stimulus to the bibliophilic fervor of the times, especially by employing important designers.

Stone & Kimball began life in 1893 in Cambridge, Massachusetts, where Herbert S. Stone and Ingalls Kimball were Harvard undergraduates. They both came from Chicago, however, and they both returned there in 1894 with their new firm. In 1896 they separated, Kimball going to New York and becoming sole owner of Stone & Kimball; Stone remaining in Chicago where he became head of a new firm entitled Herbert S. Stone & Company. In 1897 Kimball was forced by financial difficulties to sell off at public auction the properties of Stone & Kimball, and the firm came to an end. Herbert S. Stone & Company continued until 1905. Sidney Kramer, author of the definitive book on the two firms, felt that they were important in American publishing of the nineties because they put into practice,

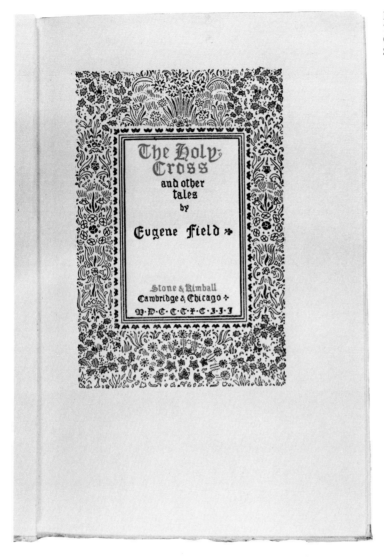

before the older houses, the new ideals of the nineties: publication of avant-garde European literature under the Copyright Act of 1891 and creation of physically beautiful volumes. And they did it in the name of idealism rather than commercialism, for they were amateurs in the best sense more than they were businessmen.[2]

The first trade notice of the new firm appeared in *Publishers Weekly* for September 9, 1893, emphasizing the significance of its western location and of its ambition to emulate Mathews' and Lane's London firm, The Bodley Head.[3] Kramer gave three reasons for their choice of Chicago as a base: the lack of competition in book publishing, the fact that their families were already there, and the proximity of the Chicago Exposition.[4] Indeed, the first publication was a guide book for the World's Fair of 1893, held in Chicago.

The second publication revealed another orientation of the young firm—bibliophily: *First Editions of American Authors: A Manual for Book Lovers Compiled by Herbert Stuart Stone with an Introduction by Eugene Field* (1893). The third publication was another version of the guide book, while the fourth was Hamlin Garland's *Main-Travelled Roads* (1893), a book of fiction. This interest in contemporary American *belles lettres* was matched by the importation from England of sheets of new English literature, the first example being Kenneth Grahame's *Pagan Papers* (1894), from Mathews and Lane, with art work by Beardsley.

Besides the guide book, printed in Chicago, and the imported English sheets, the early Stone & Kimball volumes were printed at the University Press in Cambridge. In 1894, however, when they moved back to Chicago, the partners started using the Lakeside Press, although they did not give up the University Press. In any case, the press they used is not important since the partners themselves determined the format, and that format was the small, simple Aesthetic one propagated by Mathews and Lane in London, and continued by the other literary publishers in the wake of Stone & Kimball. Thomas Bird Mosher in Maine had also been spreading the Aesthetic format since 1891, although his books were

Plate 46. James Barr (Angus Evan Abbott), *The Gods Give My Donkey Wings.* Chicago: Stone & Kimball, 1895.

98

even simpler than Stone & Kimball's. The latter's volumes themselves became simpler with time, as Kramer pointed out: ". . . there can be seen, between 1893 and 1896, a progression from a deluxe, ornamental style to one graceful but simple and functional."[5] It is in the decorations that can be found the occasional touch of Arts and Crafts: Louis J. Rhead's designs for Eugene Field's 1893 *The Holy Cross and Other Tales* (Plate 45), Pierre la Rose's bordered title page for Hugh McCulloch's *The Quest of Heracles and Other Poems* (1894), or Frank Hazenplug's for George Ade's *Fables in Slang* (1900) and *More Fables* (1900); the last two for Herbert S. Stone & Co. An 1894 Stone & Kimball letterhead also shows Arts and Crafts, both in its composition (solid set Gothic type with a red initial) and in its wording: "This cometh from . Stone & Kimball . who publish books for . Gentlemen and Gentlewomen . . ."

An example from one of the series may be taken to describe the format of a typical Stone & Kimball Aesthetic book: Angus Evan Abbott's [i.e., James Barr] *The Gods Give My Donkey Wings* (1895), printed at the Lakeside Press, was the fifth in the Carnation Series. The small book is in Caslon type on laid paper, with a special Stone & Kimball watermark, and very wide margins at the foot. The only decoration is the series title in red with a stylized carnation at the head of the centered title page and another carnation in black in the middle. The binding of beige cloth has an overall carnation pattern stamped on a green background (Plate 46).

The year 1894 marked the beginning of one of the most influential of all Stone & Kimball publications: the *Chap-Book*, a semimonthly periodical, begun on May 15 in Cambridge and continued in Chicago until July 1, 1898. Like the *Yellow Book* in England it inspired widespread interest for both its content and format. A rash of similar "little magazines" covered the United States for about ten years, and its promotion of posters gave impetus to the poster craze of the nineties. The *Chap-Book* was simple in format, more or less living up to the antique flavor of its name and therefore tending to the Arts and Crafts side of book design. It was in Original Old Style type with decorated initials, on laid paper, with good margins, in brown paper covers (Plate 47). Ernest Elmo Calkins has described the impact it made at the time on the typographically sensitive.

> It was the format, not the contents, that wrought [my] transformation. I was a printer and printing was at a low ebb, flat as the Illinois prairies and dull as Main Street. Without background, or experience, or inspiration, I was vainly struggling to express with type things vaguely imagined, to break through conventions that confined printing like iron bars. When job work was a conglomerate of every type in the shop, looking like a badly arranged specimen sheet of ugly and conflicting faces, here was a little magazine set all in one letter, that had distinction, life, and above all simplicity. The Chap-Book was an inspiration—not only to me but to hosts of others. No younger man can fully appreciate the impact of that simple and casual little magazine on a world of stodgy and commonplace printing. It turned attention toward the relation of type to the things printed with it. True, it was reminiscent of an earlier and better day. Its attractiveness was due not to any new pattern or treatment, but rather to a skillful adaptation of old forms, but it did remind us that there was in the world a reservoir of good taste in printing, either calculated or unconscious, which was not being utilized.[6]

Herbert Stone, after the demise of his publishing firm in 1905, went on until 1913

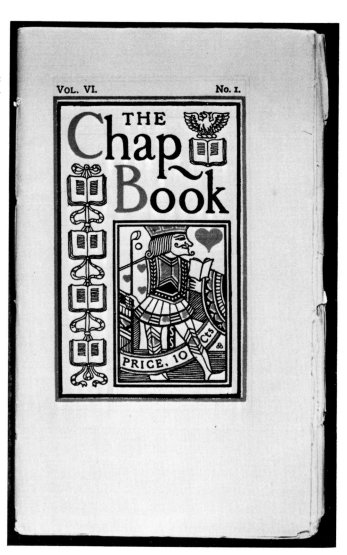

Plate 47. *Chap-Book.* Chicago:
Herbert S. Stone & Co., 1896.

editing *House Beautiful,* the periodical he had taken over in 1897. In 1915 he and Elbert Hubbard were both passengers who did not survive the sinking of the *Lusitania.*

Ingalls Kimball, besides becoming the friend and associate of Walter Gilliss in New York, established in 1897 the Cheltenham Press, which did some private printing and also became a much sought after commercial press in the field of advertising. Especially successful was the Cheltenham Old Style typeface, created in 1900–1901 by Kimball and B. G. Goodhue, the most popular font for advertising for years. Will Bradley said of the commercial work of the press that it was in a class by itself, "unsurpassed and only rarely equaled."[7]

In 1908 Kimball wrote and produced *The First Ten Years of the Cheltenham Press: Being an Acccount of Various Problems in Printing and in Advertising and of Their Solutions* in an Arts and Crafts format. It is set in Cheltenham type, within red rules on every page and with headings in black letter. The title page has the title in caps in a paragraph

100

arrangement with a large initial on a red floriate background. The imprint is in caps, flush left, as is the half title.

The other Chicago literary publisher was more intimately involved with Arts and Crafts. W. Irving Way was one of the most knowledgeable and articulate of the western bibliophiles, a friend, according to Ralph Fletcher Seymour, of the well-known English bookmen, Andrew Lang and Thomas James Wise.[8] A collector of Eugene Field, he was perhaps only less well known than that great popularizer of fine editions.

Way was born in Canada in 1853 and worked as a railway clerk before settling in Chicago in 1890 as the western representative of *Forum* magazine.[9] A member of book clubs, including the Grolier, and a regular contributor on fine books to *Inland Printer* and other periodicals, Way also started publishing in the early nineties. It was he who put out Harriet Monroe's *The Columbian Ode* (1893) in honor of the Columbian Exposition in Chicago, printed by De Vinne, with decorations by Will Bradley. When Stone's *First*

Editions of American Authors appeared in 1893, Way wanted to become his partner. When Stone elected to stay with Kimball, Way sought out capital in the form of the well-to-do Chauncey L. Williams, founding Way & Williams in 1895. Williams was to become sole owner in 1896.[10] Like the other literary publishers the new firm imported books from England, specialized in contemporary literature, and tended toward Aesthetic formats.

But Way & Williams also had direct connection with William Morris. Way made a trip to England in 1895 where he visited Morris at Hammersmith on two occasions and made a deal to be the American publisher of one of the Kelmscott books.[11] Rossetti's *Hand and Soul* was so issued in 1895, the only Kelmscott book to bear the name of an American publisher. Will Bradley has described the Way of this period:

> Way & Williams, publishers, have an office on the floor below my studio. Irving Way, who would barter his last shirt for a first edition, his last pair of shoes for a volume from the Kelmscott Press of William Morris, is a frequent and always stimulating visitor.[12]

In 1895 Way & Williams issued a book in Arts and Crafts style: Shelley's translation of *The Banquet of Plato*, designed by Bruce Rogers. In 1897, not only did Way & Williams publish Buxton Forman's *The Books of William Morris*, but also a book reflecting current Arts and Crafts work. *The Miracles of Madame Saint Katherine of Fierbois* (Plate 48), translated by Andrew Lang, was printed at the De Vinne Press, with decorations by the Englishman, Selwyn Image. Like *Hand and Soul*, it was issued in American and English editions, on handmade and Japan vellum paper. The margins are of Morrisian proportions and the binding is paper boards, half vellum, but, despite the Image woodcuts, the overall effect is of bastard Arts and Crafts. There are centered running titles in italic and the text is in a modern style type. Less hybrid examples of Way & Williams books exhibit the typical Aesthetic format. Percival Pollard's *Dreams of To-Day* (1897) has an Art Nouveau binding and a plain, Aesthetic text. Opie Read's *Bolanyo* (1897) has a cover by Maxfield Parrish and decorations by Charles Francis Browne, which include a vignette headpiece and tailpiece and a rococo title page. The text is Caslon on laid paper, with italic cap running heads.

In 1898, after only four years of Way & Williams imprints, the firm sold out to Herbert S. Stone & Co. But, as Kramer has pointed out,[13] the copyrights were not actually transferred and most of the list was, for some reason, assigned to Doubleday & McClure in 1900. Way & Williams as a publishing house probably had less general effect than Stone & Kimball, Copeland & Day, or even R. H. Russell. But Way as an individual was, without doubt, one of the moving spirits of the typographic fervor of the nineties because of his prolific writing and his importation of the only Kelmscott book to have an American publisher.

The most important firm in commercial printing in Chicago was the one used by the literary publishers. The R. R. Donnelley Company, founded in 1864 and reorganized in 1883 as R. R. Donnelley & Sons, owned in the Lakeside Press the largest and most famous Chicago printing house. As well as trade books, the Lakeside Press was hired for privately printed books where, as with many private books, evidence of Kelmscott influence can be traced. For example, *Eugene Field: An Auto-Analysis* was printed in 1896 for Frank M. Morris, Chicago antiquarian bookseller. The text is in Bookman type and the title page in Jenson. There are hand-illumined initials, some of which are Kelmscott-style, and tail-pieces throughout, with a side border for the text opening. It is on Japan vellum in a binding of gray paper boards.

It was not in commercial printing but in private presses that Chicago revealed the greatest Kelmscott influence. However, many of the key figures in the private press world were also involved in commercial endeavors.

1. W. Irving Way, "Bibliophilism in Chicago," in *The Book-Lovers Almanac for 1893* (New York: Duprat, 1892), unpaged.
2. Sidney Kramer, *A History of Stone & Kimball and Herbert S. Stone & Co. with a Bibliography of Their Publications 1893–1905,* (Chicago: University of Chicago Press, 1940), pp. 140–141.
3. "Stone & Kimball, of Cambridge, Mass., and Chicago, Ill.," *Publishers Weekly,* XLIV (September 9, 1893): 311.
4. Kramer, *Stone & Kimball,* p. 12.
5. Ibid., p. 151.
6. Ernest Elmo Calkins, "The Chap-Book," *Colophon,* III (May 1932), Part 10, unpaged.
7. Letter, Will H. Bradley to Sidney Kramer, dated August 5, 1938, quoted in Kramer, *Stone & Kimball,* p. 70.
8. Ralph Fletcher Seymour, *Some Went This Way* (Chicago: R. F. Seymour, 1945), p. 111.
9. "W. Irving Way," *Inland Printer,* XVII (April 1896): 67.
10. For information on Way, Williams, and the firm itself, see Joe W. Kraus, "The Publishing Activities of Way & Williams, Chicago, 1895-98," *Papers of the Bibliographical Society of America,* LXX (Second quarter, 1976): 221-260.
11. W. Irving Way, "A Visit to William Morris," *Modern Art,* IV (July 1, 1896): 78-81.
12. Will H. Bradley, *Will Bradley: His Chap-Book* (New York: Typophiles, 1955), pp. 32-33.
13. Kramer, *Stone & Kimball,* p. 115.

XII

Private Presses
in the Chicago Area

IN RIVER FOREST, Illinois, eleven miles from Chicago, William Herman Winslow was responsible for founding the Auvergne Press in 1895 with his neighbor, Chauncey L. Williams, the partner of Irving Way. Winslow owned the Winslow Ornamental Iron Works and in 1893 had been the first to commission Frank Lloyd Wright for the independent designing of a private home.[1] Winslow and Wright together printed by hand in 1896–1897 William Channing Gannett's *The House Beautiful*, a quintessential Arts and Crafts text, advocating a return to nature, simplicity, and honesty.

The book is lavishly decorated by Wright in red and black. All text pages are within borders with Morrisian margins, and there are several double spreads of solid ornament with no text, similar to the carpet pages of Celtic manuscripts. The double-spread title page is in red old-style caps (as is the text) within a black border with a repeating frieze of figures and leaf ornament, recalling in its rectilinearity the work of Ricketts and the Glasgow School. Wright has described it in a letter to Samuel R. Morrill, dated September 27, 1949: "Yes, my first work of the kind: an amateur feeling for a decorative pattern to harmonize with the type of the text—looking for it in the seed pods of weeds growing all about."[2]

This interesting book was more innovative than typical of the private press books of the time. Lyman Frank Baum, best known as the author of *The Wizard of Oz*, produced a more familiar-looking volume when he turned to private printing. This turn was a predictable development in his own history. Born in 1856 in Chittenango, New York, he had, as a teenager, received a printing press from his father and, with his brother, had put out a monthly publication. He later worked on several newspapers, at one point owning a printing shop in Bradford, Pennsylvania.[3] He also leaned toward handicraft: "Like William Morris, whom he read and admired, Baum had a constitutional dislike of the mass-produced item. . . ."[4] In 1898 he published his own poetry, *By the Candelabra's Glare*, "Privately Printed by L. Frank Baum in His own Workshop," in an edition of ninety-nine copies. The foreword says that he set the type, turned the press, and did the binding. The title page has an asymmetrical arrangement within a red border. The type is Jenson. The illustrators include W. W. Denslow, Frank Hazenplug, and R. F. Seymour.

The Wind-Tryst Press of Chicago was a more amateurish affair. For example, Louisa Young Foote's poem, *In the Adirondacks*, is printed in a four-page brochure without a title page. The colophon reads: ". . . printed by me, Martha Foote Crow, in our printery. . . . Fifty copies were printed, for our family and special friends only, at Christmas-time . . ." the date being 1897. This is in Jenson, the arrangement an inverted triangle, while the text is in Satanick, the ATF type modeled on Morris' Troy face, with rows of fleurons as head and tailpieces. The first page has the title in caps and a Kelmscott outline vine border on three sides. Two other titles from this press are in the Arts and Crafts mode. *The Ministry of a Child: A Book of Verses* by Martha Foote Crow (1899) again stresses in its colophon the private nature of the book: "We printed this book in a small edition, for our friends only, during January." It is in Bookman type with a centered title page. Louisa Young Foote's *The Old Homestead* (1899) is also in Bookman type. The centered title page has an incongruous, spindly row of arabesque type ornaments at the head. There is a Kelmscott initial at the text opening with large black Satanick initials for each stanza.

Another press, in St. Charles, oriented toward Arts and Crafts, was even called the Morris Press. William Morris' *In Praise of My Lady* (1902), is a tiny book typical of the private press books of the time. The colophon states that William Edward Davidson designed the title page and border (which is repeated on each page) and did the printing of 400 copies (in Jenson). The cover has a woodcut title and ornament in the manner of Blue Sky books. The title page and borders have the same flower printed in green and orange (the type is black). The title is on a scroll, with a flower impinging on the words "By William Morris" asymmetrically placed. A few of the book's elements seem disproportionate or jarring. For example, the text opening is very high and to the middle in an exaggeration of Kelmscott margins. The verso facing this page has the medievalistic: "Here Beginneth . . ." while its recto has a verse from the Rubaiyat. The printer's device at the end contains a smoking lamp and the motto: "Love and Art are Life."

Still another press, in Highland Park, put out an Arts and Crafts style book, one of the two titles it published. George Wither's *Certain Poems* was issued in 1901 by the Elm Press, named from the initials of the founder, Everett Lee Millard, and housed, according to Ransom, in a house built from elm logs and surrounded by elm trees. The binding is gold-stamped vellum with vellum ties, the paper handmade wove, and the type Jenson. The decorations are by Day McBirney with a portrait from an old engraving. The title, placed in the upper left corner, resembles a half title in its brevity. The text opening has a border of ovals containing interlaced designs with a matching initial. There are no running titles, but catchwords are used. Millard's other book was Abraham Cowley's *Essays* (1902), in 110 copies, with decorations by Peter Verburg. This is in Jenson type also but is much plainer than the preceding and therefore less Arts and Crafts. In green boards, it is on wove paper with a centered red and black title page. There are foliate initials but they are not Morrisian.

The Blue Sky Press was a more ambitious undertaking. It was founded in June 1899 with a magazine, the *Blue Sky*. The 1899 volume is in Jenson and Satanick. With Volume 2 (1900) the text is in Caslon with the Morrisian faces used for display. Thomas Wood Stevens, Alden Charles Noble, and their friends supplied the art and literature while Alfred G. Langworthy took care of the business and mechanical side of the print shop.[5] Their handmade, limited editions were offered in two grades of quality by direct circulars and

105

Plate 49. Laura Blackburn (Charles Granger Blanden), *Omar Resung*. Chicago: Blue Sky Press, 1901.

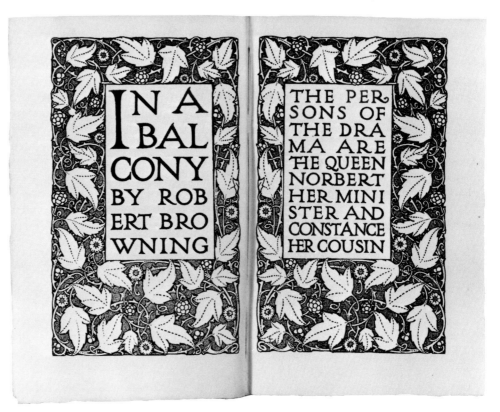

Plate 50. Robert Browning, *In a Balcony*. Chicago: Blue Sky Press, 1902.

a monthly bulletin, becoming well enough known to exhaust the editions.[6] Their books have lost none of their charm today; they remain delightful examples of the books of the turn of the century that combined Arts and Crafts touches with a simple format.

For example, they did several small pamphlets reprinted from the *Blue Sky*. Stevens' *The Unsought Shrine* (1900) was published in fifty copies with little decoration. The gray paper covers have the title and a "TWS" monogram in black, while there is an Art Nouveau printer's mark below the colophon. The title page is plain, but the initial for the text opening has a pale blue and pink floral background. Noble's *Lyrics to the Queen* (1902) is only slightly more elaborate, with hand lettering and a troubadour woodcut on the cover and red on the title page. A note by Stevens at the end says that no more numbers of the magazine would be issued because, among other reasons, Noble was leaving Chicago, and Stevens desired to print books instead of the magazine. (The press continued until 1906.)

In 1901 one of the most successful of the Blue Sky books was issued: Charles Granger Blanden's *Omar Resung*. The edition comprised two hundred copies on Van Gelder handmade laid paper and twenty-five on Japan vellum. The text is in Caslon, much used by Blue Sky, with shoulder note running titles in black letter and broad margins at the foot. The decorations for the hand-lettered title page and binding by Frank B. Rae, Jr., are floral Art Nouveau (Plate 49). The slipcased volume has the popular tall, thin shape. The same woodcut design, incorporating title and floral motifs, is printed in black on the wine-colored paper boards and in rust on the cream endpapers. Rae also did Art Nouveau designs for Edward Martin Moore's *Spoil of the North Wind* (1901), which are reminiscent of Dard Hunter's work at the Roycroft Press.

Blanden's *A Harvest of Reeds* (1902), is similar in format. The gray paper boards with a picture of a harvest moon rising over a field are printed in black and red, as is the typographic title page with a printer's device. The shoulder note running titles are in red. Still resembling this format but more elaborate is William Morris' *Sir Galahad* (1904), in an edition of five hundred on laid paper and twenty-five on Japan vellum, designed by Stevens. The dark green boards have a gold-stamped title within a Morris border. The dark green endpapers are printed in black with the title, author, and Morris border. The book, printed on one side of the paper only, is from plates entirely hand lettered under the direction of Stevens. Each page has a large running title in red at the head, while the title page is also black and red. The boldness of the art work gives a definite Arts and Craft flavor to the book.

A still more obvious follower in Kelmscott footsteps is Robert Browning's *In a Balcony* (1902) with designs by two budding typographic giants: Goudy and Dwiggins. The edition is somewhat smaller: four hundred on laid paper and fifteen on Japan vellum. The endpapers have, as usual, printed designs, and the opening page of the introduction has a grapevine headpiece with a large red initial. The speakers' names throughout are in red, the type Caslon, and the layout with Morrisian margins. The red and black double-spread title opening has vine borders and hand lettering (Plate 50).

The Blue Sky books are not at all slavishly imitative of Morris. Rather they are successful and charming reflections of the coalescence of current typographic trends: Art Nouveau, Aesthetic, and Arts and Crafts. The books of the Alderbrink Press, on the other hand were both more imitative and less successful.

Ralph Fletcher Seymour, despite his increasing orientation toward commercial work, had his beginnings in the private press tradition. He was an important figure in the Chicago book world of the turn of the century, although he never achieved national influence. His original inspiration was from the Arts and Crafts Movement, as he himself has testified:

> A new art doctrine had come out of old England. Its followers became known the world around as the Pre-Raphaelite Brotherhood. William Morris was its leader. They held that Art was of the people and belonged among the people. . . .[7]

Seymour was an Indiana boy who had gone to study at the Cincinnati Art Academy:

> I returned home well entangled in a strange net, the meshes of which were made out of Arthurian romances, plain-song, sixteenth century cathedrals, ancient tapestries and Pre-Raphaelite paintings, features of aesthetic expression which had come forth in places and times other than mine, but which once had seemingly lived and had power among long-gone men. Whether such things might be of use somewhere in this land of corn fields and cotton, factories and city towers I did not know, but I meant to try to introduce them and make them important in the every day life of Indiana. . . . By autumn, I was forced to admit that there was no place for art in Indiana.[8]

In later years he would make a pilgrimage to visit Emery Walker and Kelmscott House, but for the time being he moved to Chicago in the late nineties to become part of the world of printing. Like so many others, he not only idealized Morris ("Taken altogether better books had never been produced. . . ."[9]), but also found much to criticize in contemporary American typography, with its emphasis on mechanical cheapness.[10]

Before designing his own typeface, Seymour worked at hand lettering. In 1900 he published Keats' *The Eve of St. Agnes* in an edition printed by R. R. Donnelley and Sons from plates made from drawings designed and lettered by Seymour. It is a book which produces an ambivalent reaction today. One is aware that, charming in its clumsiness, it must have been in its own time one of those Arts and Crafts books that aroused much rancor among the purists. Undoubtedly incoherent and overdone, ugly in its drawings and tiny margins, it yet seems rather endearing, reminiscent of Blue Sky books, but much less successful. There were eight hundred copies on L. L. Brown's handmade wove, deckle-edge paper, twenty on Japan vellum, and four on real parchment. The double title page, in black and rust red, has borders, a floral background, and shield-like devices on both pages with the incongruous information that Seymour's address was the Fine Arts Building, Michigan Avenue, Chicago, Illinois, U.S.A. There is an elaborate initial at the text opening and a few others elsewhere. The running titles at the heads of the pages are in black and rust, with floral decoration. The pages are in fact quite solid, without much margin. There is a full-page fly title on the verso facing the poem opening with floral border and background. The rather clumsy lettering is old-style roman for the preface; the poem itself is in romanized Gothic with long batarde descenders. The illustrations, done in black only, are crude woodcuts. All in all, enthusiasm is more apparent than talent.

Seymour's first book in 1902 with his special Alderbrink typeface, inspired by the Kelmscott Golden and cut by Robert Weibking of Chicago, who also worked for Goudy, was a William Morris lecture, *The Art of the People*. Two hundred fifteen copies on L. L. Brown laid paper and ten on Japan vellum were printed by George F. McKiernan and

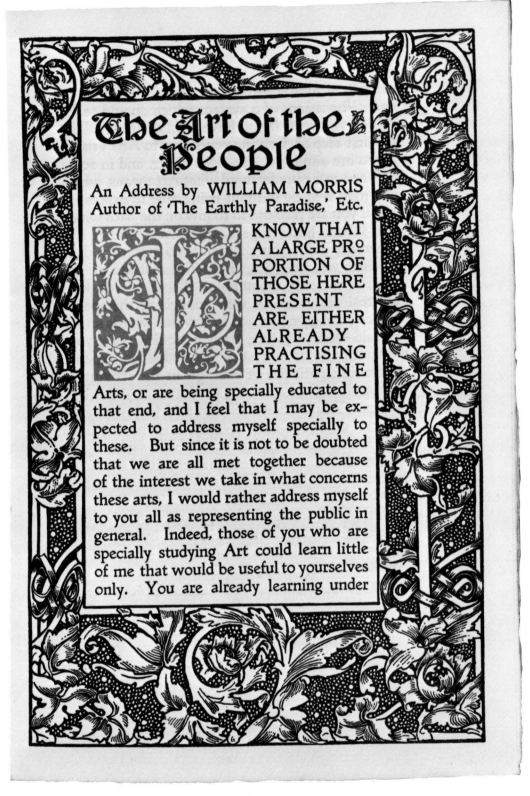

The Art of the People

An Address by WILLIAM MORRIS
Author of 'The Earthly Paradise,' Etc.

I KNOW THAT A LARGE PRŌ PORTION OF THOSE HERE PRESENT ARE EITHER ALREADY PRACTISING THE FINE Arts, or are being specially educated to that end, and I feel that I may be expected to address myself specially to these. But since it is not to be doubted that we are all met together because of the interest we take in what concerns these arts, I would rather address myself to you all as representing the public in general. Indeed, those of you who are specially studying Art could learn little of me that would be useful to yourselves only. You are already learning under

Plate 51. William Morris, *The Art of the People*. Chicago: R. F. Seymour, 1902.

Company of Chicago. The centered title page does not have a border but the opening page of the text does (Plate 51). There are red shoulder note running titles throughout, while the red and black initials are decorated with vines.

He also worked in collaboration with commercial publishers, as shown by two books in 1904 for Bobbs-Merrill of Indianapolis. A. W. Pollard's *Books in the House* was "Designed by and printed under the supervision of Ralph Fletcher Seymour at the press of R. R. Donnelley & Sons Co., in Chicago . . ." (colophon). There were five hundred copies on handmade paper and ten on Japan parchment, with, as usual, woodcut title page, headpieces, and initials. *The Book of Ruth: Taken from an Edition of the Bible Printed at Oxford in 1680* was done at the Prairie Press, Chicago, for Bobbs-Merrill, also in 1904. There were ten copies on Japan vellum and one thousand on wove paper. The black and red title page is hand lettered in Gothic, with a very Morrisian border. There are red floriated initials at the chapter openings with woodcut illustrations on the facing versos.

The Arts and Crafts approach with its heavy, blunt lines seems to have been the predominant element in Seymour's own Alderbrink Press style, as shown in Maurice Hewlett's *The Birth of Roland* (1911) with its Jensonian type and vine border. But Seymour could also produce Aesthetic work: Donald Robertson's *Beauty's Lady and Other Verses* (1910), despite its title in Gothic letters. There is an outline floral headpiece and initial at the text opening and decorative initials for some, but not all, poems. Each poem, in small, old-style type, is set high up on its own page. The running titles are in small caps at the heads of the pages, underlined with rules. The poem titles are flush left on versos, flush right on rectos.

Besides his book work, Seymour did much advertising and other commercial printing which led him toward machine printing. This seems to have bothered him, for he asked De Vinne about machine versus hand printing and received a letter in reply, dated June 18, 1907, in which De Vinne found machine printing natural and inevitable. De Vinne also sounded a death knell for the style of printing that had inspired Seymour: "Even in literary societies and clubs the love of black letter and medieval mannerisms is dying out. There seems to be increasing desire for simplicity and unpretentiousness. . . ."[11]

That Seymour never altogether forgot the Arts and Crafts style is witnessed by a book he wrote and published (copyright 1954): *Episodes in the Lives of Some Individuals Who Helped Shape the Growth of Our Midwest . . .*, which has a rather Morrisian title page. As for the primacy of the machine, here are wistful words from Seymour himself quoted in the Chicago *Sun Book Week* of May 4, 1947: "Once there was a veritable Alderbrink Press . . . but for some years my books have been mostly Linotype, 25 per cent rag paper, case bindings, and nothing much to write about."[12]

1. *The Turn of a Century 1885-1910* (Cambridge: Department of Printing and Graphic Arts, Houghton Library, Harvard University, 1970), p. 112.
2. Quoted in *The Turn of a Century 1885-1910*.
3. Martin Gardner and Russel B. Nye, *The Wizard of Oz and Who He Was* (East Lansing: Michigan State University Press, 1957), pp. 20-22.
4. Ibid., p. 30.
5. W. G. Bowdoin, "Private Presses—The Blue Sky Press," *New York Times Saturday Review*, August 1, 1903, p. 538.
6. Ibid.
7. Ralph Fletcher Seymour, *Some Went This Way* (Chicago: R. F. Seymour, 1945), p. 30.
8. Ibid., pp. 30-31.
9. Ibid., p. 104.
10. Ibid., p. 105.
11. Quoted in Seymour, *Some Went This Way*, p. 120.
12. Clipping in Alderbrink Press ephemera folder, Rare Book Room, The New York Public Library.

XIII

The Typographic Styles
of Will H. Bradley

ANOTHER participant in both the private press and commercial printing worlds, but a man of much greater stature than Seymour, was Will H. Bradley, the "American Beardsley." But Bradley was as much influenced by Morris as by Beardsley. His pictorial work shows the broad, flat, unmodeled areas of color and sometimes the perverse faces of Beardsley but often utilizes the medievalistic iconography and botanical borders of Arts and Crafts. Bradley was a leader of American Art Nouveau and one of the most influential figures in early twentieth-century American printing. Bevis Hillier has said that his artistic style, along with Tiffany glass, "remains the most admirable expression of Art Nouveau in America."[1]

Bradley was born in 1868, living for the first years of his life in Lynn, Massachusetts, where he worked as a delivery boy to save money for a small printing press. After his father's death in 1877, Bradley's mother took him to Ishpeming, Michigan. In 1880 he began work in a local printing office and by the age of fifteen had worked up to foreman. In 1885 he moved on to Chicago but returned to Ishpeming after an abortive unpaid job as a wood engraver at Rand McNally. A few months later he returned to Chicago, this time managing to become a designer at Knight & Leonard, a leading commercial printer. But he soon left them to free-lance as a designer. It was during this period that he met Goudy, and in the mid-nineties his work began to attract national and international attention. In 1895, after several years in Geneva, Illinois, he moved to Springfield, Massachusetts, to set up the Wayside Press. In 1898 Wayside was merged with the University Press. Bradley soon withdrew, however, and took up free-lance work again, building a house in Concord, Massachusetts, in 1903. After the turn of the century he did much promotional work for the American Type Founders Company and typographic arrangements for several magazines. In 1915 Hearst employed him as art director for both his publications and his motion pictures. After another free-lance interval Bradley returned to Hearst, retiring in 1930. He was also a writer of fiction, producing, for example, in 1902, *The Shards of the Silver Sword*, set in the days of King Arthur and couched in such archaic language

111

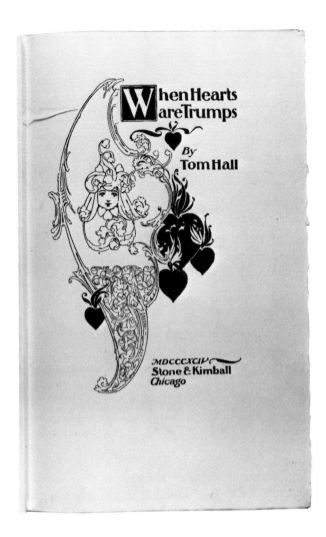

that it was rejected by publishers.[2] The archaic language of Morris' last romances comes to mind.

Beardsley's drawings for Dent's *Le Morte d'Arthur* in 1893 spread his pseudo-Kelmscott style far and wide, as did the article on him in the April 1893 *Studio*. A commentator a few years later wrote that the "Beardsley craze" generalized American interest in the Kelmscott Press, with many people never differentiating between the two.[3] Before this, Bradley was producing very conventional designs. Yet some of his motifs show the Pre-Raphaelite interest in the Middle Ages. For example, "A Few Words About the Chicago Herald" in the *Inland Printer* for January 1892 has many straightforward, old-fashioned line drawings by Bradley depicting in a realistic way the different departments of the newspaper.[4] But the title plate on coated paper preceding the article takes advantage of the newspaper's name to depict a medieval herald bestride a horse, with feudal trappings, within a shield device. The drawing is modeled and shaded, most unlike the later Bradley, as are the designs on a plate following this same article: "Original Page Ornaments Drawn Especially for the Inland Printer by Will H. Bradley." There are head and tailpieces with rococo scrolls and realistically portrayed girls and landscapes. On the other hand,

Plate 53. Richard Doddridge Blackmore, *Fringilla, or Tales in Verse*. Cleveland: Burrows Brothers, 1895.

by April 1894, after *Le Morte d'Arthur*'s publication, an advertisement for William Blades' *The Pentateuch of Printing* in the same *Inland Printer* is pure Beardsley: the swirling outlines, the lack of shading or perspective, the large areas of black opposed to large areas of white.[5]

In the interval before this switch in style, Bradley had also begun to do book work. In his autobiography he claimed that his first book assignment was for Stone & Kimball's *When Hearts Are Trumps* and the second for *The Columbian Ode*, but since he mistakenly believes the latter to have been published by Way & Williams, rather than by Way alone, he may be mistaken about the order of assignment as well.[6] In any case, Harriet Monroe's *Columbian Ode* was published in 1893, before the other book, and its Bradley designs show general Arts and Crafts influence in their strong black outlines.

Tom Hall's *When Hearts Are Trumps* (1894) was printed by John Wilson & Son in Cambridge for Stone & Kimball, in a small, Aesthetic format, on laid paper. The binding is mauve cloth, gold stamped with large hearts, the one on the front cover within a rococo frame. Playing card designs that include hearts and Gothic lettering are used on the half-title, dedication, copyright, two fly-title, and colophon pages. Each poem, in small, leaded Modernized Old Style, has its own page with the title in black letter and a blue rococo border. The hand-lettered title page has the title and author in asymmetrical position, but the uncluttered Aesthetic effect is lost because of the design of hearts and a child's face (Plate 52). Bradley also designed a striking binding for Stone & Kimball's *In Russet & Silver*, by Edmund Gosse (1894). And in 1898 he put Robert Herrick's *Love's Dilemmas* into neo-Colonial dress for Herbert S. Stone & Company.

More importantly, in 1895 Bradley did "Sundry Decorative Picturings" for R. D. Blackmore's *Fringilla*, published by The Burrows Brothers of Cleveland, and printed by John Wilson in six hundred copies on handmade laid paper. This is a brilliant book, more ambitious and successful than *When Hearts Are Trumps*, with strong Arts and Crafts details. The double-spread title page is within Kelmscott-style borders (Plate 53). There is a typical Bradley use of large black and white spaces in the frontispiece design which continues across the gutters from the verso to the recto. The opening pages of the sections have borders and matching initials, showing a strong *Morte d'Arthur* influence. The motifs are chosen with more appropriateness than Morris showed in his borders, e.g., papyrus for "Lita of the Nile." The type is Jenson, and red is used for accents throughout, although the printing shows some admixture with black. The closely knit texture of the book, one of the distinguishing characteristics of Bradley typography, goes directly to Kelmscott models, a fact recognized even when not approved: "He repeated a fault of Morris' by having the letters too near the decoration. . . ."[7] More recent critics have found that in this book "he has assimilated the influence of Whistler, Beardsley and Morris and turned it to his own use. . . ."[8] This is certainly true for Beardsley and Morris, but the influence of Whistler can be better seen in other books such as *When Hearts Are Trumps*.

Whistlerian Aestheticism can be seen even more clearly in the two versions of Richard Le Gallienne's paraphrase of the "Rubaiyat" printed in 1897 by Bradley at his Wayside Press. The one done in November for John Lane, The Bodley Head, is a large book, with Caslon type on laid paper, in white boards with spine label. Both "To the Reader" and the colophon are in italic, the latter small in size and placed high on the page. The red and black centered title page contains roman, italic, and Gothic capitals. An earlier version, printed in August and published by R. H. Russell, is a smaller, more decorated book. On laid paper, it is in green boards with a darker green arabesque design. The title page is in leaded caps, flush left and right, with a large red Persian floral design in the center (Plate 54). Other designs are used on various fly titles and opening pages throughout the book. The text is in small Caslon, and the colophon in small caps. It is a very effective little book, reminiscent of Mosher but more decorated.

Bradley's eclecticism was recognized by contemporary critics. For example, H. A. Adam wrote in the *Printer and Bookmaker:*

> . . . he has aptly been described as a sort of Beardsley and Grasset and Crane rolled into one, and there is apparently no limit to his ideas and his technical skill. The influence of the Japanese line and decorative work is prominent in some of his work. The influence of William Morris is also perceptible, and some of his drawings remind one of Albert Dürer in quality of line and sentiment.[9]

It might also be mentioned that Bradley's cover design for another 1897 book, Richard Le Gallienne's *The Quest of the Golden Girl*, published by John Lane, shows Laurence

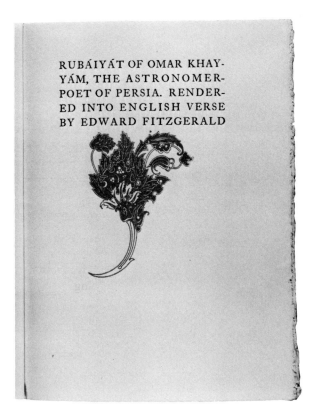

RUBÁIYÁT OF OMAR KHAY-
YÁM, THE ASTRONOMER-
POET OF PERSIA. RENDER-
ED INTO ENGLISH VERSE
BY EDWARD FITZGERALD

Plate 54. Omar Khayyam, *Rubaiyat:
Rendered into English Verse by
Edward Fitzgerald*. New York:
Published for Will Bradley by
R. H. Russell, 1897.

Plate 55. Stephen Crane,
War Is Kind. New York: Stokes, 1899.

" What says the sea, little shell ?
" What says the sea ?
" Long has our brother been silent to us,
" Kept his message for the ships,
" Puny ships, silly ships,"

15

Housman's influence in the massing of the girls' heads. And Edgar Breitenbach has found in Bradley's work the influence of Irish and Anglo-Saxon illumination.[10]

One of Bradley's most famous books is more original than any of those yet discussed. The first edition of Stephen Crane's *War Is Kind* was designed and printed by Bradley at the University Press in 1899 for Frederick A. Stokes. Here, Morris and Whistler have been left behind, Beardsley and Charles Ricketts are still evident in the illustrations, while the eccentricity of the format can be traced to the possible inspiration of Ricketts' version of Wilde's *Sphinx*. The gray boards, with a spine label, are decorated on the front with the well-known picture of a woman with a sword printed in black. The whiplash line is less evident than in earlier Bradley; the perpendicular line of Glasgow and Ricketts bindings has taken over. The cover of the tall, thin octavo is divided into elongated panels by rules, and the elongated line is repeated in the figure of the woman, her flowing hair, her sword, the trees behind her, the large vases beside her. The title page resembles the cover with its eccentric lettering and decorations of a lyre, birds, and extremely elongated candles, all within rules. There is an illustration facing the text opening, other full-page illustrations and occasional decorations throughout, but some pages are plain, even without running titles. Most of these decorations are very black, which suits the thick gray wove, deckle-edge paper on which the book is printed but does not suit the Caslon text type, which is also too thin for the heavy dark paper, especially since only a few lines of poetry are printed to a page (Plate 55). This is the only jarring note in what is otherwise a monument of American Art Nouveau bookmaking. It is a strong, harsh book, one not for all tastes. At the time one critic ended a review of Crane's writing with a single mention of Bradley: "The less said of Mr. Bradley's drawings the better."[11]

It was five years earlier that Bradley had begun to attract very favorable attention from commentators. There were two publishing enterprises that launched him into international acclaim. The *Inland Printer*, for which he had done his pre-*Morte d'Arthur* work, had given him more and more scope as his new style emerged. Volume XIII (April to September 1894), for example, has his decorative work throughout. More importantly, he was allowed to design monthly covers from April 1894 to March 1895, the first of which has Kelmscott-style white on black vines. According to Bradley, this was "the first occasion when a monthly magazine changes its cover design with each issue."[12] Since the *Inland Printer* had an international audience, one of these covers was selected as an illustration for a piece in the English *Studio* and established Bradley as a leading American designer.[13] Bradley's eccentricity was the *leitmotif* of the piece which, while admitting the strength of the Beardsley influence, claimed that Bradley was fundamentally original. It was one of the *Inland Printer* covers (December 1894) that launched Bradley into another sphere of influence. It has a "panel of lettering that four American and one German foundry immediately begin to cut as a type. Later the American Type Founders Company, paying for permission, names the face 'Bradley.'"[14] This face, a romanized Gothic, was obviously inspired by the Kelmscott Troy type, and in turn inspired other American faces, but Bradley's type remained the favorite and was widely used as a display font in turn-of-the-century printing. (The ATF Satanick, modeled on Morris' Troy, was produced in 1896.)

The other publishing concern that helped to make Bradley famous was Stone & Kimball. He was commissioned not only for the books mentioned above, but for posters. It was the famous "Twins," the first of the *Chap-Book* posters (May 1894) that brought

Plate 56. *Bradley: His Book*. Springfield: Wayside Press, 1896.

Bradley recognition and helped to start the American poster craze of 1894–1895. (Bradley did seven out of the first eight *Chap-Book* posters.) It was also in the 1894 *Chap-Book* that another early critical piece, by Herbert S. Stone himself, centered on Bradley and his "splendid sense of the value of black and white."[15]

Applause for Bradley returned to the pages of the *Inland Printer* when A. H. Mc-Quilken, the editor, wrote a piece on him for the February 1895 number.[16] The opening page is within a Kelmscott-style border by Bradley, with a matching initial. The text claimed that the *Studio's* approval of him brought high acclaim in America. McQuilken found Stone's *Chap-Book* article appreciative but patronizing.

It was the *Chap-Book* that inspired the major achievement of the Wayside Press—the artistic and literary magazine called *Bradley: His Book*, which ran for seven numbers in 1896–1897 before Bradley's financial and emotional collapse that led to and followed his abortive association with the University Press. The four-page prospectus (April 1896) is extremely Morrisian in appearance. It is printed in very solidly set black and red Jenson, the front and back with borders. The advertisement emphasized the physical rather than literary side of the magazine:

> Its literature is to be the work of many clever writers, its Art the Art of Books, etcetera, especially that which finds expression in decoration. Its printing will be pleasing, and, that the illustrations may appear upon the paper for which they were designed, some three or four varieties will be used, each page appearing in at least two colors, and from that up to six. A new cover will be designed by Mr. Bradley for each number, these also to be printed in colors, each on a different style of paper. In the hope that the advertisements may be made quite interesting, they will not be taken from more than one commercial house in the same line of business. Each will be designed with much care, appearing in this magazine before publication elsewhere.[17]

Bradley also announced that his magazine would have a poster for each number. The first edition of *Bradley: His Book* would appear in ten thousand copies, but there would be as well a fine, limited edition of fifty copies on Japanese paper, signed by Bradley, and priced at twenty dollars.[18]

The first number (May 1896) is printed in many colors, typical of Bradley advertising typography, and in a variety of typefaces, but Jenson is used for the unpaged text. Harriet Monroe's "The Night-Blooming Cereus: A Poem" is given a Morrisian layout: double-page spread in Jenson caps solidly set, with the title in red, two pictures, all within borders. An American Type Founders Company advertisement in this issue is an indication that the Morris Revival was at its height:

> Invitation to Artists. The American Type Founders Company, in entire sympathy with the development of classic typography, is prepared to co-operate with those who have made a serious study of mediaeval models, and will adapt them to modern requirements.[19]

The next number (June 1896) has a Caslon text, but Jenson is still used for advertisements. There are two of these in particular that are very Morrisian, with borders and

BRADLEY
HIS BOOK
FEBRUARY, 1897. VOL. II. No. 4

Narcissus. Jean Wright.

THE HAPPY POET PAGANS SUNG AND SAID ₰
ONCE LIVED A BOY WHOSE GRACIOUS BEAU-
TY MADE ₰ ₰ ₰ THIS DARK WORLD RADIANT
FOR A LITTLE SPACE; ₰ ₰ ₰ ₰ AND ALL WHO
LOOKED UPON HIS PERFECT FACE ₰ ₰ THEY
NEEDS MUST LOVE HIM FOR ITS LOVELINESS.

THUS MANY A NYMPH, WHOSE PASSIONATE
WARM HEART ₰ KNOWING NOT HOW TO CURB
ITS TENDERNESS ₰ BROKE WITH THE WEIGHT
OF UNREQUITED LOVE, ₰ ₰ ₰ SIGHED OUT A
PRAYER FOR PITY TO GREAT JOVE, ₰ ₰ THAT
HIS COLD YOUTH BE PIERCED BY EROS' DART.

₰ ₰ VAIN HOPE. FOR AS IT CHANCED UPON A
TIME, ₰ DEEP IN A FOREST POOL, AS CRYSTAL
CLEAR, ₰ ₰ HIMSELF HE SAW, AND HELD NO
OTHER DEAR ₰ THEREAFTER. STERN JUSTICE
WAVERING, ₰ METED A TENDER JUDGEMENT
FOR HIS CRIME; ₰ ₰ ₰ ₰ ₰ EARTH COULD ILL
SPARE SO BEAUTIFUL A THING. ₰ A DELICATE
PURE FLOWER, HE FOR ALL TIME ₰ ₰ ₰ WILL
STAR THE WOODLAND IN THE EARLY SPRING.

Plate 57. *Bradley: His Book.* Springfield: Wayside Press, 1897.

Gothic letters: Riverside Paper Company and Ault and Wiborg Inks. One of the literary items is Morris' "Gossip About an Old House on the Upper Thames," referred to by Bradley in a note which also says: "This is gradually becoming an age of 'Morris' printing. . . ."[20]

Subsequent issues continue the pattern: Caslon for text, Jenson for display. The July 1896 number (Plate 56) quoted the *New York Journal:* "[*Bradley: His Book*] gives promise of showing that America has in this young man one who can go further even than the famous Kelmscott Press."[21] Volume 2 changes to a larger format but keeps the type pattern, except for the December 1896 issue, set in Satanick, with red-bordered Kelmscott-style illustrations for "The Secret History of the Rescue of the Duchess de Dragonflies" by Tudor Jenks.

The January 1897 number, the last one to be published (only part of the February number was finished [Plate 57]), is an example of Bradley's Colonial style. The title is a combination of Caslon capitals, lower case, and italic. The running heads are in italic and there are catchwords. Bradley has described how this Colonial style came about when he visited the Boston Public Library in 1895 and was overwhelmed by the early American books and their use of Caslon.[22] Bradley displayed his Colonial printing at the first exhibition of the Boston Arts and Crafts Society. The reviewers approved and, within a year, the type foundries found their orders for Caslon increased.

Examples of this style from the Wayside Press include Washington Irving's *Rip Van*

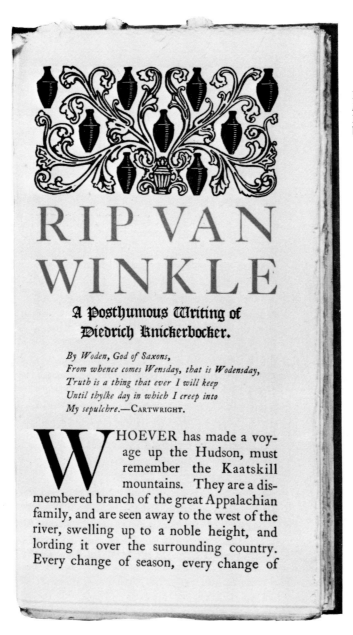

Plate 58. Washington Irving, *Rip Van Winkle.* New York: Published for the University Press by Harper, 1897.

Winkle (Plate 58) and *The Legend of Sleepy Hollow* (Plate 59). They are on thick wove paper in brown paper boards with spine labels. Heavy dark woodcuts in chap-book style by Bradley are on the front covers and used as head and frontispieces. The Caslon texts have large running heads in caps and lower case. Red is used on the title pages and text openings. These were among the Wayside assets taken over and retained by the University Press after Bradley's departure. A 1903 advertisement for the Wayside Publications of the Wayside Department of the University Press at Cambridge stated: "Each issue is intended to be a perfect expression of the Printer's Art, the decorations, the types, the paper, and the binding being chosen with a specific view of adaptability to the title itself."[23]

Another title offered by the University Press in this advertisement shows another side of Bradley's style in the late nineties: *The Book of Ruth and the Book of Esther* (Plate 60),

120

first printed by him in 1897 and published by R. H. Russell. It too is on handmade paper, in gray paper boards with a printed spine label. There are very extreme Morrisian margins, some headings in red, black woodcut initials, and much use of black fleurons. The type is Satanick. Bradley offered it at seventy-five cents in the last number of *Bradley: His Book*, with fifty copies signed and numbered, on Japan vellum, at $2.50. The accompanying blurb makes pathetic reading in view of the approaching demise of the Press:

> These are the first of a series of choice little volumes to be known as the Little Classics of the Bible. The type used is the same as that used by William Morris at the Kelmscott Press and is called "Troy." An effort has been made to make these little books pleasing examples of good bookmaking, and their reception by the public will do much to influence the future publications of this house.[24]

During the first years of the new century, when Bradley was finding himself again, he issued several small volumes from the Sign of the Vine at Concord, Massachusetts, printed for him by Heintzemann of Boston. They are in plain paper boards with printed labels on the front. *The Leather Bottel* (Plate 61) is in chap-book format with heavy black woodcuts and a large red title. Its tiny pages in transitional type have italic running heads

Plate 59. Washington Irving, *The Legend of Sleepy Hollow.*
New York: Published for the University Press by Harper, 1897.

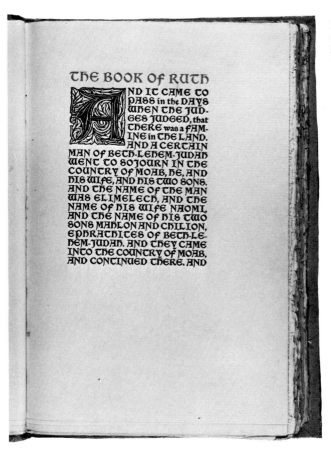

Plate 60. *The Book of Ruth and the Book of Esther*. New York: Published for Will Bradley by R. H. Russell, 1897.

Plate 61. *The Leather Bottel*. Concord: The Sign of the Vine, 1903.

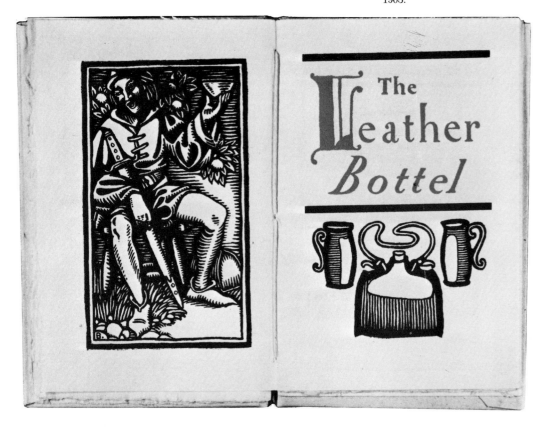

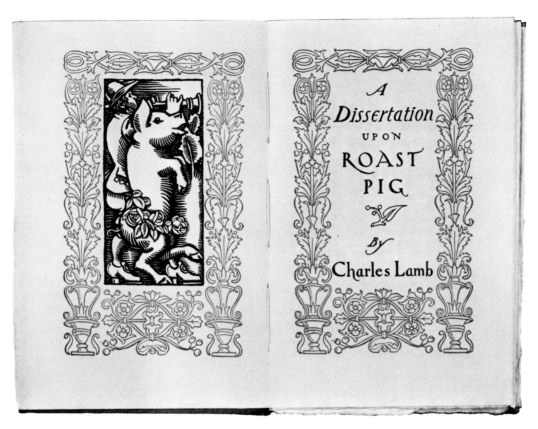

Plate 62. Charles Lamb, *A Dissertation upon Roast Pig.* Concord: The Sign of the Vine, n.d.

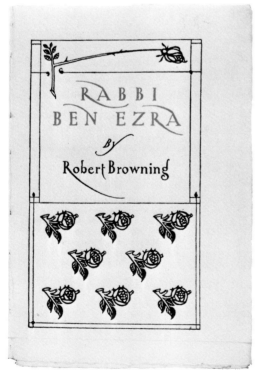

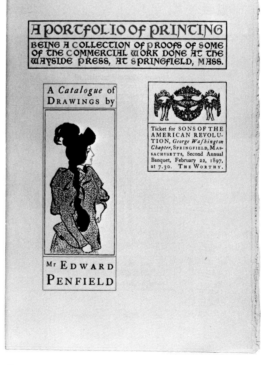

Plate 63. Robert Browning, *Rabbi Ben Ezra.*
Concord: The Sign of the Vine, n.d.

Plate 64. Will H. Bradley, *A Portfolio of Printing.*
Springfield: Wayside Press, 1897.

with type ornaments and red factotum initials. Lamb's *Dissertation upon a Roast Pig* is in modern-style type with Renaissance outline decorations in red and black, including borders for the hand-lettered title page and the heavy black woodcut frontispiece (Plate 62). There are running heads with thick and thin rules. The book is thus a hybrid, combining styles, but Bradley's artistic taste makes it hang together. Browning's *Rabbi Ben Ezra* is also a hybrid. It has modern type with large red initials and running heads with type ornaments. The hand-lettered title page is, however, Art Nouveau in feeling, with a repeated woodcut rose motif (Plate 63). It does not hold together as well as the Lamb.

It was in this period that the last evolution of Bradley's style was taking place. He has been much talked about as an artist but not analyzed for typographic development. After the early period of traditional realism, he adopted around 1893 the Beardsley/Kelmscott style of *Le Morte d'Arthur* and turned it eventually, after incorporating influences from other artists, into his own brand of Art Nouveau that culminated in the gloomy masterpiece *War Is Kind*.

The third period overlapped with the second, beginning, as Bradley has described, with his studies in 1895 at the Boston Public Library and culminating in neo-Colonialism. The fourth period also overlaps. Bradley was evolving his own brand of advertising typography while at Wayside, of which acute critics were not unaware. Joseph M. Bowles wrote in the Spring 1896 number of *Modern Art* praising his commercial work with its extra-

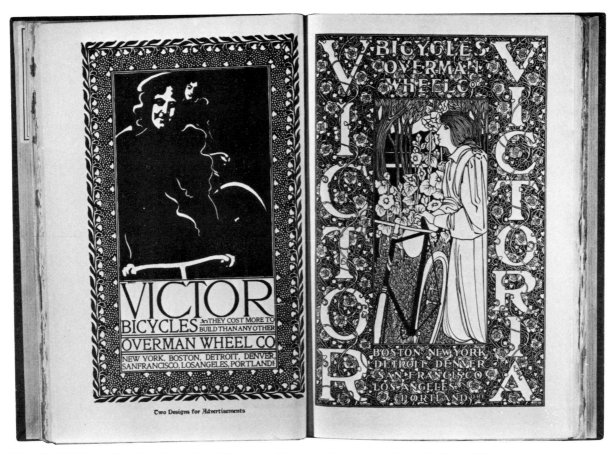

Plate 65. Will H. Bradley, *Some Examples of Printing and Drawing*. Cambridge: University Press, 1898.

ordinary use of color.[25] This early advertising style had strong Kelmscott roots, as seen in *Bradley: His Book* and in his work for Whiting's Ledger Papers. He has in fact been given credit for adapting Morris' style to commercial printing.[26]

The climax of this first phase of his commercial style can be seen in booklets Bradley prepared as advertisements: in 1897 *A Portfolio of Printing: Being a Collection of Proofs of Some of the Commercial Work Done at the Wayside Press, Springfield, Mass.* (Plate 64) and in 1898 *Some Examples of Printing and Drawing: The Work of Will Bradley, Issued in This Wise as an Advertisement by the University Press, at Cambridge, U.S.A.* (Plate 65). There are still Morrisian examples but a more independent style is evident. And when Bradley designed the twelve numbers of the *American Chap-Book* (September 1904 to August 1905) for the American Type Founders Company, it was this second commercial style that emerged as the fifth period in his typography to influence another generation of American printers. Its roots go back to Arts and Crafts in the heavy, blunt lines, rounded enough to give a slightly curvilinear impression even when arranged, as they normally are, in rectilinear fashion (Plate 66). The other great debt to Arts and Crafts is the close spacing. Decorative and typographic elements are set close to each other when

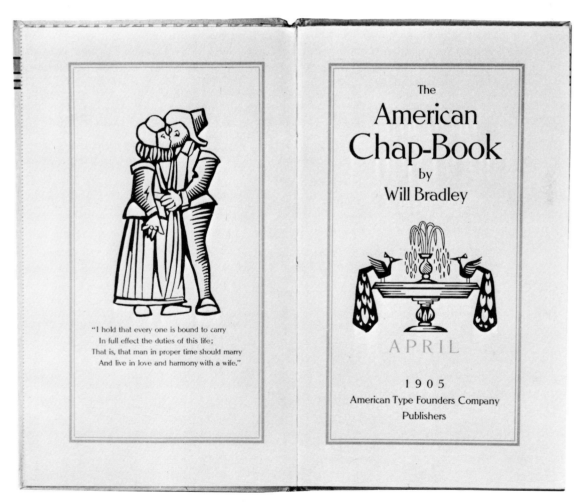

Plate 66. *American Chap-Book.* Jersey City: American Type Founders Company, 1905.

they are not actually superimposed, leaving little unfilled space on the page. This stress on decoration is accompanied by an emphasis on color, often not primary but muted, subtle tones. Tinted paper is often used, thus providing a background shade. The use of repeated motifs is yet another characteristic but they are disposed in a uniform, not random, fashion. Floral and other phyllomorphic motifs constitute the largest category. The headings are often in very large type, letter spaced.

Bradley's brilliant *American Chap-Book* served not only to promote the wares of ATF; it was actually intended as a teaching device for American printers and so served. Edmund G. Gress, for example, followed in Bradley's footsteps and helped to spread the style. His 1908 book (which had earlier appeared in the *American Printer*), *Type Designs in Color*, does not give Bradley credit but the influence is clearly visible.[27] In some of the examples of commercial design presented, Kelmscott initials are used, as in the business card for Nesmith & Son/Arts and Crafts/Mission Furniture Makers.

Bradley's extensive work in remodeling magazines gave him an unparalleled influence in that field as well. His book work was minor after the turn of the century but, since advertising and periodicals are the major elements in American graphic communication, it could be said that he did more than any one man to create the beginnings of American twentieth-century style. An *American Printer* editorial comment in 1936 made this very statement.[28] This American style would not have been the same if the school of art most quintessentially expressed by the Kelmscott Press had not existed, for Bradley's first work with vitality stemmed from the combined Morris/Beardsley influence. He went on to add neo-Colonialism to the Arts and Crafts stream, then his own brand of commercial typography that grew out of Arts and Crafts.

1. Bevis Hillier, *Posters* (New York: Stein and Day, 1969), p. 158.
2. Huntington Library, *Will Bradley: His Work—An Exhibition* (San Marino: Huntington Library, 1951), p. 17.
3. Frederic T. Singleton, "Will Bradley: Printer," *Printer and Bookmaker*, XXVI (June 1898): 184.
4. "A Few Words about the Chicago Herald," *Inland Printer*, IX (January 1892): 329-344.
5. Advertisement in *Inland Printer*, XIII (April 1894): 97.
6. Will H. Bradley, *Will Bradley: His Chap-Book* (Mount Vernon: Peter Pauper Press, 1955), p. 35.
7. William Dana Orcutt, *The Kingdom of Books* (Boston: Little, Brown, 1927), p. 151.
8. *The Turn of a Century 1885-1910* (Cambridge: Department of Printing and Graphic Arts, The Houghton Library, Harvard University, 1970), p. 108.
9. H. A. Adam, "Bradley's Influence on Printing," *Printer and Bookmaker*, XXIV (June 1897): 142-143.
10. Edgar Breitenbach, "A Brief History," in *The American Poster* (New York: October House, 1968), p. 17.
11. John Curtis Underwood, "The Bookman's Table," *Bookman*, IX (July 1899): 467.
12. Bradley, *Will Bradley: His Chap-Book*, p. 36.
13. Charles Hiatt, "On Some Recent Designs by Will H. Bradley, of Chicago," *Studio*, IV (1894): 166-168.
14. Bradley, *Will Bradley: His Chap-Book*, p. 37.
15. Herbert S. Stone, "Mr. Bradley's Drawings," *Chap-Book*, II (December 1, 1894): 62.
16. A. H. McQuilken, "Will Bradley and His Work," *Inland Printer*, XIV (February 1895): 430-433.
17. *Bradley: His Book—Prospectus* (Springfield: Wayside Press, 1896), unpaged.
18. Ibid.
19. [Advertisement], *Bradley: His Book*, I (May 1896), unpaged.
20. [Will H. Bradley] [Note] *Bradley: His Book*, I (June 1896): 61.
21. Quoted in *Bradley: His Book*, I (July 1896): 133.
22. Bradley, *Will Bradley: His Chap-Book*, pp. 41-43.
23. [Advertisement], *Printing Art*, I (April 1903): xiii.
24. [Advertisement], *Bradley: His Book*, III (January 1897): unpaged.
25. [Joseph M. Bowles] "Echoes," *Modern Art*, IV (Spring 1896): unpaged.
26. Norma Levarie, *The Art and History of Books* (New York: Heinemann, 1968), p. 280.
27. Edmund G. Gress, *Type Designs in Color* (New York: Oswald Publishing Company, 1908).
28. Editorial comment to Frederic T. Singleton, "Will Bradley: Turn of the Century Renovator of American Typography and Decorative Art," *American Printer*, CIII (August 1936): 13.

XIV

Frederic W. Goudy
& His Proteges

O F COMPARABLE stature is the final major typographic figure to have made his start
in the Chicago of the nineties—Frederic William Goudy. Less of an innovative and
creative artist than Bradley, he was nevertheless a man of great industry and persistence
who designed more typefaces than any other American, who ran a long-lived private press
(1903–1947), and whose considerable personal charm influenced more than one generation
of American printers. He, too, found in William Morris his principal inspiration. The
typography critic, Paul Johnston, has said that it was Goudy's role to be the intermediary
between Morris and the average printer.[1]

Goudy was born in Bloomington, Illinois, in 1865. In 1884 the family moved to South
Dakota where Goudy worked in his father's real estate office. He moved on to Minneapolis,
Springfield, and finally Chicago in 1890, where he worked as a bookkeeper. In 1891 he
also issued a periodical, *Modern Advertising*, with a schoolteacher friend, C. Lauron
Hooper. It was at this time that he met Will Bradley, got him to design a cover, and, as
Bradley relates, bought some printing equipment from him.[2] In 1894 Goudy and Hooper
entered on another venture, the Booklet Press, for printing advertising booklets. In the
same year the ubiquitous Irving Way introduced him to Herbert S. Stone who gave him
the commission of setting in type the *Chap-Book*, already begun from Cambridge but
to be continued from Chicago. For this job Goudy changed the name of his press to
Camelot, in line with the romantic spirit of America's leading "bibelot." It was a time
of great mental expansion for Goudy—he acquired "a new conception of art and literature
[and of typography on] a higher plane than mere commercialism."[3] Goudy also began to
frequent bookstores, receiving thereby an education:

> At this time I really began to be interested in books as books, in terms of their physical
> appearance. Fortunately, through regular visits to the large bookstore of A. C. McClurg
> & Co., I became acquainted with George Millard, who was in charge of the rare book
> department, and his assistant, Mr. Chandler. Millard noticed my interest in certain

productions of the then new private presses . . . and he went out of his way to show me the new books from these presses as they came in.[4]

Goudy was allowed to handle a Kelmscott *Chaucer* in pigskin.

The Camelot Press was responsible for the *Chap-Book* only in late 1894 and early 1895. Not long thereafter Goudy himself left it and went back to bookkeeping because of disagreement with a friend of Hooper's who had entered the establishment. The name Camelot was to appear again in 1896, however, in Goudy's first typeface, designed at the kitchen table in less than an hour and sent to the Dickinson Type Foundry in Boston, producer of Jenson. A check for ten dollars came back for this series of almost monoline capitals, enough to encourage Goudy to continue designing.

After getting married in 1897 to Bertha Sprinks, he moved to Detroit as a cashier but returned to Chicago in 1899 as a free-lance designer. In the next few years he did work for many of the leaders in the current typographic milieu—articles and a cover for *Inland Printer*, the binding of George Ade's *Fables in Slang* (1900) for Herbert S. Stone & Company, a cover for Stone's *House Beautiful*. For Thomas Bird Mosher of Maine, he did cover designs for the Vest Pocket and Old World series. He worked on a hand-lettered version of *Sonnets from the Portuguese* (1900) for Ralph Fletcher Seymour. The same year, W. W. Denslow also commissioned a hand-lettered *Mother Goose*, the letter forms of which were changed into Hearst type by the Inland Type Foundry. (Denslow also introduced Goudy to Elbert Hubbard for whom he did several bookplates, orders for which were solicited through the *Philistine*.[5]) In 1900 Goudy was employed as instructor at the Frank Holme School of Illustration where he met W. A. Dwiggins. Other typefaces were produced for commercial firms that wanted them for advertising purposes, namely Pabst for Schlesinger & Mayer in 1902 and Powell for Mandel Brothers in 1903.

In 1903 Kuppenheimer & Company asked Goudy to design a face, which he based on Morris' Golden. Goudy has recorded his earlier acquaintance with Golden, in the ATF Jenson version:

> For one of our jobs [at the Camelot Press] I ordered from Boston the then new "Jenson" type which had been copied by the Dickinson Type Foundry. . . . The type was 14 pt. size and I received a postal card acknowledgement of the order from the foundry with the added information that mine was the *first* order for it from Chicago.
>   . . . In the '90s, even now in some degree, the discipline of a living tradition was not generally part and parcel of the American printers; it remained for Morris to revive and apply this tradition . . . the influence of his motives in craft as represented by his printing is as strong today in my mind as then.[6]

As for the direct influence on his own type, he said in the announcement for his press that it evolved from several modern faces: Morris' Golden, Rogers' Montaigne, Goodhue's Merrymount, and Walker's Doves.[7] (It is interesting that he did not mention Ricketts' Vale type for, in later years, he was to give it primary credit: ". . . it was this type in the *Poems of Sir John Suckling* that really inspired my study of private types."[8]) One of Goudy's last words on the Golden type showed, however, that he had come to criticize it for its clumsy heaviness and excessive blackness.[9]

After Kuppenheimer & Company reneged on their commitment to Goudy's type based on Golden, it was returned to Goudy who then formed another press, this time with Will Ransom, one of his students. Robert Wiebking, who had just cut Ralph Fletcher Seymour's type, did the cutting of this new Village face, as it was called, and the Village Press was set up at the Goudy home in Park Ridge, Illinois. All the processes were to be done by hand; as Peter Beilenson has said: ". . . the press exactly fitted the picture which the arts-and-crafts movement of the Nineties had established as the workman's ideal."[10]

Ransom left the Press after the first book was finished and Mrs. Goudy took over his duties. The next year (1904) the Goudys moved the press east to Hingham, Massachusetts, after reading an article on "Village Handicrafts" in the Boston Society of Arts and Crafts magazine *Handicraft* and concluding that they would find there a congenial atmosphere.[11] It was, indeed, congenial but also unremunerative, and in 1906 they moved to the commercial center of New York. That same year Goudy took part in the formation of the Guild of Book Workers, another of the numerous Arts and Crafts clubs being set up. He was one of the signers of the circulars sent out to drum up interest in the foundation.[12] The first members included, besides both of the Goudys, Dwiggins and Updike. During the Guild's first exhibition (April 25–29, 1907) the Village Press was set up on the spot to demonstrate both printing and casing.

In January 1908 the Village Press was totally destroyed by fire. The Village type matrices, however, had been in a safe and were bought by F. F. Sherman.[13] Goudy kept on with his designing work and in 1909 was able to make his first trip abroad. In London he met Emery Walker, Morris' old associate; Charles T. Jacobi of the Chiswick Press; and A. W. Pollard, Keeper of Books at the British Museum, who let him handle the original Kelmscott books. One of Goudy's biographers reported that Walker showed him Kelmscott and other Morris items from his collection and added: "On their first meeting Walker said, 'Morris would have liked knowing you,' a remark that was to Goudy ample recognition of his hard work."[14] Goudy himself wrote that Walker "gave me a large photogravure portrait of Morris made by him in his own shop, which he inscribed for me and which I cherish today in my own studio."[15]

After more years in New York City, the Goudys settled in 1913 in Forest Hills Garden, Long Island, where they remained until 1923 when they moved to an old house and mill which they called Deepdene at Marlborough-on-Hudson. There Goudy began to engrave his own matrices and there the Village Press remained despite another disastrous fire in 1939. Bertha Goudy died in 1935, Fred Goudy in 1947. Before his death he had designed nearly 125 typefaces, from which task, as early as 1911, he had derived the chief part of his livelihood.

Although Goudy returned to Jensonian-style type in later faces (e.g., Italian Old Style for the Lanston Monotype Company in 1924, the year Goudy bought one of Morris' Albion presses from James Guthrie of the Pear Tree Press), it is not in his type designing that extended Morris influence can be seen. Rather, one must go back to some of his early decorative designs, his own early printing, and his writings.

His early designs for initials, published in the *Inland Printer* for 1896, show no particular Morris influence.[16] They are, indeed, quite clumsy, although the magazine offered some for sale in August 1896.[17] Editorial comment was favorable; it does not appear that Goudy met opposition at the start.

129

HERE ENDS
THE BLESSED DAMOZEL· BY
DANTE GABRIEL ROSSETTI·
REPRINTED FROM THE GERM
FOR FEBRUARY M·DCCC·L
PRINTED & BOUND BY FRED
W· AND BERTHA M· GOUDY
AT THE VILLAGE PRESS· 110
COPIES PRINTED 98 FOR SALE

The Village Press ·

Park Ridge, Illinois, December, 1903

Plate 67. Dante Gabriel Rossetti, *The Blessed Damozel.*
Park Ridge: Village Press, 1903.

The letter designs shown are simple and harmonious, and not without some strength and character. . . . Mr. Goudy follows the best traditions of the ancient schools in his study of lettering and ornament. We shall watch his progress with interest.[18]

The cover design for a Mosher book, Swinburne's *Laus Veneris* (1900), however, is in an outline vine style reminiscent of Kelmscott. His 1902 work in the Arts and Crafts style with Dwiggins on Browning's *In a Balcony* for the Blue Sky Press has already been mentioned. His work around 1908–1910 for the Hillside Press of Englewood, New Jersey, is in a similar vein. Goudy initials and headpieces were also used in the September 1908 *Your Printer* put out by the Kimball Press of Evanston, Illinois.

The style that he exhibited in the Hillside books and in *Your Printer* is similar to the work in his own Village Press books and is in the Kelmscott line. The decorations consist of natural forms, usually tangled leafy white vines, sometimes with flowers, seedpods, etc., against a slightly irregular black background, little of which shows but which follows the shape of the white forms. A few blunt black lines are used for internal modeling of the white forms so that the effect is slightly three-dimensional. All the forms are curvilinear and blunt.

The format of the early Village Press books also shows a general similarity that places them squarely in the private press movement of the turn of the century. The books are on handmade paper in limited editions, with board bindings and impeccable presswork. They are in Village type, based on Golden, fairly solidly set, with wide margins. (The 1905 *Lyf of Seynt Kenelme* in ATF Flemish is the first one not in Village.[19]) Some of the titles have decorations that place them even more firmly within Arts and Crafts.

The first book issued by Goudy and Ransom in 1903 in 231 copies was *Printing an Essay* by William Morris and Emery Walker, "intended as a tribute and acknowledgment of obligation to William Morris. . . ."[20] The beige cloth binding (by Bertha Goudy) has the title in red caps in the upper left. Large red caps are also used for the title at the text opening, along with a vine-decorated red initial. An outline leaf is used to fill in the solid setting, but the effect is not at all spotty, as in many Morris-inspired pages. The same floral ornament used on the centered title page in red is used again as a tailpiece in black. The colophon is followed by a Morrisian printer's device. Goudy was displeased when

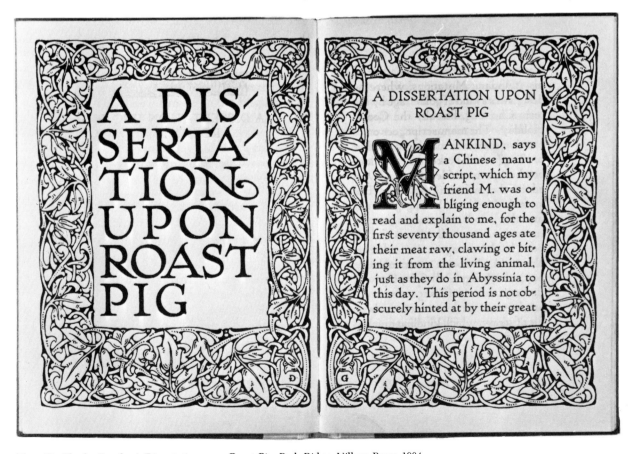

Plate 68. Charles Lamb, *A Dissertation upon Roast Pig*. Park Ridge: Village Press, 1904.

Printing was rejected by the Arts and Crafts Exhibit at the Art Institute of Chicago but flattered when he won a medal at the Louisiana Purchase Exposition in St. Louis, 1904.[21]

The Grolier Club's copy of Rossetti's *The Blessed Damozel* (1903) is on Japan vellum in a Goudy binding that is pure Arts and Crafts: vellum paper over boards with green silk ties (other copies are limp, without ties). There are two photographic illustrations but otherwise the book adheres to Arts and Crafts format, including the colophon page (Plate 67). The title page is mostly flush left and right caps, with a vine ornament. The text opening has a red initial with an irregularly shaped vine ornamentation.

Vine decoration is used heavily in headbands, initials, and tailpieces for Charles Lamb's *A Dissertation upon Roast Pig* (1904) in 215 copies. Both the title page and text openings are presented in double-page spreads within borders, "strongly reminiscent of William Morris"[22] (Plate 68).

The last title to be printed at Park Ridge, except for fugitive pieces, was *The Blind Princess and The Dawn: Two Poems* (1904). According to the colophon, a single copy was made for Mr. James Weber Linn, but an unbound proof copy exists at the New York Public Library. The title and opening text pages have Goudy vine headbands, while space has been left for hand-illumined initials at the beginning of each poem.

W. A. Dwiggins, whom Goudy had known in Chicago, joined the Goudys in Hingham after their move east and decorated two books for them. A 1904 edition of Browning's *Rabbi Ben Ezra* (Plate 69) printed in 173 copies in gray boards has a title page with a square vine decoration in red. On the facing verso there is a black woodcut frontispiece. John M. Neale's *Good King Wenceslas* (1904), with an introduction by Morris and illustrations by Arthur J. Gaskin, issued in 185 copies in gray boards with spine labels, is more Morrisian. The text is in caps, with decorated initials, all in black (Plate 70). The title page and the facing frontispiece are within borders of outline stylized vines.

The Goudys gave Morris' *The Hollow Land* (1905) an appropriately Morrisian dress. The title page and woodcut frontispiece by W. J. Enright are within large, heavy vine borders. Leaves are used as paragraph marks in the text, and the page numbers are in shoulder note position. The text opening has the title again in Gothic with a large black initial on a white and red foliate background. Two hundred twenty copies were printed at Hingham but only eighty-five or so survived the New York fire.

In New York Goudy worked as a designer for trade publishers as well as for private presses like the Hillside. An example of a colorful Morrisian book done for a publisher is Emerson's *Prudence* (1906) printed by Kenneth Ives Inc. for Morgan Shepard Company of New York and San Francisco. It is in green boards with white spine and a red and black label on the front. The double-spread title opening is within Goudy's peapod vine borders, the verso tinted green with an Emerson quotation and red floriate initial. The title on the recto is in red caps with a center decoration. There is a red vine initial at the text opening and red shoulder notes in upper and lower case.

The Village Press itself also designed and printed books for trade publishers. Sir Noel Paton's *A Christmas Carol* (1907) is one of three books done for Ivan Somerville & Company in that year. It is on Old Stratford wove paper in Bookman type. The tan boards have a square green vine design and a red title. There is a double-spread opening within green borders with the title and author on the verso and the text opening on the recto with a decorated initial.

In 1907 Goudy also finished *The Sermon in the Mount*, on which he had been working for some time. All copies were destroyed in the 1908 fire and only a fragment remains to

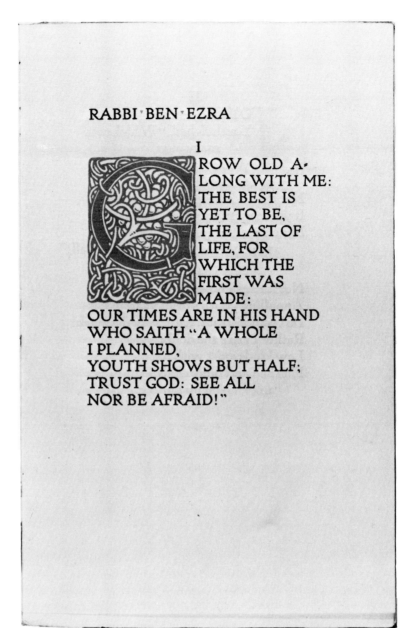

RABBI·BEN·EZRA

I
GROW OLD A‑
LONG WITH ME:
THE BEST IS
YET TO BE,
THE LAST OF
LIFE, FOR
WHICH THE
FIRST WAS
MADE:
OUR TIMES ARE IN HIS HAND
WHO SAITH "A WHOLE
I PLANNED,
YOUTH SHOWS BUT HALF;
TRUST GOD: SEE ALL
NOR BE AFRAID!"

Plate 69. Robert Browning, *Rabbi Ben Ezra: A Dramatic Monologue.*
Hingham: Village Press, 1904.

show that this would have been the most complete Kelmscott/Goudy performance of all.
The page reproduced in *Some Examples of the Work of American Designers* reveals
a magnificent black and white border with accompanying red initial and text in Village
type[23] (Plate 71). Will Ransom said that rumors spread that this would have been the most
beautiful of all the Village Press books.[24]

For H. G. Wells' *The Door in the Wall and Other Stories,* printed by Norman T. A.
Munder & Company of Baltimore for Mitchell Kennerley of New York and London
in 1911, Goudy designed not only the decorations but also a new typeface, called Kennerley

IN HIS MASTER'S STEPS
HE TROD,
WHERE THE SNOW LAY
DINTED;
HEAT WAS IN THE VERY SOD
WHICH THE SAINT
HAD PRINTED.
THEREFORE, CHRISTIAN
MEN, BE SURE
WEALTH OR RANK
POSSESSING,
YE WHO NOW WILL BLESS
THE POOR,
SHALL YOURSELVES
FIND BLESSING.

19

Plate 70. John M. Neale, *Good King Wenceslas*. Hingham: Village Press, 1904.

Old Style, destined to be one of his most popular. It was this type that launched him as a successful seller of types, and in his Village Letter Foundery specimens he quoted a hyperbolic statement from the San Francisco *Examiner:* "The type is a new design by Goudy, the only man since William Morris to show any distinction as a type designer."[25]

Goudy himself continued to quote from and write about Morris. In *Typographica No. 3* (1916), an advertising piece for the Village Press set by Bertha Goudy and printed by C. E. Ruckstuhl of New York, Morris' "The Ideal Book" was reprinted with Goudy's statement: "It voices the publisher's own ideals so fully that any other excuse for the reprint seems unnecessary."[26]

In the third number of the periodical he edited, *Ars Typographica* (Spring 1920), he reiterated his faith in Morris' work "as the pioneer in the Renaissance of printing now under way. . . ."[27]

It was for the Morris memorial edition of the German journal *Philobiblon* in 1934 that Goudy wrote his longest tribute to his master. He took a judicious, balanced point of view, deploring those who slavishly copied Morris' style but admitting to the strong indirect influence emanating from Morris' work. He implied that, while it is acceptable to have been inspired by Kelmscott, one must move away and find one's own path, keeping in mind the broad lessons of Morris. The article ended, after discussing Morris' influence on Rogers and Updike, with the statement that Morris was "one of the outstanding figures of the Nineteenth Century, and in printing, it may be, the greatest figure since Gutenberg."[28] A few years later he borrowed his own summation from Morris: "I would wish, as was said of Morris, my epitaph might intimate that 'he sought to do good work within the limits of his own craft.'"[29]

It is difficult to measure his influence. The Village Press books were not innovative and have probably had little, if any, effect. The decorative work he did for others was of small impact. Many of his perhaps overly numerous typefaces caused few ripples, but a few, such as Kennerley, have had wide use. Virtually all reflect qualities of sound design and craftsmanship with a sane respect for the past and a healthy regard for the future. Perhaps it has been his writings, his own genial personality, the whole sum of his approach to typography, that have provided a focal point for post-Morris printing in America. Bradley went over to commercialism and Hollywood; Updike and Rogers were aristocrats. Without the original artistry of Bradley or Rogers, or the learned mind of Updike, Goudy provided the common touch.

One manifestation of Goudy's humanity was his professional launching of two protégés destined for fame themselves. Will Ransom who began the Village Press with Goudy was thereby started on an outstanding typographic career. In particular, he went on to become the dean of writers about private presses with his standard work on the subject, *Private Presses and Their Books*.[30] He was born in 1878 in Michigan. His parents later moved to the state of Washington where as a boy he learned to love printing from a job on a local newspaper. He went on from that to hand-illumined manuscripts.[31] Philip John Schwarz, who has studied Ransom's diaries, says that there were three influences affecting him at the time. Besides the work of Elbert Hubbard at his Roycroft Press, the books of Thomas B. Mosher impressed him, especially for their content, as did the issues of the *Inland Printer*, "the midwestern trade journal through whose pages the concept of the 'book beautiful' or ideal book was transmitted to America from England just prior to the turn of the century."[32]

In 1901 Ransom set up the Handcraft Shop in Snohomish, Washington, and printed his first book, *The Lady of Shalott*. "One copy was sent to Elbert Hubbard in exchange for a signed portrait on Japanese vellum, which Ransom immediately sent to Seattle to be framed."[33] The brown suede binding and oblong format of the book resemble Roycroft volumes. The title page has a trellis design hand colored in yellow, green, and mauve. There are multicolored designs on all the pages, which are set in black batarde type with wide margins. The second book, Wilde's *Ave Imperatrix!* (1902) also clearly shows the Roycroft influence, especially in the hand-illumined initials throughout. Jenson type is used on handmade wove paper. The decorations by John D. Clancy include a grapevine border on a vellum leaf tipped in before the text. Each text page has the same asymmetrical tree and vine motif within which the verse is set.

Ransom met Irving Way, became acquainted with Kelmscott books, and decided to study at the Art Institute in Chicago. In 1903, when he arrived, he went to look up Way, found Goudy instead, and was introduced by him to Seymour. On leaving there, he went to an Arts and Crafts exhibit where he saw a pigskin-bound Kelmscott *Chaucer*. At the end of the semester he joined Goudy at the Village Press. There he helped to make the first book, *Printing*.[34] The Newberry Library also has a book from 1903, printed, hand colored,

135

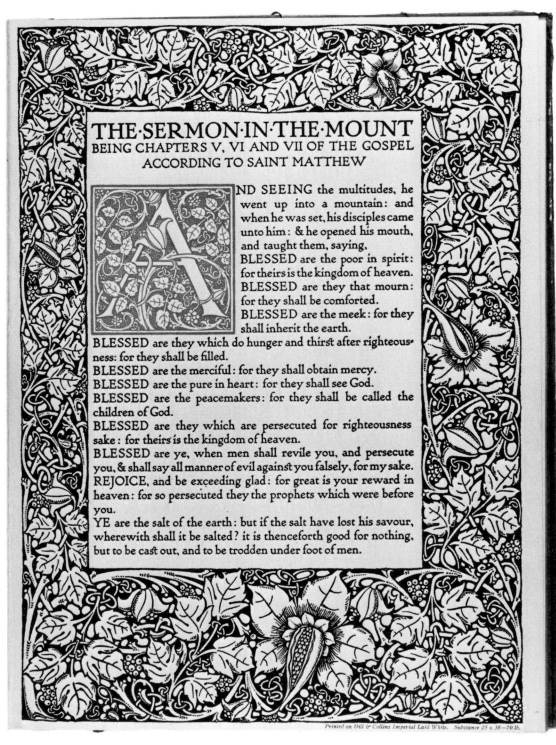

Plate 71. *The Sermon in the Mount.* New York: Village Press, 1907.

bound, and published by Ransom: Walter Savage Landor's *A Vision and the Dream of Petrarca.*

The other young typographer who worked closely with Goudy in the early years was destined to make an even greater mark on American bookmaking: William Addison Dwiggins. Like Ransom, he was a student of Goudy's in Chicago, collaborated with him on a few books, and went on to his own work and subsequent fame.

Dwiggins was born in 1880 in Martinsville, Ohio, and went at nineteen to Chicago where he worked in an engraving plant and attended Frank Holme's School of Illustration. In 1902 he worked with Goudy on the Blue Sky *In a Balcony.* When Goudy moved to Hingham, Dwiggins joined him in 1904 and worked on two Village Press books. After Goudy left for New York, Dwiggins stayed on in Hingham, in time commuting to a Boston studio as a free-lance artist. He became friendly with the Boston Society of Printers and met Henry Lewis Johnson, Carl Heintzemann for whom he laid out music titles, and Daniel Berkeley Updike. "They steered me," he has been quoted as saying.[35]

In 1906 he put out a hand-lettered version of the Ninety-first Psalm, printed from blocks at the Heintzemann Press under Dwiggins' supervision and sold by him at Hingham Centre. The small book is in red and black round Gothic lettering, with one large and four small initials which somewhat resemble Morrisian work. Dwiggins did a lot of work in the early years of the century for Alfred Bartlett, the Boston publisher. One of Bartlett's publications was this same psalm, made even more Arts and Crafts by the addition of white on black borders for every page, albeit with Renaissance motifs. A similar booklet, *The Parable of the Prodigal Son,* with hand-lettered text and designs by Dwiggins was published by Bartlett in 1905. The text opening has an illustrative headpiece and a large initial within black and white arabesques. There are more illustrations in the text and much use of leaves as line fillers.

Dwiggins began to take a more individualistic view of art after his first Arts and Crafts efforts, indicated by a letter dated "November Something, 1922," to Rollins:

> . . . Art has nothing to do with democracy. You must get that out of your head. . . . It has been revealed to me by a sojourn in the middle west that art is to be pursued solely as a personal matter. People do not want it, and it is entirely all right that they shouldn't. Old man Morris led us all astray by his dream of a popular or democratic art activity. It isn't there, old cock, and for one I am content that it isn't there. Sweat the popular art poison out of your blood, and start in pleasing yourself, and you have cured ONE trouble in your state of affairs. . . .[36]

Between the World Wars, Dwiggins went on to make a brilliant career as one of the most influential book designers in the country, especially in the field of trade books. It was he who made the Knopf books the most physically attractive volumes from any general American publisher. His work was both highly original and based on current art trends. Its influence is still felt. Dwiggins died in 1956, one of the second wave of turn-of-the-century typographers deriving initial inspiration from Kelmscott before finding their own style.

Chicago's place in the Morris Revival was primarily one of a breeding ground as can be seen from the above descriptions of early beginnings. Effects of the Revival were evident there from about 1894, somewhat later than Boston but earlier than New York.

1. Paul Johnston, "Frederic W. Goudy: American Typographer," *Fleuron*, VII (1930): unpaged.
2. Will H. Bradley, *Will Bradley: His Chap-Book* (Mount Vernon, New York: Peter Pauper Press, 1955), pp. 28-29.
3. Frederic W. Goudy, *A Half-Century of Type Design and Typography* (New York: Typophiles, 1946), Vol. I, pp. 31-32.
4. Ibid., p. 30.
5. Ibid., p. 49.
6. Quoted in Melbert B. Cary, Jr., *A Bibliography of the Village Press* (New York: Press of the Woolly Whale, 1938), pp. 10-11.
7. Quoted in Frederic W. Goudy, *The Story of the Village Type* (New York: Press of the Woolly Whale, 1933), p. 6.
8. Goudy, *A Half-Century*, note on p. 51.
9. Frederic W. Goudy, *Typologia* (Berkeley & Los Angeles: University of California Press, 1940), pp. 149-150.
10. Peter Beilenson, *The Story of Frederic W. Goudy* (Mount Vernon, New York: Peter Pauper Press, 1965), p. 34.
11. Ibid., p. 37.
12. Guild of Book Workers, *First Year Book and List of Members 1906-07* (New York: Guild of Book Workers, 1907), unpaged.
13. Goudy, *The Story of the Village Type*, p. 12.
14. Bernard Lewis, *Behind the Type* (Pittsburgh: Carnegie Institute of Technology, 1941), p. 66.
15. Goudy, *A Half-Century*, p. 73.
16. [Reproductions of Initials] *Inland Printer*, XVII (April, May, June 1896): 92, 204, 313.
17. [Note] *Inland Printer*, XVII (August 1896): 587.
18. "The Initial Designs by Goudy," *Inland Printer*, XVII (June 1896): 317.
19. Roland O. Baughman, *Frederic William Goudy 1865-1947: A Commemorative Exhibition* (New York: Columbia University Libraries, 1966), p. 6.
20. Cary, *Bibliography*, p. 31.
21. Goudy, *The Story of the Village Type*, p. 8.
22. Baughman, *Goudy*, p. 5.
23. Joseph M. Bowles, ed., *Some Examples of the Work of American Designers* (Philadelphia, New York, Boston: Dill & Collins Co., 1918), unpaged.
24. Will Ransom, Foreword to *Spinach from Many Gardens* (New York: Typophiles, 1935), p. 4.
25. *A Novel Type Foundery* (New York: Village Press, 1914), unpaged.
26. [Frederic W. Goudy] *Typographia No. 3* (New York: Village Press, 1916), unpaged.
27. Frederic W. Goudy, "Printing as an Art," *Ars Typographica*, I (Spring 1920): 40.
28. Frederic W. Goudy, "William Morris: His Influence on American Printing," *Philobiblon*, VII (1934): 191.
29. Introduction by Goudy to Vrest Orton, *Goudy: Master of Letters* (Chicago: Black Cat Press, 1939), p. 23.
30. Will Ransom, *Private Presses and Their Books* (New York: Bowker, 1929).
31. The Newberry Library in Chicago has the Ransom archives which include a book of poems by J. W. Riley, *From Riley* (1899), Ransom's own *When Three Is Company: A Spring Fancie* (1900) (a decorated typescript), and Maurice Hewlett's *A Sacrifice at Prato* (1900).
32. Philip John Schwarz, "Will Ransom: The Early Years," *Journal of Library History*, III (April 1968): 140.
33. Ibid., p. 143.
34. Ibid., pp. 144-152.
35. In Paul A. Bennett, "W. A. Dwiggins, Who 'Writes, and Draws, Fair,'" *Linotype News*, XII (September 1933): 5.
36. Quoted in Paul A. Bennett, ed., *Postscript on Dwiggins* (New York: Typophiles, 1960), Vol. I, p. 91.

XV

New York
& Trade Publishing

NEW YORK, the major printing and publishing center of the country, proved in the nineties relatively conservative. It possessed only one notable literary publisher, R. H. Russell, while commercial printing was led by two old-fashioned firms, De Vinne and Gilliss, whose reputations for fine work had been formed well before the advent of Morris. Following directly in their pattern was the other influential New York establishment, the Marion Press run by Frank E. Hopkins, a former employee of De Vinne. There was private press activity but none of it very significant, except for the Elston Press in the suburb of New Rochelle. The most important designer from New York, Thomas Maitland Cleland, also began with a private press.

However, even in general trade publishing Morris' influence does appear. For the Kelmscott series of James Pott & Company, the description in the 1901 *Publishers' Trade List Annual* states:

> An entirely new edition in unique and artistic leather binding, Roycroft style, printed on deckle edge, Old Stratford paper, with illustrations on plate paper, by the following well-known artists: G. W. Bardwell and H. Gregory. Square 12mo, in box, $1.00.[1]

Besides this specific example of a namesake series, there were two principal ways in which Morris' influence affected commercial book format: the use of Jenson type and bordered title pages added to otherwise ordinary sheets. An example in the first category is the second edition of Anthony Hope's *Phroso: A Romance* (copyright 1897) published by Stokes with illustrations by Henry B. Wechsler. It is very nineteenth century in appearance with a pictorial cloth cover, a centered title page with various kinds of type, vignetted engravings as well as plates on coated paper, and a thin, spindly type for the text. However, Jenson is used for most of the title page, the contents, half title, chapter titles, running heads, and Opinions of the Press. Jenson was even combined with the Aesthetic format

I have seen full many a sight
Born of day or drawn by night:
Sunlight on a silver stream,
Golden lilies all a-dream,
Lofty mountains, bold and proud,
Veiled beneath the lacelike cloud;
But no lovely sight I know
Equals Dinah kneading dough.

15

Plate 72. Paul Lawrence Dunbar, *Candle-Lightin' Time.* New York: Dodd, Mead, 1901.

as in the Reverend G. Campbell Morgan's **The Hidden Years at Nazareth** (copyright 1898) published by Fleming H. Revell Company in New York, Chicago, and Toronto. It has the small, thin, saddle-book shape with a decorated green on white cloth cover. The text is in a leaded old-style type. Jenson is used for some of the asymmetric title page, the half title, introductory biblical quotation, and shoulder note running titles.

Jenson type was not restricted to display although that was its main use. Examples of it as a text type can be seen in a series of highly decorated books put out by Dodd, Mead from 1899 to 1906 and printed by the University Press in Cambridge. These were the poems of Paul Lawrence Dunbar, the black dialect writer. The books had covers and borders on every page by a single artist and were sometimes illustrated with photographs by the Hampton Institute Camera Club. The 1899 *Poems of Cabin and Field* has foliate borders by Alice Morse in light green, some of which include such items as ears of corn and opossums. The headings are in old-style type, the title page calligraphic, and the text Jenson.

140

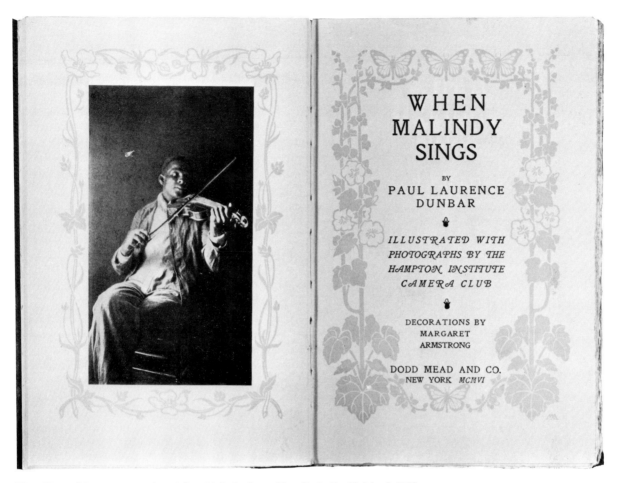

Plate 73. Paul Lawrence Dunbar, *When Malindy Sings.* New York: Dodd, Mead, 1906.

Margaret Armstrong decorated the 1901 *Candle-Lightin' Time* (Plate 72). The pattern is the same: calligraphic title page, borders throughout, and Jenson type. *When Malindy Sings* (1906) has a title page in type (Plate 73) and was also decorated by Margaret Armstrong. (Incidentally, an earlier use of Jenson in connection with Dunbar turns up from a jobbing press in Toledo, Ohio. *Majors and Minors* was printed in 1895 by Hadley and Hadley Printers and Binders. The text is in modern type but Jenson is used for display. This shows the amazingly rapid spread of Jenson, for 1895 was the very year it was offered for sale.)

The other concession to the Arts and Crafts style favored by trade publishers was an even easier one: the addition of a bordered title page. Often on coated paper, it was obviously designed separately from the text sheets and even sometimes repeated the information on a separate undecorated title page. Red ink was often used as well as black. The wording might either be centered or set in solid blocks. The borders themselves varied, of course, both in motif and treatment, ranging from close imitations of Morris to designs rather far removed. The usual effect of these added title pages is one of incongruity; the disparity between them and the text, often in modern-style type, is all too apparent. Furthermore, this type of book, since it is essentially a refurbishing operation for old sheets, is often not dated. Even if there is an internal date it can sometimes be misleading.

For example, from the New York publishing house of Thomas Y. Crowell, Robert Louis Stevenson's *Poems* (copyright 1900) may have been printed close to that date. Besides the added title page within borders, it is in old-style type with a cover reminiscent of Margaret Armstrong. But Longfellow's *Evangeline* (copyright 1893) was probably issued later than that in the added-title-page format. On the other hand, James Allen's *As a Man Thinketh* is not dated at all. The text is in modern-style type but the added title page is in green and rust Gothic lettering within a vine border.

Other examples of undated but obviously turn-of-the-century books with bordered title pages show a range of New York publishers: Milton's *Poetical Works* from Thomas Whittaker, Irving's *Knickerbocker History of New York* from the Cosmada Library, Hawthorne's *Wonder Book* from Mershon, W. E. Aytoun's *Lays of the Scottish Cavaliers* from the Home Book Company, and Henry Drummond's *Addresses* and O. W. Holmes' *One Hoss Shay and Other Poems* from H. M. Caldwell (New York and Boston).

The same sort of thing can be traced to other American publishing centers: Sir Thomas Browne's *Religio Medici* from Little, Brown of Boston (in this case, the border is signed—by T. B. Hapgood), Emerson's *Representative Men* from M. A. Donahue & Company of Chicago, De La Motte Fouque's *Undine* from Henry Altemus of Philadelphia, or Shakespeare's *King Henry V* from David McKay of Philadelphia. David McKay also issued at least one book of this type with a date: Sir Edward Bulwer-Lytton's *Richelieu or the Conspiracy*, copyright 1901, printed by Sherman & Company of the same city.

An extended use of the undated added title page can be found in the works of Ruskin, taken over in 1898 by Estes & Lauriat of Boston, in the form of the Cabinet & Sterling editions published by Merrill & Baker of New York, and continued by Dana Estes & Company, which succeeded to Estes & Lauriat.[2] These series also show other Morris influence. For example, the red and black typographic title page of "*Praeterita . . .*" in the Illustrated Cabinet edition of Dana Estes does not have a border, but both the title and the imprint are in Satanick, set in solid block arrangement, filled out by flowers.

In sum, trade publishers often conceded to the Arts and Crafts fashion in rather superficial ways. But in New York there was a small literary publisher more concerned with finely designed books than many larger firms. An American publishing leader has said that the firm of R. H. Russell emulated the Stone & Kimball books.[3] Be that as it may, the firm survived only a little longer than its famous colleague. When Russell was bought out by Harper & Brothers in 1903, he gave the explanation that the times were not propitious for small houses without periodicals to compete with large ones.[4]

The firm began in 1893 when the elder Robert Howard Russell left the De Witt Publishing Company and set up R. H. Russell & Son. The younger Russell was particularly interested in art and saw to it that Russell books reflected current trends in that field. For example, D. B. Updike was commissioned to design a charming example of the Aesthetic style: Madison Cawein's *Shapes and Shadows* (1898) printed from plates by Redfield Brothers of New York. It is in Caslon type on laid paper with a black and red ruled title

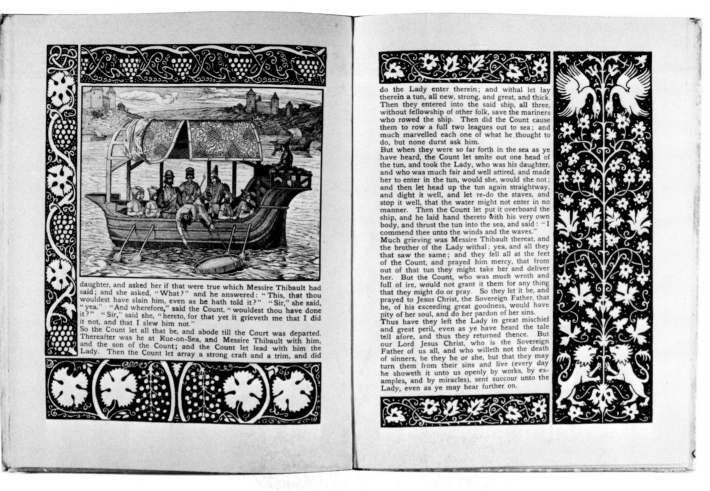

Plate 74. William Morris, *The History of Over Sea*. New York: R. H. Russell, 1902.

page that includes a rather rococo shield device for Russell. The floral decorations, in darker green on a green cloth binding, are also rococo in feeling. Italic running titles are at the heads of the pages, within rules.

In the same year Russell brought out a book equally typical of Arts and Crafts: Tennyson's *Idylls of the King* with woodcut illustrations and decorations by George Wooliscroft Rhead and Louis Rhead. This highly ornate book is in red and black. Each page, except where there are illustrations, is bordered, with Celtic interlacing as the major motif. The text is in Satanick type. The use of coated paper somewhat mars the book's effect.

Louis Rhead's work was used again by Russell in 1902 for *The History of Over Sea*, printed by John Wilson & Son, Cambridge. It is a large, flat book, again on coated paper. The paper board binding is printed in red and green fleur-de-lis pattern, with silk ties. The black and red title page is in Gothic type, within borders, facing a bordered frontispiece. The illustrations within the text are also bordered as are their facing pages (Plate 74). The other pages are solid set in Bookman type with Kelmscott margin proportions and an ornamented initial at the text opening.

Somewhat less of an Arts and Crafts book is Morris' *The Doom of King Acrisius* (1902) in a square format, with illustrations by Burne-Jones. Leaves are used on the black and red title page and on the bindings to fill out the title and author paragraph. There are vine-decorated initials in the text. The binding is gold stamped on white cloth, repeating the title-page design which has large leaves in each corner within a very rectilinear layout. The type is Caslon. Morris' *Pygmalion and the Image* (1903) is a companion to this volume.

Still another 1902 book is a good example of Arts and Crafts translated into trade terms: Mrs. S. B. Herrick's *A Century of Sonnets*. The format is copied from the Copeland & Day sonnet series: one poem high on the page, in Bookman type with an outline foliate initial. The red and black title page has a vine border and leaf line fillers. The cream-colored paper boards have a design in gold reminiscent of Ricketts' *Silverpoints* cover: flowers and leaves repeated over a background of undulating lines. In the last analysis R. H. Russell, as a publisher, was quite attracted by the Arts and Crafts style, putting out more books of this type than any of the other literary publishers except for the Copeland & Day English Love Sonnet series.

1. James Pott and Company section, *Publishers' Trade List Annual* (New York: Bowker, 1901), p. 4.
2. Raymond L. Kilgour, *Estes and Lauriat: A History 1872-1898 with a Brief Account of Dana Estes and Company 1898-1914* (Ann Arbor: University of Michigan Press, 1957), pp. 171–174.
3. George H. Doran, *Chronicles of Barrabas 1884-1934* (New York: Harcourt, Brace, 1935), p. 83.
4. Quoted in Charles A. Madison, *Book Publishing in America* (New York: McGraw-Hill, 1966), p. 169.

XVI

Theodore Low DeVinne's Opinion of Arts & Crafts

COMMERCIAL printing in New York at the turn of the century was dominated by the most famous printer in America, Theodore Low De Vinne. Born in Stamford, Connecticut, in 1828, he began work in 1843 as a newspaper apprentice in Newburgh, New York. In 1848 he came to New York City, joining in 1850 the firm of Francis Hart, of which he became a partner in 1858. After Hart's death in 1877, the firm was reorganized, becoming in 1883 T. L. De Vinne & Company. Until his retirement in 1908, De Vinne was involved in the major typographic movements of the times. His firm, an eminently successful one, did printing for Scribner's and the Century Company, among other publishers. It was noted for the high quality of its work from a technical point of view; its printing of wood engravings was particularly remarkable. De Vinne was open to technical innovation as well. He was the first printer to order coated paper for better impressions of the new halftones. Throughout his career he was a prolific writer on both the practice and history of typography, advocating a classically simple approach to design. He was an important figure in the organization of the New York Typothetae in 1865 and of the Grolier Club in 1884. Of the fifty-five volumes issued by the latter before De Vinne's death in 1914, forty-five were from his press.[1]

An early writer on the Kelmscott Press, De Vinne continued to mention Morris frequently in his numerous publications. He even met and interviewed the master of Kelmscott around 1892. There are several views that De Vinne consistently held about the Morris movement, which may be said to characterize his attitude.

In the first place, he approved of Morris' use of bolder, blacker type:

Pickering's revival of Caslon's old-style type, and William Morris's equally happy revival of the forms of the early Italian printers, came none too soon. To many young readers the new Morris types were an unexpected revelation of the strength, beauty, and readability of a really masculine form.[2]

De Vinne used the term feminine to denote the weakness of the modern-style types. He advocated masculine printing and had himself returned to old-style type before Morris, perhaps under the Chiswick stimulus, or possibly simply from his own broad knowledge of typographic history. In the revival of Caslon and other old-style types, De Vinne was an influential force.

He was even instrumental in making modern-style type more bold. The Century type, done under his aegis, is still used and probably inspired Kimball's Cheltenham, an immensely popular face. In his introduction of Century, De Vinne linked it to Morris, claiming a general preference, among "advertisers, as well as . . . bibliophiles," for bolder types.[3]

Secondly, superb craftsman that he was, he appreciated the value of Kelmscott books from a technical viewpoint: the quality of the materials and, especially, the presswork.

> . . . For an amateur in difficult trades, his workmanship is surprising, if not unexampled. A prominent American typefounder . . . testifies that he has . . . made types that in lining, fitting, and adjustment show the skill of the expert. . . . his types and decorations and initials are in admirable accord . . . the evenness of color he maintains on his rough paper is remarkable, and . . . his registry of black with red is unexceptionable. No one can examine a book made by Morris without the conviction that it shows the hand of a master.[4]

In the third place, De Vinne was not impressed with Morris' composition and page design. He found the letters too closely spaced, the use of fleurons as line fillers annoying, and the decoration sometimes excessive. In particular, the lack of leading between the lines made, for De Vinne, a page too black and therefore illegible—the cardinal typographical sin. For example, in his book on title pages, he called Morris' spacing rules "fetters to symmetrical composition" and his fleurons "a positive offence."[5]

His fourth and last point was the unfortunate effect of Morris on his imitators, many of whom rushed blindly down the path of pseudo-incunabular printing. This seemed to De Vinne a deliberate affectation of crudeness. He was basically a believer in technological progress for whom the mystique of the handpress held no value. The rudeness of archaic types and woodcuts was uncouth, not charming, and could be valuable only for the limited use of allusive typography.

> How does one make a book attractive? The novice in book-making hopes to do it by ornamentation, by a new and startling cut of type, by some eccentric arrangement of types, by a servile imitation of the worst features of mediaeval printing, by borders, red ink, headbands, initials—what not?[6]

These four points remained fairly constant indicators of De Vinne's opinion of Morris, but the balance of that opinion shifted in the late nineties from an enthusiastic reception to disillusionment, evident in his review of a Portuguese book at the Paris exhibition of 1900. De Vinne applauded Didot, stating that Morris had turned back "all the wheels of improvement."[7]

Turning to De Vinne's own bookmaking, one must remember that, especially in the later years when he was busy with his numerous other activities, he did not always directly supervise the design of even those books for which no specified artist was responsible. Frank E. Hopkins, who worked for De Vinne between 1888 and 1898 and who was himself responsible for design, has told how De Vinne did not see the books for which the press extolled him until the reviews came out, when he would ask to see a copy of the latest example of his "finished art."[8] His reluctance to assume the duties of designer, quite in the vein of the old-time printer the Revivalists were anxious to abolish, is illustrated by a story recounted by William Dana Orcutt:

> The first commission I received to design a book came quite by accident. I was lunching in New York with Paul Reynolds, the well-known literary agent. After discussing the personal business that had brought us together, Reynolds remarked:
>
> "I had a curious experience yesterday. W. B. Yeats, the Irish poet, is one of my clients, and he sent me a little manuscript with the request that I have it printed for him in attractive style, not for publication, but for him to give to his friends. I took it to the De Vinne Press, and read Mr. De Vinne Yeats' letter.
>
> "'How do you wish to have it made?' Mr. De Vinne asked me.
>
> "Now, I don't know anything about *making* books," Reynolds continued, "and I told him so. He smiled genially and handed the letter back to me. 'Better write Mr. Yeats and ask him how he wants the book made,' De Vinne said; 'then we would be very glad to manufacture the volume for him.'"
>
> "Would you care to let me have a crack at it?" I inquired with the confidence of youth.
>
> "You'd take a load off my mind," Reynolds laughed; and the manuscript came to me for design and manufacture. Incidentally, this experience turned me into a designer first, and a book manufacturer afterwards.
>
> This incident, as I write it, sounds incredible in view of the fact that today no bookmaking establishment of any pretensions is without a typographic consultant, whose research and taste are placed at the disposal of its clients.[9]

The fact remains that the De Vinne Press under De Vinne's direction did put out books in a variety of styles. One of these was the Chiswick/Aesthetic manner of the exhibition catalogues produced for the Grolier Club from 1886. An example is *Commercial Bookbindings: An Historical Sketch, with Some Mention of an Exhibition of Drawings, Covers, and Books, at the Grolier Club, April 5 to April 28, 1894.* The booklet is in old-style type on laid paper with wide margins. Besides the press device at the end, the only decoration is an unframed Renaissance initial with shading at the text opening, rather incongruously set off by an outline foliate headband.

Renaissance arabesque initials are used at the beginning of each poem in an 1897 De Vinne book, *Some Verse* by A.C.B. (i.e., Alice Cary Bussing), remarkable for the extent to which it resembles some of the books published by Mosher in Maine. It has a tall, thin shape, although still small in size, in a vellum paper binding, the title within a design of violets. Each poem, in old-style type, is centered on its own page (Plate 75). The title page is also centered, with a violet in the middle. The paper for the one hundred copies is the kind used by Mosher—Van Gelder. De Vinne may not have believed in feminine typography, but his Press could certainly turn out an Aesthetic book with all the delicate attributes of that style.

Plate 75. Alice Cary Bussing, *Some Verse.*
New York: De Vinne Press, 1897.

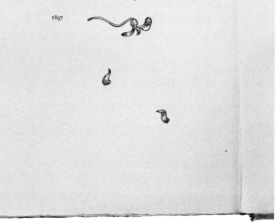

BON VOYAGE.

TO I. W.

DEAR Ocean, cease thy sighing for a space ;
Calm thy broad bosom for a little while ;
Let the fair light of thy most radiant smile
Reflect heaven's glory on thy placid face.
May stormless stars watch nightly in their place
O'er the great ship that onward, mile on mile,
Forges its way toward that lordly isle,
The empire seat of Britain's conquering race.
Guard well that ship's dear burden ! Show her all
Thy glories ; let her know thy nameless charm
As thy true lovers do. And when once more
She trusts herself to thee, and leaves the thrall
Of Old-World wonders, bear her, safe from harm,
Back to the Sunset Land, her native shore !

1897

In the other vein of late nineteenth-century typography, the De Vinne Press was also long accustomed to old-fashioned printing in the bold manner. An early book that remarkably foreshadows the Colonial style of the nineties and may be called an example of the Antique style described earlier is: *An Antidote against Melancholy: Compounded of Choice Poems, Jovial Songs, Merrie Ballads &c.*, an 1884 Christmas book for the Pratt Manufacturing Company of New York. (An earlier, similar book, *A Paradise of Daintie Devices* (Christmas 1882), had been so successful that this second one was prepared.) An added title page, the same as the paper cover, has black and red lettering within a woodcut border of Renaissance motifs. The typographic title page has an arabesque border and ornament, also in black and red (Plate 76). "To the Reader" is in large Caslon type, leaded widely, with a decorative initial. This book, harking back to seventeenth- and eighteenth-century models, is closer to the Arts and Crafts spirit than the neo-Gothic *Philobiblon* of 1889.

A category of titles in which Arts and Crafts has often appeared is Christmas books. Henry Van Dyke's *The Lost Word: A Christmas Legend of Long Ago* (New York, Scribner's, 1898) was printed by De Vinne with designs by Amy Richards. The olive green cloth

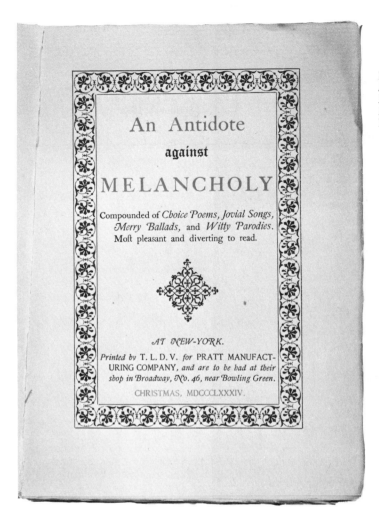

binding (Plate 77) and the black and red title page both have grapevine borders, but the result is not very Morrisian. Even less so are the text pages within borders composed of flowers and fish. The photogravure illustrations from drawings by Corwin Knapp Linson do not add to the unity. Another more successful Christmas book was Richard Watson Gilder's *A Christmas Wreath* (New York, Century Company, 1903) with pictures and designs by Henry McCarter (Plate 78). The binding is gold-stamped vellum boards with crimson endpapers. Again there are borders on every page but with more variety: some are black silhouettes on white backgrounds, some white designs on black backgrounds, while others are simply outlines. Unity is maintained by using the same motifs: vases, flowers, and arabesques. The type is Jenson throughout.

This was by no means the first time De Vinne and Jenson type had come together; according to Hopkins, he was even responsible for the name.

A representative of the Dickinson Type Foundry of Boston brought in a proof of a new font of type they had cut, which they wished to name the Morris type because it was in effect a copy of one of Mr. William Morris' types. Mr. De Vinne argued

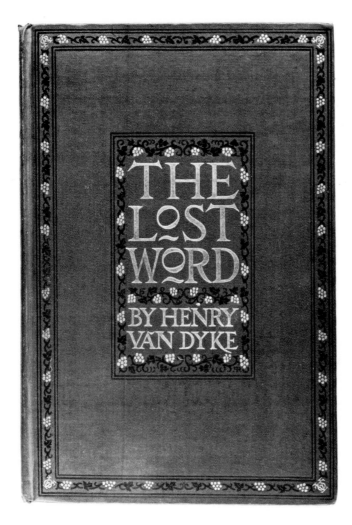

strongly against it; said the Morris type was not an original face but was plainly modeled after Jenson, and he suggested that Jenson's name was more appropriate. It was named Jenson.[10]

For De Vinne's opinion of the ATF types copying Morris, one can turn to *Old Faces of Roman and Medieval Types Lately Added to the De Vinne Press* (1897) the wrapper of which has the title within a Kelmscott-style border of acanthus leaves and Kelmscott initials throughout the specimens. The introductory section is printed in Jenson and says in part:

> The Jenson is a fair reproduction of the face made by Nicholas Jenson in 1471, and soon after adopted by typefounders of all countries as the basis or standard of good form for Roman letter. It is not unlike and will compare favorably with the Golden type of William Morris. . . .
> The Satanick is a revival of the Round Black-letter of Round Gothic, in general use as a book text before the production of Jenson's form of Roman. This is the style preferred by William Morris for his best books. For reprints of medieval work it will always be a desirable face.[11]

An early example of De Vinne's use of Jenson is to be found in a charming book of 1895: Spenser's *Epithalamion* (New York, Dodd, Mead, 450 copies) with drawings by George Wharton Edwards in the manner of Walter Crane. The red and black title page is hand lettered, but the text, on Japan vellum, is in Jenson. Everything is decorated, even the copyright notice on the verso of the title page. The dedication and half-title pages have full-page illustrations. Each text opening has poetry only on the verso, within a pictorial border, facing a full-page illustration on the recto.

The title page, but not the text, of the *Catalogue of the Books in the Library of the Typothetae of the City of New York* (February 1896) is in Jenson type. In fact, it has a total Arts and Crafts layout: block arrangement, flush left and right, in caps with an historiated initial. There are even two words in lower case—in the—to make the spacing come out right, a practice not often condoned by De Vinne.

De Vinne did use Jenson for other texts, as in the 1898 *Pilgrim's Progress*, done for the Century Company with designs by the three British Rhead brothers: George, Frederick, and Louis. The book is also an example of the *horror vacui* elsewhere deplored by De Vinne. Each page has a border except for some full-page illustrations (Plate 79). There are large initials on decorated backgrounds and panels of grapevine decoration. Even the copy-

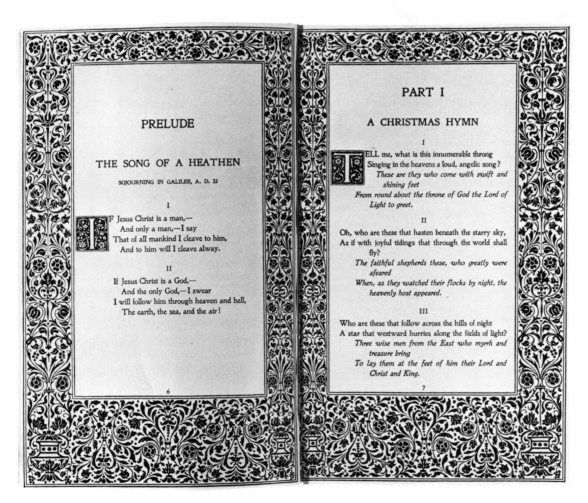

Plate 78. Richard Watson Gilder, *A Christmas Wreath*. New York: Century, 1903.

Plate 79. John Bunyan, *The Pilgrim's Progress from This World to That Which Is to Come.*
New York: Century, 1898.

right page has a picture, as in the Spenser. Another example of De Vinne's use of Jenson as a text face is Ernest Seton-Thompson's *The Trail of the Sandhill Stag* (New York, Scribner, 1900), which also has Kelmscott initials in green and black and other decorations by Mrs. Seton-Thompson (Plate 80).

Again, a book De Vinne was hired to print privately in 1900 repeated the use of Jenson. *An Account of the Pilgrimage to the Tomb of General Grant* by Burritt Darrow is an almost total Kelmscott pastiche. Printed on cream-colored laid paper in two hundred copies, it has a title page within a Kelmscott border, facing a photographic frontispiece. The title, beginning with a Kelmscott initial, is in black and red caps, flush left and right, with fleuron line fillers. The text opening, however, strikes the incongruous note De Vinne usually managed to achieve: the headpiece has white on black Renaissance monsters with heads of warriors, busts of winged women, and tails of serpents on either side of a medallion head of Hector. (An earlier privately printed book, Henry Van Dyke's *The Toiling of Felix* (1898) is virtually undecorated, but the text is in Jenson.)

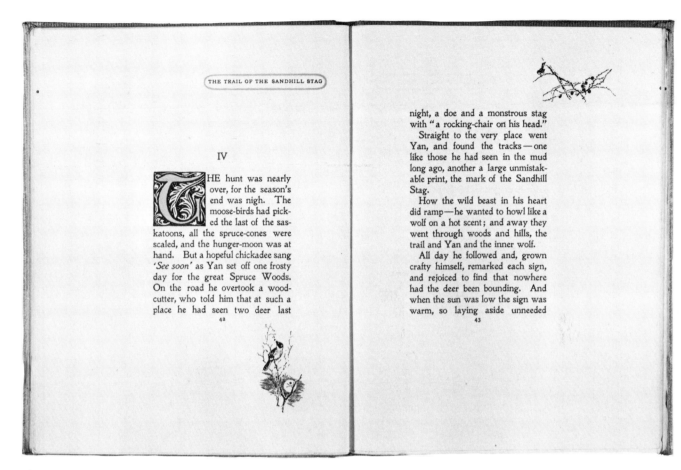

Plate 80. Ernest Seton-Thompson, *The Trail of the Sandhill Stag*. New York: Scribner's, 1900.

The first use of De Vinne's own Venetian type, the Renner, took place in 1900 with Boccaccio's *Life of Dante* for the Grolier Club. That De Vinne was responsible for such a type at this time is surely not unrelated to the general movement. One critic believes that it was negatively inspired by Morris: "... it was an attempt to do what Morris had done and to do it better; to show Morris in effect what he should have done."[12]

A title from 1903 shows De Vinne's use of Satanick type, modeled on Morris' Troy face: *A Book of Shakespeare's Songs*, decorated by Edward Edwards for G. Schirmer. It is a large book in two hundred copies on Italian handmade wove paper, printed in red and black Satanick. Edwards' decorations are superbly done: woodcut illustrations in the style of Walter Crane on versos face recto text pages, both within elaborate borders.

De Vinne's own interest in incunabula predated Morris; he had written *The Invention of Printing* in 1876. John Clyde Oswald recounted the following undated incident: "I once asked him, in his study, to show me what he considered to be the best printed book he had ever seen. He got down from the shelves a volume ... printed late in the fifteenth century."[13] Henrietta C. Bartlett also pointed out in the auction catalogue of De Vinne's library that De Vinne "was a great admirer of the early Venetian printers and had many examples

153

from their presses."[14] This catalogue lists only two Kelmscott Press books: *The Golden Legend* and *Poems by the Way*, although there are several other Morris items: the 1897 Aymer Vallance book about Morris, an 1898 Chiswick Press issue in Golden type of one of his speeches, the 1900 Mosher *Child Christopher*, and the 1902 *Art of the People*, published by R. F. Seymour. (Two Elston Press printings of Morris writings, with De Vinne's bookplates, are now in the Wing Collection of the Newberry Library.)[15]

Commentators on De Vinne have consistently agreed in their evaluations, both about De Vinne's own work and his relationship with Morris: that the De Vinne Press did excellent work from a craft point of view and was a decided influence for the better in American typography, that De Vinne was not a great designer for he lacked both originality and infallible taste, and that he was affected by the Morris movement but was not one of its ardent followers. D. B. Updike, writing in 1923, touched on all three of these points:

> Personally, the mechanical execution of De Vinne's books appears to me more admirable than their artistic conception; for I do not consider that in such matters he had great taste. His work was often flawless, but by the same token cold. He belonged, perhaps, too much to the school of Didot and had too little sympathy with the good elements in that "revival of printing" which took place during the latter part of his career.[16]

Carl Purington Rollins, often an astringent viewer of typography, commented that De Vinne "was not unaffected by the Morris influence,"[17] but wrongly went on to say that De Vinne did not use the American versions of Kelmscott type. His use of Jenson and Satanick has been pointed out above. Rollins' final assessment of De Vinne was: "Conventional types conventionally arranged, and printed with precision: this is the worst and the best that may be said of De Vinne's printing."[18]

Another commentator, Michael Koenig, in his judgment of De Vinne, has been too generous: "It can be argued that De Vinne was the greatest American printer and that he exerted probably the greatest influence of any one man upon American printing."[19] On the contrary, De Vinne was the last and greatest representative of the old-time printers, a man whose scholarship enabled him to codify the practices of the past. As an inspiration to the next wave of printers, his name has not often been mentioned. Stylistically, he was a leader in the reaction against weak modern types and crowded title pages. Otherwise, he left no particular style to follow; he was more concerned with the mechanics of printing than the aesthetics. And this was the very point the young printers of the turn of the century were making: it was time for printers to be aware of both.

De Vinne thought of himself as a lover of beautiful books, but in practice he felt the customer's will to be paramount. "Mr. Lawrence's orders about this book may overrule mine." [Letter to Hopkins, February 24, 1895.] "But it is their right to have what they like, and we must give it." [Letter to Hopkins, August 19, 1895].[20] He remained the old-fashioned jobbing printer on a grand scale. Like any good jobbing printer, he made technological innovations when they seemed to promise bigger profits. De Vinne was ending his career in the period when technology was placing the possibility of technically superb printing in the hands of any competent well-equipped workman. The mechanical difficulties that De Vinne struggled with in the mid-nineteenth century were being overcome, along with the paucity of typefaces and illustration media. The very richness of possibility in this new printing era called for the artist-designer who could see his own path of unity and

154

coherence through the maze. For example, Updike and Rogers did not profess to know all the mechanical ins and outs of printing, but they did know that designers were needed. De Vinne, like Nash in the West, Bodoni in the eighteenth century, or Mardersteig now, became a hero to printers because of his high standards, his uncontroversially classic approach, his comprehensive knowledge, his self-assurance, and his worldly honors of money, fame, and academic awards.

1. See Michael Koenig, "De Vinne and the De Vinne Press," *Library Quarterly*, XLI (January 1970): 1–24.
2. Theodore Low De Vinne, "Do You Know the Letters?," in *Liber Scriptorum* (New York: Authors' Club, 1893), p. 195.
3. Theodore Low De Vinne, "The Century's New Type," in *Specimens of the Century Romans* (Jersey City: American Type Founders, N.D. [ca. 1894–1895]), unpaged.
4. Theodore Low De Vinne, "The Printing of William Morris," *Book Buyer*, XIII (January 1897): 921.
5. Theodore Low De Vinne, *Title-Pages as Seen by a Printer* (New York: Grolier Club, 1901), pp. 250–251.
6. Theodore Low De Vinne, "The Printing of Books," *Outlook* (December 4, 1897): 808.
7. Theodore Low De Vinne, "A Book that Won the Grand Prize," *New York Times Saturday Review* (October 27, 1900): 736.
8. Frank E. Hopkins, *The De Vinne & Marion Presses* (Meriden: Columbiad Club, 1936), p. 42.
9. William Dana Orcutt, *From My Library Walls* (London: John Murray, 1946), pp. 172–173. The Yeats book was probably *The King's Threshold* (1904) printed by the University Press for John Quinn, the wealthy patron of the arts who was a friend of Yeats. It has no decoration except for some use of red ink and is, by no means, an outstanding example of book design.
10. Hopkins, *The De Vinne & Marion Presses*, p. 39.
11. *Old Faces of Roman and Medieval Types Lately Added to the De Vinne Press* (New York: De Vinne, 1897), unpaged.
12. Koenig, "De Vinne," p. 11.
13. John Clyde Oswald, in *Catalogue of Work of the De Vinne Press* (New York: Grolier Club, 1929), p. 15.
14. Henrietta C. Bartlett, Introduction to *The Library of the Late Theodore Low De Vinne* (New York: Anderson Galleries, 1920), p. 3.
15. Another small indication of De Vinne's interest in Morris is his undated scrapbook entitled *Miscellaneous Cuts* at the Grolier Club. The very first paste-in is a reduced cut of the opening page of the Kelmscott *Poems by the Way*. The second one is two dolphin and anchor marks from the Chiswick Press.
16. Daniel Berkeley Updike, "The De Vinne Press," *Literary Review* (January 20, 1923): 405–406.
17. Carl Purington Rollins, "Theodore Low De Vinne," *Signature*, N.S., X (1950), 15.
18. Ibid., p. 21.
19. Koenig, "De Vinne," p. 20.
20. Quoted in Thomas A. Larremore, and Amy Hopkins Larremore, *The Marion Press* (Jamaica: Queens Borough Public Library, 1943), pp. 80, 82.

XVII

Commercial & Private Presses in the New York Area

WALTER GILLISS and his brother Frank founded a press in New York in 1870 that was noted for fine printing long before the nineties, and was connected with Arthur Turnure's *Art Age*. The Gilliss brothers also printed for the Grolier Club, the Metropolitan Museum of Art, and bibliophiles such as Hoe, Morgan, and W. L. Andrews. The press was renowned not for any particular style but simply for impeccable workmanship. Walter Gilliss was influenced by De Vinne,[1] to whom McMurtrie found him "superior in taste and judgment,"[2] and he was largely unaffected by the Morris Movement.[3]

One book of his has been pointed out as showing Morris influence: *The Treatyse of Fysshynge wyth an Angle. From the Book of St. Albans, Printed by Wynkyn de Worde at Westminster in the Year MCCCCLXXXXVI. With an Introductory Essay upon the Contemplative Man's Favorite Recreation by William Loring Andrews*.[4] This was published by Scribner's in 1903. It has a vellum binding with silk ties, a bordered title page, woodcut illustrations, and specially cast type, patterned after Wynkyn de Worde's (Plate 81). In this use of an incunabular mode, Gilliss may be said to follow in Morris' footsteps, but the book is more an example of allusive typography than it is of the Morris style.

However, there is one aspect of the nineties in which Gilliss may have played an important role—the revival of old-style, particularly Caslon, type. As Gilliss recounts it, when he began printing Turnure's *Vogue* in 1892, the Caslon type was to be imported until it was found that an 1870 specimen book of MacKellar, Smith & Jordan of Philadelphia showed an identical type called Original Old Style. In 1858 Laurence Johnson of Philadelphia, a predecessor of MacKellar, Smith & Jordan, had bought the type in order to reproduce it in the United States, where it became the first old-style to be shown since 1822. The first large fonts were sold in 1892 to Gilliss, after which *Vogue* attracted printers' attention.[5]

The Marion Press was less affected by the Morris Revival than De Vinne but more so than Gilliss. Frank E. Hopkins was born in 1863 in New York City, son of a printer who later moved to Connecticut and New Hampshire. In 1883 he began to attend Boston Uni-

156

versity but had to leave in his junior year to support his family. He returned to the printing world of New York where, after other jobs, he began to work in 1888 with De Vinne's press. There he soon became the unofficial book designer, taking an evidently unwelcome load from De Vinne's shoulders. In a painstaking book written by Hopkins' daughter and son-in-law, he is given credit for design work on such volumes as the famous 1892 *Book of Common Prayer*, or, more modestly, Louise Chandler Moulton's *Arthur O'Shaughnessy*, printed for Stone & Kimball in 1894.[6]

In 1896 he began to print at home in Jamaica on a handpress in his attic, naming the new establishment after his daughter Marion. Since De Vinne had the feudal idea that hired help belonged to their employers even on their own time, he made Hopkins choose between working for De Vinne & Company and running the Marion Press. In February 1898, Hopkins resigned and went into business on his own. He had met wealthy bibliophiles at De Vinne's and had in fact begun publishing, four volumes having already been issued in collaboration with Paul Lemperly and Francis Adon Hilliard. Now he found much of his business coming from that same world: the Rowfant Club of Cleveland, the Caxton Club of Chicago, the Carteret Club of Newark. On a more commercial level, he was approached by still another bibliophile: "Mr. Thomas B. Mosher of Portland, Maine, requested me to undertake the printing of all his publications, a handsome offer which I felt obliged to decline because of the press of other work. I regretted afterwards that I did so."[7] As with other offers to back his press, Hopkins declined in order to maintain his newly gained inde-

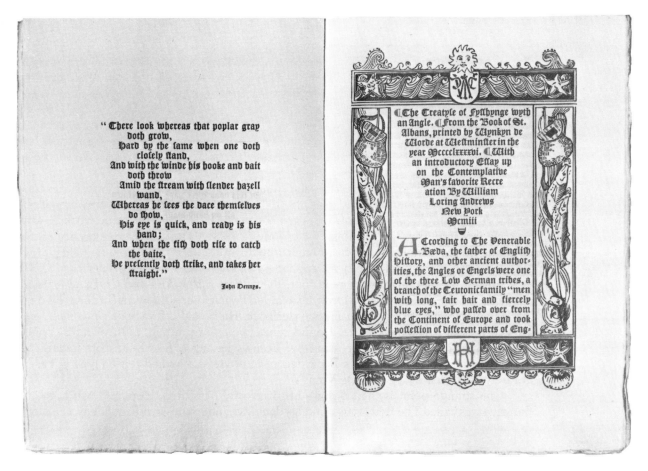

Plate 81. William Loring Andrews, *The Treatyse of Fysshynge wyth an Angle*. New York: Scribner's, 1903.

pendence. After a life of both struggle and success, Hopkins died in 1933 and the Marion Press came to an end.

His chroniclers, who were quite aware of the ubiquitous Morris trend of the times, felt that Hopkins' typography was formed by his work at De Vinne's and by his own taste, not by current fashions.

> To his days at De Vinne's and the impinging of the environment there upon his personality and his "New England conscience," certain definite tendencies can be traced: the desire to plan tastefully and simply and print perfectly at whatever cost; the dislike of ornamented types or embellished pages; love of correct composition and faultless presswork, featured by rich, brilliant inking; and, finally, an unusually vigorous skepticism towards Morris and the Kelmscott school.[8]

> Long before the Kelmscott Press was set up, Hopkins had yielded to the typographic urge by printing . . . his juvenile journals. . . . So that if Morris' example furnished Hopkins any impetus at all, it was merely as one of several contributing factors. . . . Hopkins' stimulus to print *artistically* came as much from within as did Morris'. And before any Kelmscott opus appeared, the young man was actually at work on books for De Vinne, who insisted, as a matter of routine, on strong type, fine paper and the best composition and presswork. Marion imprints owe these qualities, therefore, to De Vinne rather than to Morris. . . .

> Always he denied vigorously that his press derived from or owed any obligation to Hammersmith. No great admirer of Morris' types, decoration or bindings, he said so, openly. . . .[9]

What the Larremores did not realize was that Hopkins did not remain totally unaffected by the spirit of the times, since his books may be classed among turn-of-the-century exponents of the Aesthetic trend. For example, *One Hundred Quatrains from the Rubaiyat of Omar Khayyam—A Rendering in English Verse by Elizabeth Alden Curtis. With an Introduction by Richard Burton*, was printed in six hundred copies for the Brothers of the Book in 1899. It is on deckle-edge, laid paper, in old-style type, with a symmetrical red and black title page. The page layout is Aesthetic, including disproportionately large tail margins.

The conservative restraint of this and other books from the Marion Press was a conscious achievement on Hopkins' part. In 1907 he wrote: "Meaningless ornamentation, tricks of typography, and eccentricities are not to our taste."[10] In the same work he also quoted a review from the *Evening Post* of July 5, 1898: "'The unobtrusive beauty of the typography of "Two Poems of Sea-Fights with Spain" . . . is refreshing in the midst of so much William Morris eccentricity misapplied nowadays in honor of the printer's art. . . .'"[11]

Finally, as the Larremores point out, there *were* a few Arts and Crafts touches in Hopkins' work.[12] Like William Morris, he avoided large paper editions but ordered his own handmade paper with a Marion Press watermark. He bound a few books in vellum, one of which even had thongs to tie. He did some two-color printing, mostly on title pages and used black letter types occasionally. Besides having a few Kelmscott initials, he frequently chose Bradley's *Chap-Book* decorations. He also owned Jenson type but used it rarely after first trying it at De Vinne's.

One strange point is that, despite his disavowal of Morris, Hopkins' own home in Jamaica was called The Red House, and his daughter and son-in-law do not deny a connec-

Plate 82. Elizabeth Barrett Browning, *Sonnets from the Portuguese*. New York: Elston Press, 1900.

tion with its English predecessor. Perhaps Hopkins was more influenced in his life style by Morris than even he knew. It would seem that this private/commercial press earned a living without losing its stylistic independence. This achievement in itself fulfilled one major Morrisian ideal—one that Morris would have preferred over mere imitation of Kelmscott formats.

There were even more individual presses than the Marion around New York, some of which turned out brilliant work, others mediocre. In the latter category, the Cadmus Press printed Henry Van Dyke's *Books, Literature and the People* (1900) in Caslon type with a decorated red initial and a red and black centered title page. The page layout seems marred by too wide leading. Another inept attempt is an edition of William Morris' *The Ideal Book*, printed for George H. Broughton, Jr., at the Calumet Press in 1899. After the red and black title page with fleurons and a border of acorns, the opening page has a large red initial. There are red initials for each paragraph, and the red running heads are filled out with acorns. The type is Caslon. That the inspiration for this book was Morris himself is verified from the foreword: "The effort has been made to produce a little book which would have pleased the author. . . ."

More successful in its work was the Grannis Press of New York, run by Percy Grannis, father of Chandler B. Grannis, former editor of *Publishers Weekly*. In 1901 he printed for the Laurel Press 450 copies of Spenser's *Amoretti* in brown paper boards and Bookman

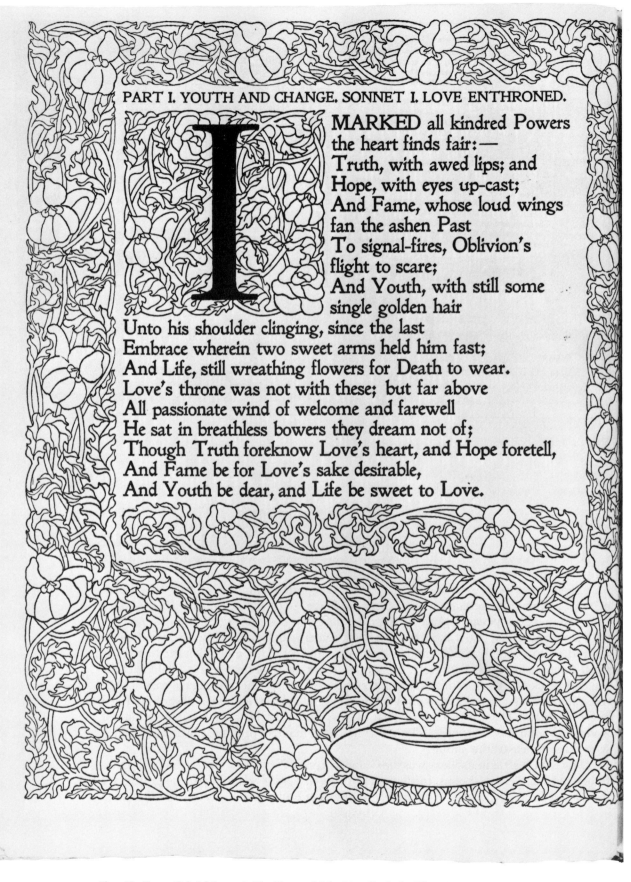

PART I. YOUTH AND CHANGE. SONNET I. LOVE ENTHRONED.

I MARKED all kindred Powers
the heart finds fair:—
Truth, with awed lips; and
Hope, with eyes up-cast;
And Fame, whose loud wings
fan the ashen Past
To signal-fires, Oblivion's
flight to scare;
And Youth, with still some
single golden hair
Unto his shoulder clinging, since the last
Embrace wherein two sweet arms held him fast;
And Life, still wreathing flowers for Death to wear.
Love's throne was not with these; but far above
All passionate wind of welcome and farewell
He sat in breathless bowers they dream not of;
Though Truth foreknow Love's heart, and Hope foretell,
And Fame be for Love's sake desirable,
And Youth be dear, and Life be sweet to Love.

Plate 83. Dante Gabriel Rossetti, *The House of Life*. New Rochelle: Elston Press, 1901

type. The title page is in centered caps with no decoration, while the text pages have large outline initials with intertwined vines. There is one poem to a page, placed quite high. The effect is reminiscent of Copeland & Day's English Love Sonnet series in Boston a few years earlier. In 1905 the Grannis Press published with its own device *Olympus and Fuji Yama: A Study in Transcendental History* by Layton Crippen. This is decidedly an Aesthetic book, with an asymmetrical title page.

Another reasonably successful attempt at bookmaking took place in the New York suburb of Flushing. William Morris' *Gossip about an Old House on the Upper Thames* was reprinted from the *Quest* by J. E. Hill in 1901, with a frontispiece by C. M. Gere which had been used at the Kelmscott Press, illustrations by E. H. New, and Kelmscott-style initials by Hill himself, who had done earlier work of this sort for Updike. One hundred copies were printed in a heavy roman face on Japan vellum and bound in marbled paper boards.

Two more elaborate but still pleasing books were put out by different publishers but decorated by the same man, William Cushing Bamburgh, and therefore similar in effect. The first one is Chaucer's *The Nonnes Preestes Tale of the Cok and Hen* (1902) with an introduction by Bamburgh, published by the Grafton Press of Frederick H. Hitchcock and printed at the De Vinne Press. It is on Whatman wove paper, in Gothic type, with the glossary in Bookman. The second one is *Three Masques* by Ben Jonson (1903), published by Robert Grier Cooke, and printed on Provence handmade laid paper in old-style type. Bamburgh did hand-lettered black and red title pages and large ornamented red initials for both books. He illuminated by hand twenty-six lettered copies in each edition, which also included four copies on Japan vellum. The books are similar in size, while both have copperplate engraved portraits of the author as frontispieces and bindings of vellum paper boards with the title gold stamped in Gothic letters.

The most important of the New York private presses was in a suburb. The Elston Press began in Manhattan in 1900, but its owner, Clarke Conwell, moved it to New Rochelle in 1901. Conwell, with the aid of his designer and wife, Helen Marguerite O'Kane, was one of the most brilliant of the Kelmscott disciples. His books exemplify the best in the private press spirit: with traditional models as a point of departure, they achieve freshness of their own. They were printed by handpress in limited editions on handmade paper and Japan vellum, bound in boards or cloth or vellum with ties.

The first book from the press, Elizabeth Barrett Browning's *Sonnets from the Portuguese* (1900), is a superb achievement in the controlled mastery of a complicated page. The poems, in Satanick type, are set within borders by O'Kane that match the boldness of the letterforms (Plate 82).

The third book, Rossetti's *House of Life* (1901), was the first one to be done in New Rochelle. It is on American handmade paper printed on one side only in a "new font especially cast for this book" (from Elston Press brochure), of Jenson. Although most of the Elston books have red and black, this one is black only but there are numerous decorations by O'Kane. The double-spread title page has the title on the verso, the author on the recto against a background of flowers resembling Kelmscott arabesques. Both pages are within outline floral borders, as are the text pages (Plate 83). Each sonnet has a solid black initial against a background of flowers, while the titles of the sonnets have floral line fillers. The illustration facing the text opening shows Burne-Jones-like figures in a garden.

The next book from the Press, Langland's *The Vision of William Concerning Piers the Plowman* (1901), is in what Conwell called the Chaucer font, i.e., Satanick. The red

161

Plate 84. William Morris, *Sir Galahad: A Christmas Mystery.* New Rochelle: Elston Press, 1902.

shoulder note running titles are in Latin and the text in two columns with black paragraph marks. The O'Kane borders and floriated initials are very Morrisian while the illustrations are again reminiscent of Burne-Jones: elongated figures, almost identical faces, backgrounds without white space. *The Tale of Gamelyn* (1901) is also in Chaucer type, but it is the last one before the acquisition of Caslon Old Roman, "especially cast for the Press in England" (Elston Press brochure). It is also a plain book, showing Conwell's capabilities of restraint.

In 1902 Conwell published several William Morris reprints: *The Art and Craft of Printing*; *Some Notes on Early Woodcut Books, With a Chapter on Illuminated Manuscripts*; *Five Arthurian Poems*; and *Sir Galahad: A Christmas Mystery* (Plate 84), the last in Gothic type. The first two are fairly plain, the last two have O'Kane decorations in the Kelmscott manner. The balance between decoration and restraint can be seen in other books. Milton's *Comus* (1902) has a red and black double-spread title with grapevine borders by O'Kane, while Pope's *The Rape of the Lock* in the same year has no real title page at all, only a half title in black and a fly title in red. The book's sole decoration is a leafy rose paragraph mark in red. There was a trend toward simplicity in the later years of the Press before it ended in 1904. Laurence Twine's *The Patterne of Painefull Adventures*

162

(1903) is a plain book, while the only decorations in Shelley's *The Cenci* (1903) are the black and white initials by O'Kane.

O'Kane also did work for commercial publishers. For example, A. Wessels Company of New York published Morris' *Pre-Raphaelite Ballads* in 1900 in Satanick type with red initials. The edition note states that there are 500 numbered copies on "Old Stratford" paper and 250 on Imperial Japanese, of which Numbers 1–10 are bound in full English vellum with initials drawn and hand illuminated by O'Kane. There are also printed borders throughout and illustrations by her. The borders have large botanical motifs that are more Beardsley than William Morris, while the illustrations recall both Burne-Jones and Beardsley.

Conwell's press was not totally appreciated at the time. FitzRoy Carrington had this to say about *Sonnets from the Portuguese:* "Like many another disciple of Morris, Mr. Conwell has thought that by increasing the blackness of type and decorations he would achieve greater beauty and legibility, but this has not been the result and the effect is somewhat heavy."[13] But the years have lightened the effect. Conwell's and O'Kane's work now looks, as do some of the other products of turn-of-the-century presses, like Arts and Crafts happily mingled with Art Nouveau.

Still another New York private press was run by a young man who was to become one of America's great names in graphic art. Thomas Maitland Cleland was born in Brooklyn in 1880 but his family moved to Manhattan where, at the age of fifteen, he attended briefly the Artist Artisan Institute on West Twenty-third Street. At sixteen he bought a copy of Walter Crane's *Of the Decorative Illustration of Books*, in which he read about William Morris. Later he saw a copy of the Kelmscott *Chaucer* in the window of Scribner's bookstore, to which he returned on several occasions. An employee of Scribner's, Lewis Hatch, asked him in to look at the books and even got him work as a designer for the Caslon Press of Frederic T. Singleton, a short-lived commercial press set up after Singleton had worked at Bradley's Wayside. Cleland then got a press for himself and began printing in his father's basement. "Many ambitious projects for the illustrating and printing of medieval romances were born at this time and died for lack of the capital to buy paper or type."[14] A book he issued did attract attention in Boston, however, and Cleland moved his press there, setting up at 69 Cornhill and calling it the Cornhill Press. He published three more books before returning to New York where he assumed the art editorship of *McClure's Magazine* for a time, eventually becoming one of the outstanding American free-lance designers, particularly in the field of advertising.

Cleland's early work differs sharply from his later; there is no more clear-cut example of an American typographer starting in the Arts and Crafts tradition but abandoning it totally once he had found his true style—for Cleland, the style of the eighteenth century, especially French and Italian. His early designs are heavy woodcuts in the chap-book mode and may well owe Bradley a debt, as James Eckman has suggested in a "Heritage of the Graphic Arts" lecture on Cleland in New York, September 15, 1971. Indeed, Cleland wrote Bradley a letter, dated August 6, 1950, acknowledging such a debt.[15]

For example, Cleland did a woodcut with bold, sturdy lines for the cover of the official catalogue of the 1900 semicentennial celebration of the New York Typographical Union No. 6, showing the back of a pressman as he pulls the handle of a handpress. A contemporary account described it as "printed in black and red on a rough-surface paper, and . . . illustrated with wood cuts, the whole being in imitation of 'ye olden style.'"[16] Another example can be found in Elbert Hubbard's *Philistine* from East Aurora, New York. The

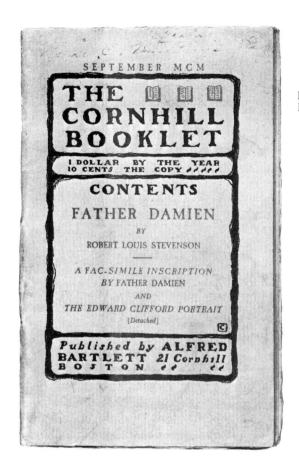

Plate 85. *Cornhill Booklet.*
Boston: Alfred Bartlett, 1900.

May 1900 number has on the recto of the first leaf following the cover a full-page advertisement in Bookman type for the National Phonograph Company of New York, with leaves as line fillers and a black and red heavy-line woodcut of a man smoking a long pipe and listening to a phonograph. Finally the *Cornhill Booklet*, published by Alfred Bartlett of 21 Cornhill, Boston, in 1900, has red type on its cover within a plain black frame, with heavy, irregular old-style lettering and leaves, signed "C," which may indicate Cleland (Plate 85). (The two earlier examples were signed "TMC," but his later work was often signed simply "C.")

In his book work the same influences can be seen. Will Ransom has passed on Cleland's version of the ambiance when he was beginning:

> T. M. Cleland . . . recalls an early experience which indicates very clearly the youthful viewpoint of the time. In 1898 he came into possession of a small Gally Universal press . . . and installed it in the home cellar. "Here I printed a few circulars, a very diminutive little book for private circulation . . . and a slightly more ambitious job for which I drew a very queer initial and tailpiece. Both of these were printed in black letter types and were very hard to read and I had a notion at the time that being so made them especially romantic and beautiful." Some such notion as that was pretty general in those days.[17]

The first little book referred to was Josephine Preston Peabody's *In the Silence*, for which the colophon says that one hundred copies were printed for Miss Peabody and her friends in New York in June 1900. It is on laid paper in gray wrappers. The black letter type is relieved by red Lombardic initials on the title page and at the beginnings of stanzas. The half title and the fly title are both placed in the upper left corners. The centered title page has two acorn arrangements. It is a tentative effort.

The next one was Tennyson's *The Lady of Shalott*, begun, according to the above account, in New York but finished, according to the colophon, at 69 Cornhill, Boston, in September 1900, in 240 copies. This also is a small book on laid paper in Gothic type with red for display. There are blue wrappers over boards. Acorns are used, not as line fillers but at the beginning of the refrain lines. The opening initial has a pictorial background of a castle and there is a woodcut tailpiece showing the Lady of Shalott in her barque.

Cornhill Press is named in the imprint for Lady Dilke's *The Shrine of Death and The Shrine of Love*, printed in 290 copies during January 1901. The dark gray paper boards have a beige cloth spine and a title in red caps, flush left. This is an archetypical Arts and Crafts book, in Bookman type on laid paper. The title page is as plain as possible, in flush left caps, but the double-spread openings for the two sections have outline woodcut vine borders, large red decorated initials, and illustrations on the verso in the style of Italian fifteenth-century books (Plate 86). The text pages are stark: no running titles, pagination, fleurons, or decorated initials, but fairly wide margins. The presswork for the woodcuts is admirable, less so for the text pages where pages of differing blackness can be found facing each other. But Cleland's drawings for the cuts show rapid artistic progress.

The final book published by the Cornhill Press, Laurence Housman's *Blind Love* (500

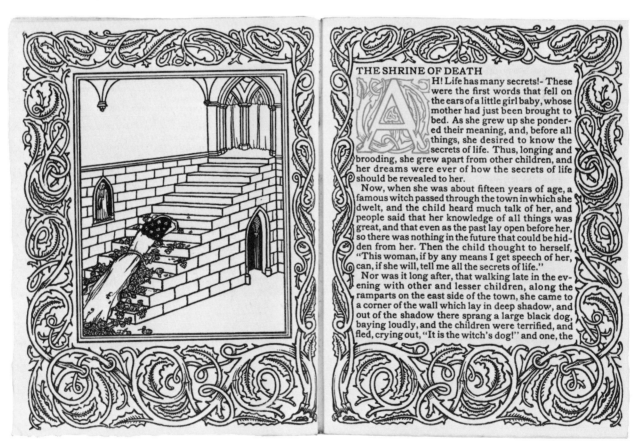

Plate 86. Lady Dilke, *The Shrine of Death and The Shrine of Love.* Boston: Cornhill Press, 1901.

copies, March 1901), is in a different style to suit its Aesthetic author, but it is still in the private press mood of the time. Again on laid paper with absolutely plain text pages, it is in Caslon type with a simple, centered title page. The medieval spirit has been left behind for rose-trellis decoration on the opening text initial and the tailpiece following the colophon (Plate 87).

Cleland did not immediately abandon his Arts and Crafts style. In 1903 he designed Bliss Carman's *The Word at St. Kavin's*, from Temple Scott's Monadnock Press of Nelson, New Hampshire. Three hundred copies were printed in old-style type on Alton handmade wove paper by the Heintzemann Press and bound in dark red suede. The lines of poetry are widely leaded and the fore and tail margins are wide, but this open space does not give an Aesthetic feeling since the type is rather large. It is the double-spread title page that establishes the Arts and Crafts atmosphere. There are woodcut borders of double rules and leafy branches surrounding a woodcut frontispiece in fifteenth-century outline style and a title page in red caps. The text opens with the title in red caps and a large ornamental initial. The other stanzas have large red initials. The only other decoration is a printer's device after the colophon. (Another 1903 book is the two-volume *Poems of Dante Gabriel Rossetti* printed by the Merrymount Press for the Pafraets Book Company of Troy, New York. The title page has a Cleland woodcut, printed in red, of a spray of roses with thorns. Its heavyish rounded lines suggest Arts and Crafts.)

About this same time, Cleland was developing a style more in keeping with the sixteenth-century Renaissance. *Arcady in Troy* by George B. Warren (1904) has a charming woodcut title page that places the title and imprint within a green architectural frame of trellis, fountain, and foundation. This was done for the Merrymount Press, for which Cleland did several other books.

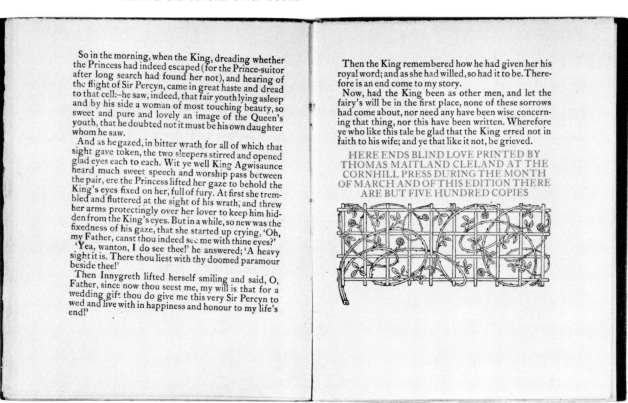

So in the morning, when the King, dreading whether the Princess had indeed escaped (for the Prince-suitor after long search had found her not), and hearing of the flight of Sir Percyn, came in great haste and dread to that cell:-he saw, indeed, that fair youth lying asleep and by his side a woman of most touching beauty, so sweet and pure and lovely an image of the Queen's youth, that he doubted not it must be his own daughter whom he saw.

And as he gazed, in bitter wrath for all of which that sight gave token, the two sleepers stirred and opened glad eyes each to each. Wit ye well King Agwisaunce heard much sweet speech and worship pass between the pair, ere the Princess lifted her gaze to behold the King's eyes fixed on her, full of fury. At first she trembled and fluttered at the sight of his wrath; and threw her arms protectingly over her lover to keep him hidden from the King's eyes. But in a while, so new was the fixedness of his gaze, that she started up crying, 'Oh, my Father, canst thou indeed see me with thine eyes?'

'Yea, wanton, I do see thee!' he answered; 'A heavy sight it is. There thou liest with thy doomed paramour beside thee!'

Then Innygreth lifted herself smiling and said, O, Father, since now thou seest me, my will is that for a wedding gift thou do give me this very Sir Percyn to wed and live with in happiness and honour to my life's end!'

Then the King remembered how he had given her his royal word; and as she had willed, so had it to be. Therefore is an end come to my story.

Now, had the King been as other men, and let the fairy's will be in the first place, none of these sorrows had come about, nor need any have been wise concerning that thing, nor this have been written. Wherefore ye who like this tale be glad that the King erred not in faith to his wife; and ye that like it not, be grieved.

HERE ENDS BLIND LOVE PRINTED BY THOMAS MAITLAND CLELAND AT THE CORNHILL PRESS DURING THE MONTH OF MARCH AND OF THIS EDITION THERE ARE BUT FIVE HUNDRED COPIES

Plate 87. Laurence Housman, *Blind Love*. Boston: Cornhill Press, 1901.

Very much the maverick and iconoclast, as James Eckman has so vividly described,[18] Cleland followed no party line in his few public announcements. On the whole, he tended to identify with the forces of modernism. In 1915, in an address to the American Library Association, he revolted from the handicraft mystique: ". . . a modern cylinder press is in all respects a finer machine [than a handpress] and is capable of doing better work of any description, and doing it incomparably faster and in larger quantities."[19] Many years later, in 1941, for the "My Favorite Book—And Why" feature of the *Dolphin*, when Cleland named the Limited Editions Club *Tristram Shandy* as his favorite of the books he had designed, he still expressed a feeling for practicality:

> Within the advancing years I have grown out of that early enthusiasm for books, as *objets d'art*, with which most of us were inspired by the works of the Kelmscott Press. I have not lost any fraction of my admiration for the craftsmanship of William Morris; in fact, it has increased as I have observed the failure of any of us to surpass or even equal it.
>
> But books, since the invention of printing has made them universal, should be something to read and not merely admired in a glass case.[20]

On the whole, New York City does not give evidence of a nucleus of people interested in Morris and increasing that interest by mutual reflection as in Boston and Chicago. There was a limited reaction on the part of the trade publishers, including the short-lived firm of R. H. Russell, while commercial printing remained largely indifferent to Morris, except for the sporadic flirtations of De Vinne. The private press group was not particularly cohesive; the two most important members being very peripheral: Clarke Conwell moved to a suburb, Cleland went off to Boston. This lack of an enthusiastic center probably accounts in part for the limited nature of the New York City response to Morris. Elsewhere in New York state, however, flourished a man often referred to as the American William Morris.

1. James M. Wells, "Book Typography in the United States of America," in Kenneth Day, ed., *Book Typography 1815-1965* (London: Ernest Benn, 1966), p. 339.
2. Douglas C. McMurtrie, Editorial Comment, *Ars Typographica*, II (October 1925): 175.
3. Hellmut Lehmann-Haupt, *The Book in America* (2nd ed.; New York: Bowker, 1951), p. 183.
4. Thomas A. Larremore, and Amy Hopkins Larremore, *The Marion Press* (Jamaica: Queens Borough Public Library, 1943), p. 238, note 262.
5. Walter Gilliss, *Recollections of the Gilliss Press and Its Work During Fifty Years 1869-1919* (New York: Grolier Club, 1926), p. 59.
6. Larremore and Larremore, *The Marion Press*, pp. 91 & 101.
7. Frank E. Hopkins, *The De Vinne & Marion Presses* (Meriden: Columbiad Club, 1936), p. 58.
8. Larremore and Larremore, *The Marion Press*, p. 77.
9. Ibid., pp. 114-115.
10. *A List of Books Printed at the Marion Press 1896-1906* (Jamaica: Marion Press, 1907), p. 6.
11. Ibid., p. 9.
12. Larremore and Larremore, *The Marion Press*, p. 115.
13. FitzRoy Carrington, "Private and Special Presses," *Book Buyer*, XXIII (1901): 100.
14. Alfred E. Hammill, *The Decorative Work of T. M. Cleland* (New York: Pynson Printers, 1929), pp. x, xii.
15. Item 80 in *Will Bradley: His Work—An Exhibition* (San Marino: Huntington Library, 1951), p. 27.
16. "'Big Six's' Booklet," *Printer and Bookmaker*, XXIX (December 1899): 208.
17. Will Ransom, *Private Presses and Their Books* (New York: Bowker, 1929), p. 78.
18. James Eckman, *Week Ends with Tom Cleland* (Rochester, Minnesota: Doomsday Press, 1971).
19. Thomas Maitland Cleland, "The Fine Art of Printing," *Printing Art*, XXVI (September 1915): 30.
20. Thomas Maitland Cleland, "Typographic Distinction," *Dolphin*, IV (Winter 1941): 201.

XVIII

Elbert Hubbard:
"An American William Morris"

ONE OF THE MOST ardent American followers of the Kelmscott style, certainly its most prolific propagator, and perhaps the most widely influential, worked, not in one of the metropolitan centers, but in a small town in western New York. The community of the Roycrofters in East Aurora was the creation of one man, Elbert Hubbard, although it survived his death on the *Lusitania* in 1915 by twenty-three years, under his son, Elbert Hubbard II. Not only were the social ideals of the Arts and Crafts Movement—the need for enjoyable, creative hand labor, the ability of the average man to produce artistic work—basic ideals of this community, but the style of the artifacts made there was of English inspiration—directly, in that Hubbard and his artisans were aware of the work produced by Morris; indirectly, in that a return to early sources for handicraft techniques and models, one of Morris' most important teachings, was also an integral part of the Roycroft philosophy. (In 1921 the Roycroft catalogues were still explaining the antiquity of the crafts of bookbinding, copper work, and modeled leather.) Nowhere can this be seen more clearly than in the printing of books, always their most important activity.

Hubbard came to Arts and Crafts late in life. Born in Bloomington, Illinois, in 1856, he grew up in a small town not far away. As a teenager, he became an itinerant soap salesman in the Midwest, moving to Buffalo at the age of nineteen. (He settled in East Aurora, a nearby town, in 1884.) Later in life, he claimed all sorts of trades and occupations for this youthful period, but his biographers point out that there is proof only for his having sold soap.[1] The Larkin Soap Manufacturing Company prospered and, when Hubbard sold out his interest in 1892, he was a well-to-do man. As he wrote to his mother at the time: "I have concluded that he who would excel in the realm of thought must not tarry in the domain of dollars."[2]

His attention had already been drawn to the history of printing. At a meeting of an informal men's club in East Aurora to which he belonged, Harry P. Taber, later to be the printer of Hubbard's first book, gave a talk on the subject, "illustrating it with

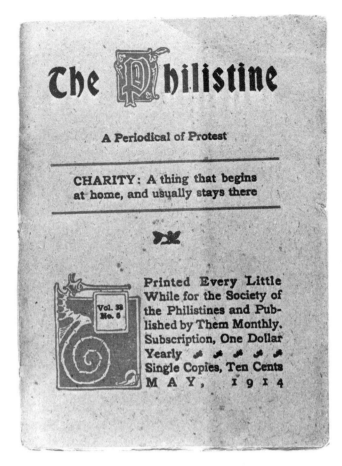

Plate 88. *Philistine*. East Aurora: Elbert Hubbard, 1914.

specimens of fine typography from the early Venetian printers—Aldus, Jenson, and their predecessors, the monastery *scriptorium*. . . ."[3] It sounds as though this talk may have been partly inspired by Emery Walker's famous lecture or by Morris himself.

After a brief fling at Harvard in 1893, he took off for his first European trip in 1894, including a visit to the Kelmscott Press at Hammersmith and a meeting with Morris himself. Hubbard recognized this meeting as a turning point, referring to it both in his autobiographical piece for *Cosmopolitan*[4] and in his brief notice for the English *Who's Who*.

Back in America Hubbard began in 1894 the first of his periodicals. The *Little Journeys to the Homes of the Great* came out monthly for fourteen years. The first two were printed at the local press, then G. P. Putnam arranged to print them. (Hubbard took them back in 1900.) Their success was such that the circulation reached nearly a thousand in six months; this encouraged Hubbard to begin another periodical, the *Philistine* (Plate 88), in 1895, a venture undertaken to give him an outlet for his own ideas since his writing had been rejected by the established magazines. The *Philistine* continued until his death and had the largest circulation of any of the little magazines of the time.

During this same period, Hubbard was establishing the Roycroft Press. He had bought a handpress soon after his return from England, and in 1895 acquired the equipment of local printers who were going out of business.[5] The name came from the seven-

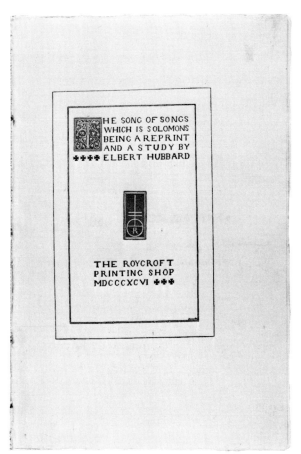

Plate 89. *The Song of Songs Which Is Solomon's*, East Aurora: Roycrofters, 1896.

teenth-century English printers, Thomas and Samuel Roycroft, but the influence of Morris is undoubted. ("To fill in the time we printed a book; we printed it like a William Morris book—printed it just as well as we could.")[6]

The first book, *The Song of Songs* (1896), turned out to be a rather free, and not very successful, interpretation of the Kelmscott style. The title page is in black and red, the latter being used for a decorative initial with scrollwork and for the Roycroft device, patterned on one used by Jenson. The black printing comes from a woodblock, clumsily handlettered by Hubbard's wife with both the title and imprint in block form, filled in by Maltese crosses (Plate 89). The next page states that six hundred copies were printed, each one numbered and signed. The first part of the book is taken up by a "Study" written by Hubbard, the opening page of which has an initial "I" within a Kelmscott-style side border. Most succeeding pages are arranged as inverted triangles, with Kelmscott-style initials at the beginning and a leaf or fleur-de-lis at the end. The biblical text, however, is undecorated, undistinguished typography, perhaps in deference to the lushness of the text itself. The colophon at the end of the book is in black capitals, with red fleurs-de-lis as decoration, the only other touch of red:

> And here, then, is finished this noble book . . . printed after the manner of the Venetian with no power save that of human muscle by Harry P. Taber. . . . Begun

on September the third day, MDCCCXCV, and finished—Thank God!—on January the twentieth day, MDCCCXCVI.

(This exaggeration of Morris' pseudomedieval language is typical of Roycroft colophons and title pages.) The type is Bookman, the paper handmade laid, and the binding heavy gray paper boards with buckram spine and matching endpapers. The overall effect of the book is distinctly amateurish, but it was not long before the typical Roycroft style had been formed.

George Bernard Shaw's *On Going to Church* was issued the same year (1896). It has brown paper boards with white buckram spine, handmade laid, deckle-edge paper, and Bookman type for the text. The title page is in black and red, with the title and author in Jenson type, flush left and right, filled out by acorns. The text pages have leaves and flowers, some hand illumined, scattered through for decoration, while many of the paragraphs begin with Kelmscott-style initials, also hand illumined. Although Roycroft books came out in differing formats, these characteristics of handmade materials, old-style type, and hand-colored initials are the basic elements of Roycroft books, with the addition of chamois covers. Typically, Hubbard has "gone Morris one better" by adding a further medievalism not found in Kelmscott books—hand illumination.

The other points on which Hubbard consistently differed from Morris are in the direction of modernity: well leaded rather than solid black pages; a separate, full title page; and avoidance of Jensonian-style type for the text. In fact, Roycroft never had any special types and simply used commercially available ones. Again, unlike Kelmscott, Monotype machines were used fairly early, although the first books were hand set. On the other hand, Hubbard, like Morris, did have handmade paper with his own watermark made especially for him and imported from Italy, Holland, and England.[7]

To give Hubbard credit, it must be remarked that the illumination had a practical, as well as esthetic, origin. To help with his printing activities, Hubbard hired some local men and women, which meant that he had many hands available that had to be kept occupied. The entire history of the Roycrofters does not concern us here, but it should be mentioned that, from this small beginning, Hubbard went on to employ over four hundred people at a time, turning out a whole line of home furnishings and personal items, especially in copperware and modeled leather. Roycroft was at the head of the American Arts and Crafts Movement, including the so-called Mission style of furnishings, popular at the turn of the century. Roycroft was, in other words, a bridge between the English Arts and Crafts, itself stemming from Morris & Company, and the most widespread American style in the years just before World War I.

But printing remained the single most important activity of Roycroft. *Little Journeys* and the *Philistine* both entered numerous American homes in quasi-Morrisian dress. (The *Fra*, Hubbard's other periodical, begun in 1908, was of much larger format and retained Arts and Crafts characteristics, although combined with Art Nouveau.) Books in limited editions were issued steadily and sold well, thanks both to the public's recognition that here were "artistic" books for the common man and to the enormous impact of Hubbard's controversial personality. He traveled over the country, delivering public lectures, dressed in a picturesque costume probably based, at least in part, on Morris' habitual attire. He entertained visitors, famous and obscure, at the Roycroft Inn. He wrote prolifically, and after *A Message to Garcia* in 1899, which was printed eventually in literally millions of copies, his name was a household word.

171

Plate 90. Elbert Hubbard,
*Little Journeys to the Homes
of English Authors: William Morris.*
East Aurora: Roycrofters, 1900.

He probably had little to do with the actual making of the books. Knowledgeable about printing, he was nevertheless not a designer; the designers who worked for him had the major responsibility for the appearance of Roycroft books. Samuel Warner and W. W. Denslow were the first important ones, and Warner was the more Morrisian.

Typical of his work is the *Little Journey to the Home of William Morris* (January 1900), the first one to be printed by the Roycrofters after Putnam ceased to publish the *Little Journeys*. The title-page border and initials in the text give a Kelmscott appearance at first glance, especially since the rest of the format contributes to that. The wide margins, Bookman type, shoulder note running titles, and the scattering of fleurons on the pages are all reminiscent. On closer inspection, one sees that the stylized, symmetrical floral backgrounds also recall Beardsley (Plate 90). Warner, who had studied in London and was a fellow of the Royal Society of Artists before coming to East Aurora in 1895,[8] may well have seen Beardsley's decorations for *Le Morte d'Arthur*, which Dent brought out in 1893.

This resemblance is even more striking in the 1899 *Aucassin and Nicolete*, where the title of this medieval piece is set within a very Art Nouveau border which appears to be made up of wings. The headpieces on pages 11 and 23 (Plate 91), printed in red, also have a Beardsleyesque sharpness of outline, while the printer's device at the end returns to black and white stylized flora. The colophon does not state that this book is by Warner, but the title page and device are surely his design. This book is typical of the more luxu-

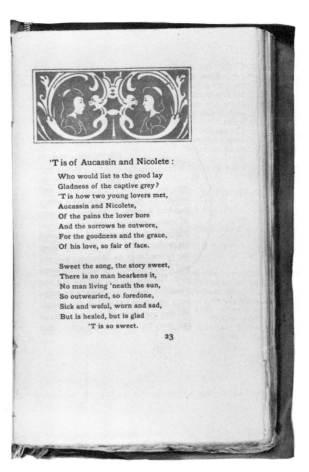

Plate 91. *Aucassin and Nicolete: Being a Love Story Translated out of the Ancient French by Andrew Lang.* East Aurora: Roycrofters, 1899.

'T is of Aucassin and Nicolete :

Who would list to the good lay
Gladness of the captive grey?
'T is how two young lovers met,
Aucassin and Nicolete,
Of the pains the lover bore
And the sorrows he outwore,
For the goodness and the grace,
Of his love, so fair of face.

Sweet the song, the story sweet,
There is no man hearkens it,
No man living 'neath the sun,
So outwearied, so foredone,
Sick and woful, worn and sad,
But is healed, but is glad
   'T is so sweet.

23

rious Roycroft volumes. The binding is beige chamois suede with an embossed picture of the protagonists on the front cover, their names stamped in gold. This binding material is often given the ugly technical name of limp ooze or referred to disrespectfully as window cleaners, or mouse skin. There are rather garish yellow silk doublures and marker. Black, red, and green inks are used for the Bookman type, while the shoulder note running titles are in Gothic. The initials have hand-colored backgrounds and the text opening a very large and elaborate capital "Y," done entirely by hand in vermilion and gold, the rather shaky flourishes of which intrude on the printed page.

That Warner could be more traditionally Morrisian can be seen in two books from 1900. Ruskin's *King of the Golden River* is in Caslon type on a cream-colored laid paper that does not have the desirable crispness of some other papers used at Roycroft and which fails to provide the sought-after black and white contrast. The title-page borders and initials are, however, the Morrisian white vines on black backgrounds. Again, the effect is somewhat destroyed since, facing the title page, is a photoengraved portrait of Ruskin. This use of photographs along with the Arts and Crafts format is not untypical of Roycroft.

A much more successful book, indeed one of the most beautiful of all Roycroft products, is Tennyson's *Maud,* totally derivative in style. The title-page border and initials by Warner are again white vines on black backgrounds, and the type used is Satanick. The initials, especially, are among the handsomest of Warner's designs (Plate

173

I HATE the dreadful hollow behind the little wood,
Its lips in the field above are dabbled with blood-red heath,
The red-ribb'd ledges drip with a silent horror of blood,
And Echo there, whatever is ask'd her, answers "Death."

For there in the ghastly pit long since a body was found,
His who had given me life—O father! O God! was it well?—
Mangled, and flatten'd, and crush'd, and dinted into the ground:
There yet lies the rock that fell with him when he fell.

Did he fling himself down? who knows? for a vast speculation had fail'd,
And ever he mutter'd and madden'd, and ever wann'd with despair,
And out he walk'd when the wind like a broken worldling wail'd
And the flying gold of the ruin'd woodlands drove thro' the air.

1

Plate 92. Alfred Tennyson, *Maud.*
East Aurora: Roycrofters, 1900.

Plate 93. *Gray's Elegy: A Lyric Poem.*
East Aurora: Roycrofters, 1903.

92). Adding to the book's beauty is the quality of the materials. The paper is beautifully crisp and white; the binding is a pleasing shade of burgundy chamois with matching silk doublures and marker. The presswork, both inking and register, is also impeccable, which is not always the case in Roycroft books. And finally, the taste used in putting the book together extends to the fine touch of printing the title on the title page in a red darker than usual to match the binding. The fly titles for the parts are also in this red, as is the colophon.

Warner was rather eclectic in his title-page proportions. In *Maud* the border was designed so that the space for the title is slightly to the upper left, i.e., the left and top parts of the border are narrower than the right and bottom parts. This is in accord with Kelmscott doctrine on the proper proportions for margins. At other times, Warner placed the title in the exact center of the border, with all four parts equal, as in the William Morris *Little Journey*. Or again, he partly reversed the Kelmscott proportions, with the narrow sections at the top and right, as in the Patrick Henry *Little Journey* (1903).

Warner's masterpiece is probably the Art Nouveau borders he designed for Robert Browning's *The Last Ride* (1900). Printed on one side only of the wove paper, these charming, pictorial, hand-colored borders vary from page to page. This book was issued in the classic Arts and Crafts real vellum binding, with beige silk ties threaded through slits in the vellum. However, unlike the plain endpapers of other private presses, Hubbard's publication has red silk doublures. The borders were re-used for a 1903 edition of Gray's *Elegy* (Plate 93).

The well-known artist W. W. Denslow worked for Hubbard between 1896 and 1900.[9] He drew the famous cartoons, many including Fra Elbertus (as Hubbard was known at Roycroft), which adorned the back of the *Philistine*. In 1900 he made his fortune with illustrations for *The Wizard of Oz*. His designing for the Roycrofters was not particularly Morrisian, but there is an amusing Antique book. Coleridge's *Ancient Mariner* (1899) was erroneously described in the Roycroft catalogue for that year as being in the style of a 1761 production of Horace Walpole's Strawberry Hill Press,[10] but it *is* an eighteenth-century pastiche. The binding is the familiar beige chamois with pictorial embossing and yellow silk doublures, but the title page strikes a novel note. It is in panel form, within rules, black and red, mostly Caslon type, but with other faces thrown in. The burlesque language of the title page (too long to repeat here) can be surmised from the following note two pages farther on: "Various of ye pictures are did by hande by ye First Ladies of East Aurora at a Bee: where ye Ladies were kindly supervised by ye Deacon Denslow." The book is printed in red, green, and black, with touches of gold put in by hand. Each page is within rules with a side panel, a very satisfactory device for marginal comment. The decorations are numerous and far from boring. Especially brilliant is one in which the ship's reflection in the water forms the pattern of a skull (Plate 94).[11]

The Roycroft designer who was to figure most importantly in later bookmaking came to East Aurora in 1903 as a young man of nineteen. Dard Hunter, according to his autobiography, grew up in an atmosphere of printing; his father owned a newspaper first in Steubenville, Ohio, then after 1900 in Chillicothe, Ohio. Hunter said in his reminiscences that, just before entering college

> . . . my father, also keenly interested in fine printing, purchased a book that had a pronounced influence upon me. This unusual volume, with richly decorative borders

and initials, had been printed in England several years previously by William Morris, an artist and craftsman about whom I knew little. I became so fascinated by the book and by father's description of the Kelmscott Press that I was eager to visit England, where such books had been made.[12]

He went to Ohio State University instead, where he saw more Kelmscott and Doves Press books. His brother was reading the *Philistine* which gave him an interest in East Aurora. If he could not go to England, he could at least go to upper New York state. When he did, the Hubbards allowed him to settle down. In the library were two Kelmscott books which he studied. "I had become more and more interested in this Hammersmith press and read everything I could find relating to the life and work of William Morris."[13] Hunter went on to tell an anecdote about May Morris' visit to America. She spoke at the Woman's Club in Buffalo, where Hunter went to hear her. "In her lecture Miss Morris was sarcastic and critical of America and spoke of the lack of culture in this country."[14] Afterwards Hunter gave her an invitation from Hubbard.

When she unfolded the letter and saw the signature her eyes flashed. Looking up at me, she said: "I most certainly will not go to East Aurora, nor do I have any desire to see that obnoxious imitator of my dear father." With an air of disdain she crumpled the note in her hand and gave it back to me.[15]

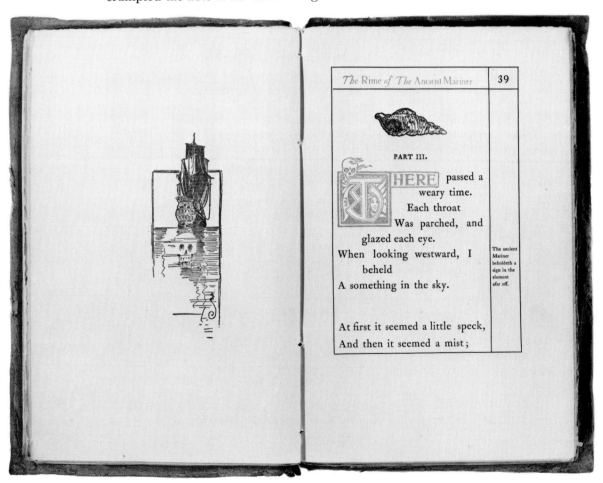

Plate 94. Samuel Taylor Coleridge, *Ye Ancient Mariner*. East Aurora: Roycrofters, 1899.

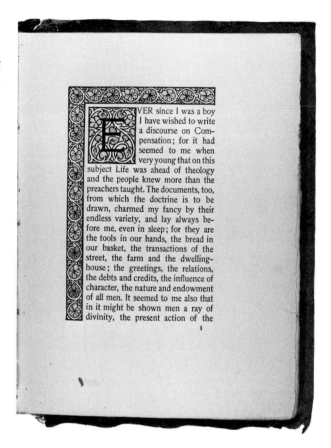

Plate 95. Ralph Waldo Emerson, *Compensation*. East Aurora: Roycrofters, 1904.

In 1904 or 1905 Hunter began to design books for the Roycroft Press. Irving's *Rip Van Winkle* (1905) is usually said to be his first book, but Lloyd Emerson Siberell thought that Hubbard's *The Man of Sorrows* (1904) was designed by Hunter.[16] It does not look particularly typical of Hunter, but Emerson's *Compensation* (Plate 95), also 1904, looks very much like his work. The decorations are hand colored in blue, yellow, green, and light orange. Their small flowers bring to mind Hunter's work for *Justinian and Theodora* or his cover design for *The Motto Book* (Plate 96).

He soon developed his own distinct style, which is recognizably part of the larger picture of Art Nouveau. *Justinian and Theodora* (1906) by Hubbard and his wife Alice has been called the Roycroft masterpiece.[17] Its orange, red, and black double title page, headpieces, initials, and colophon are indeed striking. The motif is regularly repeated flowers, with, on the title page, elongated stems (Plate 97). The same decorations were re-used in Hubbard's *The Doctors* (1909). Another outstanding Hunter book is Hubbard's *White Hyacinths* (1907), which again has a double title page within a green and white floral border. The same hyacinth motif is repeated throughout in initials and tailpieces and as part of a binding design, re-used for Hubbard's *Health and Wealth* (1908). These works, although with floral motifs, are not really part of the older curvilinear whiplash line Art Nouveau; they belong more to the newer school of Glasgow and Vienna, where the rectilinear, elongated line was important. Hunter himself mentioned that he designed books in this style in 1909 after a trip to Vienna[18] but his leanings toward it can be seen in earlier work.

177

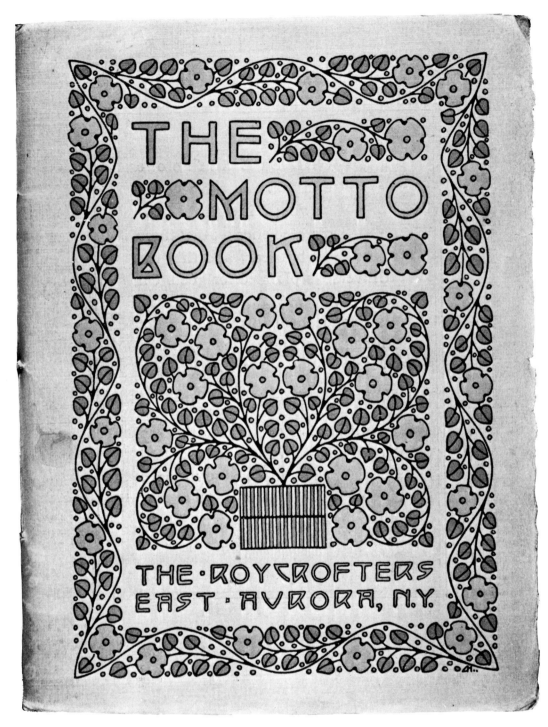

Plate 96. Elbert Hubbard (Fra Elbertus), *The Motto Book: Being a Catalogue of Epigrams.*
East Aurora: Roycrofters, 1909.

Other influences are visible. For example, Koch has pointed out a possible inspiration from Will Bradley in the title page for Emerson's *Nature* (1905). The text pages of *Nature*, with pictorial initials, also recall Bradley (Plate 98). That there was some direct Kelmscott inspiration as well in Hunter's work can be seen in *Love, Life and Work* (1906). The double title page is within outline vine borders, reminiscent of Morris (Plate 99). In this book the work is unsigned but, strangely enough, the same border is used in Victor Hugo's *Battle of Waterloo* (1907), this time for a single title page, and is signed "DH."

Hunter professed not to care for his own early work at East Aurora. "While the Roycroft Shop was a pleasant place for a young fellow to work, I do not now feel that I accomplished anything worth while there, and I probably would have gained a better knowledge of typography had I spent my tender years elsewhere."[20] But today his books seem genuine and charming products of American Art Nouveau. In 1910 Hunter went back to Europe to study graphic art in Vienna and work as a designer in London, where he made a pilgrimage to Hammersmith. On his return to America he set up his own papermill at Marlborough-on-Hudson, becoming at the time the only person in North America to be making handmade paper. He also designed his own typeface, cut the punches, struck the matrices, and cast the type. After doing his own composition and presswork, he turned out books that were truly one-man productions. Of this period

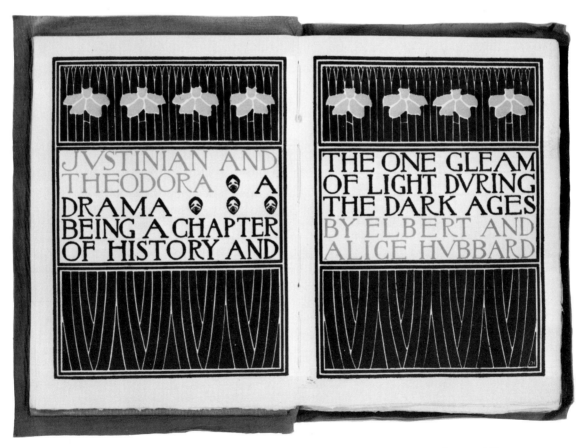

Plate 97. Elbert Hubbard and Alice Hubbard, *Justinian and Theodora: A Drama—Being a Chapter of History and the One Gleam of Light during the Dark Ages.* East Aurora: Roycrofters, 1906.

he wrote: "I was constantly under the influence of William Morris and his Kelmscott Press. . . ."[21]

That the Morrisian doctrine of handicraft was part of his thinking at the time can be documented from contemporary sources. He published a piece called "The Lost Art of Making Books" in 1915, which carries this doctrine to its logical conclusion.

In the private press books too many individuals are represented. . . . the book should be the work of one man alone. In this way, and only this, will the volume be truly his. There must be a better understanding between the three arts of paper-making, type-founding, and printing, and when this better understanding exists we will produce the much talked of, but seldom seen, book harmonious.[22]

A few years later, in an autobiographical account entitled "The Story of Dard Hunter," he wrote in equally strong words that if you must use a power press and print dry with machine-cast type, you have no right to use handmade paper. "All constituents should be either hand-made or machine-made; not a combination of the two."[23] Frank Weitenkampf's *The Etching of Contemporary Life* (1916), produced for the Chicago Society of Etchers, is an example of Hunter's one-man books. The laid paper has the Society's seal and "DH" within a heart as watermarks. The colophon states that the paper and type were made by him "in the manner" of the sixteenth century, and the decorations also look like the French Renaissance with floral motifs on stippled backgrounds. The old-style type is distinctive, and at the same time reminiscent of other private press types.

Besides making one-man books, Hunter became the world's leading authority on fine papermaking. His interest in bookmaking, originated in his father's newspaper office, stimulated by the sight of Kelmscott books, and developed in the Roycroft workshops, led him not only to study in Europe but to travel all over the world observing local methods of papermaking. It led also to a career that called forth such comments as Paul A. Bennett's: "Dard Hunter has accomplished more than any individual I know in the field of the graphic arts"; and Elmer Adler's: "The place that Dard Hunter occupies in the history of the book is unique."[24]

Hubbard had earlier employed other designers for a few books, such as Louis J. Rhead for the title page of the 1900 edition of Robert Louis Stevenson's *The Essay on Walt Whitman* (Plate 100). But after Hunter there were no more distinguished artists working on Roycroft books. Raymond Nott (who was at East Aurora as early as 1909, since his work appears in *The Motto Book* of that date) was a resident designer, but his work is neither original nor attractive. For example, Alice Hubbard's *The Myth in Marriage* (1912) has a red and black title page within borders, red headpieces, tailpieces, initials, and printer's device by Nott. There is much too much red in this little book and it shows through the paper. The colophon, which is now very matter-of-fact and without the humor of Hubbard's medievalistic language, gives A. V. Ingham the credit for the typography. He had been a printer for some twenty years in well-known houses and at Roycroft since about 1909,[25] but his work here is unimpressive. The best thing about the book is its modeled leather cover.

It is virtually certain that Hubbard himself paid much less attention to the printing in this period than he had earlier. Since the fantastic success of *A Message to Garcia* with the business community, Hubbard had increasingly forsaken his earlier Morrisian emphasis on the common man and become an apologist for big business. Roycroft itself was, of course, a big business, and much job printing had to be done to keep the presses and workmen busy. Hubbard himself was away a good part of the time on his lecture tours and still writing prolifically. Without a superior artist like Hunter, Roycroft books were bound to go into decline. Nor is it surprising that, after Hubbard's death in 1915, the books kept on declining. *Abe Lincoln and Nancy Hanks* (1920) by Hubbard, is still neatly printed in Caslon type on Roycroft paper, but the only design in evidence is an unprepossessing one stamped on the brown cloth cover. The two illustrations are equally unsuccessful. Altogether it is a colorless book that the elder Hubbard would hardly have tolerated. As one person said of him: "Hubbard was fond of bright colors and a page well filled with scrawly entwined vines or anything startling in its boldness. He always wanted plenty of typographic fireworks, and, if possible, some red illumination."[26]

As we have seen, some of the Roycroft books followed the Kelmscott style very closely (*Maud*), others followed it only in the wider sense of using antiquarian models (*Ye Ancient Mariner*), while others reflected contemporary art styles more than antique ones (*Justinian and Theodora*), but virtually all of them followed Morris in a general way, as implied by the essential Roycroft characteristics. Roycroft books consisted of handmade materials, even those composed and printed mechanically; they were bound in leather or paper boards, not cloth; they emphasized decoration, with the use of color, with fleurons, and with ornamented title pages, initials, and colophons; they were usually in an old-style typeface; and the text page layout usually had wide margins and the running title in the form of a shoulder note.

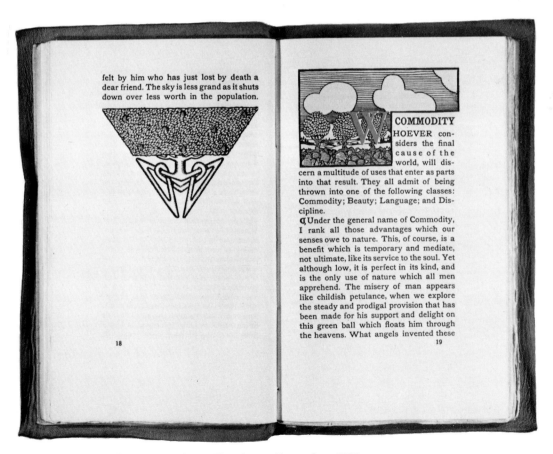

Plate 98. Ralph Waldo Emerson, *Nature*. East Aurora: Roycrofters, 1905.

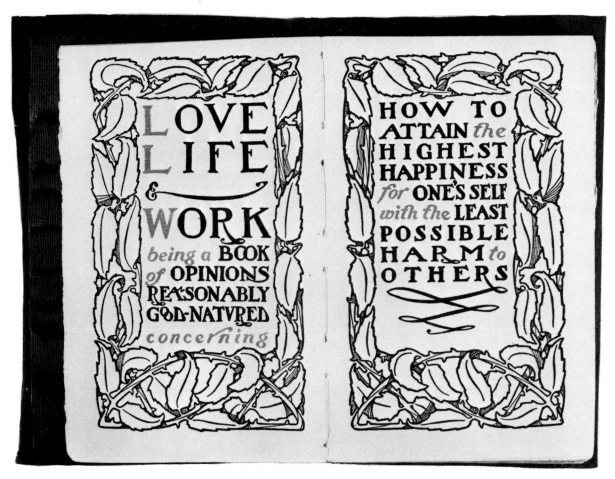

Plate 99. Elbert Hubbard, *Love, Life and Work*. East Aurora: Roycrofters, 1906.

Besides Hubbard's public declaration of himself as a follower of Morris, other proofs of his devotion are numerous. A room in the Roycroft Inn was named after Morris, and Hubbard sometimes read from his works in the evenings.[27] He published Morris' writings and wrote about Morris himself. The first *Little Journey* printed at Roycroft (January 1900) described his life and personality, albeit in a garbled fashion. References to Morris abounded in the pages of the *Philistine* and the *Fra* (which had a picture of him on its cover for November 1911). One such article brought a response from an English socialist that reveals both Hubbard's use of his imagination and the violent reaction it often provoked:

It is perhaps worth while calling attention here to an article by Elbert Hubbard, in the Philistine, December 1903. . . . Mr. Hubbard devotes many pages to a circumstantial account of the relations which existed between William Morris and Karl Marx, their intimate friendship, rivaling that of Damon and Pythias, ended by a bitter quarrel. Every word of that account is untrue. The two men never met and Morris never saw Marx in his life! . . . In all literature I know of nothing more scandalous than Hubbard's article.[28]

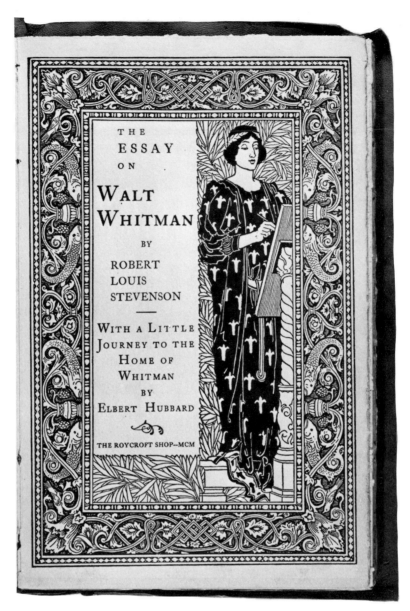

Plate 100. Robert Louis Stevenson, *The Essay on Walt Whitman.*
East Aurora: Roycrofters, 1900.

Hubbard's unique combination of medievalism and salesmanship is dramatically demonstrated in what amounts to a hand-rubricated advertisement in the form of a four-page circular printed by the Roycrofters. The folder is in red and black Bookman type on a quarter sheet of handmade wove paper, and is probably datable to the last years of the nineteenth century by the presence of Denslow's seahorse in the Roycroft device. There are various fleurons printed in black and a tailpiece in blue, while red and blue paragraph marks and flourished initials are inserted by hand. The text is *Fruit of the Roycroft* by Amy Leslie, famous drama critic of the Chicago *Daily News.* It says in part:

183

The first printed books were the best. . . . No books printed from type are equal in beauty and artistic excellence to the manuscript volumes made by the monks of the Middle Ages, and the first printed books were made in imitation of these. . . .

And now the Roycroft is following in the footsteps of the monks. It is printing such books as America has never before had leisure to make. . . .

. . . Books too beautiful to defile by price are put out from these presses, books too exquisite to read, books lovely to see.[29]

Despite his protestations about the value of handicraft, Hubbard found it necessary to compromise between the hand and the machine. As described in the *Philistine* for December 1914: "My first intent was to print entirely by hand. But gradually we got over the idea . . . [with] quantities that we never possibly could have turned out by hand."[30] This compromise between hand and machine is essentially the familiar battle between quality and quantity, art and money, idealism and business. That this is the core of the ambiguity in Hubbard's life and personality none of his biographers doubts. He made a lot of money in the soap business, left it for the "higher life," which included the Brotherhood of Man as well as Art, then wrote *A Message to Garcia*, became the Voice of Business, and made a lot more money. However, it seems that when World War I broke out, Hubbard felt big business was responsible and once more changed his views.[31]

Hubbard attempted to resolve this dichotomy between idealism and business in his writings describing the failures of cheap-book publishers.[32] When defending Kelmscott high prices, he was surely sincere in saying: "Cheap products make cheap men." And when listing five benefits received by society from a Morris book, he was intending a defense of Roycroft as well.[33]

While Roycroft prices, too, could be high (the 1912 catalogue offered *An American Bible*, "The finest of the Roycroft Modeled-Leather books," at $300 a copy), deluxe copies of the *Little Journeys* sold for a dollar apiece, "On hand-made paper, bound in limp chamois, silk lined, silk marker, hand-illumined."[34] Many, if not most, of the books sold for two dollars, unless in a special binding or on special paper. While this was not low for a small book at the turn of the century, it was not remarkably high, either. Carloads were delivered to the East Aurora station every day for transport all over the country.

Hubbard's main statement of idealism about books came in 1900 in his volume called *So Here Then Are the Preachments Entitled The City of Tagaste and A Dream and a Prophecy. The City of Tagaste* is a fable of a culture, now in ruins, that had closely resembled Hubbard's view of America. It is a serious fable, although the Hubbard humor is irrepressible:

And so books became so cheap that men utilized them to throw at the cat. Instead of spelling it missal—they spelled it missile.[35]

All the bookmaking processes have been mechanized:

And so in a factory where ten thousand books a day were made, there was neither a printer, an illustrator, an illuminator nor a binder. There were sad-eyed girls and yellow, haggard boys who stood all day & fed sheets into a machine, week after week, month after month, twelve hours a day, and they were paid just enough money to keep them from starvation.[36]

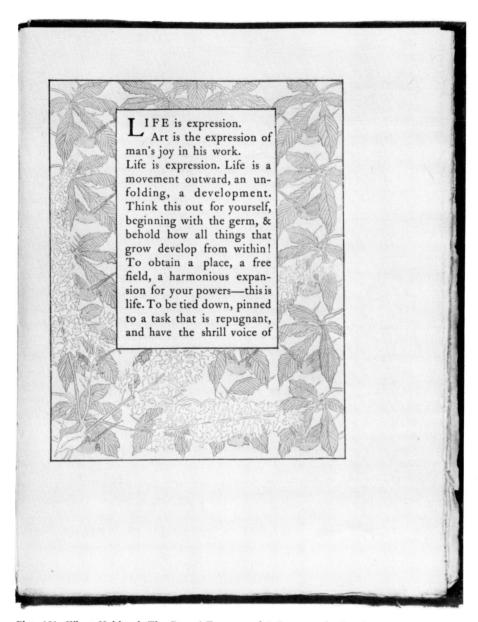

LIFE is expression.
Art is the expression of man's joy in his work.
Life is expression. Life is a movement outward, an unfolding, a development. Think this out for yourself, beginning with the germ, & behold how all things that grow develop from within! To obtain a place, a free field, a harmonious expansion for your powers—this is life. To be tied down, pinned to a task that is repugnant, and have the shrill voice of

Plate 101. Elbert Hubbard, *The City of Tagaste and A Dream and a Prophecy.*
East Aurora: Roycrofters, 1900.

Those who work with their heads rather than their hands have acquired all the wealth, managing in the process to pollute the environment and to devastate the forests to make their cheap books and print huge newspapers full of useless bad news. *A Dream and a Prophecy* is a positive rather than negative fable which seems to outline what the Roycrofters were trying to do: the return to nature and the simple life, the work with both hand and brain, the possession of few but beautiful objects, the return to the past for the best models. Even Hubbard's language is less bombastic and less colloquial than usual in these essays. The book itself is a beautifully produced volume, in Caslon

185

type on crisp white wove paper, in a quarto format, gray boards, half suede, with lovely floral borders, perhaps by Warner (Plate 101), since the device at the end of the book looks like his work. The volume seems like the high point of Hubbard's idealism, both in philosophy and in bookmaking.

Contemporary opinion of Hubbard tended to extremes, as it had of Morris. On the positive side, Hubbard could point to the tremendous sales of his books and claim that "from very crude attempts at decoration we have attained to a point where the British Museum and the 'Bibliotheke' at the Hague have deigned to order and pay good golden guineas for specimens of our handicraft."[37] The Roycroft catalogues carried Some Extracts from Letters from the Elect, in which many notables of the day praised the books, some formally, having obviously been given complimentary copies, and some enthusiastically, ordering copies for their friends. Felix Shay, the business manager of Roycroft, wrote that the books won "prizes and awards in international competitions at Paris, Berlin, Amsterdam and Antwerp!"[38] There was strong praise, rather early, in the press of the time. For example, "The Roycroft Printing Shop" in the *Printer and Bookmaker* opened with: "Although the average layman may know but little of the Roycroft Printing Shop, it is doubtful if many bibliomaniacs are unaware of its existence and the attractiveness of its productions."[39] The article went on to quote from Frank H. Severance in the Buffalo *Express*: "London has its Kelmscott Press, Birmingham its Baskerville, and Buffalo—has cause to claim with pride its Roycroft." There were even English admirers of Hubbard, such as Cedric Bonnell who made an address which was reprinted from the Nottingham *Daily Express* (February 12, 1904), as *An American William Morris*.[40]

On the other hand, there was a continuing flow of criticism of Roycroft right from the beginning. The very first book, *The Song of Songs*, was unfavorably reviewed in *Modern Art*. This review showed how Hubbard's salesmanship put the wrong taste in some people's mouths. Bowles referred to the extravagant claims made in the announcement circular and went on to criticize the book in detail, winding up with the statement: "Had it been called an effort toward an ideal, as all our work in this country must be for a long time yet, no one could have criticized it."[41] A review of the second Roycroft book, *The Journal of Koheleth: Being a Reprint of the Book of Ecclesiastes*, in the first issue of the *New York Times Book Review*, was strikingly similar. It alluded to Hubbard's advertising before going on to severe doubts about his workmanship.[42] The design can also be criticized (Plate 102). FitzRoy Carrington, a contemporary observer of the fine printing scene, wound up two articles on "Private and Special Presses" in the *Book Buyer* with doubts that it would be worthwhile to write about Roycroft:

> If you *must* buy such things, subscribe for "The Bilioustine," published by William S. Lord, of Evanston, Illinois. The *edition de luxe* is bound in burlap, and the publisher guarantees that every copy is baled and stencilled by hand. His announcement brings these notes to a close. Here it is: "To Lovers and Book Lovers. This edition of *The Bilioustine* is the swellest thing that the Boy Grafters have yet done; and that is saying a great deal. It has about it the delicate perfume of the Ideal, the elusive flavor of the Missal. . . . [43]

In the professional printing world, George French was an equally virulent opponent of Hubbard. He criticized his books in articles in the *American Printer*, in one of which he claimed that the Roycroft so-called limited editions were fraudulent, that as many as fifteen hundred copies might have been distributed when only a few hundred had been announced.[44]

But these are mild comments compared to the wrath of Carl P. Rollins, himself an admirer of Morris. The fury of his scorn has probably helped to create the almost complete contempt in which Roycroft books have been held in the middle third of the twentieth century. In his *Saturday Review of Literature* column, Rollins entitled a 1934 section "Footnote on Morris's Influence on American Printing and Printers":

> . . . Hubbard's printing was unbelievably bad: it was bad in itself, it was ludicrous as a copy of Kelmscott work. As a follower of the Arts and Crafts movement he was beneath contempt, both artistically and ethically. . . .
>
> And yet—fantastic as it may seem it is true that the great exploiter of Morris, his most busy introducer to the American people, was the mountebank of East Aurora![45]

There has been still a third strand of thought about Roycroft that is a compromise of pro and con. This school claims no merit for the books themselves but is impressed with the good Hubbard accomplished by interesting people in books. For example, the *Cranbrook Papers* had a piece by "Aurelius" that discussed Roycroft:

Plate 102. *The Journal of Koheleth: Being a Reprint of the Book of Ecclesiastes.*
East Aurora: Roycrofters, 1896.

Mr. Hubbard has borrowed not a little from the spirit of Morris, but much less from the substance. . . . [Yet] Americans owe much to Mr. Hubbard, for in a few short years, perhaps by choosing wisely and not aiming above the heads of the people, he has reached them the better and has cultivated in many thousands a keen interest in and a love for good books.[46]

Dard Hunter, whose own purism about having the whole book handmade may well have been formed in reaction to Roycroft, kept a steady middle-ground estimate of Hubbard, of whom he was personally fond. In his autobiography Hunter summed up his feelings:

Even though the books produced at the Roycroft Shop were bizarre and lacked taste and refinement, they were, nevertheless, a step in the right direction. These books were better made than most of the work done in this country at the time, and people who had never before thought of collecting books began assembling the Roycroft issues. Mr. Hubbard probably had more influence in the development of book-collecting than any other person of his generation.[47]

Nonetheless, the negative point of view is still very much with us: ". . . poorly printed on rough, heavy paper, using ugly types with the nastiest of art nouveau decoration, and bound in . . . cheap soft suede. . . ."[48]

It is time for serious critics to reappraise Hubbard's books. The Roycroft paper was heavy and rough only in the way all handmade laid papers are; the types were mostly Bookman and Caslon, the former one of the most widely used fonts at the turn of the century, the latter one of the all-time great faces, going back to the eighteenth century. The borders were indeed Art Nouveau, made by designers who became famous graphic artists. The bindings were indeed of cheap leather (at one and two dollars a copy), but fine leather bindings were available. Some of the books were pretentious; many were not. Hubbard's taste was often flamboyant, but many of his books are nevertheless attractive. The only recent thoroughgoing supporter of Roycroft has been Robert Koch. Strangely enough, even he seems unaware that Hubbard was and is controversial, although he knows more about the books than anyone else. "By 1900 it was generally agreed that the most beautiful books ever produced in the United States were being turned out at East Aurora."[49]

The ambivalent mood seems, on the whole, still prevalent, as in Champney's excellent book or in an *American Heritage* article by Robert L. Beisner, which takes the point of view that Hubbard was a faker but also had a good side.[50] Hubbard did certainly have the saving grace of humor that allowed him to laugh at himself as well as at the world. An example is the *Essay on Silence* by Fra Elbertus, a small book bound in brown chamois with matching silk doublures, and crisp, white, absolutely blank pages. A leaf is folded inside, purporting to be a review by George Whopper James in the *Graftsman*:

This essay is bound to stimulate thought and meditation. . . . Open it anywhere and it is equally interesting. It is one of the best things the Fra has done, and so different from some of his other writings in that it is wholly unobjectionable.

Whatever one's judgment of Hubbard, his volumes were the most widespread American Arts and Crafts books. They lay on the parlor tables of innumerable middle-class homes, and young people dreamed of making fine volumes themselves.

1. E.g., David Arnold Balch, *Elbert Hubbard: Genius of Roycroft* (New York: Stokes, 1940), pp. 70–71; Freeman Champney, *Art & Glory: The Story of Elbert Hubbard* (New York: Crown, 1968), pp. 30–31.
2. Quoted in Felix Shay, *Elbert Hubbard of East Aurora* (New York: Wm. H. Wise, 1926), p. 29.
3. H. Kenneth Dirlam and Ernest E. Simmons, *Sinners, This Is East Aurora* (New York: Vantage, 1964), pp. 15–16.
4. "An Interesting Personality: Elbert Hubbard," *Cosmopolitan*, XXXII (January 1902): 309–320.
5. Champney, *Art & Glory*, pp. 58–60.
6. Elbert Hubbard, "A Social and Industrial Experiment" (reprint of the *Cosmopolitan* article), in *The Roycroft Books: A Catalog and Some Remarks* (East Aurora: Roycrofters, 1902), p. 17.
7. Dard Hunter, "Elbert Hubbard and 'A Message to Garcia,'" *New Colophon*, I (January 1948): 29.
8. Robert Koch, "Elbert Hubbard's Roycrofters as Artist-Craftsmen," *Winterthur Portfolio*, III (1967): 69.
9. Ibid., p. 71.
10. *A List of Books Made during the Year 1899* (East Aurora: Roycrofters, 1899), p. 5.
11. A 1900 reprint of *A Message to Garcia*, undertaken as a New Year's greeting for the H. R. Barker Manufacturing Company, illustrates Roycroft utilization of material. The cover is the butcher paper, familiar from *Philistines* and *Little Journeys*, the title page has one of Warner's Kelmscott-style borders, while the text opens with Denslow's initial for the beginning of the *Ancient Mariner*, again hand colored. Each page is put within rules, with a side panel. Someone, probably Hubbard, has written marginal comments on the text to be printed in red within these panels.
12. Dard Hunter, *My Life with Paper* (New York: Knopf, 1958), p. 28.
13. Ibid. p. 35.
14. Ibid.
15. Ibid., p. 36.
16. Lloyd Emerson Siberell, "Chillicothe's Dard Hunter," *Book Collector's Packet*, II (July 1938): 2.
17. Koch, "Elbert Hubbard's Roycrofters," p. 80.
18. Hunter, *My Life with Paper*, p. 47.
19. Koch, loc. cit.
20. Dard Hunter, "Peregrinations & Prospects," *Colophon*, Part VII (September 1931): 4–5.
21. Hunter, *My Life with Paper*, p. 66.
22. Dard Hunter, "The Lost Art of Making Books," *Miscellany*, II (1915): 3–6.
23. Dard Hunter, "The Story of Dard Hunter," *Ben Franklin Monthly*, XXI (March 1923): 26.
24. Both quoted on the dust jacket of *My Life with Paper*.
25. "The Roycrofters of East Aurora," *American Bulletin*, N.S., No. 4 (August 1910): 1.
26. Lois C. Levison, "A Maker of Books," *Quarto Club Papers*, II (1927–28): 12.
27. Hubbard, "A Social and Industrial Experiment," p. 21.
28. John Spargo, *The Socialism of William Morris* (Westwood, Mass.: Ariel Press, [1906?]), p. 20 Note.
29. Amy Leslie, *Fruit of the Roycroft* (East Aurora: Roycrofters, n.d.), unpaged.
30. Quoted in Champney, *Art & Glory*, p. 120.
31. Champney, *Art & Glory*, pp. 193–194.
32. Hubbard, "A Social and Industrial Experiment," pp. 20–25.
33. Elbert Hubbard, *Little Journeys to the Homes of English Authors: William Morris* (East Aurora: Roycrofters, 1900), p. 13.
34. From an advertisement on the wrapper of the Patrick Henry *Little Journey*, 1903.
35. Elbert Hubbard, *So Here Then are the Preachments Entitled The City of Tagaste and A Dream and a Prophecy* (East Aurora: Roycrofters, 1900), p. 2.
36. Hubbard, *The City of Tagaste and A Dream and a Prophecy*, p. 3.
37. Hubbard, "A Social and Industrial Experiment," p. 19.
38. Shay, *Elbert Hubbard*, p. 174.
39. "The Roycroft Printing Shop," *Printer and Bookmaker*, XXV (November 1897): 152.
40. Cedric Bonnell, *An American William Morris and the Romance of the "Roycrofters"* (Nottingham: N.S.O.V. [Nottingham Sette of Odd Volumes?], Opuscula, XVII, 1904).
41. [Joseph M. Bowles] "Echoes," *Modern Art*, IV (April 1, 1896), n.p.
42. "Finely Printed Bible Books," *New York Times Book Review*, I (October 10, 1896): 2.
43. FitzRoy Carrington, "Private and Special Presses," *Book Buyer*, XXIII (1901): 218.
44. George French, "The Pro and Con of Roycroftie," *American Printer*, XXXIV (April 1902): 121–122.
45. Carl Purington Rollins, "The Compleat Collector," *Saturday Review of Literature*, XI (September 29, 1934): 151.
46. "Aurelius" in *Cranbrook Papers* (Detroit: Cranbrook Press, 1901), p. 25.
47. Hunter, *My Life with Paper*, p. 43.
48. Roderick Cave, *The Private Press* (London: Faber and Faber, 1971), p. 155.
49. Koch, "Elbert Hubbard's Roycrofters," p. 71.
50. Robert L. Beisner, " 'Commune' in East Aurora," *American Heritage*, XXII (February 1971): 72–77, 106–109.

XIX

Thomas Bird Mosher:
The Aesthetic Pirate

ANOTHER publisher whose name is often linked with Morris is Thomas Bird Mosher. Like Elbert Hubbard, he produced a large number of books—approximately four hundred titles—and is often said to have influenced the course of American bookmaking. Unlike Hubbard, Mosher's essential style did not resemble that of Morris. But Mosher and Morris were both products of the general urge toward beautiful books so evident in the eighties. Indeed, they both began publishing in the same year (1891) so that it is not sure that Mosher had seen a Morris book before at least the planning of his own, which was announced in the December 19, 1891, *Publishers Weekly*. His first book was in the general style of his later ones. This first title was George Meredith's *Modern Love*, in 400 ordinary copies and 50 large paper. The vellum cover has an asymmetric layout, but the black and red title page is in block arrangement. There is a resemblance to the Bodley Head titles coming out in London in the Aesthetic style. Mosher's choice of this simpler style is not surprising. He was as passionately interested in literature as Morris but was not himself a designer or creative artist. He did not have the innate drive toward pattern that Morris had. Moreover, he was concerned with keeping his books at a low price: "To more widely extend the love of exquisite literary form, it must be shown by example that choice typography and inexpensiveness need not lie far apart."[1]

Mosher was born in Biddeford, Maine in 1852, the son of a sea captain with whom he traveled between 1866 and 1870. His father made him leave his dime novels at home and read only good literature while at sea, to which Mosher later attributed his love for literary excellence. After his travels, Mosher had to earn a living rather than go on to formal schooling. Just before turning forty, he decided to try his hand at doing what he really desired to do: publish the books he loved.

He was not a printer himself, but he did supervise the printing closely. Miss Flora M. Lamb, his long-time secretary, wrote in a letter to Norman H. Strouse in 1937:

> Mr. Mosher chose his own type faces and arrangements, quality of paper and format. He asked no help from anyone on this. He also owned all the decorations

in the way of head bands and tail pieces, etc. Furnishing them for the printer together with all fancy initials, letters and designs. The designs for book-covers, catalogues, etc., were drawn by different artists. . . .[2]

There were three firms of printers employed by Mosher: the Brown Thurston Company for the three volumes of the English Reprint series, Smith & Sale for most of the others, and George D. Loring for most of the Brocade series and an occasional one in another series, such as Fiona Macleod's [i.e., William Sharp] *Deirdrê and the Sons of Usna* (Plate 103), second edition (1909), in the Old World series. Mosher's concern with format can be seen from an unpublished letter:

> I shall then possibly issue another short series of cheaper books—booklets in size—but *not* the ordinary sort of *inside* that booklets, so far, seem to possess. I have seen some recent revived specimens of typography that I believe can be applied to advantage.[3]

And his pride in his materials can be seen in still another letter comparing the paper his *Bibelot* was printed on to that of Stone & Kimball's *Chap-Book:*

> It is a paper that costs me as much if not more than theirs: and I far prefer mine to any machine made, wood-pulp imitation of a genuine deckle-edge hand made rag paper such as they use!
> Nor do I like their [sic] color of it, or the finish; and as to *their* press work as compared with mine, why if they really *do* think theirs is the best, I'm sorry for such amazing lack of knowledge![4]

The Mosher series, fourteen in all, plus the long-running periodical, the *Bibelot* (1895–1914), and the carefully designed catalogues, give a superficial impression of variety. They range widely in size from the large Quarto series, only nine in number (or the large paper copies from other series), to the tiny Vest Pocket series. Most of them were available, not only on differing papers (usually Van Gelder and Japan vellum), but also in different bindings. The Brocade series books were issued in flowered slipcases that recall their name. Decoration is used sparingly but sometimes with great effect, as on the cover and title page of *Fancy's Following* by Anodos [i.e., Mary Elizabeth Coleridge] (1900). Art Nouveau poppies in red with green stems and leaves are equally striking on the blue wrappers and on the white title page.

But this variation does not hide a profound stylistic similarity pervading the Mosher books, despite Mosher's belief in his own originality:

> Mosher once boasted to a correspondent, by way of explaining the charm of his book, "that I have had the wit to think out new formats," and again he said, "there is something of my own in these editions which makes the Mosher Books sell.[5]

Typography critics have been too prone to accept this evaluation, even some of those who do not like the Mosher books. Actually, Mosher was almost totally unoriginal: except for the few Art Nouveau touches provided by hired artists, his books are almost completely in the Aesthetic tradition, which goes back through the Chiswick Press, to

191

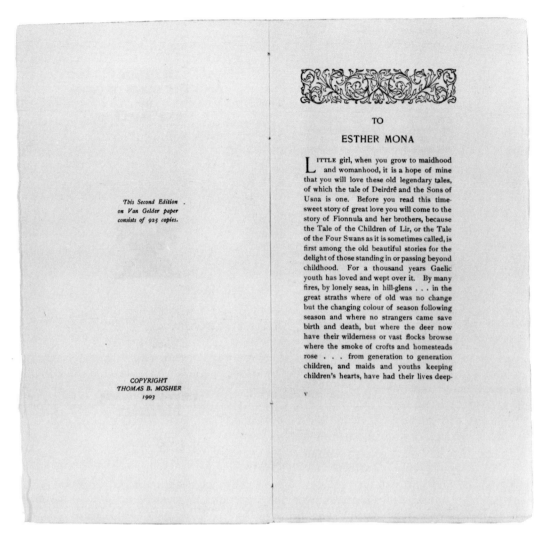

TO

ESTHER MONA

Little girl, when you grow to maidhood and womanhood, it is a hope of mine that you will love these old legendary tales, of which the tale of Deirdrê and the Sons of Usna is one. Before you read this time-sweet story of great love you will come to the story of Fionnula and her brothers, because the Tale of the Children of Lir, or the Tale of the Four Swans as it is sometimes called, is first among the old beautiful stories for the delight of those standing in or passing beyond childhood. For a thousand years Gaelic youth has loved and wept over it. By many fires, by lonely seas, in hill-glens . . . in the great straths where of old was no change but the changing colour of season following season and where no strangers came save birth and death, but where the deer now have their wilderness or vast flocks browse where the smoke of crofts and homesteads rose . . . from generation to generation children, and maids and youths keeping children's hearts, have had their lives deep-

v

Plate 103. William Sharp (Fiona Macleod), *Deirdrê and the Sons of Usna*. Portland: Mosher, 1909.

which Mosher admitted his debt, to the French Renaissance. The determining characteristics of the Mosher style are small format, handmade paper, small old-style type, both roman and italic, board or vellum bindings, little ornament and that usually Renaissance in motif, no illustration, simple title pages. As Will Ransom said in later years, speaking of the turn of the century:

> In typography and format the Mosher books justly may be called both sane and charming. With almost the restraint of Cobden-Sanderson, Mr. Mosher used very little decoration. Even color appears very seldom. And that choice took strength of character and a certain conviction in those days when typography was running pretty wildly to decorative and colorful, even weird, effects.[6]

In fact, the overall monotony of this chaste simplicity is relatively unrelieved by

Plate 104. J. M. Barrie,
George Meredith: A Tribute.
Portland: Mosher, 1909.

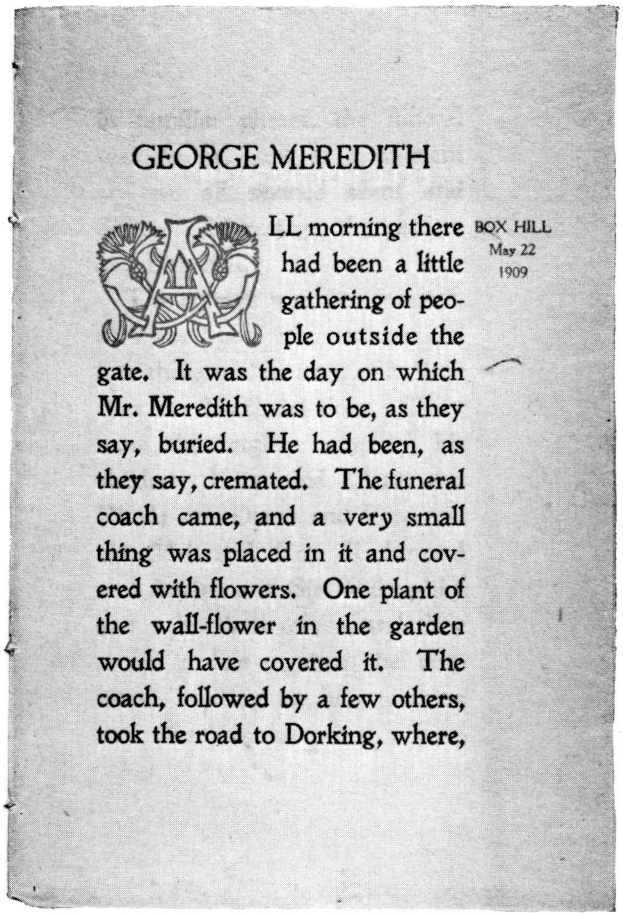

GEORGE MEREDITH

A LL morning there
had been a little
gathering of peo-
ple outside the
gate. It was the day on which
Mr. Meredith was to be, as they
say, buried. He had been, as
they say, cremated. The funeral
coach came, and a very small
thing was placed in it and covered with flowers. One plant of
the wall-flower in the garden
would have covered it. The
coach, followed by a few others,
took the road to Dorking, where,

BOX HILL
May 22
1909

the variety alluded to previously, although the difference between two reticent touches of decoration or the points of variance among the series can become fascinating to the connoisseur. The common ground many of Mosher's admirers share is precisely their wide acquaintance with Mosher books. They know them so well that they take the sameness for granted. Their other common point is their emphasis on the low price of the books. Virtually everyone agrees that Mosher spread through the English-speaking world the knowledge of good literature, in volumes that sold well because they looked like gift books but cost little.

Mosher has always been known as a literary "pirate," for helping himself to other people's work without their permission, although he then sent them voluntary royalty checks. Whether the possibly small size of these checks had anything to do with the small prices charged by Mosher has not been determined. One of his letters reveals his tactics:

Alas, dear Mr. Stedman, my "Aucassin and Nicolete" is very nigh all in type. 'Tis too late to ask Mr. [Andrew] Lang, except in the way of, if he will or will not accept five guineas, and that I fear he'd decline *after* the steal. I've had one experience with asking permission that sort of sickened me of anything except taking the high seas and becoming a Paul Jones of letters.[7]

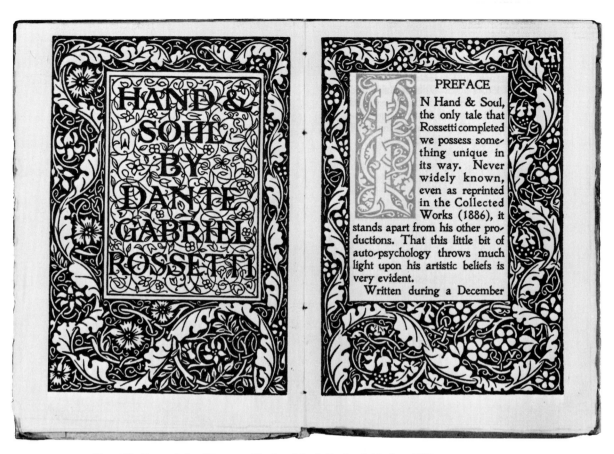

Plate 105. Dante Gabriel Rossetti, *Hand and Soul*. Portland: Mosher, 1899.

Of those two eccentric men, Hubbard and Mosher, selling books on a large scale from East Aurora and Portland, one from 1895 to 1915, the other from 1891 to 1923 (both establishments continued after their founders' deaths but not on the same scale of production or popularity), each chose instinctively one of the two major styles of format then in vogue and continued using it consistently. Both styles were brought into American homes which had rarely, if ever, before received such carefully unified books.

The fact that Mosher found the Aesthetic style more congenial than the Arts and Crafts does not mean at all that he was unaware of the latter or unappreciative of Morris. On the contrary, he was virtually a disciple of Morris, who was one of the major names on Mosher's list. The Hatch bibliography reveals nineteen titles by Morris (one with Pater as co-author), some of them in more than one edition, plus five translations by him and two items about him in the *Biblelot*.[8] It has even been said that Mosher's publishing advanced Morris' American reputation,[9] although this is dubious since Roberts Brothers had been issuing his books from the sixties, while Mosher's publication of Morris coincided with the even greater fame of the Kelmscott Press.

There were seven Kelmscott Press books in Mosher's personal library,[10] and Jenson type formed part of his repertory, as in the cover titles for the Brocade series. One of the Morris translations in this series, *The Tale of King Florus and the Fair Jehane* (1898), has a spine title in Jenson caps and a block arrangement of the same on the front, in-

194

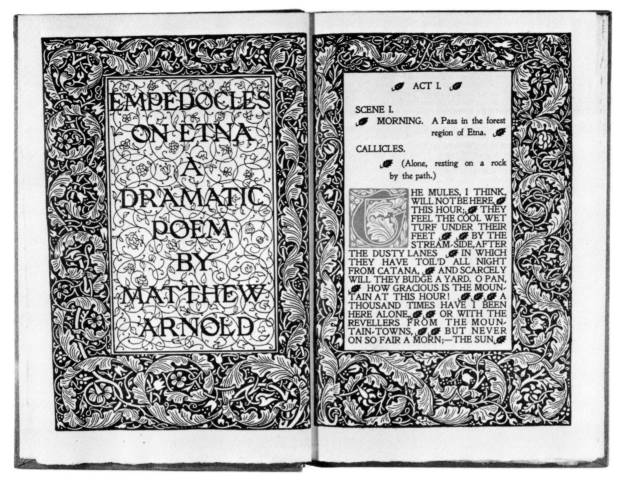

Plate 106. Matthew Arnold, *Empedocles on Etna: A Dramatic Poem.* Portland: Mosher, 1900.

cluding a red floral initial and a fleuron line filler. Jenson was also used for colophons in some of the Old World series, such as the 1895 *Rubaiyat* and *Aucassin and Nicolete.* Mosher did not usually use Jenson as a text face but he did at least once. *George Meredith: A Tribute by J. M. Barrie* is a small, unpaged pamphlet printed in 1919 on Kisogawa handmade paper in 950 copies. The type is Jenson and there are further Arts and Crafts touches in the pierced red "bloomers," or floral initials, opening the foreword and text, and in the red shoulder note accompanying the text opening (Plate 104).

Two Mosher items are total imitations of Morris. Rossetti's *Hand and Soul* (Plate 105) (the title published jointly by Morris and Irving Way) (1899), was the seventh in the Miscellaneous series. Mosher's *A List of Books* justified its publication:

The Kelmscott Press edition having passed out of print (copies now selling at four guineas in London), and a more recent reprint from the Vale press proving in many ways decidedly unsatisfying, Mr. Mosher offers an edition of his own in format based upon that of the Morris volume, but at a price within reach of the American book-lover.

The edition is as follows: 450 copies on genuine Kelmscott Press hand-made paper, with four Morris borders, text printed in red and black, done up in old-style blue boards, white labels and in slide case.[11]

These copies were priced at $1.50 and 100 copies on Japan vellum at $2.50, an excellent buy given the quality of the reproduction. Strouse quotes an interesting letter of Mosher's, dated February 13, 1900:

I was very glad indeed to send you a copy of *Hand and Soul*, and would say in regard to its being a facsimile of the Kelmscott edition that it is as nearly so as possible to make it. The only changes are in printing the big initials in red. . . .

Mr. Irving Way who brought out the Morris edition in this country recently wrote me desiring to know how I succeeded in getting so close a duplicate. It was done by using our best efforts on the press work and by procuring special inks, which I think on comparison fully come up to the Morris ink.

One thing we did which Morris did not and that is dry-press the sheets. This means that after the book is printed it is put in between sheets of paste board and the impression of the types taken out. Morris believed this was not the right thing to do, but all American printers are dead against him and I think justly so.[12]

Number XIII in the Miscellaneous series was the 1900 printing of Matthew Arnold's *Empedocles on Etna* (Plate 106), described by Mosher in this fashion:

Had William Morris lived one can scarcely doubt that he would have given us a reprint of Empedocles worthy of the theme and himself.

It is with this view in mind that Mr. Mosher offers at a price within reasonable limits, an example of Kelmscott Press work for which one of the choicest—*Coleridge's Poems*—has been drawn upon for borders, initials, and format.

The edition is as follows: 450 copies on genuine Kelmscott Press hand-made paper, with Morris borders and initials, printed in Golden text, done up in old-style boards, white labels and in slide case.[13]

This time the price was $2.50, with fifty copies on Japan vellum at $5.00. Again the initials are in red (once done at Kelmscott for Blunt's *Love Lyrics* and then abandoned), but the effect, as for *Hand and Soul*, is remarkably close to Morris (and to Ricketts).

The line Mosher took on his own may be illustrated by the preceding volume in the Miscellaneous series: Morris' *Child Christopher and Goldilind the Fair* (1900). It is a rather large book in blue boards on Van Gelder paper. The red and black title page is centered within rules, with Mosher's device in the middle and a Renaissance headband on a stippled background. There is a large red initial at the text opening and other Renaissance head and tailpieces. Each page is within rules with a running title at the head and shoulder notes on the sides. Like so many of the Mosher books, it is not unattractive but seems cool and antiseptic.

Carl Weber said that Kelmscott influence exists in the first volume of the Miscellaneous series, A. E.'s *Homeward Songs by the Way* (1895),[14] but it is now difficult to see. The rather crudely done decorations have Renaissance motifs and are closer to Aesthetic book design than Arts and Crafts. Their fame comes from the fact that they are the first book decorations done by Bruce Rogers for an eastern publisher. It is true that at about this time he was producing Arts and Crafts work for *Modern Art*, but, in working for Mosher, he seems to have tried to approximate Mosher's usual style.

There have been many favorable comments on Mosher's influence but few have gone as far as the famous book collector A. E. Newton in 1928. Eventually "every printer and publisher in the country copied more or less his [Mosher's] style." "Morris has his disciples—Rudge, Rogers, Nash, Updike, Goudy—but no less a debt is owed Mosher by those who may be called commercial publishers, and it is these who disseminate the taste of the nation; indeed, it seems to me our printers owe as much to Mosher as to Morris."[15] This is another way of saying that trade publishing has followed the Aesthetic line.

The Hubbard-Mosher parallel extends to their reputations. Idolized by a section of the population for several years after their deaths (albeit different sections), each one eventually suffered a loss of respect and fame, now perhaps to be restored under the aegis of ardent collectors, notably Robert Koch for Hubbard and Norman Strouse for Mosher. Good taste becomes perhaps less necessary with the distance of time, so that Hubbard's extravagance now looks charming and Mosher's restraint a trifle chilly. The clean, pure silhouettes of the latter's books are, nevertheless, an antidote to all those limp suede bindings of Hubbard's. And we can marvel that at the turn of the century the two American individualistic publishers with the widest audiences reflected so neatly the dichotomy in the art of the book at the time.

1. Thomas Bird Mosher, "Introduction," *Bibelot*, I (January 1895), unpaged.

2. Quoted in Norman H. Strouse, *The Passionate Pirate* (North Hills, Pa.: Bird and Bull Press, 1964), p. 63.

3. Letter, Thomas Bird Mosher to Edmund Clarence Stedman, April 13, 1893, Stedman Manuscripts Collection, Columbia University Libraries.

4. Letter, Thomas Bird Mosher to Edmund Clarence Stedman, April 22, 1895, Stedman Manuscripts Collection, Columbia University Libraries.

5. Ray Nash, "Biographical Essay," in Benton Hatch, *A Check List of the Publications of Thomas Bird Mosher of Portland Maine 1891-1923* (Northampton, Mass.: Printed at the Gehenna Press for the University of Massachusetts Press, 1966), p. 24.

6. Will Ransom, "In the Tradition," quoted from *Publishers Weekly*, March 24, 1928, in *The Mosher Books* (Portland: Mosher, 1928), p. 3.

7. Letter, Thomas Bird Mosher to Edmund Clarence Stedman, September 17, 1895, Stedman Manuscripts Collection, Columbia University Libraries.

8. Hatch, *A Check List of the Publications of Thomas Bird Mosher*.

9. Max Putzel, *The Man in the Mirror: William Marion Reedy and His Magazine* (Cambridge: Harvard University Press, 1963), p. 61.

10. Note by Editor [Carl Weber] to Edward F. Stevens, "The Kelmscott Influence in Maine," *Colby Library Quarterly*, Series I, VI (March 1944): 92.

11. *A List of Books* (Portland: Mosher, 1901), unpaged. This same catalogue, in addition to the slighting remark about the Vale Press quoted above, speaks of the "trifling prettiness" of the Vale *Blessed Damozel*. But Mosher also admired Ricketts, as shown by the flattery of imitation: the 1898 reprint of the *Germ* has a honeysuckle border on its wrapper from the Vale *Suckling* and the 1899 *Wine Women and Song* has a violet border on its wrapper from the Vale *Campion*, which was used on other Mosher books. The cover of Mosher's 1906 catalogue copies Ricketts' binding design for John Gray's *Silverpoints* (1893). Ricketts said in *A Defence of the Revival of Printing* (1899), that *Silverpoints'* tall, thin shape, which found many imitators, was based upon Aldine models, in turn probably based upon Persian saddle-books. Mosher claimed an Aldine format for his Bibelot series books, which are also tall and thin and which also began to come out in 1893. Is this a case of borrowing or of independent inspiration? At least we know that Mosher was familiar with *Silverpoints* by 1906.

12. Strouse, *The Passionate Pirate*, pp. 64-65.

13. *A List of Books* (Portland: Mosher, 1901), unpaged.

14. Note by Editor [Carl Weber] to Stevens, "The Kelmscott Influence in Maine," p. 93.

15. A. Edward Newton, "The Book Itself," quoted from *This Book Collecting Game*, 1928, in *The Mosher Books* (Portland: Mosher, 1929), pp. 3-4.

XX

Presses in the Rest of the Country

WHILE Mosher and Hubbard are the best known and most prolific of turn-of-the-century publishers outside of Boston, New York, and Chicago, others were influenced by Morris, such as the Golden Press in Los Angeles, which advertised, in the 1908 *Bibelot*, Luke North's *Rubaiyat of Cheerfulness*, in five hundred copies at two dollars.

> Printed from hand-set Caslon type, pages decorated with special grape-vine designs, on heavy India-tint antique paper, rough edges, limp leather binding, full ooze sheep, beautifully decorated, lined with pongee silk—a book that we are not afraid to compare with the best of the Mosher or Roycroft volumes sold at the same price, yet entirely distinctive & characteristic.[1]

In commercial printing, two other major American cities are important: Philadelphia, which had been an early center of American bookmaking, and San Francisco, the book center of the western coast. In Philadelphia, the Jenson Press and the Butterfly Press were part of the Printing Revival: semiprivate presses run by printing idealists, available for commercial hire but also producers of bookplates, posters, hand-illuminated books, little magazines, and occasionally titles of their own. In San Francisco, John Henry Nash stands out as an eminently successful commercial printer known for the superb quality of his work, the design of which followed the Doves Press mode of the later Revival.

Between these eastern and western centers, private presses sprang up over the nation in the late nineties and early twentieth century under the inspiration of the Kelmscott Press, although it should be borne in mind that there were numerous other private presses founded in the United States during this period without a style close to Morris. In a general sense they are part of the Revival since they demonstrate an interest in fine printing, but they do not show Kelmscott stylistic influence. Such presses, which seem to have clustered in the Northeast, include Frederick C. Bursch's two offices in Greenwich, Connecticut; Lewis Buddy's Kirgate Press in Canton, Pennsylvania; Hervey White's Maverick Press in Woodstock, New York; the Queen's Shop in Brookline, Massachusetts; the

Dana brothers' Elm Tree Press in Woodstock, Vermont; the Flower brothers' Solitarian Press in Hartland, Vermont; and others. Still another press roamed over both the South and West—Frank Holme's Bandar Log Press. Holme was a newspaper artist from Chicago who became ill with tuberculosis and moved to warmer climates in search of better health. The books he produced were not physically modeled on Kelmscott work, but their creator was aware of the Arts and Crafts atmosphere of his time. Here is a burlesque colophon:

This rare and limited edition was done into type and the refined and elegant illustrations were done into wood cuts on best grade North Carolina yaller poplar lumber with an IXL jackknife (two blades), and the whole business was done into its present shape in the month of December, A.D. 1901, by F. Holme, who at that time had nothing else to do, and the whole job was done in Asheville, North Carolina, and at [printer's mark] The Bandar Log Press. But 174 copies have been printed, after which the types were put back where they belonged and the refined and elegant wood blocks were done into kindling wood in an endeavor to counteract the balmy climate of the Sunny South.[2]

Among private presses influenced by Morris, Philip V. O. Van Vechten and William H. Ellis, who ran a newspaper and job printing office in Wausau, Wisconsin, turned to private work in the period from 1896 to 1904. They published books under the imprint of the Philosopher Press at the Sign of the Green Pine Tree, for which Helen Bruneau Van Vechten often did the presswork. Feeling themselves in the Arts and Crafts mainstream, they advertised some of their books—Rossetti's *Jenney*, Stevenson's *A Lodging for the Night*, Emerson's *Self-Reliance*—as having Kelmscott initials. In fact, their books range the gamut from absolutely plain, characterless typography to total Kelmscott imitation, as shown in the following descriptions.

Neal Brown's *Critical Confessions* (1899) is an undecorated, undistinguished book in transitional type, with a centered title page and running titles in italic capitals. Tennyson's *Elaine* (1900) has outline, uncolored decorations by Agnes Bassett that are geometrical in form, often with interlacing that is vaguely Celtic. The type is the irregularly edged old style called Fifteenth Century or Caslon Antique. A similar, lightly decorated book is *Fifty Rubaiyat of Omar Khayyam Paraphrased from Literal Translations by Richard Le Gallienne* (1901) printed for James Carleton Young of Minneapolis. Kelmscott initials are used for each quatrain; otherwise the book is not Morrisian. The type is widely leaded Schoeffer Oldstyle on laid paper. In a restrained Arts and Crafts style, Elia W. Peattie's *The Love of a Caliban: A Romantic Opera in One Act* (1898) has gold-printed white paper boards. Three hundred copies were printed on handmade paper, with decorations by P. V. O. Van Vechten and Gardner C. Teall. The title page is in Fifteenth Century type with the title and imprint paragraphs set flush left. Touches of red include an initial for the Note. The shoulder note running titles are in Gothic type. There are black floriate initials in the text. Emerson's *Self-Reliance* (1901) is totally Kelmscott. In blue boards, half vellum, it was issued in 370 copies on laid paper with Venetian type. The double spread at the beginning has the title on the verso in roman caps on an arabesque background within a Kelmscott border. The facing recto for the text opening has a matching border, a Kelmscott initial, the title in red caps, and fleuron line fillers. There are many Kelmscott initials throughout.

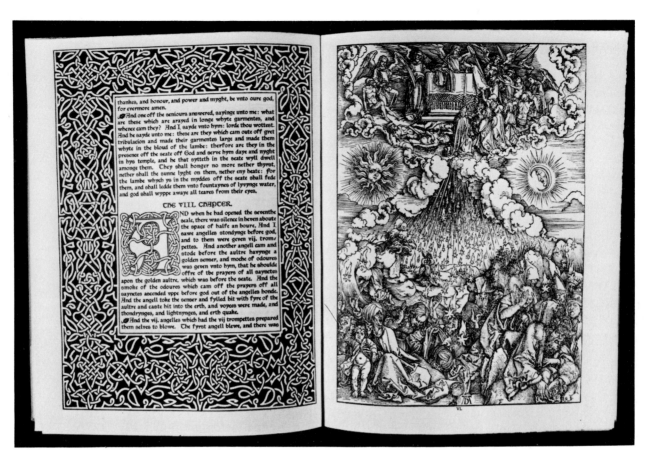

Plate 107. *The Revelation of St. John the Divine.* Detroit: Cranbrook Press, 1901.

The Philosopher Press made itself known nationwide for the excellence of its press-work; in Michigan we find a similar press run on an elaborate scale. At the turn of the century George G. Booth set up a private press in Detroit directly inspired by Kelmscott and Roycroft. His father-in-law was James E. Scripps, publisher of the Detroit *Evening News* on which Booth himself was employed, but the smell of ink and the noise of presses were not enough to hide the dearth of culture in the mid-western city. According to Paul McPharlin, author of a thorough article on the subject,[3] Booth was familiar with Morris' work and wished to follow in his footsteps. After a visit to East Aurora where he was disappointed to see power printing, he began to set up his own hand printing establishment, sparing no pains or money to make it look like a Flemish Renaissance printing office, with furniture of carved black oak.[4] The press was named after the town of Kent from which Booth's forebears had come, Cranbrook. A periodical called *Cranbrook Papers* was founded at the same time, with decorations by Booth and pseudonymous contributions from his

200

friends. Booth also did the book decorations but needed workmen to aid him in the actual printing. He found with difficulty a hand compositor, took over one of the newspaper employees for a part-time pressman, and later hired a Viennese bookbinder. In the Roycroft manner, local female talent was employed for watercoloring the decorations.

Handmade paper was brought in from the L. L. Brown Company of Massachusetts, ink from New York, and a handpress from Chicago. A good stock of Jenson and Satanick type was purchased from American Type Founders. The books issued with these materials during the two years of Cranbrook's life were a biography of Lincoln, Caxton's *The Dictes and Sayings of the Philosophers*, *The Revelation of St. John the Divine* with Durer's illustrations, *Three Wise Men* (writings of Marcus Aurelius, Francis Bacon, and Benjamin Franklin), More's *Utopia*, the bound volume of the ten numbers of the *Cranbrook Papers*, and three books by Booth: *The Cranbrook Press*, *Cranbrook Tales*, and *The Pleasures of Planting*. As Booth found that his other business kept him from supervising the Press, printing came to an end in 1902 before Booth got around to the facsimile Kelmscott *Chaucer* he had projected. Booth's Arts and Crafts sentiments led him later to endow for public benefit a large estate containing schools, an outdoor theater, museums, gardens, and a church by Goodhue.[5]

The Cranbrook books provide excellent examples of both the advantages and disadvantages of Morrisian inspiration. They are admirable for the quality of their materials and craftsmanship—Booth deserves credit for having learned this lesson well. But the decorative design falls short; Booth could do nothing about his own lack of talent. Like De Vinne's attempts at medievalism, thay are subtly, not egregiously, bad. There is an air of naïvete (apparent also in Booth's writing) and a lack of harmony about them.

The Dictes and Sayings of the Philosophers (1901), is in Satanick type with many black leaves within its solid-set pages. The decoration—opening borders, initials, tailpieces— are in the outline strapwork characteristic of Booth's designs. The reader of today may well share the unfavorable opinion of a contemporary critic: "Personally I much prefer those pages in 'The Dictes and Sayings' which are devoid of all ornamental borders and wish that the unmeaning and unpleasing leaves scattered through the text might have been omitted likewise."[6]

Another book in Satanick is *The Revelation of Saint John the Divine* (1901). All pages, except those with Durer's illustrations, have white on black strapwork borders, with similar initials for the chapter openings (Plate 107). The same critic called Booth to task for printing the Durer woodcuts in reduced size on paper so rough that they were not satisfactorily reproduced. McPharlin, although sympathetic to Booth, found fault with this book: "While the tone of the type and borders matched that of the classic woodcuts, there was a feeling of unbalance between the bordered and the unbordered pages; and Booth's strong decorations, though it was unintentional, competed with the Durer pictures."[7]

Booth's *The Cranbrook Press* (1902) is also a relatively plain book. The title page is set with fleurons in an inverted pyramid arrangement facing a woodcut frontispiece of the press. The text in Jenson opens with an illuminated initial. In this book he gave credit and praise to Morris: "I think William Morris may be said to have excelled all printers, both ancient and modern. . . . I must bear witness to the influence his work had upon what I have undertaken."[8]

The Cranbrook Papers (1901) is perhaps the most impressive of Booth's books with its impeccably composed and printed Jenson, its hand illumination, and its three-quarter vellum binding. A piece in this book, "Aurelius," mentioned earlier in connection with Elbert Hubbard, concluded that, despite the inferiority of his books, Hubbard had been successful in teaching Americans to love fine books. The same could not be said of Booth. When he dissolved the press, many copies of his small limited editions remained unsold.[9]

The Clerk's Press was first established in 1908 by the Reverend Charles Clinch Bubb in Fremont, Ohio. Later works done in Cleveland show a simple, restrained Kelmscott style. For example, *Selected Passages from the 'Forget-Me-Not': A Jest in Sober Earnest* (1915) is a small pamphlet in thirty-two copies printed on Tuscany handmade laid paper. The type is Jenson and the title page in caps is set in a solid block with a Jenson initial hand-colored in red and green. The printer's device on the verso of the colophon page is the same orb and cross variety used by the Roycrofters. The poems, incidentally, are by some unfortunate woman, of whom the clerical printer makes cruel fun. A 1914 book, *A Little Candlemass Garland Gathered out of Various Books for the Annual Meeting of the Rowfant Club*, is in similar format with the archaic use of "V" and "U" on the title page. (This same mannerism appears in the other book.) Like '*Forget-Me-Not*,' it has a mauve cover, solid cap title, Jenson type, red and green initials, Tuscany paper, leaves as line fillers, and Morrisian margins. There were seventy-six copies.

Cincinnati also boasted a private press—the Byway Press of A. E. Goetting. *The Saga of Hen Thorir Done into English out of the Icelandic by William Morris and Eirikr Magnusson* was printed in 350 copies on French handmade paper in 1903. The initials and tailpieces by Goetting are not Kelmscott style. The type is Gothic and the binding brown paper boards. The medieval inspiration is there, but the result does not owe much to Kelmscott.

In New Jersey two presses were producing some of the most interesting work of the period. The first of these is the Alwil Press of Ridgewood, reminiscent of the Blue Sky Press in Chicago; indeed, the leading spirit of Alwil, Frank B. Rae, Jr., was also a designer for Blue Sky. The similarity of the two presses lies in the very thing that constitutes their chief attraction—the woodcut Art Nouveau floral decorations.

An early piece of Alwil work is Estelle Lambert Matteson's *Phryne and Cleopatra* (1900) published by the Stilletto Publishing Company of New York in five hundred copies. On rather yellowish wove paper, it is hand colored and hand printed in Jenson type. The title page is simple but both poems also have frontispiece title pages, then borders for each text page from designs by Rae. The ones for *Phryne* are mostly light green, with touches of red and yellow and random variations in tone from page to page. *Cleopatra's* borders, however, seem to go deliberately from light blue to dark blue with touches of yellow. Their main motif is an asp. The effect is not subdued, certainly, but totally charming.

A later and simpler, although far from unrestrained, book is Emerson's *Essay on Nature* (1902), finished, according to the colophon, in Palisades, New York, April 1903. This, too, is in Jenson and is printed on only one side of the paper. The red and black title page includes a floriated initial. Each page of the text has the running title "Nature" in red woodcut lettering, the same cut as on the cover of the book. Each page also has a half border in green of a branch with rose and leaves (Plate 108). The result is pleasantly and naively colorful.

In 1901 the Alwil Shop put out a series of brochures, including Thomas Wood Stevens' *The Unsought Shrine and Titian, the Boy* and Egbert Willard Fowler's *Dream-Rest*. Both

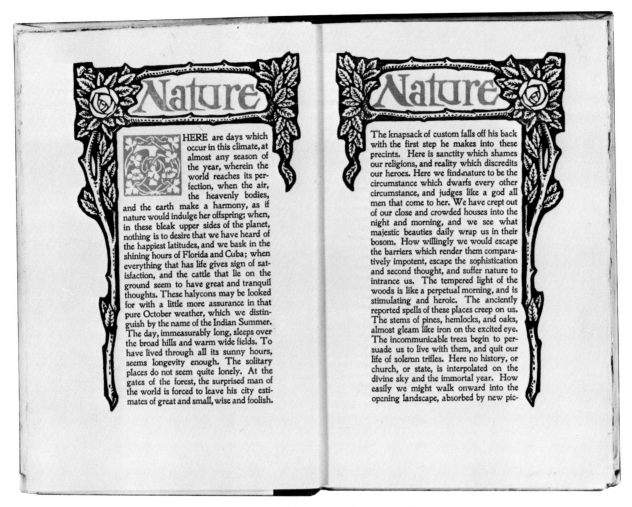

Plate 108. Ralph Waldo Emerson, *The Essay on Nature*. Ridgewood: Alwil Shop, 1902.

are simply done pamphlets with texts in Jenson and woodcut borders of rose vines on the title pages. The price was ten cents, with deluxe copies on Van Gelder paper and hand colored at one dollar. The Alwil Shop's link with the Arts and Crafts Movement can be seen in a piece entitled "Shop Talk," printed in *The Unsought Shrine* brochure, and probably written by Rae.

> In a work such as we are doing here at Alwil Shop, the personal touch is indispensable. A craft that is also an art should rely much upon the craftsman, and unless he is free to put some stroke of personality into his labor he is drawn to the level of a mere automaton. It is this degrading of the artisan that makes present day products so lifeless, and it is what Morris and Ruskin, Crane, the Rookwood Pottery and a small band of desperate enthusiasts in the Middle West have endeavored to arrest and overcome.[10]

The next year, in a little magazine piece, Rae wrote appreciatively of Morris before going on to castigate Morrisian imitators and call for modern books:

203

Following him was a motley crew of as weak rogues as could well be found. Strong men, too, followed, but the rogues were loud-voiced. Everything heavy and black in types, massive and rough-hewn in wood, everything old, everything dark in tone, everything straight and severe, no matter how bad, how crude, how out of place, was hawked in the name of Morris.[11]

The Alwil Shop itself accomplished Rae's ideals. Its books take the Arts and Crafts tradition as a point of departure but are fresh achievements of American Art Nouveau, not merely derivative work. Rae was unaware that other Morris followers had also achieved such freshness.

At the other New Jersey press, in Englewood, Frederic M. Burr printed books from 1906 to 1915 under the Morris influence. For his Hillside Press he usually chose Jenson type, handmade paper, and bindings of boards with labels. He sometimes used title-page borders and ended with colophons. His design was not up to the master's although his materials were excellent. His first book in 1906 was Browning's *Andrea Del Sarto*. In Jenson on English laid paper, it was printed in only thirty copies. The title page is weak: the lines (mostly in red) are set flush left with fleurons, but there is too much white space within the outline vine border. The page is also marred by the black wreath in the middle.

The second book, Morris' *Svend and His Brethren* (1906), is hardly more successful. Again in Jenson on French laid paper, this book has an unexceptionable but weak title page within panels. Burr's presswork is faulty: the register of the red and black title at the text opening is not exact. (Burr also printed Morris' *Sir Galahad* in 1915.) Much more interesting is the third book, Amelia J. Burr's *The Point of Life: A Play in Three Acts* (1907) on Italian wove paper. The text is in Jenson (Plate 109). The double-spread title page has a border that was designed by Mabel H. Duncan. With swirling Art Nouveau lines, it is a bold, heavy design that jumps out at the reader until it becomes overwhelming. The same border was used for the same author's *Plays in the Market Place* (1910) in which the headpieces and printers' devices are by F. W. Goudy. Goudy also did the designs for Amelia J. Burr's *The Sleep of Beppo—A Poem* (1909). This is a small pamphlet on dark green Italian paper printed in white with Jenson type. Goudy's decorations are in red and gold. It was probably charming when new; now the white ink is coming off, the red ink is difficult to see, and the gold is tarnished. Two much simpler books with Goudy decorations are Maurice Hewlett's *A Sacrifice at Prato* and F. M. Burr's *A Criminal in Stone*, both 1908. The former is in Bookman type on Van Gelder paper, the latter in Jenson on Kelmscott paper. Goudy's decorations for the Hewlett book are in his Kelmscott vine style. The title page for the Burr book seems even more derivative. Below the black hand-lettered title there is a large, square, red decoration that fills the page in a manner reminiscent of the Goodhue design for Updike's Crowell books. Instead of a vase as the central point of departure for the interlacing vines, this one has a Cupid-like figure in the same position with a similar tangle of vines emerging from it and including open seedpods, as did Goodhue's. The Hillside books are appealing, but they lack the colorful charm of the Alwil books. Goudy's bookwork pales beside that of Rae.

A southern example of Morris influence is provided by a Yankee transplant. William Lewis Washburn left school in 1879 to work as a printer in Hartford, Connecticut. In 1883, when his father moved the family to Aiken, South Carolina, he got work on various southern newspapers, ending up in 1887 at the Aiken *Journal and Review*. The Palmetto Press was begun in 1899 as a hobby in his own newspaper office. In 1904 his interest in the paper was bought out and the Palmetto Press was moved to Arkansas, New York, and New Jersey. In the period 1929 to 1938 he became known for the miniature books he published.[12]

His earliest work shows a steadily increasing reflection of current typographic trends. For example, Theodore O'Hara's *Bivouac of the Dead* (1900) is a pamphlet in white wrappers with no particular Morris influence. There is a slight feeling of Arts and Crafts in the 1900 *Sonnets from the Portuguese*. The black and red title page contains a leaf and fleur-de-lis that are continued throughout the text, making very spotty text pages. The preface opens with a red Kelmscott-style initial and a red headpiece. One hundred fifty copies were printed on Ruisdael laid paper "after divers trials and tribulations and with much love of the work. . . ." (colophon).

In 1901 Washburn put out Morris' *Svend and His Brethren* in a total Arts and Crafts format. The black and white title page, designed by Miss A. T. Colcock, has solid-set type within a border composed of large leaves and snakes twining around swords. The text is in a heavy old-style type with Gothic shoulder note running titles and Kelmscott initials. Seventy-nine copies were printed on Kelmscott laid paper, bound in light blue, half holland boards, and "Dedicated to all lovers of William Morris and his books" (colophon).

From Pennsylvania comes an Arts and Crafts book done by the Monk's Head Press, run by Edwin S. Potter from 1901 to 1902 in Philadelphia. *The Tale of a Nun* (1901) in paper boards with label, has a half title set flush left in caps and a title page with two hand-colored lilies. There are decorated initials in the text, which is set solid with fleurons as paragraph marks.

Philadelphia, the leading American book city until the ascendency of Boston and New York in the mid-nineteenth century, was also the location of two members of a less well-known manifestation of the Revival of Printing—the jobbing press founded by individuals specifically concerned with fine printing. These presses, distinguished from purely private ones by their commercial availability, sprang up in connection with little magazines in which editorials expressed the credo of fine printing. Pictorial art work in various media was stressed as well as literary offerings, and the advertisements were especially designed by the owners. These presses often issued their own book publications as well as being for hire for other people's books. Other types of graphic art were offered, especially posters, broadsides, and bookplates.

The little magazine issued by the Jenson Press from 1894 to 1895 was called *Moods*. Its first number brought national attention:

> The local papers, without exception, have waxed enthusiastic over its handsome appearance. In a recent conversation with the director of the Jenson Press your correspondent was informed that the company contemplated the early publication of several handsome limited editions in the distinct style foreshadowed in *Moods*.[13]

Volume 2 (1895) of *Moods* (subtitle: *Wherein the Artist and the Author Pleaseth Himself*), edited by M. E. St. Elmo Lewis, shows it to be a microcosm of the art movements of the time. The writers include three of the Gothic Revivalists of Boston: B. G. Goodhue, Norman Hapgood, and Ralph Adams Cram; the artists those Philadelphians later to be prominent as Realists: Robert Henri, W. J. Glackens, and John Sloan. The major typeface used is, of course, Jenson, with black letter for display, printed on coated paper. (The first volume was in old-style on wove paper). The press describes itself as "Makers of Unique Volumes" and "Designers of Bookplates." On the first page, Charles Dexter Allen's *Bookplates* is announced as forthcoming later in summer. On the second page a poster by Joseph L. Gould, Jr., for the first volume of *Moods*, is offered at seventy-five cents, while there are two editions of John Sloan's poster for the second volume at $1.50 and fifty cents. On the third page, "To Authors, Publishers and Bibliophiles . . ." announces that the Jenson Press will make editions for authors and bibliophiles of new or out-of-print books. It will also furnish designs for illustrations, cover pages, etc., and will act as publishing agent.

Morris himself was aware of the Jenson Press, although the difference between the two volumes of *Moods* was not made clear in this interview. Morris was asked:

"Have you heard of the firm in America which calls itself The Jenson Press?"
"Oh, yes, and I have seen some of its work. As a matter of fact, it is not Jenson at all. The same type almost exactly was used by Caslon, and later by the Chiswick Press. On the paper on which the Americans usually print, with its highly glazed surface, the so-called Jenson type looks absurd."[14]

The Butterfly Press was a later but similar institution, run by four Philadelphians: Margaret Hunter Scott, Alice Rogers Smith, Amy Margaret Smith, and George Wolfe Plank. The *Butterfly Quarterly*, which they edited, ran from 1907 to 1909. In the first number, despite references to Aestheticism—a facsimile of a Wilde letter is tipped in and the woodcut butterfly on the cover, although heavier, is reminiscent of Whistler's signature—the format is more or less Arts and Crafts. The type is a very heavy roman called Morland. The illustrations are heavy line woodcuts by Plank, sometimes hand colored. The editorial in the first number points up the bibliophilic aspects of the magazine: "It will continue to be the aim of the Editors to present only such *literary & artistic* matter as may properly be called *bookish*. . . . The edition is limited to 500 numbered copies. . . ." An advertisement for the press offers leaflets, announcements, and cards with hand-colored woodcuts. In the fourth number, a further offer is made of books on vellum, hand illumined in burnished gold and watercolors, bound by the artists. In 1908 the Butterfly Press issued William Hooper Howells' *The Rescue of Desdemona and Other Verse* with woodcuts by Plank, similar to those in the magazine.

In San Francisco, the booksellers Paul Elder and Morgan Shepard had an extensive program of publishing after the turn of the century. Their productions were almost always typographically outstanding, reflecting current art fashions. Some of their broadsides show Arts and Crafts influence, as do some of their books; for example, Shepard's *The Standard Upheld and Other Verses* (1902). The title page is within a white vine on black background border, with a block imprint and title and the date centered in roman numerals. There is a large red leaf in the middle and red initials both on the title page and at the text opening (Plate 110). Another 1902 book printed for Elder and Shepard is a striking example of Art Nouveau. Edward Robeson Taylor's *Into the Light* has a title page and frontispiece within black and red floral borders and the text pages within red ones. The flexible cover has a gold, green, and red floral design. The result is perhaps overly dramatic but undeniably effective.

These two books give no designer's name, but from 1901 Elder and Shepard worked with the best known of all the California printers, John Henry Nash. Nash's biographer relates the steps that led up to his San Francisco success.[15] Born in Woodbridge, Ontario,

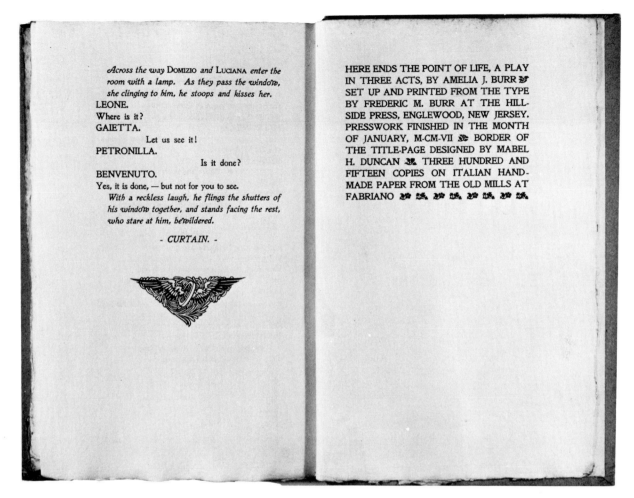

Plate 109. Amelia J. Burr, *The Point of Life: A Play in Three Acts.* Englewood: Hillside Press, 1907.

in 1871, Nash was inspired to become a printer by his uncle's library. He was employed in Toronto and Denver before moving to the Bay city in 1895, with its cosmopolitan population and tradition of fine printing, where he worked for the Hicks-Judd Company, Stanley-Taylor, the Sunset Press, and the Twentieth Century Press, of which he was half owner. When Shepard left Elder, the latter proposed an even closer alliance with Nash, and the Tomoyé Press was formed in 1903. The Morrisian inspiration in this undertaking has been brought out by Nell O'Day, Nash's librarian and bibliographer.[16]

After the earthquake and fire of 1906, Elder and Nash reestablished themselves in New York City, where the latter met and was influenced by Theodore L. De Vinne, who told him never to abandon the composing-stick, and H. L. Bullen, who showed him his great Typographic Library at the American Type Founders Company in Jersey City. Elder set up a bookstore on East Nineteenth Street which included an Arts and Crafts Book Room, where Tomoyé Press books were exhibited.[17] In 1909 the two returned to San Francisco.

The Tomoyé books show general Arts and Crafts influence, as in two books by Jennie Day Haines, *Ye Gardeyne Book* (1906) and *Weather Opinions* (1907), which are printed in

207

Plate 110. Morgan Shepard, *The Standard Upheld and Other Verses.* San Francisco: Elder & Shepard, 1902.

Plate 111. Paul Elder, comp., *Mosaic Essays.* San Francisco & New York: Tomoyé Press, 1906.

black and green with borders or rules on the text pages, and pictorial title pages reminiscent of Walter Crane. The famous series of Western Classics, done in New York, are strangely like De Vinne's work in that they are technically excellent, while the designs do not hang together coherently. The 1910 *Sonnets from the Portuguese*, however, is more successful. It resembles the Western Classics in format and paper (very white, handmade wove). The sonnets are in italic with delicate woodcut side borders, Still there is a jarring element: the colophon is worded in archaic, tongue-in-cheek language that belies the dignity of the book.

A Tomoyé title of specifically Arts and Crafts style is *Mosaic Essays* (copyright 1906) compiled by Elder. Its binding, endpapers, and double-spread title page all have designs by Robert Wilson Hyde that shade over into Art Nouveau (Plate 111), in a way reminiscent of Dard Hunter. The red and black text is spotted throughout with leaves.

Elder and Nash broke up in 1911, the latter going on to form Taylor, Nash and Taylor. In 1915 Nash left to join the Blair-Murdock Company, which, however, ceased to exist in 1916. From then on, Nash was on his own and soon became the most famous printer in America, showered with riches and honors that recall the spoils of Bodoni in the eighteenth century, when his Parma office was a stop on the Grand Tour. Like Bodoni, Nash catered to the powerful and made a specialty of grandiose, monumental printing, the sort that very easily comes to pomposity. On the other hand, the impression he made on businessmen helped to provide a climate favorable to printing, at least during the twenties. And the artistry of his work was once an inspiration to the next wave of fine printers.

But did Nash's own inspiration come directly from William Morris? Certainly he was aware of Morris' importance, once spending $1,000 for a Kelmscott *Chaucer* for his typographic library.[18] This same library contained a portrait of Morris along with those of Gutenberg, Bodoni, De Vinne, and others.[19] And certain Morrisian ideas were part of Nash's credo. He disliked machine work and found hand work vastly superior. He insisted upon the finest materials, using mainly, like Mosher in Maine, Van Gelder paper from Holland. He believed in impeccable presswork, including a firm impression of the type. The composition had to be tight, with no spots or rivers of white on the pages. Venetian type, notably Cloister, was his preference. In fact, two of the same Venetian printers, Ratdolt and Jenson, who had inspired Morris, were also taken by Nash as models. However, when all is said and done, it is not Kelmscott work that was more immediate to Nash than fifteenth-century Venice but the Doves Press of Cobden-Sanderson, itself inspired by Kelmscott but using lighter pages without decoration. Of course, if it had not been for Morris, the Venetian incunabular printers would not have been so well known nor so revered, but neither should it be said, as has been done, that Nash imitated William Morris heavy-handedly throughout his career.[20]

He was capable of straight imitation when the occasion demanded, as for the Morris Keepsake in the Zellerbach Paper Company's series of Printer's Keepsakes in the twenties,[21] or an announcement for a Kelmscott exhibit at the Little Museum of La Miniatura in Pasadena (1929) (colophon: San Francisco: This announcement is John Henry Nash's contribution to the William Morris Memorial Fund), or another notice for the Morris Centenary at Mills College in 1934.

But the landmarks of Nash's career were in the Doves Press style. As early as 1916 he printed Cobden-Sanderson's *The Ideal Book*, to high praise from the author. There is a touch of decoration, but it is definitely unornamented typography that is the central focus. In 1921 Nash printed *The Kelmscott and Doves Presses* by R. E. Cowan, one of the catalogues of the library of William Andrews Clark, Jr. The book is reminiscent of Doves, not Kelmscott. In 1928, one of the most famous of Nash's books, *The Life and Personality of Phoebe Apperson Hearst* by Winifred Black Bonfils, printed for William Randolph Hearst, provides one of the best examples of the dangers of Nash's printing, in which the subject matter did not always determine the typographic treatment. Hearst commissioned both the writing, by a newspaper reporter, and the printing of this biography of his mother. The monumental treatment given the text by Nash makes the lightweight text appear ludicrous instead of pleasant. On rather creamy laid paper, the text is in Cloister with headbands and a frontispiece by William Wilke, very feebly done. There are fly titles for each chapter and huge margins. The large book is bound in gold-stamped white vellum and is in a brown cloth protective bag.

The 1929 three-volume *Divine Comedy* is similar in format. It is on wove paper, with the same bindings and protective bags. The text is also Cloister but placed within blue rules which provide an added interest to the pages. The book is impeccably done and more successful than *Phoebe Apperson Hearst* because the text seems more appropriate for the pretentious treatment.

An earlier book that did have more of a Morrisian flavor is W. Irving Way's *Migratory Books: Their Haunts and Habits* (1924), printed for the bookseller Ernest Dawson of Los Angeles. The text is again Cloister, with a large floriated initial at its opening and italic running titles in shoulder note form printed in a rust color. The paper covers are also rust with a printed label, and there is a matching leaf on the title page. In fact, the book is charming, except for the exaggerated margins, a defect also noticeable in the books described earlier. The gutter and top edges are too narrow in comparison with the others, so that the fore edge seems wide and the foot altogether too big.

Whatever one may think of Nash's taste, his importance in California printing is undeniable. "Nash so dominated the fine printing movement in San Francisco that one admirer . . . turned the entire fine printing movement upside down by referring in apparent sincerity to William Morris as a Victorian Nash!"[22] As various writers have pointed out,[23] the early Venetian style lasted later in the West than in other parts of the country. This was probably for several reasons. In the first place, the West was not hit so hard or so soon by the Kelmscott impact; the incunabular inspiration, once started, dragged on longer, however. Secondly, the West is cut off from the eastern centers of publishing and bookmaking, so that the printing done there has always gone to the two extremes: commercial jobbing and quality private presses. The latter have helped to perpetuate Jensonian inspiration. Thirdly, there was John Henry Nash, providing magnificent typography in the Doves style, but more a craftsman, like De Vinne, than an artist.

These have been the highlights in the nationwide picture of excitement about Arts and Crafts printing at the turn of the century. The literature contains indications that jobbing printers in small towns were also caught up in this excitement: they wrote letters to the printing journals about Jenson type, they composed title pages in block arrangements with fleurons. But the tide turned in the years before World War I from Kelmscott to Doves inspiration—in the West with John Henry Nash, in the East with the Boston Society of Printers.

1. [Advertisement], *Bibelot*, XIV (1908), unpaged.
2. Quoted in Ralph Fletcher Seymour, *Some Went this Way* (Chicago: R. F. Seymour, 1945), p. 49.
3. Paul McPharlin, "The Cranbrook Press," *Dolphin*, No. 4, part III (Spring 1941): 268-278.
4. Ibid., pp. 270-271.
5. Ibid., p. 275.
6. Fitzroy Carrington, "Private and Special Presses," *Book Buyer*, XXIII (1901): 100.
7. McPharlin, "The Cranbrook Press," p. 275.
8. George C. Booth, *The Cranbrook Press* (Detroit: Cranbrook, 1902), pp. 11-12.
9. McPharlin, "The Cranbrook Press," p. 278.
10. [Frank B. Rae, Jr.] In Thomas Wood Stevens, *The Unsought Shrine* . . . (Ridgewood: Alwil, 1901), unpaged.
11. Frank B. Rae, Jr., "Setters of Types," *Impressions Quarterly*, III (March 1902): unpaged.
12. Harry B. Weiss, "The Miniature Books of William Lewis Washburn," *Book Collector's Packet*, III (September 1938): 20-21.
13. Dale, "Philadelphia Letter from our Regular Correspondent," *Engraver and Printer*, VII (April 1895): 83.
14. I. H. I. "The Kelmscott Press—An Illustrated Interview with Mr. William Morris," *Bookselling*, I (November 1895): 4.
15. Robert D. Harlan, *John Henry Nash: The Biography of a Career* (Berkeley: University of California Press, 1970).
16. Nell O'Day, *A Catalogue of Books Printed by John Henry Nash* (San Francisco: Nash, 1937), p. vi.
17. Harlan, *John Henry Nash*, p. 12.
18. Ibid., p. 130.
19. Ibid., p. 76.
20. James M. Wells, "Book Typography in the United States of America," in Kenneth Day, ed., *Book Typography 1815-1965* (London: Ernest Benn, 1966), p. 361.
21. Harlan, *John Henry Nash*, p. 56.
22. Ibid., p. 127.
23. E.g., Louise Farrow Barr, *Presses of Northern California and Their Books 1900-1933* (Berkeley: Book Arts Club, University of California, 1934).

XXI

Some American Versions of Kelmscott Types

THE American Type Founders Company (ATF), formed by the merger of many individual foundries in 1892, obtained one of its great successes with the first copy anywhere of a Morris type—the Jenson type of 1895. Henry Lewis Bullen, the ATF librarian who had a hand in its later program of historic type revivals, has left an account of the genesis of the Jenson face in which he gives the full credit to Joseph W. Phinney, of the Dickinson Type Foundry in Boston, an ATF branch.

> Mr. Phinney was the first to thoroughly—even more than William Morris—recognize the merit and significance of this revised design. He applied, not once, but thrice and urgently, for permission to pay for the privilege of reproducing the design, but Mr. Morris did not want to popularize it or make its reformatory influence available in general typography, but rather to keep it for the narrow purpose of enhancing the value of his limited edition publishing business. Mr. Phinney, therefore, felt himself absolved, and proceeded under his legal right to cut the design in a magnificent series of fourteen sizes, with a corresponding italic series and a condensed series, neither of which had been attempted by Mr. Morris. . . . Nor was Jenson Old Style a slavish copy, for each character of every size was cut with the original print from the ancient Jenson types as a guide. The first showing of the series had an effect on typographic taste in America that was instantaneous and most valuable and still remains effective.[1]

That Phinney understood the spirit as well as the letter of Morris' typography is shown by a further quotation from Bullen: ". . . in nothing was he more criticized by the old-time founders than on his insistence on close 'fitting' one character with another."[2] In another piece, years later, Bullen described the aftermath of Phinney's efforts:

> In 1895, a handsome twenty-four-page large quarto specimen was issued, the composition by John B. Williams. . . . It presented the new type designs and decorative materials in the style of the Kelmscott Press. It was not only a specimen of types, but

211

a guide to better typography. The response of the printers was a complete surprise to the typefounders. No one typefoundry could supply the demand. The task was divided among three of them. On the other hand, many tons of hitherto brisk-selling type faces were made unsalable, ultimately going into the metal pots—a tremendous, if expensive, compliment to the art of Morris. Since then commercial typography in America has steadily improved with few divagations. Thus was accomplished a reform which Morris himself had not foreseen. There is as much artistry to be found in American commercial printing and the bagatelles—booklets, broadsides and the like—as in our book printing.[3]

At the time the new face received a mixed reaction from the critics. Irving Way, with his usual perspicacity, saw that it would be popular: "The new font . . . is not unlikely . . . to work its way into favor, if, indeed, it does not become quite popular, among those very people who were once loudest in their condemnation of Mr. Morris."[4] So did an anonymous reviewer in the same number of the *Inland Printer:* "Among the recent faces of type offered the appreciative printer, the Jenson series . . . will probably be much admired and sought after."[5] But some months later R. Coupland Harding, the regular type critic for the same periodical, showed his displeasure:

Eccentricity and quaintness which are tolerable, or even admirable, in a few display lines or a brief circular, may be quite out of place in a body-font. . . . It is here that—with all respect to their artistic taste—I venture to join issue with such authorities as Mr. Walter Crane and Mr. William Morris. The Jenson old style of the Dickinson foundry . . . is an example. I confess that I do not like the face at all. This, however, is a matter of taste, but I do not think there can be much question as to the distressing effect a page or two of this letter would have on the eyes of a reader.[6]

The American Type Founders Company featured Jenson in their first collective specimen book, *Specimens of Type Ornaments and Borders . . .* , n.d. (but the price list is dated October 1895). Its immediate popularity is shown by Gelett Burgess' poem called "In Jenson Type":

In Jenson type my printer knows
The height of typographic pose;
  The black-faced letters cross the page
  Like mummers of some by-gone age,
In solemn, sad, funereal rows.

No matter what is said, "it goes"—
Though doggerel verse or puerile prose—
  If but its wretched rantings rage
    In Jenson type.

Go, foolish rhyme, and dress your woes
In this prevailing garb of those
  Who call all well that fits the gauge
  Set by the medieval sage—
You, too, may conquer, I suppose,
  In Jenson type.[7]

The desire to share in this popularity became evident when other houses began bringing out their own versions, such as the Mazarin of Barnhart Brothers and Spindler in Chicago, reviewed by Harding, who seems to have learned resignation:

> The success of the Jenson series has brought out a rival face—the Mazarin. Like the Jenson, it has been suggested by the "golden type" of the Kelmscott Press. . . . Appropriate ornaments and initials are also shown. I have seen only a few of these, but the initials are handsome, and the borders have a richness of effect which is very pleasing.[8]

The Mazarin came out in 1895, as did the Morris Old Style of the Crescent Type Foundry of Chicago. In 1896 another copy was called Kelmscott by the Inland Typefoundry, St. Louis.

Jenson was still important in the 1912 ATF Specimen Book; indeed, it was still featured in the 1923 *Manual of Linotype Typography*, designed by William Dana Orcutt and E. E. Bartlett. "The Jenson face is now rarely used for bookwork, principally because it requires special treatment in order to produce a pleasing effect. For small books and limited editions, however, it is a face which book-lovers admire."[9]

In 1895 ATF also brought out a romanized Gothic face, modeled on Will Bradley's lettering for the December 1894 *Inland Printer* cover, and called Bradley. This, too, met with great success and was widely used for display typography, including the title pages of books. There were other similar faces at just the same time, as can be seen from a review of Harding's:

> Last month I wrote in praise of the new face "St. John," by the Inland Typefoundry, early specimens of which appeared in *The Inland Printer* for August. In the following issue I now find two faces, "Bradley" by MacKellar and "Abbey Text" by Farmer & Son, bearing an exceedingly close resemblance to the St. John. It is not the first time that I have noticed a curious coincidence of the kind—two or more houses coming out almost simultaneously with novelties almost identical in their main features. . . . I have no doubt that, as letters of this class are characteristic of Mr. Bradley's work, that to him may be assigned the credit of originating the design, of which the two other faces appear to be variants.[10]

Still other romanized Gothics were Tell Text and Tudor Text, put out in 1896 by Barnhart Brothers and Spindler, Chicago. The reason for all these similar types is probably that there was a desire for such a face aroused by Morris' Troy type. In any case, ATF brought out in 1896 Satanick, modeled directly on Morris' Gothic font. The American Type Founders Company advertised it to accompany Jenson Old Style and Jenson Italic, stressing its romanization: "The face has the legibility of Roman type, the letters being modeled so as to avoid every surplus line, adhering to simplicity and strength in shapes and proportions."[11]

The type companies also produced sets of ornamented initials and borders (based on fifteenth-century models), some to accompany the above fonts, some issued alone. (The Jenson was accompanied by decorations based directly on Morris' designs for the Kelmscott Press.)

1. "Quadrat," [i.e., Henry Lewis Bullen] "Discussions of a Retired Printer," *Inland Printer*, XXXIX (June 1907): 354–355.
2. Ibid., p. 355.
3. Henry Lewis Bullen, "William Morris: Regenerator of the Typographic Art," *Inland Printer*, LXIX (June 1922): 372.
4. "Irving" [i.e., W. Irving Way] "Books, Authors, and Kindred Subjects," *Inland Printer*, XIV (March 1895): 547.
5. "Recent Type Designs," *Inland Printer*, XIV (March 1895): 574.
6. R. Coupland Harding, "Review of Type Designs," *Inland Printer*, XVI (November 1895): 170.
7. Gelett Burgess, "In Jenson Type," *Inland Printer*, XVI (January 1896): 442. Reprinted from the *Philistine*.
8. R. Coupland Harding, "Review of Type Specimens," *Inland Printer*, XVII (April 1896): 69.
9. *Manual of Linotype Typography* (Brooklyn: Mergenthaler Linotype Co., n.d.), p. 144.
10. R. Coupland Harding, "Review of Type Designs," *Inland Printer*, XVI (January 1896): 409.
11. "Progressive Type Making," *Typographic Advertiser*, XLI (October 1896): 10.

XXII

Chronology & Perspectives

IT IS POSSIBLE now to see the outlines of the Morris Revival in America from the beginning of the Kelmscott Press to the early twentieth century. The first Kelmscott book, finished in April 1891, was given wider American distribution in the fall of that year by Roberts Brothers, Morris' American publishers, when they produced a facsimile of *The Glittering Plain*. The doctrine of Arts and Crafts was also disseminated in the States in 1891 by Walter Crane's visit. Updike began work at the Riverside Press division of Houghton Mifflin and designed his own first book, *On the Dedications of American Churches*. This was the year, too, of the International Copyright Law with its protection of foreign authors, which heralded the efflorescence of literary publishers in the nineties. (But Mosher, the literary publisher who began in 1891, gave only token payments to foreign authors, when he gave any at all.)

Following this background year of 1891, 1892 saw the first important American reaction to Kelmscott. The two avant-garde periodicals *Mahogany Tree* and *Knight Errant* appeared in Boston, where Goodhue was also working on the designs for Copeland and Day's *The House of Life*, and Updike was turning out a trade book, *A Day at Laguerre's*, in Kelmscott format. Comment in the press was building up, one influential piece being De Vinne's on "Masculine Printing."

With 1893, the year of Beardsley's *Le Morte d'Arthur*, reaction to Kelmscott reached such a volume that this may be designated the first year of the Morris Revival proper. The press barrage, both pro and con, informed everyone in the book world of Kelmscott. *Modern Art* was spreading Arts and Crafts philosophy with designs by Rogers, who was also doing his first work for books. Updike had broken away from Riverside and issued his own first circular to solicit business. *The Book of Common Prayer* in its decorated form, supervised by Updike and designed by Goodhue, was issued. The literary publishers began their programs in all three major cities. New York had R. H. Russell, while in Boston Copeland & Day put out two Arts and Crafts books: *The Decadent* and *The House of Life*. Stone & Kimball began publishing in both Boston and Chicago, including one

215

of their few Arts and Crafts title pages: *The Holy Cross*. Also in Chicago, Irving Way was responsible for *The Columbian Ode* in a publishing endeavor preliminary to Way & Williams.

In 1894 Stone & Kimball moved entirely to Chicago and put out another Arts and Crafts title: *The Quest of Heracles*, as well as the influential periodical, the *Chap-Book*, which spread the craze for both posters and little magazines. This was the first year the Kelmscott Revival was strongly felt in Chicago, as it had been in Boston the previous year. Goudy ran his Booklet/Camelot Press, doing the printing for some of the *Chap-Book* numbers, while Bradley designed new monthly covers for the *Inland Printer*, a feature never before adopted by magazines. Kelmscott influence was being referred to in the press, and it was spreading outside the big cities. Hubbard began publishing his *Little Journeys* from East Aurora, and *Modern Art* was being issued from Indianapolis. This was the year that Bowles made his plea for artist-printers in its pages and Updike unwittingly answered with his second circular and its book-designer credo. This was printed in Jenson type, the American Type Founders Company copy of Morris' Golden, the first appearance of this type and the herald of really wide-scale Kelmscott imitation.

The very next year, 1895, was a peak time in the Revival. Jenson type was offered for sale to the public and other imitations of Golden type appeared. Bradley type, with its resemblance to Morris' Troy, was also cut, as well as imitations of it. Hubbard began issuing his *Philistine* and Mosher his *Bibelot*, while *Modern Art* moved to Boston and adopted a total Arts and Crafts format. Updike formed the Merrymount Press, the Jenson Press was working in Philadelphia, and Bradley started his Wayside Press outside of Boston, a location which gave him the chance of seeing Colonial books with Caslon type in the Boston Public Library. Copeland & Day were using the talents of Goodhue for *Esther* and *Nine Sonnets Written at Oxford*. Irving Way, after his visit to Morris in England, formed Way and Williams and distributed the Kelmscott *Hand and Soul*. He also commissioned Rogers to design *The Banquet of Plato*. Rogers did other significant book designing in 1895, with *Homeward Songs by the Way* for Mosher and Gruelle's book on the Walters Collection for Bowles. Another landmark book of this year was Bradley's *Fringilla*, with his most Kelmscott-inspired book designs. In the face of this wave of Kelmscott imitation, the initial disapproval of Morris in the press was somewhat less marked, to be resumed in a later period of disillusionment after the turn of the century.

The year 1896 continued the peak of the Morris Revival; in fact, the two years 1895 and 1896, marked the first high point of Kelmscott imitation and adulation. The American Type Founders Company offered Satanick, its copy of Troy type, and Goudy began his type designing with Camelot. Bradley published his Arts and Crafts periodical, *Bradley: His Book*, while Hubbard turned to books for the first time with *The Song of Songs*. Updike designed a notable early instance of allusive typography in *The Governor's Garden*, while his *Altar Book* of this year stands out as the one most beautiful and complete of all American imitations of the Kelmscott style. The Philosopher Press began work in Wisconsin, marking the beginning of the widespread private press movement in the wake of Morris.

In 1897 there was an abatement of avant-garde activity, with the ending of Stone & Kimball and of *Bradley: His Book*, and the last of the Copeland & Day English Love Sonnet series. But there was the beginning of an upsurge in commercial response to Kelmscott with De Vinne's catalogue of old faces added to his press that extolled the Morris imitations and the first book in Updike's Arts and Crafts style for the publisher Crowell.

Perhaps the Boston Arts and Crafts exhibition of this year, the first in America, helped to move the style from avant-garde to more public circles.

The same trend continued in 1898. On the one hand, the avant-garde lost Way & Williams, the Wayside Press, and the *Chap-Book*, which all came to an end. On the other, the Kelmscott style in commercial printing can be seen in such books as the *Pilgrim's Progress* printed by De Vinne for Century. In 1899 both Copeland & Day and Lamson, Wolffe closed their doors, but Mosher published his first Morris-style book, *Hand and Soul*. His sales were booming, as were Hubbard's. Private press activity began to pick up in this year with the formation of the Blue Sky and Palmetto Presses.

The year 1900 was another peak in the Morris Revival. The turn of the century marked a high point in the second wave of Kelmscott influence, both in commercial and private press printing. The work of the first leaders, Updike, Rogers, and Bradley, was taking other forms, most notably with Rogers' Riverside Press Limited Editions which showed antiquarian but not Arts and Crafts influence; these books had great influence themselves on other American bookmakers. Goudy, who was the great leader of the second wave, did Arts and Crafts designing for Herbert S. Stone and Mosher in 1900, and Mosher published his other Kelmscott book, *Empedocles on Etna*. In commercial printing, De Vinne brought out his Renner type and printed a Kelmscott pastiche, *The Tomb of General Grant*. This was still the period of the added Arts and Crafts title pages, and trade publishers were bringing out volumes such as *Pre-Raphaelite Ballads*, designed by H. M. O'Kane for A. Wessels & Company. Seymour was beginning to issue Arts and Crafts books in Chicago, while the private press scene in the East saw the formation of three important presses: Elston, Cornhill, and Alwil. This was a prime year for Roycroft with *Maud, City of Tagaste*, and other outstandingly well-designed books.

In 1901 continued commercial interest can be seen in James Pott & Company's Kelmscott series, while private presses continued with the Handcraft Shop, Elm, Monk's Head, and Cranbrook Presses. In 1902 R. H. Russell and Elder & Shepard brought out Kelmscott-style books, while Seymour published his first title in his own Alderbrink type. The year 1903 was most notable for the formation of Goudy's Village Press which climaxed the turn-of-the-century heyday of such Morris-inspired presses. Dard Hunter started working at Roycroft and the *Printing Art* was founded in Boston. R. H. Russell went out of business, but the Tomoye press of Elder and Nash began. There were still great Kelmscott trade books, such as *Shakespeare's Songs* printed by De Vinne.

In 1904 Updike printed his *Tacitus* in Merrymount type, marking his post-Kelmscott allegiance to the Doves style. Bradley began his *American Chap-Book*, the chief disseminator of his influential advertising style. The year 1905 marked the end of Herbert S. Stone & Company, but the beginning of the Society of Printers, while 1906 was the year of the latter's exhibition for which Updike and Rogers wrote their apologia for Doves. Other traces of the Morris Revival can be found up until World War I, but this praise for the unornamented typography of Doves by the two great leaders, Updike and Rogers, marked the beginning of the end of Kelmscott imitation. There would be other antiquarian books but rarely modeled directly on Morris. The Morris Revival was continued in two general forms: interest in fine printing and the heavy, blunt line in typography. The latter was important in the twenties and carried over in a sense to Bauhaus work, which in turn has been one of the biggest influences in twentieth-century typography.

To sum up, after the prototype for the Morris Revival in America appeared in 1891, the American response began in 1892, reached the scale of a movement in 1893, and came to a peak in 1895–1896 among the avant-garde leaders. It then became absorbed in commercial printing and trade publishing, this second wave reaching a peak around 1900 at the same time the private press movement was beginning its period of importance. Kelmscott imitation was dying out in favor of Doves by 1906, and was gone by the War. But that Kelmscott imitation had not been a fad; it was a response to a need, evident in the precursors of the eighties, in the widespread adoption during the nineties, and in subsequent twentieth-century developments.

Twentieth-century perception of the Morris Revival has as its first form the inevitable reaction to earlier praise. Early in the century market prices of Kelmscott books fell, following an initial rise after Morris' death in 1896. A contemporary commentator remarked: "The truth is, collectors have tired of them and will have none of them. That they may regain some of their lost prestige is possible, but that they will ever reach the high values of four or five years ago is improbable."[1]

Running through many of the later comments, both British and American, is the predilection for the opposing, more classical, style of typography, the Aesthetic. Holbrook Jackson compared Morris unfavorably to Whistler and termed the Kelmscott volumes "models of what a book should not be."[2] Paul Johnston thought the Chiswick Press much better and more influential than the Kelmscott.[3] A. J. A. Symons wrote his piece on "An Unacknowledged Movement in Fine Printing" in the *Fleuron* of 1930, which has already been referred to.

On the other hand, there has been an even greater stream of abiding faith in Morris and the good he did for typography. A notable statement of this positive theme in twentieth-century reaction to Morris can be found in Margaret Bingham Stillwell's 1916 piece in the *Bulletin of the New York Public Library* on "The Heritage of the Modern Printer," where she claimed that commercial printing and publishing were better because of Morris.[4] Printers themselves gave Morris credit for improving their craft. For example, a 1920 handbook in the Typographic Technical Series for Apprentices stated: "We owe much of our present wide-spread reverence for good design in printing to his [Morris'] influence. . . ."[5] In 1922, Henry Lewis Bullen wrote in the *Inland Printer:* "Among typographers Morris's influence, generally by indirection . . . is seen in almost every piece of good printing of our time in almost every country."[6] This line has been reiterated by innumerable other writers including Stanley Morison, the British typographic historian, and Giovanni Mardersteig, the great Italian printer.[7] John Winterich has given it lively, if hyperbolic, expression:

> Today's novel or biography, today's dictionary and encyclopedia, today's school textbook, today's telephone book and checkbook are all likely to be better examples of good taste, good typography, and good craftsmanship because, toward the close of the nineteenth century, William Morris built the Kelmscott *Chaucer.*[8]

Many commentators have rightly felt that the period when Morris' books as models were eagerly followed lasted for an intense but brief time. Their archaic style was, in the long range, useful because it helped to create an abiding interest in early printing. But as many have pointed out it was Morris' teachings about the quality of materials and craftsmanship, rather than his designs, that proved an inspiration to twentieth-century printers. (Where I disagree with other writers on this period is in the evaluation of the Arts and Crafts books themselves, the ones that attempted to follow in Morris' footsteps. These books have been casually dismissed by virtually every critic, sometimes with a few exceptions made, such as for the Elston Press, but almost always with special condemnation for Elbert Hubbard, as artistically unworthy. As I have pointed out, some of them were indeed artistically unworthy, but to condemn them as a group is mistaken. They are highly interesting, and sometimes beautiful, examples of one of the most astonishing episodes in printing history. The other artifacts produced by the American Arts and Crafts Movement, such as furniture, metal and leatherwork, have been given recognition; it is time to look at the books, too, without prejudice.)

If the ideas of Morris have indeed shed lasting benefit, in what ways has the American printing scene been superior in this century? For one thing, in this day when mechanization has almost completely taken over there has been less need to justify printing as an art. One notable indication of the public acceptance of artistic books has been the establishment of the American Institute of Graphic Arts in 1914 and from 1923 its continuing project of choosing the fifty best-designed books of the year, giving them publicity, and putting them on exhibition.

Secondly, the improvement of printing can be seen in commercial, jobbing work. As Bruce Rogers put it, "the most lasting contribution made by the arts and crafts movement was one which would have startled its leaders: the principle that good design, when coupled with an intelligent use of machinery, could produce first-rate work."[9] What this meant for jobbing printers was put into very specific terms by John Cotton Dana in 1929:

> The value of printing output in the city [Newark] was $1,857,652 in 1900, and increased to $14,811,376 in 1925. . . .
>
> The improvement in quality in these 25 years has been far more striking than has the increase in quantity. Not a few shops in Newark now turn out printing of high grade.
>
> That improvement has come, as it has come in all parts of the country, chiefly because of the spread of general intelligence and of wider appreciation of the fact that when art is applied to typography the product is more profitable to the purchaser.[10]

Part of the reason for the improvement of such printing was the Printing House Craftsmen Movement, a latter-day Arts and Crafts development. The first Club of Printing House Craftsmen was founded in New York in 1909. By 1912 there were clubs in Philadelphia, Boston, Pittsburgh, and Chicago; eventually, clubs were formed all over the nation for the promotion of fellowship and the exchange of knowledge about historical printing as well as modern design.[11]

The improvement in trade books has come with the acceptance of the need for a designer, following the Morrisian emphasis on artistic unity. In this area Knopf has been a trail-blazer, not only by hiring designers of the caliber of Dwiggins for unlimited editions, but also by printing, in the Arts and Crafts manner, explanatory colophons, giving details of materials and design. In 1927 the *Times Literary Supplement* in England described the new calling of typographer, or book designer, which had grown up in the wake of Arts and Crafts, naming Bruce Rogers as the best-known practitioner on the Anglo-American scene.[12] Holbrook Jackson also pointed out the importance of the designer for modern book production. He believed that acceptance of the designer stemmed from Morris' control of the whole book at the Kelmscott Press, although his own hands did not do all the work.[13]

219

Awareness of historic printing has been another result of the Morris Revival. Stanley Morison in his capacity as typographic consultant to the British Monotype Corporation, the Cambridge University Press, and the *Times*, played an important role in the improvement of Anglo-American trade books. Influenced by the Revival himself and deeply interested in historic typefaces, he saw that they were provided in the up-to-date form of Monotype faces, used for much book printing in the twentieth century, thus merging mechanization and historicism.

There is a third area of printing, between trade publishing and private presses, where Morris' example has had lasting effect: the area of fine commercial presses. Updike continued to run his Merrymount Press in Boston until his death in 1941. William Edwin Rudge, mentioned in connection with Rogers, produced for many years at his press in Mount Vernon, New York, as fine work as could be found anywhere. Elmer Adler with his Pynson Printers in New York City also set a standard of excellence. In the same city, Joseph Blumenthal's Spiral Press was one of the best in the country until its demise. There have been similar presses elsewhere. That amazing phenomenon, George Macy's Limited Editions Club, which succeeded in selling fine books on a monthly basis in the heart of the Depression, could not have been dreamed of without the work of these presses and similar ones in other countries. Moreover, the audience for these books might not have existed without the impetus of the Revival and its aftermath.

Private presses, with their emphasis on all three aspects of the physical book—craftsmanship, materials, and design—have become a permanent phenomenon. Their influence on other printing is impossible to measure, but its existence has been attested by a well-known California printer and designer, Adrian Wilson: "Since the time when William Morris' Kelmscott Press initiated a revival of interest in the mystique of fine printing and the book as a work of art . . . small private presses have exerted a strong influence on the standards of the commercial book."[14] Many purposes have been served by these presses: personal expression, publication of noncommercial texts (especially poetry), maintenance of standards of craftsmanship impossible on a mass scale, experimentation in design, and even the preservation of historical printing styles in the use of allusive typography.

One habit of the private presses has often been criticized, however, that of publishing yet again the old chestnuts of literature, in formats that make the books *objets d'art* rather than material for reading. No other writer on typography has offered an apology for this but I believe that it can be justified in terms of still another result of the Morris Revival: the validity of printing as an interpretive art. Morris himself hinted at it in an interview of 1895:

"And now, Mr. Morris, will you kindly tell us why you started the Kelmscott Press?"
"Oh! simply because I felt that for the books one loved and cared for there might be attempted a presentation, both as to print and paper, which should be worthy of one's feelings. . . ."[15]

Holbrook Jackson hit on another aspect of the same concept in stressing the non-utilitarian nature of fine printing: "The best books produced as a result of that impulse towards good printing are protests of beauty against ugliness rather than precepts and examples for ordinary practice. They bear much the same relation to books in general as monuments do to life in general."[16]

To explain what I mean by printing as interpretation, I must go back to basic principles.

Literature can be received through either hearing or sight: if aurally, we are likely to expect and appreciate an artist-interpreter; if visually, we can do the same. *War and Peace* on newsprint is no more the identical experience as in a Limited Editions Club version than it is when read by a tongue-tied person as compared to Laurence Olivier. If the printer is thought of as an interpretive artist, similar to an actor, there is a justification for multiple renderings of *Sonnets from the Portuguese* or the *Rubaiyat:* each artist has the right to give his own version of the classics. Since 1900 more people have accepted this view in practice but without consciously expressing the principle.

The major typographic spokesmen of this century have taken a very opposite view. Since the Arts and Crafts period, there has been prominent a classical approach to printing, which might be summed up as the Crystal Goblet School, after Beatrice Warde's famous essay of that name. If you are a lover of fine wine, you prefer to drink it from a thin, clear, crystal goblet that interposes itself as little as possible, rather than from a more costly vessel of gold and jewels. Typography's proper role is to play the crystal goblet to the text it is presenting. Mrs. Warde's friend Stanley Morison was the foremost exponent of this school; their combined influence has been formidable. In fact, Roderick Cave has pointed out that Beatrice Warde's statement, "Printing should be invisible," resembles the Doves Press approach to typography, emphasizing restraint and lack of decoration.[17] Moreover, this emphasis on neutrality accords well with an industrial age's concept of the book as a tool; a means to an end rather than an end in itself. The mechanization of printing has increased the multiplication of books to the point of regarding them as expendable. This has been a theme throughout the history of printing; the farther we get from the costly manuscript the more we hesitate to lavish time-consuming art on the ordinary book.

But in the day of the cheap volume, there is a counter-balancing need for limited editions from presses which still know the touch of human hands. Perhaps the real function of the Morris Revival has been to remind us of this. The close of the nineteenth century was the very period when mechanization—power presses, automatic typesetting, photographic reproduction—was noticeably replacing hand processes. People turned to medievalistic books as godsends because they were reaching back for the values of the manuscript period. Their concern over the triumph of the machine and the ugliness of mass production was expressed by the creation of handcrafted, decorated, dark books, reminiscent of Gothic Europe. These characteristics became symbols for the old values of beauty and hand production, so that they were even translated into terms of mass-produced books made by machines. The Morris Revival was a symbolic reaffirmation of human art in the face of the impersonal machine.

But the Arts and Crafts style, brilliantly useful for a time precisely because of its archaisms, could not last for long. The Aesthetic style, more legible, more adaptable to machine production, less decorated, has had a greater and longer-lasting influence. The two styles represented not only the dichotomies of the Middle Ages versus the Renaissance but also individuality, decoration, exuberance, imagination, the Romantic versus standardization, utilitarianism, restraint, rationalism, the Classical.

Arts and Crafts, while it lasted, was a fresh start, a rejuvenation for printing in its return to sources. As Holbrook Jackson has pointed out: "Revivals in art attempt to restore vitality by throwing back to periods when design and production had primitive vigour."[18] A suggestion of what was to come was given in the pages of the July 1889 *American Bookmaker:* "One of the most curious phases of printing and bookbinding is shown in the return to ancient forms, now so common. What is new is out of favor; that which is old, even if badly formed, is in request."[19] Medievalism provided symbolic relief for the widespread fear of the Industrial Revolution's effect on books.

1. William G. Menzies, "The Present Value of the Publications of the Kelmscott Press," *Connoisseur*, XII (1905): 42.
2. Holbrook Jackson, *The Printing of Books* (London: Cassell, 1947 [first edition 1938]), pp. 92, 175.
3. Paul Johnston, "Modern Fine Book Printing in America," *American Printer*, XC (March 1930): 37.
4. Margaret Bingham Stillwell, "The Heritage of the Modern Printer," *Bulletin of the New York Public Library*, XX (October 1916): 737–750.
5. Harry Lawrence Gage, *Applied Design for Printers* (Chicago: United Typothetae of America, 1920), p. 54.
6. Henry L. Bullen, "William Morris: Regenerator of the Typographic Art," *Inland Printer*, LXIX (June 1922): 369.
7. Both quoted in William Morris Society, *The Typographical Adventure of William Morris* (London: William Morris Society, 1957), p. 32.
8. John T. Winterich, *The Works of Geoffrey Chaucer: A Facsimile of the William Morris Kelmscott Chaucer* (Cleveland: World, 1958), p. xii.
9. Bruce Rogers, footnote to James M. Wells, ed., "Letters from Bruce Rogers to Henry Watson Kent," *Printing and Graphic Arts*, III (February 1955): 9.
10. John Cotton Dana in Newark Public Library, *The Richard C. Jenkinson Collection of Books Chosen to Show the Work of the Best Printers*, Book II, (Newark: Newark Public Library, 1929), pp. vi–vii.
11. August Dietz, "The Printing House Craftsmen Movement in America," in A. Ruppel, ed., *Gutenberg Festschrift* (Mainz: Gutenberg-Gesellschaft, 1925), p. 207.
12. "Modern Typography," *Times Literary Supplement Printing Number* (October 13, 1927): 3-4.
13. Jackson, *The Printing of Books*, pp. 33–35.
14. Adrian Wilson, *The Design of Books* (New York: Reinhold, 1967), p. 143.
15. I. H. I., "The Kelmscott Press: An Illustrated Interview with Mr. William Morris," *Bookselling*, I (November 1895): 3.
16. Jackson, *The Printing of Books*, p. 14.
17. Roderick Cave, *The Private Press* (London: Faber and Faber, 1971), p. 147.
18. Holbrook Jackson, "The Aesthetics of Printing," *Gutenberg-Jahrbuch*, XXV (1950): 395.
19. [Editorial] *American Bookmaker*, IX (July 1889): 16.

APPENDIX

Morris' Statements on Book Design

The excerpts that follow are arranged in categories in descending order of importance, according to the amount of space given them by Morris. The number in parentheses following each excerpt refers to the number in the list of sources at the end of this appendix.

TYPE

General

. . . it is of the first importance that the letter used should be fine in form. . . . (1)

. . . if you want a legible book, the white should be clear and the black black. . . . You may depend upon it that a gray page is very trying to the eyes. (3)

Smoothness of cut and symmetry of form are not really needed in types. The eye craves some angularity and irregularity; without them the printed page becomes wearisome. (15)

The books made by expert mediaeval copyists, and by famous early printers, are good models of style. (15)

I began printing books with the hope of producing some which would have a definite claim to beauty, while at the same time they should be easy to read and should not dazzle the eye, or trouble the intellect of the reader by eccentricity of form in the letters. (6)

As to the fifteenth century books, I had noticed that they were always beautiful by force of the mere typography, even without the added ornament, with which many of them are so lavishly supplied. (6)

The early printers were wonderful fellows for seizing the main ideas, and they gradually worked out, taking the script letters for their basis, sets of types in Gothic and Roman forms, which we have hardly equalled to-day. Of course we have improved on the Roman letters, and the best work of the Caslons can hardly be excelled. But what I want to point out is that the beauty of the form is with such printers as Jenson, Pannartz, Coburger, and others, almost perfectly realized. My own types hardly differ from theirs in essentials. They are not the same, of course, but they are not altogether original. It would be impossible to obtain absolute originality where the sphere of action, so to speak, of the designer, is so very limited. (14)

Size

The book should be as easily readable to the mature man as to the schoolboy. The employment of small types (unavoidable for newspapers, Bibles, dictionaries, etc.) is to be regretted. Large type is to be preferred, and hair-lines avoided. (15)

Commercialism again compels the use of type too small in size to be comfortable reading: the size known as 'Long primer' ought to be the smallest size used in a book meant to be read. (1)

. . . you cannot have a book either handsome or clear to read which is printed in small characters . . . small pica seems to me the smallest type that should be used in the body of any book. (3)

Roman

Types should be black and bold. The great faults of modern Roman types are feebleness and grayness. (15)

The full-sized lower case letters, "a," "b," "d," & "c," should be designed on something like a square to get good results . . . each letter should have its due characteristic drawing; e.g., the thickening out for a "b," should not be of the same kind as that for a "d"; a "u" should not merely be an "n" turned upside down; the dot of the "i" should not be a circle drawn with compasses, but a delicately drawn diamond, and so on. To be short, the letters should be designed by an artist and not an engineer. (3)

Jenson

Of Jenson it must be said that he carried the development of Roman type as far as it can go. . . . (1)

Most of Jenson's letters are designed within a square, the modern letters are narrowed by a third or thereabouts; but while this gain of space very much hampers the possibility of beauty of design, it is not a real gain, for the modern printer throws the gain away by putting inordinately wide spaces between his lines, which, probably, the lateral compression of his letters renders necessary. (1)

. . . what I wanted was letter pure in form; severe, without needless excrescences; solid, without the thickening and thinning of the line, which is the essential fault of the ordinary modern type, and which makes it difficult to read; and not compressed laterally, as all later type has grown to be owing to commercial exigencies. There was only one source from which to take examples of this perfected Roman type, to wit, the works of the great Venetian printers of the fifteenth century, of which Nicholas Jenson produced the completest and most Roman characters from 1470 to 1476. . . . I did not copy it servilely; in fact, my Roman type, especially in the lower case, tends rather more to the Gothic than does Jenson's. (6)

Aldus

[Aldine] type is artistically on a much lower level than Jenson's. . . . (1)

Caslon

Caslon's type is clear and neat, and fairly well designed. . . . (1)

224

The design of the letters of this modern 'old style' [i.e., Caslon re-cut by Miller & Richard of Edinburgh in 1850] leaves a good deal to be desired, and the whole effect is a little too gray, owing to the thinness of the letters. It must be remembered, however, that most modern printing is done by machinery on soft paper, and not by the hand press, and these somewhat wiry letters are suitable for the machine process, which would not do justice to letters of more generous design. (1)

. . . legibility is the first thing to be aimed at in the forms of the letters; this is best furthered by the avoidance of irrational swellings and spiky projections, and by the using of careful purity of line. Even the Caslon type when enlarged shows great shortcomings in this respect. . . . (1)

Modern

[Bodoni and Didot style types of the eighteenth century] are dazzling and unpleasant to the eye owing to the clumsy thickening and vulgar thinning of the lines. . . . (1)

The sweltering hideousness of the Bodoni letter, the most illegible type that was ever cut. . . . (3)

Gothic

. . . black letter . . . developed more completely and satisfactorily on the side of the 'lower-case' than capital letters. . . . (1)

[The 1462 Bible] imitates a much freer hand, simpler, rounder, and less spiky, and therefore far pleasanter and easier to read. (1)

The Roman face of type, with its many admitted merits, is not the culmination of good taste and common sense. For many books the old black and angular Gothic faces are better. The eye that may be the first offended by the eccentricity of its capital letters, soon recognizes these eccentricities as useful in preventing insipid monotony. (15)

I would . . . put in a word for some form of gothic letter . . . [not too] prepensely gothic [but] transitional. (3)

. . . a good deal of the difficulty of reading gothic books is caused by the numerous contractions in them, which were a survival of the practice of the scribes; and in a lesser degree by the over abundance of tied letters, both of which drawbacks I take it for granted would be absent in modern types founded on these semi-gothic letters . . . in my opinion the capitals are the strong side of roman, and the lower case of gothic letter. . . . (3)

. . . the task I set myself was to redeem the Gothic character from the charge of unreadableness. . . . So I entirely eschewed contractions, except for the "&," and had very few tied letters. . . . I designed a black-letter type which I think I may claim to be as readable as a Roman one, and to say the truth I prefer it to the Roman. (6)

COMPOSITION

Letter and Word Spacing

Also I am beginning to learn something about the art of typesetting; and now I see what a lot of difference there is between the work of the conceited numskulls of to-day and that of the 15th and 16th century printers merely in the arrangement of the words, I mean the spacing out: it makes all the difference to the beauty of a page of print. (Letter, December 1888, to F. S. Ellis.) (8)

. . . double column seems to me chiefly fit for black letter, which prints up so close. (Letter, 31 December 1890, to F. S. Ellis.) (8)

In good printing the spaces between the words should be as near as possible equal. (1) The general *solidarity* of a page is much to be sought for: modern printers generally overdo the 'whites' in the spacing, a defect probably forced on them by the characterless quality of the letters. For where these are boldly and carefully designed, and each letter is thoroughly individual in form, the words may be set much closer together, without loss of clearness. No definite rules, however, except the avoidance of 'rivers' and excess of white, can be given for the spacing, which requires the constant exercise of judgment and taste on the part of the printer. (1)

One thing should never be done in ideal printing, the spacing out of letters, that is, putting an extra white between them. . . . No more white should be used between the words than just clearly cuts them off from one another; if the whites are bigger than this, it both tends to illegibility and makes the page ugly. (3)

Leading

. . . if the practice of 'leading' were retrenched larger type could be used without enhancing the price of the book. (1)

. . . the 'face' of the letter should be as nearly conterminous with the 'body' as possible . . . the modern practice of 'leading' should be used as little as possible, and never without some definite reason. . . . (6)

Margins

. . . whenever they saw a book that was rightly put upon the paper, even if the type was bad and the paper not good, the book would look rather pleasant than otherwise; whereas if the book were not properly put upon the paper it would always seem that something was wrong. When they had paid attention to these points they would have books which any one could read with pleasure, and he thought it was something to feel that they were reading a little bit through their eyes as well as through their mind. (Cheers.) (10)

The two facing pages of an opened book are correlated and should be reasonably close together. The back margins of ordinary books are too wide. (15)

The modern printer . . . considers the single page as the unit, and prints the page in the middle of his paper—only nominally so, however, in many cases, since when he uses a headline he counts that in. . . . (1)

. . . we only occasionally see one page of a book at a time; the two pages making an opening are really the unit of the book; and this was thoroughly understood by the old book producers . . . the binder edge (that which is bound in) must be the smallest member of the margins, the head margin must be larger than this, the fore larger still, and the tail largest of all. (3)

. . . concerning large paper copies. I am clean against them, though I have sinned a good deal in that way myself; but that was in the days of ignorance. . . . If the margins are right for the smaller book, they must be wrong for the larger; and you have to offer the public the worse book at the bigger price. If they are right for the large paper, they are wrong for the small. . . . (3)

A friend, the librarian of one of our most important private libraries, tells me that after careful testing he has come to the conclusion that the medieval rule was to make a difference of 20 percent from margin to margin. (6)

PAPER

. . . the paper should be good, which is a more important point than might be thought, and one on which there is a most complete contrast between the old and the modern books. . . . (2)

The paper that is used for ordinary books is exceedingly bad even in this country, but is beaten in the race for vileness by that made in America, which is the worst conceivable. (1)

One fruitful source of badness in paper is . . . eking out a thin volume by printing it on thick paper almost of the substance of cardboard. . . . On the whole, a small book should be printed on paper which is as thin as may be without being transparent. (1)

. . . the fact must not be blinked that machine-made paper cannot in the nature of things be made of so good a texture as that made by hand. (1)

Hand-made paper, with its infelicities of rough edges, hard face, and uneven size and thickness, is more trustworthy than that made by machine. It is a better background for strong types. You cannot print modern types upon hand-made paper, and upon a machine with the best result. You must wet the paper and print upon a hand-press by the old methods. (15)

Our ideal book must, I think, be printed on hand-made paper as good as it can be made; penury here will make a poor book of it. Yet if machine-made paper must be used, it should not profess fineness or luxury; but should show itself for what it is. (3)

For my part, I decidedly prefer the cheaper papers that are used for the journals, so far as appearance is concerned, to the thick, smooth, sham-fine papers on which respectable books are printed, and the worst of these are those which imitate the structure of hand-made papers. (3)

A small book should not be printed on thick paper, however good it may be. You want a book to turn over easily, and to lie quiet while you are reading it. . . .
The fact is, a small book seldom does lie quiet. . . . Whereas, a big folio lies quiet and majestic on the table . . . with its leaves flat and peaceful. . . . (3)

. . . 1st, that the paper must be wholly of linen (most hand-made papers are of cotton today), and must be quite 'hard,' i.e., thoroughly well sized; and 2nd, that though it must be 'laid' and not 'wove' . . . the lines caused by the wires of the mould must not be too strong, so as to give a ribbed appearance. . . . So I took as my model a Bolognese paper of about 1473. (6)

DECORATION

I do not know anything more dispiriting than the mere platitudes of printer's ornaments: trade ornaments. (2)

. . . the value of a well-drawn line, crisp and clean, suggesting a simple and beautiful *silhouette*. (2)

. . . the ornament, whatever it is, whether picture or pattern-work, should form *part of the page*, should be part of the whole scheme of the book. (1)

. . . books whose only ornament is the necessary and essential beauty which arises out of the fitness of a piece of craftsmanship for the use which it is made. (3)

. . . the Mediaeval craftsman had two sides to his artistic mind, the love of ornament, & the love of story. (7)

Decoration is permissible and often praiseworthy, but it must be real decoration and not frippery. It must not be patchwork. It must be in harmony with the types—must help, not hinder. (15).

Simple arrangements of types are more pleasing to the educated reader than those that are artificial and fussy. (15)

It was only natural that I, a decorator by profession, should attempt to ornament my books suitably; about this matter I will only say that I have always tried to keep in mind the necessity for making my decorations a part of the page of type. (6)

[The pictures'] two main merits are first their decorative and next their story-telling quality; and it seems to me that these two qualities include what is necessary and essential in book-pictures. (5)

. . . the art of the Middle Ages [in Germany] fell dead in a space of about five years, and was succeeded by a singularly stupid and brutal phase of that rhetorical and academical art, which, in all matters of ornament, has held Europe captive ever since. (5)

UNITY

The question . . . is this, Whether we are to have books which are beautiful as books; books in which type, paper, woodcuts, and the due arrangement of all these are to be considered, and which are so treated as to produce a harmonious whole, something which will give a person with a sense of beauty real pleasure whenever and wherever the book is opened, even before he begins to look closely into the illustrations; or whether the beautiful and inventive illustrations are to be looked on as separate pictures embedded in a piece of utilitarianism, which they cannot decorate because it cannot help them to do so. (2)

. . . in this country . . . a great deal of work intending to ornament books reasonably is turned out . . . which, in fact, is seldom satisfactory unless the whole page, picture, ornament, and type is reproduced literally from the handiwork of the artist, as in some of the beautiful works of Mr. Walter Crane. (2)

The illustrations should not have a mere accidental connection with the other ornament and the type, but an essential and artistic connection. (2)

. . . the designer[s] . . . , the wood-engraver, and the printer, all of them thoughtful, painstaking artists, and all working in harmonious cooperation for the production of a work of art. This is the only possible way in which you can get beautiful books. (2)

Any fashion of type, composition, or presswork, any fad in paper or binding that interferes or distracts, is a mistake. (15)

ARCHITECTURAL ANALOGY

. . . the only work of art which surpasses a complete Medieval book is a complete Medieval building. (2)

. . . a book quite unornamented can look actually and positively beautiful, and not merely un-ugly, if it be, so to say, architecturally good, which by the by, need not add much to its price. . . .

First, the pages must be clear and easy to read; which they can hardly be unless, Secondly, the type is well designed; and Thirdly, whether the margins be small or big, they must be in due proportion to the page of letter. (3)

The ornament must form as much a part of the page as the type itself . . . and in order to succeed . . . it must submit to certain limitations, and become architectural. . . . (3)

. . . a book ornamented with pictures that are suitable . . . may become a work of art second to none, save a fine building duly decorated, or a fine piece of literature. (3)

CRAFTSMANSHIP

If any real school of wood-engraving is to exist again, the wood-cutter must be an artist translating the designer's drawing. (2)

The design must be suitable to the material and method of reproduction. . . . (2)

The first thing necessary was to have a certain number of artists who had an intense desire to produce work suitable for book ornament; and those artists would, in some way, force the public to give them an opportunity for producing those books. (2)

. . . printed books might once again illustrate to the full the position of our Society that a work of utility might be also a work of art, if we cared to make it so. (1)

The thought of the author is of first importance to the reader. The deliberate obtrusion of technical skill by any mechanic who contributes to the making of the book, is an impertinence. (15)

The hand-press for small editions is more efficient and useful than any form of printing machine. (15)

[Printing] was born full grown and perfect, but began to deteriorate almost at once. For one thing, of course, it was invented just at the end of the mediaeval period, when everything was already pretty far gone. And its history, as a whole, has practically coincided with the growth of the commercial system, the requirements of which have been fatal, so far as beauty is concerned, to anything which has come within its scope. (13)

SOURCES

1. (With Emery Walker), "Printing," in *Arts and Crafts Essays* (London: Rivington, Percival, 1893), pp. 111–133. A rewriting of Walker's 1888 talk before the Arts and Crafts Exhibition Society.
2. "The Woodcuts of Gothic Books," in May Morris, *William Morris: Artist, Writer, Socialist*, Vol. 1 (New York: Russell & Russell, 1966—reprint of 1936 edition), pp. 318–338. A paper read before the Society of Arts, 26 January 1892; "Some German Woodcuts of the Fifteenth Century" is an abridgment.
3. "The Ideal Book," in May Morris, op. cit., pp. 310–318. A paper read before the Bibliographical Society, 19 June 1893.
4. "Some Notes on the Illuminated Books of the Middle Ages," *Magazine of Art* XVII (1894): 83–88. In May Morris, op. cit., pp. 338–346.
5. "On the Artistic Qualities of the Woodcut Books of Ulm and Augsburg in the Fifteenth

Century," *Bibliographica* I (1895): 437–455. In May Morris, op. cit., pp. 346–356.

6. *A Note by William Morris on His Aims in Founding the Kelmscott Press*, 11 November 1895, first printed in "The Kelmscott Press," *Modern Art* IV (April 1896): 36–39. Published in 1898 as the last book of the Kelmscott Press.

7. *Some Thoughts on the Ornamented MSS of the Middle Ages* (New York: The Press of the Woolly Whale, 1934). Taken from a manuscript at the Huntington Library.

8. *The Letters of William Morris to His Family and Friends*, edited with introduction and notes by Philip Henderson (London: Longmans, Green, 1950).

9. Unpublished lecture: "Printed Books, Ancient and Modern," October 21, 1893, referred to in Eugene D. Lemire, *The Unpublished Lectures of William Morris* (Detroit: Wayne State University Press, 1969), p. 320.

10. Unpublished lecture: "On the Printing of Books," 2 November 1893, for which there exists a notice in the *Times* of 6 November 1893, p. 4. Also see "William Morris on the Printing of Books," *Publishers Weekly* XLIV (December 30, 1893): 1065–1066.

11. "The Poet as Printer: An Interview with Mr. William Morris," *Pall Mall Gazette* LIII (November 12, 1891): 1–2.

12. *Daily Chronicle* interview referred to in "Editorial Notes," *Engraver and Printer* III (March 1893): 87–88.

13. A.B., "William Morris at the Kelmscott Press," *English Illustrated Magazine* XIII (April 1895): 47–55.

14. I.H.I., "The Kelmscott Press: An Illustrated Interview with Mr. William Morris," *Bookselling* I (November 1895): 2–14.

15. Theodore Low De Vinne, "The Printing of William Morris," *Book Buyer* XIII (January 1897): 920–923.

BIBLIOGRAPHY

Design Examples

PRINTED BOOKS

1. Ade, George. *Fables in Slang*. Chicago: Herbert S. Stone, 1900.
2. ———. *More Fables*. Chicago: Herbert S. Stone, 1900.
3. Aldrich, Thomas Bailey. *Friar Jerome's Beautiful Book*. Boston: Houghton Mifflin, 1896.
4. Allen, James. *As a Man Thinketh*. New York: Crowell, n.d.
5. [Andrews, William Loring]. *The Treatyse of Fysshynge wyth an Angle*. New York: Scribner's, 1903.
6. *The Altar Book: Containing the Order for the Celebration of the Holy Eucharist According to the Use of the American Church*. Boston: Merrymount Press, 1896.
7. *An Antidote Against Melancholy: Compounded of Choice Poems, Jovial Songs, Merrie Ballads &c.* New York: Pratt Manufacturing Company, 1884.
8. Applegate, Bergen, trans. and ed. *Paul Verlaine: His Absinthe-Tinted Song*. Chicago: Alderbrink Press, 1916.
9. Arnold, Matthew, *Empedocles on Etna: A Dramatic Poem*. Portland: Mosher, 1900.
10. *Aucassin and Nicolete*. Translated by Andrew Lang. New Rochelle: Elston Press, 1902.
11. *Aucassin & Nicolete: Being a Love Story Translated out of the Ancient French by Andrew Lang*. East Aurora: Roycrofters, 1899.
12. *This Is of Aucassin and Nicolette: A Song-Tale of True Lovers*. Boston: Copeland & Day, 1897.
13. Aytoun, W. E. *Lays of the Scottish Cavaliers*. New York: Home Book Company, n.d.
14. B., A. C. [Alice Cary Bussing]. *Some Verse*. New York: De Vinne Press, 1897.
15. Barlow, Joel. *The Columbiad: A Poem*. Philadelphia: Fry and Kammerer, 1807.
16. [Barr, James]. Abbott, Angus Evan. *The Gods Give My Donkey Wings*. Chicago: Stone & Kimball, 1895.
17. Barrie, J. M. *George Meredith: A Tribute*. Portland: Mosher, 1909.
18. Baum, Lyman Frank. *By the Candelabra's Glare: Some Verse*. Chicago: Privately printed, 1898.
19. Bible. *The Book of Ruth: Taken from an Edition of the Bible Printed at Oxford in 1680*. Indianapolis: Bobbs-Merrill, 1904.
20. ———. *The Book of Ruth and the Book of Esther*. New York: Published for Will Bradley by R. H. Russell, 1897.
21. ———. *The 91st Psalm*. Hingham: W. A. Dwiggins, 1906.
22. ———. *The 91st Psalm Reprinted from the King James Version*. Boston: Alfred Bartlett, 1909.
23. ———. *The Parable of the Prodigal Son*. Boston: Alfred Bartlett, 1905.
24. ———. *The Revelation of St. John the Divine*. Detroit: Cranbrook Press, 1901.
25. ———. *The Song of Songs which is Solomon's: Being a Reprint and a Study by Elbert Hubbard*. East Aurora: Roycrofters, 1896.
26. [Blackburn, Laura]. Blanden, Charles Granger. *A Harvest of Reeds*. Chicago: Blue Sky Press, 1902.
27. ———. *Omar Resung*. Chicago: Blue Sky Press, 1901.
28. Blackmore, Richard Doddridge. *Fringilla: Or Tales in Verse*. Cleveland: Burrows Brothers, 1895.
29. Blake, William. *Songs of Innocence and Experience*. Chicago: Alderbrink Press, 1906.
30. *The Blind Princess and the Dawn: Two Poems*. Park Ridge: Village Press, 1904.
31. Blunt, Wilfrid Scawen. *Esther: A Young Man's Tragedy, together with the Love Sonnets of Proteus*. Boston: Copeland & Day, 1895.
32. Bolton, Charles Knowles. *On the Wooing of Martha Pitkin: Being a Versified Narrative of the Time of the Regicides in Colonial New England*. Boston: Copeland & Day, 1896.
33. Bonfils, Winifred Black. *The Life and Person-*

ality of Phoebe Apperson Hearst. San Francisco: John Henry Nash, 1928.

34. *The Book of Common Prayer.* New York: De Vinne Press, 1893.

35. *A Book of Shakespeare's Songs.* New York: G. Schirmer, 1903.

36. Booth, George G. *Something About the Cranbrook Press and on Books and Bookmaking.* Detroit: Cranbrook Press, 1902.

37. [Bradley, Will H.]. *A Portfolio of Printing: Being a Collection of Proofs of the Commercial Work Done at the Wayside Press, Springfield, Mass.* Springfield: Wayside Press [1897].

38. _____. *Some Examples of Printing and Drawing: The Work of Will Bradley, Issued in this Wise as an Advertisement by the University Press, at Cambridge, U.S.A.* Cambridge: University Press [1898].

39. *Bradley: His Book* [Prospectus]. Springfield: Wayside Press, 1896.

40. [Brown, Alice]. *The Rose of Hope.* Boston: Copeland & Day, 1896.

41. Brown, Anna Robertson. *What Is Worth While?* New York: Crowell, 1897.

42. Brown, Neal. *Critical Confessions.* Wausau: Philosopher Press, 1899.

43. Browne, Thomas. *Religio Medici.* Boston: Little, Brown, n.d.

44. Browning, Elizabeth Barrett. *Sonnets from the Portuguese.* Boston: Ticknor, 1886.

45. _____. *Sonnets from the Portuguese.* Boston: Copeland & Day, 1896.

46. _____. *Sonnets from the Portuguese.* New York: Elston Press, 1900.

47. _____. *Sonnets from the Portuguese.* Aiken: Palmetto Press, 1900.

48. _____. *Sonnets from the Portuguese.* Boston: Small, Maynard, 1902.

49. _____. *Sonnets from the Portuguese with Lyric Interludes.* San Francisco: Paul Elder and Co., 1910.

50. Browning, Robert. *Andrea Del Sarto: A Dramatic Monologue.* Englewood: Hillside Press, 1906.

51. _____. *In a Balcony.* Chicago: Blue Sky Press, 1902.

52. _____. *The Last Ride.* East Aurora: Roycrofters, 1900.

53. _____. *Rabbi Ben Ezra.* Concord: The Sign of the Vine, n.d.

54. _____. *Rabbi Ben Ezra: A Dramatic Monologue.* Hingham: Village Press, 1904.

55. Bulwer-Lytton, Edward. *Richelieu or the Conspiracy.* Philadelphia: McKay, 1901.

56. _____. *The World as It Is.* Jamaica: Marion Press, 1898.

57. Bunyan, John. *The Pilgrim's Progress from this World to that which Is to come.* New York: Century, 1898.

58. Buonarroti, Michelangelo. *Sonnets and Madrigals.* Cambridge: Riverside Press, 1900.

59. Burgess, Gelett. *Vivette or the Memoirs of the Romance Association.* Boston: Copeland & Day, 1897.

60. Burne-Jones, Edward. *In the Dawn of the World.* Boston: Charles E. Goodspeed, 1903.

61. Burr, Amelia J. *Plays in the Market Place.* Englewood: Hillside Press, 1910.

62. _____. *The Point of Life: A Play in Three Acts.* Englewood: Hillside Press, 1907.

63. _____. *The Sleep of Beppo: A Poem.* Englewood: Hillside Press, 1909.

64. Burr, Frederic M. *A Criminal in Stone.* Englewood: Hillside Press, 1908.

65. Bury, Richard de. *Philobiblon.* 3 vols. New York: Grolier Club, 1889.

66. Carman, Bliss. *Behind the Arras: A Book of the Unseen.* Boston: Lamson, Wolffe, 1895.

67. _____. *The Word at St. Kavin's.* Nelson, New Hampshire: Monadnock Press, 1903.

68. Carman, Bliss, and Richard Hovey. *Songs from Vagabondia.* Boston: Copeland & Day, 1894.

69. Cawein, Madison. *Shapes and Shadows.* New York: R. H. Russell, 1898.

70. Chaucer, Geoffrey. *The Nonnes Preestes Tale of the Cok and Hen.* New York: Grafton Press, 1902.

71. _____. *The Parlement of Foules.* Cambridge: Riverside Press, 1904.

72. Cobden-Sanderson, Thomas James. *The Ideal Book.* San Francisco: John Henry Nash, 1916.

73. [Coleridge, Mary Elizabeth]. "Anodos." *Fancy's Following.* Portland: Mosher, 1900.

74. Coleridge, Samuel Taylor. *Ye Ancient Mariner.* East Aurora: Roycrofters, 1899.

75. Cowley, Abraham. *Essays.* Highland Park, Illinois: Elm Press, 1902.

76. [Cram, Ralph Adams]. *The Decadent: Being the Gospel of Inaction: Wherein are Set Forth in Romance Form Certain Reflections Touching the Curious Characteristics of these Ultimate Years, and the Divers Causes Thereof.* Boston: Copeland & Day, 1893.

77. Cranbrook Society. *Cranbrook Papers: First Book.* Detroit: Cranbrook Press, 1901.

78. Crane, Stephen. *The Black Riders.* Boston: Copeland & Day, 1895.

79. _____. *War Is Kind.* New York: Stokes, 1899.

80. Crippen, Layton. *Olympus and FujiYama: A Study in Transcendental History.* New York: Grannis Press, 1905.

81. Crow, Martha Foote. *The Ministry of a Child: A Book of Verses.* Chicago: Wind-Tryst Press, 1899.

82. Dante Alighieri. *The Divine Comedy.* Translated by Melville Best Anderson. 3 vols. San Francisco: John Henry Nash, 1929.

83. [Darrow, Burritt]. *An Account of the Pilgrimage to the Tomb of General Grant.* New York: Privately printed, 1900.

84. *A Description of the Pastoral Staff Belonging to the Diocese of Albany, New York, Anno Domini MDCCCXCVII: With Representations of the Chief Parts of the Staff.* Boston: Merrymount Press, 1900.

85. *The Dictes & Sayings of the Philosophers.* Detroit: Cranbrook Press, 1901.

86. Dilke, Amelia Frances (Strong), Lady. *The Shrine of Death and the Shrine of Love.* Boston: Cornhill Press, 1901.

87. Drummond, Henry. *Addresses.* New York: Caldwell, n.d.

88. Dunbar, Paul Lawrence. *Candle-Lightin' Time.* New York: Dodd, Mead, 1901.

89. _____. *Majors and Minors.* Toledo: Hadly and Hadly Printers, 1895.

90. _____. *Poems of Cabin and Field.* New York: Dodd, Mead, 1899.

91. _____. *When Malindy Sings. . . .* New York: Dodd, Mead, 1906.

92. Elder, Paul, comp. *Mosaic Essays.* San Francisco and New York: Tomoyé Press, 1906.

93. Emerson, Ralph Waldo. *Compensation.* East Aurora: Roycrofters, 1904.

94. _____. *The Essay on Nature.* Ridgewood: Alwil Shop, 1902.

95. _____. *Nature.* East Aurora: Roycrofters, 1905.

96. _____. *Prudence.* New York and San Francisco: Morgan Shepard, 1906.

97. _____. *Representative Men.* Chicago: Donahue, n.d.

98. _____. *Self-Reliance.* Wausau: Philosopher Press, 1901.

99. [Field, Eugene]. *Eugene Field: An Auto-Analysis.* Chicago: Frank M. Morris, 1896.

100. _____. *The Holy Cross and Other Tales.* Cambridge and Chicago: Stone & Kimball, 1893.

101. [Finley, John H.]. *Ellen: Her Book, Being a Collection of Rhymes about Ellen Boyden Finley & Some of her Childhood Friends.* Galesburg, Illinois: Cadmus Press, 1897.

102. Foote, Louisa Young. *In the Adirondacks.* Chicago: Wind-Tryst Press, 1897.

103. _____. *The Old Homestead.* Chicago: Wind-Tryst Press, 1899.

104. Fouque, De La Motte. *Undine.* Philadelphia: Altemus, n.d.

105. Fowler, Egbert Willard. *Dream-Rest.* Ridgewood: Alwil Shop, 1901.

106. Gannett, William C. *The House Beautiful.* River Forest, Illinois: Auvergne Press, 1897.

107. Gilder, Richard Watson. *A Christmas Wreath.* New York: Century, 1903.

108. Gruelle, R. B. *Notes: Critical & Biographical.* Indianapolis: J. M. Bowles, 1895.

109. Guerin, Maurice. *The Centaur.* Translated by George B. Ives. Montague: Montague Press, 1915.

110. Guiney, Louise Imogen. *Nine Sonnets Written at Oxford.* Boston: Copeland & Day, 1895.

111. _____. *Patrins: To Which Is Added an Inquirendo into the Wit & Other Good Parts of His Late Majesty King Charles the Second.* Boston: Copeland & Day, 1897.

112. Haines, Jennie Day. *Ye Gardeyne Boke.* San Francisco: Paul Elder, 1906.

113. _____. *Weather Opinions.* New York: Paul Elder, 1907.

114. Hall, Tom. *When Hearts Are Trumps.* Chicago: Stone & Kimball, 1894.

115. *Hand and Brain: A Symposium of Essays on Socialism by William Morris, Grant Allen, George Bernard Shaw, Henry S. Salt, Alfred Russel Wallace, and Edward Carpenter.* East Aurora: Roycrofters, 1898.

116. Harrison, Mrs. Burton. *The Merry Maid of Arcady, His Lordship and Other Stories.* Boston: Lamson, Wolffe, 1897.

117. Hawthorne, Nathaniel. *Our Old Home: A Series of English Sketches.* Boston: Houghton Mifflin, 1899.

118. _____. *A Wonder Book.* New York: Mershon, n.d.

119. Heredia, José-Maria de. *The Trophies.* Translated by Frank Sewall. Boston: Small, Maynard, 1900.

120. Herrick, S[ophie] B[ledsoe], ed. *A Century of Sonnets.* New York: R. H. Russell, 1902.

121. Hewlett, Maurice. *The Birth of Roland.* Chicago: Alderbrink Press, 1911.

122. _____. *A Sacrifice at Prato: An Old-Fashioned Narrative,* Englewood: Hillside Press, 1908.

123. Holmes, Oliver Wendell. *One Hoss Shay and Other Poems.* New York: Caldwell, n.d.

124. Hope, Anthony. *Phroso: A Romance.* 2d ed. New York: Stokes, 1897.

125. Housman, Laurence. *Blind Love.* Boston: Cornhill Press, 1901.

126. Howells, William Dean. *A Day's Pleasure and Other Sketches.* Boston: Houghton Mifflin, 1881.

127. Howells, William Hooper. *The Rescue of Desdemona and Other Verse.* Philadelphia: Butterfly Press, 1908.

128. Hubbard, Alice. *The Myth in Marriage.* East Aurora: Roycrofters, 1912.

129. Hubbard, Elbert. *Abe Lincoln and Nancy Hanks.*

East Aurora: Roycrofters, 1920.

130. _____. *The City of Tagaste and a Dream and a Prophecy*. East Aurora: Roycrofters, 1900.

131. _____. *The Doctors: A Satire in Four Seizures*. East Aurora: Roycrofters, 1909.

132. _____. *Little Journeys to the Homes of English Authors: William Morris*. East Aurora: Roycrofters, 1900.

133. _____. *Little Journeys to the Homes of English Authors: Thomas B. Macaulay*. East Aurora: Roycrofters, 1900.

134. _____. *Love, Life & Work*. East Aurora: Roycrofters, 1906.

135. _____. *The Man of Sorrows: A Little Journey to the Home of Jesus of Nazareth*. East Aurora: Roycrofters, 1904.

136. _____. *A Message to Garcia: Being a Preachment*. East Aurora: Roycrofters, 1899.

137. [_____]. Fra Elbertus. *The Motto Book: Being A Catalogue of Epigrams*. East Aurora: Roycrofters, 1909.

138. [_____]. *Respectability: Its Rise and Remedy*. East Aurora: Roycrofters, 1905.

139. _____. *White Hyacinths*. East Aurora: Roycrofters, 1907.

140. _____. *A William Morris Book*. East Aurora: Roycrofters, 1907.

141. Hubbard, Elbert, and Alice Hubbard. *Justinian and Theodora: A Drama Being a Chapter of History and the One Gleam of Light During the Dark Ages*. East Aurora: Roycrofters, 1906.

142. Huckel, Oliver. *Parsifal: A Mystical Drama by Richard Wagner Retold in the Spirit of the Bayreuth Interpretation*. New York: Crowell, 1910.

143. _____. *Tannhäuser: A Dramatic Poem by Richard Wagner Freely Translated in Poetic Narrative Form*. New York: Crowell, 1906.

144. Hugo, Victor. *The Battle of Waterloo*. East Aurora: Roycrofters, 1907.

145. Huntington, William Reed. *Sonnets and a Dream*. Jamaica: Marion Press, 1899.

146. Irving, Washington. *Knickerbocker History of New York*. New York: Cosmada Library, n.d.

147. _____. *The Legend of Sleepy Hollow*. New York: Published for the University Press by Harper, 1897.

148. _____. *Rip Van Winkle*. New York: Published for the University Press by Harper, 1897.

149. _____. *Rip Van Winkle*. East Aurora: Roycrofters, 1905.

150. _____. *Sketch Book*. Artist's Edition. New York: Putnam, 1864.

151. Jonson, Ben. *Three Masques*. New York: Robert Grier Cooke, 1903.

152. Keats, John. *The Eve of St. Agnes*. Chicago: Ralph Fletcher Seymour, 1900.

153. _____. *Odes & Sonnets*. Philadelphia: Lippincott, 1888.

154. [Kimball, Ingalls]. *The First Ten Years of the Cheltenham Press: Being an Account of Various Problems in Printing and in Advertising and of Their Solution*. New York: Cheltenham Press, 1908.

155. *King Arthur and the Table Round*. Notes by William Wells Newell. 2 vols. Boston: Houghton Mifflin, 1897.

156. Knight, William Allen. *The Signs in the Christmas Fire*. Boston: Pilgrim Press, 1909.

157. Lamb, Charles. *A Dissertation upon Roast Pig*. Concord: The Sign of the Vine, n.d.

158. _____. *A Dissertation upon Roast Pig*. Park Ridge: Village Press, 1904.

159. Landor, Walter Savage. *A Vision and the Dream of Petrarca*. Chicago: Will H. Ransom, 1903.

160. Langland, William. *The Vision of William Concerning Piers the Plowman*. New Rochelle: Elston Press, 1901.

161. *The Leather Bottel*. Concord: The Sign of the Vine, 1903.

162. Leech, Carolyn Apperson. *When Mona Lisa Came Home*. Chicago: Alderbrink Press, 1914.

163. Le Gallienne, Richard. *Robert Louis Stevenson: An Elegy and Other Poems Mainly Personal*. Boston: Copeland & Day, 1895.

164. Leslie, Amy. *Fruit of the Roycroft*. East Aurora: Roycrofters, n.d.

165. Lindsay, William. *At Start and Finish*. Boston: Small, Maynard, 1899.

166. *A Little Candlemass Garland Gathered Out of Various Books*. Cleveland: Clerk's Private Press, 1914.

167. Longfellow, Henry Wadsworth. *Evangeline*. New York: Crowell, 1893.

168. McCulloch, Hugh, Jr. *The Quest of Heracles and Other Poems*. Cambridge and Chicago: Stone & Kimball, 1894.

169. Matteson, Estelle Lambert. *Phryne and Cleopatra*. Ridgewood: Alwil Shop, 1900.

170. Meredith, George. *Modern Love*. Portland: Mosher, 1891.

171. Milton, John. *Comus: A Maske*. New Rochelle: Elston Press, 1902.

172. _____. *The Poetical Works*. New York: Thomas Whittaker, n.d.

173. *The Miracles of Madame Saint Katherine of Fierbois*. Translated by Andrew Lang. Chicago: Way & Williams, 1897.

174. Monroe, Harriet. *The Columbian Ode*. Chicago: W. Irving Way, 1893.

175. [Moore, Edward Martin]. *Spoil of the North Wind*. Chicago: Blue Sky Press, 1901.

176. More, Thomas. *Utopia*. Detroit: Cranbrook Press, 1902.

177. Morgan, G. Campbell. *The Hidden Years at Nazareth*. New York: Fleming H. Revell, 1898.

178. Morris, William. *The Art and Craft of Printing*. New Rochelle: Elston Press, 1902.

179. _____. *The Art of the People*. Chicago: R. F. Seymour, 1902.

180. _____. *Atalanta's Race and Other Tales from the Earthly Paradise*. Boston: Ticknor, 1888.

181. _____. *Child Christopher and Goldilind the Fair*. Portland: Mosher, 1900.

182. _____. *The Doom of King Acrisius*. New York: R. H. Russell, 1902.

183. _____. *A Dream of John Ball*. East Aurora: Roycrofters, 1898.

184. _____. *The Earthly Paradise: A Poem*. Author's Edition. Boston: Roberts Brothers, 1893.

185. _____. *Five Arthurian Poems*. New Rochelle: Elston Press, 1902.

186. _____. *Gossip about an Old House on the Upper Thames*. Flushing: J. E. Hill, 1901.

187. [_____]. *The History of Over Sea*. New York: R. H. Russell, 1902.

188. _____. *The Hollow Land*. Hingham: Village Press, 1905.

189. _____. *The Ideal Book*. New York: Calumet Press, 1899.

190. _____. *In Praise of My Lady*. St. Charles, Illinois: Morris Press, 1902.

191. _____. *The Life and Death of Jason: A Poem*. Author's Edition. Boston: Roberts Brothers, 1886.

192. _____. *The Lovers of Gudrun: A Poem*. Boston: Roberts Brothers, 1870.

193. _____. *Pre-Raphaelite Ballads*. New York: Wessels, 1900.

194. _____. *Pygmalion and the Image*. New York: R. H. Russell, 1903.

195. [_____]. *The Saga of Hen Thorir*. Cincinnati: Byway Press, 1903.

196. _____. *Sir Galahad*. Chicago: Blue Sky Press, 1904.

197. _____. *Sir Galahad: A Christmas Mystery*. New Rochelle: Elston Press, 1902.

198. _____. *Some Notes on Early Woodcut Books with a Chapter on Illuminated Manuscripts*. New Rochelle: Elston Press, 1902.

199. _____. *The Story of the Glittering Plain*. Reprinted in Facsimile. Boston: Roberts Brothers, 1891.

200. _____. *The Sundering Flood*. New York: Longmans, Green, 1898.

201. _____. *Svend and His Brethren*. Aiken: Palmetto Press, 1901.

202. _____. *Svend and His Brethren: A Tale of the Ancient Days*. Englewood: Hillside Press, 1906.

203. _____. *The Tale of King Florus and the Fair Jehane Done out of the Ancient French into English*. Portland: Mosher, 1898.

204. _____. *The Water of the Wondrous Isles*. New York: Longmans, Green, 1897.

205. _____. *The Wood Beyond the World*. Boston: Roberts Brothers, 1895.

206. Morris, William, and Emery Walker. *Printing: An Essay*. Park Ridge: Village Press, 1903.

207. [Neal, Alice B.]. *Patient Waiting No Loss, or, the Two Christmas Days by "Cousin Alice."* New York: Appleton, 1853.

208. Neale, John M. *Good King Wenceslas*. Hingham: Village Press, 1904.

209. Noble, Alden Charles. *Lyrics to the Queen*. Chicago: Blue Sky Press, 1902.

210. O'Hara, Theodore. *Bivouac of the Dead*. Aiken: Palmetto Press, 1900.

211. *Oliver and Arthur*. Cambridge: Riverside Press, 1903.

212. Omar Khayyam. *Fifty Rubaiyat*. Paraphrased by Richard Le Gallienne. Wausau: Philosopher Press, 1901.

213. _____. *One Hundred Quatrains from the Rubaiyat: A Rendering in English Verse by Elizabeth Alden Curtis*. Gouverneur, New York: Brothers of the Book, 1899.

214. _____. *Rubaiyat: A Paraphrase from Several Literal Translations by Richard Le Gallienne*. New York: John Lane, The Bodley Head, 1897.

215. _____. *Rubaiyat: Rendered into English Quatrains by Edward Fitzgerald*. Edited by Nathan Haskell Dole. Boston: L. C. Page, 1899.

216. _____. *Rubaiyat: Rendered into English Verse by Edward Fitzgerald*. New York: Published for Will Bradley by R. H. Russell, 1897.

217. *On the Dedications of American Churches: An Enquiry into the Naming of Churches in the United States, Some Account of English Dedications, and Suggestions for Future Dedications in the American Church*. Cambridge: Riverside Press, 1891.

218. *Our Lady's Tumbler: A Tale of Mediaeval France*. Translated by Isabel Butler. Boston: Copeland & Day, 1898.

219. Paton, Sir Noel. *A Christmas Carol*. New York: Ivan Somerville, 1907.

220. Peabody, Josephine Preston. *In the Silence*. New York: Privately printed by Thomas Maitland Cleland, 1900.

221. Peattie, Elia W. *The Love of a Caliban: A Romantic Opera in One Act*. Wausau: Philosopher Press, 1898.

222. Perry, Marsden J. *A Chronological List of the Books Printed at the Kelmscott Press*. Boston: Merrymount Press, 1928.

223. Petrarch, Francesco. *The Triumphs*. Translated by Henry Boyd. Boston: Little, Brown, 1906.

224. Pollard, Alfred W. *Books in the House: An Essay on Private Libraries and Collections for Young and Old.* Indianapolis: Bobbs-Merrill, 1904.

225. Pope, Alexander. *The Rape of the Lock.* New Rochelle: Elston Press, 1902.

226. Rader, William. *The Elegy of Faith.* New York: Crowell, 1902.

227. Read, Opie. *Bolanyo: A Novel.* Chicago: Way & Williams, 1897.

228. Rivers, George R. R. *The Governor's Garden.* Boston: Joseph Knight, 1896.

229. Robertson, Donald. *Beauty's Lady and Other Verses.* Chicago: Alderbrink Press, 1910.

230. Rodd, Rennell. *Rose Leaf and Apple Leaf.* With an introduction by Oscar Wilde. Philadelphia: J. M. Stoddart, 1882.

231. Rosenfeld, Morris. *Songs from the Ghetto.* New and enlarged edition. Boston: Small, Maynard, 1900.

232. Rossetti, Dante Gabriel. *The Blessed Damozel.* Park Ridge: Village Press, 1903.

233. _____. *Hand & Soul.* Portland: Mosher, 1899.

234. _____. *The House of Life.* Boston: Copeland & Day, 1894.

235. _____. *The House of Life.* New Rochelle: Elston Press, 1901.

236. _____. *Poems.* 2 vols. Troy, New York: Pafraets, 1903.

237. Ruskin, John. *The King of the Golden River.* East Aurora: Roycrofters, 1900.

238. _____. *"Praeterita": Outlines of Scenes and Thoughts, Perhaps Worthy of Memory, in My Past Life.* Boston: Dana Estes, n.d.

239. [Russell, George] A. E. *Homeward Songs by the Way.* Portland: Mosher, 1895.

240. Sand, George. *Fadette.* New York: Crowell, n.d.

241. *Selected Passages from the 'Forget-Me-Not': A Jest in Sober Earnest.* Cleveland: Clerk's Private Press, 1915.

242. Seton-Thompson, Ernest. *The Trail of the Sandhill Stag.* New York: Scribner's, 1900.

243. Seymour, Ralph Fletcher. *Episodes in the Lives of Some Individuals Who Helped Shape the Growth of Our Midwest.* Chicago: R. F. Seymour, 1954.

244. Shakespeare, William. *King Henry V.* Philadelphia: David McKay, n.d.

245. *Shakespeare's Sonnets.* Boston: Copeland & Day, 1897.

246. [Sharp, William] Macleod, Fiona. *Deirdrê and the Sons of Usna.* Portland: Mosher, 1909.

247. Shaw, George Bernard. *On Going to Church: Being the Preachment which Treats of Church-Going, Art, and Some other Themes.* East Aurora: Roycrofters, 1896.

248. Shelley, Percy Bysshe, trans. *The Banquet of Plato.* Chicago: Way & Williams, 1895.

249. _____. *The Cenci.* New Rochelle: Elston Press, 1903.

250. Shepard, Morgan. *The Standard Upheld and Other Verses.* San Francisco: Elder and Shepard, 1902.

251. [Sherman, Francis]. *A Prelude.* Boston: Copeland & Day, 1897.

252. Smith, F. Hopkinson. *A Day at Laguerre's and Other Days: Being Nine Sketches.* Boston: Houghton Mifflin, 1892.

253. *The Song of Roland.* Cambridge: Riverside Press, 1906.

254. Spenser, Edmund. *Amoretti.* New York: Laurel Press, 1901.

255. _____. *Epithalamion.* New York: Dodd, Mead, 1895.

256. Stevens, Thomas Wood. *The Unsought Shrine.* Chicago: Blue Sky Press, 1900.

257. _____. *The Unsought Shrine and Titian the Boy.* Ridgewood: Alwil Shop, 1901.

258. Stevenson, Robert Louis. *The Essay on Walt Whitman.* East Aurora: Roycrofters, 1900.

259. _____. *Poems.* New York: Crowell, 1900.

260. Swinburne, Algernon Charles. *Laus Veneris.* Portland: Mosher, 1909.

261. Tabb, John B. *Two Lyrics.* Boston: Craftsman's Guild, 1900.

262. Tacitus. *Agricola.* Boston: Merrymount Press, 1904.

263. *The Tale of Gamelyn.* New Rochelle: Elston Press, 1901.

264. *The Tale of a Nun.* Philadelphia: Monk's Head Press, 1901.

265. Taylor, Edward Robeson. *Into the Light.* San Francisco: Elder and Shepard, 1902.

266. Tennyson, Alfred. *Elaine.* Wausau: Philosopher Press, 1900.

267. _____. *Idylls of the King.* New York: R. H. Russell, 1898.

268. _____. *The Lady of Shalott.* Boston: Printed by Thomas Maitland Cleland, 1900.

269. _____. *The Lady of Shalott.* Snohomish, Washington: Handcraft Shop, 1901.

270. _____. *Maud.* East Aurora: Roycrofters, 1900.

271. *Thanksgiving after the Communion of the Body and Blood of Christ: Compiled from Ancient and Modern Sources By a Layman of the American Church.* With an Introduction by Rev. George McClellan Fiske, D.D. Boston: Merrymount Press, 1896.

272. *Three Wise Men: Extracts from the Celebrated Works of M. Aurelius Antoninus, Francis Bacon and Benjamin Franklin.* Detroit: Cranbrook Press, 1901.

273. Twine, Laurence. *The Patterne of Painefull Adventures.* New Rochelle: Elston Press, 1903.

274. Typothetae of the City of New York. *Catalogue of the Books in the Library of the Typothetae of the City of New York.* New York: Typothetae, 1896.

275. Van Dyke, Henry. *The Builders and Other Poems.* New York: Scribner's, 1900.

276. _____. *The First Christmas Tree: A Story of the Forest.* New York: Scribner's, 1897.

277. _____. *The Lost Word: A Christmas Legend of Long Ago.* New York: Scribner's, 1898.

278. _____. *The Poetry of the Psalms.* New York: Crowell, 1900.

279. _____. *Ships and Havens.* New York: Crowell, 1897.

280. _____. *The Toiling of Felix: A Legend on a New Saying of the Christ.* New York: Privately printed, 1898.

281. Village Press. *A Novel Type Foundery: Specimen of the Types, Borders and Page Ornaments Designed & Sold by Frederic W. Goudy.* New York: Village Press, 1914.

282. [Warren, George B.]. *Arcady in Troy.* Boston: Merrymount Press, 1904.

283. Way, W. Irving. *Migratory Books: Their Haunts & Habits.* Los Angeles: Ernest Dawson, 1924.

284. Weitenkampf, Frank. *The Etching of Contemporary Life.* Marlborough-on-Hudson: Dard Hunter, 1916.

285. Wells, H. G. *The Door in the Wall and Other Stories.* New York: Mitchell Kennerley, 1911.

286. Wilde, Oscar. *Ave Imperatrix! A Dirge of Empire.* Snohomish, Washington: Handcraft Shop, 1902.

287. Wilson, Woodrow. *The Free Life.* New York: Crowell, 1908.

288. Wither, George. *Certain Poems.* Highland Park, Illinois: Elm Press, 1901.

289. Wright, John S. *Botany in Pharmacy.* Indianapolis: Eli Lilly and Company, 1893.

290. Yale, Catherine B. *Nim and Cum.* Chicago: Way & Williams, 1895.

291. Yeats, William Butler. *The King's Threshold.* Cambridge: University Press, 1904.

292. Zelie, John Sheridan, and Carroll Perry. *Bill Pratt the Saw-Buck Philosopher.* Williamstown: Privately printed, 1895.

MANUSCRIPTS

293. [Ransom, Will]. "From Riley." Manuscript, Christmas 1899. Ransom Archives, Newberry Library.

294. [_____]. "When Three Is Company: A Spring Fancie." Typescript, May 1900. Ransom Archives, Newberry Library.

295. [_____]. Maurice Hewlett, "A Sacrifice at Prato." Manuscript, Christmas 1900. Ransom Archives, Newberry Library.

Textual Sources

BOOKS AND PARTS OF BOOKS

The Aesthetic Movement and the Cult of Japan. London: Fine Art Society, 1972.

Aldis, Harry G. *The Printed Book.* 3d ed. Cambridge: Cambridge University Press, 1951.

Altick, Richard D. *The English Common Reader: A Social History of the Mass Reading Public 1800–1900.* Chicago: University of Chicago Press, Phoenix Books, 1957.

American Art Nouveau: The Poster Period of John Sloan. Lock Haven, Pennsylvania: Hammermill Paper Company, 1967.

American Dictionary of Printing and Bookmaking. New York: Howard Lockwood & Co., 1894.

American Institute of Graphic Arts. *Daniel Berkeley Updike and the Merrymount Press.* New York: A.I.G.A., 1940.

_____. *The Village Press: A Retrospective Exhibition, 1903–1933.* New York: A.I.G.A., 1933.

[_____]. *The Work of Bruce Rogers, Jack of All Trades: Master of One.* New York: Oxford University Press, 1939.

American Posters of the Nineties. Lunenburg, Vermont: Stinehour Press, 1974.

American Type Founders Company. *American Specimen Book of Type Styles.* Jersey City: ATF, 1912.

Anderson, Donald M. *The Art of Written Forms: The Theory and Practice of Calligraphy.* New York: Holt, Rinehart, and Winston, 1969.

The Art and Work of the Art Workers Guild. London: National Book League, 1975.

Arts and Crafts Exhibition Society. *Catalogue of the First Exhibition.* London: The New Gallery, 1888.

The Arts & Crafts Movement: Artists Craftsmen & Designers 1890–1930. London: Fine Art Society, 1973.

Aslin, Elizabeth. *The Aesthetic Movement: Prelude to Art Nouveau*. New York: Praeger, 1969.

Balch, David Arnold. *Elbert Hubbard: Genius of Roycroft*. New York: Stokes, 1940.

Ballou, Ellen B. *The Building of the House: Houghton Mifflin's Formative Years*. Boston: Houghton Mifflin, 1970.

Barr, Louise Farrow. *Presses of Northern California and Their Books 1900-1933*. Berkeley: The Book Arts Club: University of California, 1934.

Bartlett, Edward Everett. *The Typographic Treasures in Europe*. New York: Putnam, 1925.

Baughman, Roland. *Frederic William Goudy 1865-1947: A Commemorative Exhibition*. New York: Columbia University Libraries, 1966.

Beilenson, Peter. *The Story of Frederic W. Goudy*. New York: Peter Pauper Press, 1965.

Bennett, Paul A. *Bruce Rogers of Indiana*. Providence: Doomsday Press, 1936.

Bennett, Paul A., ed. *Postscripts on Dwiggins*. 2 vols. New York: Typophiles, 1960.

Berthoff, Warner. *The Ferment of Realism*. New York: Free Press, 1965.

Bianchi, Daniel B. *D. B. Updike & John Bianchi: A Note on Their Association*. Boston: Society of Printers, 1965.

Bishop, Henry G. *The Practical Printer*. 3d ed. Oneonta, New York: Henry G. Bishop, 1895.

Bland, David. *The Illustration of Books*. London: Faber and Faber, 1962.

Bloomfield, Paul. *William Morris*. London: Arthur Barker, 1934.

Bolton, Theodore. *American Book Illustrators*. New York: Bowker, 1938.

Bonnell, Cedric. *An American William Morris and The Romance of the "Roycrofters."* Nottingham: N.S.O.V., 1904.

Bradley, Will H. *Will Bradley: His Chap-Book*. Mount Vernon: Peter Pauper Press, 1955.

Brooks, Van Wyck. *The Confident Years: 1885-1915*. New York: Dutton, 1952.

_____. *John Sloan: A Painter's Life*. New York: Dutton, 1955.

Brown University Library. *William Morris and the Kelmscott Press. An Exhibition Held in the Library of Brown University, Providence, Rhode Island, from October 9 to December 31, 1959. To Which Is Appended an Address by Philip C. Duschnes before the Friends of the Library of Brown University, December 7, 1959*. Providence: Brown University Library, 1960.

Bullen, Henry Lewis. *Keeping the Printing Plant Young*. (Title Page Competition.) Cambridge: Printing Art, 1910.

California Design 1910. Pasadena: California Design Publications, 1974.

Carvalho, David N. *Forty Centuries of Ink*. New York: Banks Law Publishing Co., 1904.

Cary, Elisabeth Luther. *William Morris: Poet, Craftsman, Socialist*. New York: Putnam, 1902.

Cary, Melbert B., Jr. *A Bibliography of the Village Press, 1903-1938*. New York: Press of the Woolly Whale, 1938.

Cave, Roderick. *The Private Press*. London: Faber and Faber, 1971.

Champney, Freeman. *Art & Glory: The Story of Elbert Hubbard*. New York: Crown, 1968.

[Chaucer, Geoffrey]. *The Works of Geoffrey Chaucer: A Facsimile of the William Morris Kelmscott Chaucer with the Original 87 Illustrations by Edward Burne-Jones. Together with an Introduction by John T. Winterich and a Glossary for the Modern Reader*. Cleveland: World, 1958.

Clark, Sir Kenneth. *The Gothic Revival: An Essay in the History of Taste*. Harmondsworth: Penguin Books, 1964.

Clark, Robert Judson, ed. *The Arts and Crafts Movement in America 1876-1916*. Princeton: Princeton Art Museum, 1972.

Clark, William Andrews, Jr., Library. *The Kelmscott and Doves Presses. Collected and compiled by Robert Ernest Cowan . . . With an Introduction by Alfred W. Pollard*. San Francisco: John Henry Nash, 1921.

Clattenburg, Ellen Fritz. *The Photographic Work of F. Holland Day*. Wellesley: Wellesley College Museum, 1975.

Cleland, Thomas Maitland. *The Decorative Work of T. M. Cleland: A Record and Review. With a Biographical and Critical Introduction by A. E. Hamill and a Portrait Lithograph by Rockwell Kent*. New York: Pynson Printers, 1929.

_____. *Harsh Words*. New York: Typophiles, 1940.

Compton-Rickett, Arthur. *William Morris: A Study in Personality*. London: Herbert Jenkins, 1913.

Cook, Clarence C. *The House Beautiful: Essays on Beds and Tables, Stools and Candlesticks*. New York: Scribner's, 1895.

Cram, Ralph Adams. *My Life in Architecture*. Boston: Little, Brown, 1936.

Crane, Walter. *An Artist's Reminiscences*. New York: Macmillan, 1907.

_____. *William Morris to Whistler*. London: Bell, 1911.

Crow, Gerald H. *William Morris: Designer*. London: The Studio, 1934.

Day, Lewis F. *William Morris and His Art*. (Easter Art Annual, 1899.) London: J. S. Virtue, 1899.

Denman, Frank. *The Shaping of Our Alphabet: A Study of Changing Type Styles*. New York: Knopf, 1955.

De Vinne, Theodore Low. "The Century's New Type."

In *Specimens of the Century Romans*. Jersey City: American Type Founders Company, n.d.

_____. "Do You Know the Letters?" in *Liber Scriptorum*. New York: Authors Club, 1893.

_____. *The Practice of Typography*. 4 vols. New York: Century, 1900–1904.

_____. *Printing in the Nineteenth Century*. New York: Lead Mould Electrotype Foundry, 1924.

_____. *Title-Pages as Seen by a Printer*. New York: Grolier Club, 1901.

_____. *Old Faces of Roman and Medieval Types Lately Added to the De Vinne Press*. New York: De Vinne Press, 1897.

Dickason, David H. *The Daring Young Men: The Story of the American Pre-Raphaelites*. Bloomington: Indiana University Press, 1953.

Dietz, August. "The Printing House Craftsmen Movement in America." In *Gutenberg Festschrift*, edited by A. Ruppel. Mainz: Gutenberg-Gesellschaft, 1925.

Dirlam, H. Kenneth, and Ernest E. Simmons. *Sinners, This Is East Aurora: The Story of Elbert Hubbard and the Roycroft Shop*. New York: Vantage Press, 1964.

Dreyfus, John. *Bruce Rogers and American Typography*. New York: Cambridge University Press, 1959.

Duffey, Bernard. *The Chicago Renaissance in American Letters*. East Lansing: Michigan State College Press, 1954.

Dunlap, Joseph R. *The Book That Never Was*. New York: Oriole Editions, 1971.

_____. *On the Heritage of William Morris: Some Considerations Typographic & Otherwise*. New York: Typophiles, 1976.

Duschnes, Philip C. *Bruce Rogers: A Gentle Man from Indiana*. New York: Duschnes, 1965.

Faulkner, Peter. *William Morris and W. B. Yeats*. Dublin: Dolmen Press, 1962.

Faulkner, Peter, ed. *William Morris: The Critical Heritage*. London: Routledge & Kegan Paul, 1973.

Forman, Harry Buxton. *The Books of William Morris Described with Some Account of His Doings in Literature and in the Allied Crafts*. New York: Burt Franklin, 1969. (Reprint of 1897 edition.)

Franklin, Colin. *The Private Presses*. London: Studio Vista, 1969.

Freeman, John Crosby. *The Forgotten Rebel: Gustav Stickley and His Craftsman Mission Furniture*. Watkins Glen, New York: Century House, 1966.

French, George. *The Imperial Press: A Critique*. Cleveland: Cleveland Printing and Publishing Co., 1902.

_____. *Printing in Relation to Graphic Art*. Cleveland: Imperial Press, 1903.

Gage, Harry Lawrence. *Applied Design for Printers*. Chicago: United Typothetae of America, 1920.

Gardner, Martin, and Russell B. Nye. *The Wizard of Oz & Who He Was*. East Lansing: Michigan State University Press, 1957.

Germann, Georg. *Gothic Revival in Europe and Britain: Sources, Influences and Ideas*. London: Lund Humphries, 1972.

Gilliss, Walter. *Recollections of the Gilliss Press and Its Work During Fifty Years 1869-1919*. New York: Grolier Club, 1926.

The Golden Age of American Illustration 1880-1914. Wilmington: Delaware Art Museum, [1972].

Goodhue, Bertram Grosvenor. *Book Decorations*. New York: Grolier Club, 1931.

Goudy, Frederic W. *A Half-Century of Type Design and Typography: 1895-1945*. New York: Typophiles, 1946.

_____. *The Story of the Village Type*. New York: Press of the Woolly Whale, 1933.

[_____]. *Typographica Number Three*. New York: Village Press, 1916.

_____. *Typologia*. Berkeley: University of California Press, 1940.

Gray, Nicolete. *Nineteenth Century Ornamented Typefaces*. 2d ed. Berkeley and Los Angeles: University of California Press, 1976.

Grennan, Margaret Rose. *William Morris: Medievalist and Revolutionary*. New York: King's Crown Press, 1945.

Gress, Edmund G. *The Art & Practice of Typography*. New York: Harper, 1931.

_____. *Fashions in American Typography 1780 to 1930*. New York: Harper, 1931.

_____. *Type Designs in Color*. New York: Oswald, 1908.

Grolier Club. *Catalogue of Work of the De Vinne Press*. New York: Grolier Club, 1929.

Guild of Book Workers. *First Year Book and List of Members 1906-1907*. New York: Guild of Book Workers, 1907.

Gullans, Charles B., comp. *A Checklist of Trade Bindings Designed by Margaret Armstrong*. Los Angeles: University of California Library, 1968.

Gutenberg-Gesellschaft. *Morris-Drucke und Andere Meisterwerke Englischer und Amerikanischer Privatpressen*. Mainz: Gutenberg-Gesellschaft, 1954.

Haas, Irvin, comp. and ed. *Bibliography of Modern American Presses*. Chicago: Black Cat Press, 1935.

Hamilton, Charles F. *As Bees in Honey Drown: Elbert Hubbard and the Roycrofters*. South Brunswick and New York: A. S. Barnes, 1973.

Hamilton, Frederick W. *A Brief History of Printing in America*. Chicago: United Typothetae of America, 1918.

_____. *Type and Presses in America*. Chicago: United Typothetae of America, 1918.

Hansen, Hans J., ed. *Late Nineteenth Century Art*. New York: McGraw-Hill, 1972.

Harding, George L. *D. B. Updike and the Merrymount Press.* San Francisco: The Roxburghe Club, 1943.

Harlan, Robert D. *John Henry Nash: The Biography of a Career.* Berkeley: University of California Press, 1970.

Hart, James D. *The Popular Book: A History of America's Literary Taste.* New York: Oxford University Press, 1950.

Hart-Davis, Rupert, ed. *The Letters of Oscar Wilde.* New York: Harcourt, Brace and World, 1962.

Hatch, Benton. *A Checklist of the Publications of Thomas Bird Mosher of Portland Maine 1891-1923.* Amherst: University of Massachusetts Press, 1966.

Heath, Mary Hubbard. *The Elbert Hubbard I Knew.* East Aurora: Roycrofters, 1929.

Henderson, Philip. *William Morris.* Rev. ed. London: Longmans, Green, 1963.

———. *William Morris: His Life, Work and Friends.* New York: McGraw-Hill, 1967.

Hillier, Bevis. *Posters.* New York: Stein and Day, 1969.

Holme, Charles, ed. *The Art of the Book.* London: The Studio, 1914.

Hopkins, Frank E. *The De Vinne & Marion Presses.* Meriden: Columbiad Club, 1936.

Hornung, Clarence P. *Will Bradley: His Graphic Art.* New York: Dover, 1974.

Hough, Graham. *The Last Romantics.* London: Methuen, 1961 (first published, 1947).

Hubbard, Elbert. *The Roycroft Shop: A History.* East Aurora: Roycrofters, 1908.

Hunt, John Dixon. *The Pre-Raphaelite Imagination 1848-1900.* Lincoln: University of Nebraska Press, 1968.

Hunter, Dard. *My Life with Paper: An Autobiography.* New York: Knopf, 1958.

Huntington, Henry E., Library. *Will Bradley: His Work—An Exhibition.* San Marino: Huntington Library, 1951.

———. *The Work of the Merrymount Press and Its Founder Daniel Berkeley Updike (1860-1941).* San Marino: Huntington Library, 1942.

[Isaacs, J. H.] "Temple Scott." *The Work of Frederic W. Goudy: Printer and Craftsman.* New York: Charles H. Barnard, 1912.

Jackson, Holbrook. *The Eighteen Nineties: A Review of Art and Ideas at the Close of the Nineteenth Century.* New York: Knopf, n.d.

———. *The Printing of Books.* London: Cassell, 1947 (first ed., 1938).

James, Philip. *English Book Illustration 1800-1900.* London: King Penguin, 1947.

Johnson, Alfred Forbes. *Decorative Initial Letters.* London: Cresset Press, 1931.

———. *Type Designs: Their History and Development.* 3d ed. London: Andre Deutsch, 1966.

Johnson, John. *The Printer: His Customers and His Men.* London: Dent, 1933.

Johnston, Paul. *Biblio-Typographica: A Survey of Contemporary Fine Printing Style.* New York: Covici-Friede, 1930.

Joyner, George. *Fine Printing: Its Inception, Development, and Practice.* London: Cooper and Budd, 1895.

Jussim, Estelle. *Visual Communication and the Graphic Arts.* New York: Bowker, 1974.

Kelly, Rob Roy. *American Wood Type 1828-1900.* New York: Van Nostrand Reinhold, 1969.

Kent, Henry Watson. *What I Am Pleased to Call My Education.* New York: Grolier Club, 1949.

Kilgour, Raymond L. *Estes and Lauriat: A History 1872-1898. With a Brief Account of Dana Estes and Company 1898-1914.* Ann Arbor: University of Michigan Press, 1957.

———. *Messrs. Roberts Brothers Publishers.* Ann Arbor: University of Michigan Press, 1952.

Knaufft, Ernest. *The Early Art Training of B. R. at Purdue University.* New York: Press of the Woolly Whale, 1935.

Kramer, Sidney. *A History of Stone & Kimball and Herbert S. Stone & Co. With a Bibliography of Their Publications, 1893-1905.* Chicago: University of Chicago Press, 1940.

Lane, Albert. *Elbert Hubbard and His Work.* Worcester: Blanchard Press, 1901.

Larkin, Oliver W. *Art & Life in America.* Rev. and enl. ed. New York: Holt, Rinehart and Winston, 1960.

Larremore, Thomas A., and Amy Hopkins Larremore. *The Marion Press: A Survey and a Check-List, with Incidental Alarums, and Excursions Into Collateral Fields.* Jamaica: Queens Borough Public Library, 1943.

Leatham, James. *William Morris, Master of Many Crafts: A Study.* 4th ed. Turiff, Aberdeenshire: Deveron Press, 1934.

Lee, Francis Watts, ed. *William Morris, Poet, Artist, Socialist: A Selection from his Writings Together with a Sketch of the Man.* New York: Humboldt, 1891.

Lee, Marshall. *Bookmaking: The Illustrated Guide to Design and Production.* New York: Bowker, 1965.

Lehmann-Haupt, Hellmut. *The Book in America: A History of the Making and Selling of Books in the United States.* 2d ed. New York: Bowker, 1952.

Lemire, Eugene D., ed. *The Unpublished Lectures of William Morris.* Detroit: Wayne State University Press, 1969.

Lenning, Henry F. *The Art Nouveau.* The Hague: Martinus Nijhoff, 1951.

Levarie, Norma. *The Art & History of Books.* New York: James H. Heineman, 1968.

Lewis, Bernard. *Behind the Type: The Life Story of Frederic W. Goudy.* Pittsburgh: Carnegie Institute of Technology, 1941.

Lewis, John Noel Claude. *The Twentieth Century Book: Its Illustration and Design.* New York: Reinhold, 1967.

The Library of the Late Theodore Low De Vinne. New York: Anderson Galleries, 1920.

Lindsay, Jack. *William Morris: His Life and Work.* London: Constable, 1975.

A List of Books Printed at the Marion Press, 1896–1906. Jamaica: Marion Press, n.d.

A List of Books Published by Copeland and Day. Boston: Copeland & Day, 1895.

A List of Publications for Sale en Bloc, 1899. Boston: Copeland & Day, 1899.

Lyon, Peter. *Success Story: The Life and Times of S. S. McClure.* New York: Scribner's, 1963.

Macaulay, James. *The Gothic Revival 1745–1845.* Glasgow and London: Blackie, 1975.

Mackail, John William. *The Life of William Morris.* 2 vols. London: Longmans, Green, 1899.

McLean, Ruari. *Modern Book Design from William Morris to the Present Day.* London: Faber and Faber, 1958.

_____. *Victorian Book Design and Colour Printing.* 2d ed. Berkeley and Los Angeles: University of California Press, 1972.

McMurtrie, Douglas C. *The Book: The Story of Printing and Bookmaking.* New York: Oxford University Press, 1943.

_____. *Book Decoration.* Pelham, New York: Bridgman, 1928.

Madison, Charles A. *Book Publishing in America.* New York: McGraw-Hill, 1966.

Madsen, Stephan Tschudi. *Art Nouveau.* New York: McGraw-Hill, 1967.

_____. *Sources of Art Nouveau.* New York: Wittenborn, 1956.

The Manual of Linotype Typography. Brooklyn: Mergenthaler Linotype Company, 1923.

Margolin, Victor. *American Poster Renaissance.* New York: Watson-Guptill, 1975.

Martin, Jay. *Harvests of Change: American Literature 1865–1914.* Englewood Cliffs: Prentice-Hall, 1967.

Matthews, Brander. *Bookbinding Old and New.* New York: Macmillan, 1895.

May, J. Lewis, *John Lane and the Nineties.* London: John Lane, The Bodley Head, 1936.

The Merrymount Press: Its Aims, Work, and Equipment. Boston: Merrymount, n.d.

Morison, Stanley. *Four Centuries of Fine Printing.* 2d ed. rev. New York: Farrar, Straus, 1949.

_____. *Letter Forms: Typographic and Scriptorial.* London: Nattali & Maurice, 1968.

_____. *Type Designs of the Past and Present.* London: The Fleuron, 1926.

_____. *The Typographic Arts: Two Lectures.* Cambridge: Harvard University Press, 1950.

_____. *The Typographic Book 1450–1935.* Chicago: University of Chicago Press, 1963.

Morison, Stanley, and Holbrook Jackson. *A Brief Survey of Printing History and Practice.* London: The Fleuron, 1923.

Morison, Stanley, and Rudolph Ruzicka. *Recollections of Daniel Berkeley Updike.* Boston: Club of Odd Volumes, 1943.

Morris, May, ed. *William Morris: Artist, Writer, Socialist.* 2 vols. New York: Russell & Russell, 1966. (Reprint of 1936 edition.)

Morris, William. *An Address Delivered by William Morris at the Distribution of Prizes to Students of the Birmingham Municipal School of Art on February 21, 1894.* London: Longmans, 1898.

_____. *Art and Its Producers and The Arts & Crafts of Today: Two Addresses Delivered Before the National Association for the Advancement of Art.* London: Longmans, 1901.

_____. *The Collected Works of William Morris with Introductions by His Daughter May Morris.* 24 vols. London: Longmans, Green, 1910–1915.

[_____]. *The Letters of William Morris to His Family and Friends.* Edited with introduction and notes by Philip Henderson. London: Longmans, Green, 1950.

_____. *Selected Writings and Designs.* Edited by Asa Briggs. With a supplement by Graeme Shankland. Baltimore: Penguin Books, 1962.

Morris & Company. *A Brief Sketch of the Morris Movement and of the Firm Founded by William Morris to Carry Out His Designs and the Industries Revived or Started by Him.* London: Morris & Co., 1911.

Morris & Co. [Exhibition from the Collection of Sanford and Helen Berger.] Stanford: Stanford University Press, 1975.

[Mosher, Thomas Bird, ed.]. *Amphora: A Second Collection of Prose and Verse Chosen by the Editor of the Bibelot.* Portland: Mosher, 1926.

[_____]. *A List of Books.* Portland: Mosher, 1901.

The Mosher Books. Portland: Mosher, 1928.

Mott, Frank Luther. *A History of American Magazines: 1885–1905.* Cambridge: Harvard University Press, 1957.

Muir, Percy. *Victorian Illustrated Books.* London: Batsford, 1971.

Mumford, Lewis. *The Brown Decades: A Study of the Arts of America 1865–1895.* 2d rev. ed. New York: Dover, 1955. (Reprint of 1931 edition.)

Nash, Ray. *Printing as an Art: A History of the Society of Printers, Boston, 1905–1955.* Cambridge: Harvard University Press, 1955.

Naylor, Gillian. *The Arts and Crafts Movement.* Cambridge: MIT Press, 1971.

Nelson, James G. *The Early Nineties: A View from The Bodley Head.* Cambridge: Harvard University Press, 1971.

Nesbitt, Alexander. *The History and Technique of Lettering.* New York: Dover, 1957.

———, ed. *200 Decorative Title-Pages.* New York: Dover, 1964.

Newark Public Library. *The Richard C. Jenkinson Collection of Books Chosen to Show the Work of the Best Printers.* Book II. Newark: Newark Public Library, 1929.

Nineteenth Century America: Furniture and Other Decorative Arts. New York: Metropolitan Museum of Art, 1970.

O'Day, Nell. *A Catalogue of Books Printed by John Henry Nash.* San Francisco: John Henry Nash, 1937.

Orcutt, William Dana. *From My Library Walls: A Kaleidoscope of Memories.* London: John Murray, 1946.

———. *In Quest of the Perfect Book: Reminiscences and Reflections of a Bookman.* Boston: Little, Brown, 1926.

———. *The Kingdom of Books.* Boston: Little, Brown, 1927.

———. *The Magic of the Book: More Reminiscences and Adventures of a Bookman.* Boston: Little, Brown, 1930.

———. *Master Makers of the Book: Being a Consecutive Story of the Book from a Century before the Invention of Printing through the Era of the Doves Press.* New York: Doubleday, Doran, 1928.

Orton, Vrest. *Goudy: Master of Letters.* Chicago: Black Cat Press, 1939.

Oswald, John Clyde. *A History of Printing: Its Development Through Five Hundred Years.* New York: Appleton, 1928.

———. *Printing in the Americas.* New York and Chicago: Gregg, 1937.

Pennell, Joseph. *The Graphic Arts: Modern Men and Modern Methods.* Chicago: University of Chicago Press, 1921.

Pevsner, Nikolaus. *Pioneers of Modern Design: From William Morris to Walter Gropius.* 3rd ed. Baltimore: Penguin Books, 1965.

Pollard, Alfred W. *Fine Books.* New York: Putnam, 1912.

———. *Last Words on the History of the Title-Page.* London: Nimmo, 1891.

———. *Modern Fine Printing in England and Mr. Bruce Rogers.* Newark: Carteret Book Club, 1916.

Pottinger, David. *Printers and Printing.* Cambridge: Harvard University Press, 1941.

Putzel, Max. *The Man in the Mirror: William Marion Reedy and His Magazine.* Cambridge: Harvard University Press, 1963.

[Ransom, Will]. *Kelmscott, Doves and Ashendene: The Private Press Credo.* Los Angeles: Book Club of California, 1952.

———. *Private Presses and Their Books.* New York: Bowker, 1929.

Reed, Walt, comp. and ed. *The Illustrator in America 1900–1960's.* New York: Reinhold, 1966.

Rheims, Maurice. *The Flowering of Art Nouveau.* New York: Abrams, 1966.

Ricketts, Charles. *A Defence of the Revival of Printing.* London: Ballantyne Press, 1899.

Rogers, Bruce. *Pi: A Hodge-Podge of the Letters, Papers and Addresses Written During the Last Sixty Years.* Cleveland: World, 1953.

Rollins, Carl Purington. *A Leaf from the Kelmscott Chaucer.* New York: Philip C. Duschnes, 1941.

———. *Off the Dead Bank.* New York: Typophiles, 1949.

———. *Souvenirs of My Inky Past.* New York: New York Public Library, 1950.

Rothenstein, William. *Men and Memories.* 2 vols. New York: Coward-McCann, 1931–1932.

Roycrofters. *A List of Books Made During the Year 1899.* East Aurora: Roycrofters, 1899.

———. *The Roycroft Books: A Catalog and Some Remarks.* East Aurora: Roycrofters, 1902.

———. *The Roycroft Catalog 1912: Books, Leather, Copper.* East Aurora: Roycrofters, 1912.

Ruskin, John. *The Art Criticism of John Ruskin.* Edited by Robert L. Herbert. Garden City: Doubleday Anchor Books, 1964.

Schaefer, Herwin. *Nineteenth Century Modern: The Functional Tradition in Victorian Design.* New York: Praeger, 1970.

Schmidt-Künsemüller, Friedrich Adolf. *William Morris und die Neuere Buchkunst.* Wiesbaden: Harrassowitz, 1955.

Schmutzler, Robert. *Art Nouveau.* Translated by Edouard Roditi. New York: Abrams, 1962.

Selz, Peter, and Mildred Constantine, eds. *Art Nouveau: Art and Design at the Turn of the Century.* New York: Museum of Modern Art, 1959.

Seymour, Ralph Fletcher. *Some Went This Way: A Forty Year Pilgrimage Among Artists, Bookmen and Printers.* Chicago: R. F. Seymour, 1945.

Shaw, George Bernard. *The Sanity of Art.* New York: Boni and Liveright, 1907.

Shay, Felix. *Elbert Hubbard of East Aurora.* New York: Wise, 1926.

Sheehan, Donald. *This Was Publishing: A Chronicle of the Book Trade in the Gilded Age.* Bloomington: Indiana University Press, 1952.

Shove, Raymond H. *Cheap Book Production in the United States, 1870 to 1891.* Urbana: University of Illinois Library, 1937.

Simon, Howard. *500 Years of Art & Illustration.* Cleveland: World, 1942.

Skelton, Robin, and Ann Saddlemyer, eds. *The World of W. B. Yeats*. Seattle: University of Washington Press, 1965.

Society of Printers. *The Development of Printing as an Art*. Boston: Society of Printers, 1906.

Southward, John. *Progress in Printing and the Graphic Arts During the Victorian Era*. London: Simpkin, Marshall, Hamilton, Kent & Co., 1897.

Spargo, John. *The Socialism of William Morris*. Westwood, Massachusetts: Ariel Press, n.d.

Sparling, Henry Halliday. *The Kelmscott Press and William Morris: Master-Craftsman*. London: Macmillan, 1924.

Spencer, Charles, ed. *The Aesthetic Movement 1869–1890*. London: Academy Editions, 1973.

Spencer, Robin. *The Aesthetic Movement: Theory and Practice*. London: Studio Vista, 1972.

Spencer, Truman J. *The History of Amateur Journalism*. New York: The Fossils, 1947.

Steele, Robert. *The Revival of Printing*. London: Riccardi Press, 1912.

Stein, Roger B. *John Ruskin and Aesthetic Thought in America, 1840–1900*. Cambridge: Harvard University Press, 1967.

Stern, Fritz, ed. *The Varieties of History from Voltaire to the Present*. Cleveland: World, Meridian Books, 1956.

Stillwell, Margaret Bingham. *The Influence of William Morris and the Kelmscott Press*. Providence: E. A. Johnson, 1912.

Stott, Mary Roeloffs. *Elbert Hubbard: Rebel with Reverence*. Watkins Glen, New York: Century House, 1975.

[Strouse, Norman H.]. *An Exhibition of Books from the Press of Thomas Bird Mosher from the Collection of Norman H. Strouse*. Philadelphia: The Free Library, 1967.

———. *The Passionate Pirate*. North Hills, Pennsylvania: Bird and Bull Press, 1964.

Tarr, John C. *Printing To-Day*. Rev. ed. London: Oxford University Press, 1949.

Taylor, John Russell. *The Art Nouveau Book in Britain*. London: Methuen, 1966.

Tebbel, John. *A History of Book Publishing in the United States*. Volume II: "The Expansion of an Industry 1865–1919." New York: Bowker, 1975.

Teiser, Ruth, and Catherine Harroun, eds. *Printing as a Performing Art*. San Francisco: Book Club of California, 1970.

Theodore Low De Vinne: Printer. New York: Privately printed, 1915.

Thompson, E. P. *William Morris: Romantic to Revolutionary*. London: Lawrence and Wishart, 1955.

Thompson, Paul. *The Work of William Morris*. New York: Viking, 1967.

Thompson, Susan Otis. "The Arts and Crafts Book."

In Robert Judson Clark, ed. *The Arts and Crafts Movement in America 1876–1916*. Princeton: Princeton Art Museum, 1972.

Three Letters from BR: EW. Portland: Southworth-Anthoensen Press, 1941.

Triggs, Oscar Lovell. *Chapters in the History of the Arts and Crafts Movement*. Chicago: The Bohemia Guild of the Industrial Art League, 1902.

Tschan, André. *William Morris*. Berne: Monotype Corporation, 1962.

The Turn of a Century 1885–1910: Art Nouveau—Jugendstil Books. Cambridge: Department of Printing and Graphic Arts, Houghton Library, Harvard University, 1970.

Twyman, Michael. *Printing 1770–1870: An Illustrated History of Its Development and Uses in England*. London: Eyre and Spottiswoode, 1970.

Typophiles. *Barnacles from Many Bottoms Scraped and Gathered for BR*. New York: Typophiles, 1935.

———. *Spinach from Many Gardens: Gathered by the Typophiles and Fed to Frederic W. Goudy on His Seventieth Anniversary*. New York: Typophiles, 1935.

Ulrich, Carolyn F., and Karl Kup. *Books and Printing; A Selected List of Periodicals 1800–1942*. New York: New York Public Library, 1943.

Updike, Daniel Berkeley. *The Black Art: A Homily*. Chicago: Camelot Press, 1895.

[———]. *A Few Words About Printing, Bookmaking, and Their Allied Arts: Being a Short Description of Some of the Work Done by Mr. Berkeley Updike, at Number Six Beacon Street, Boston, Massachusetts*. Boston: Updike, 1894.

———. *In the Day's Work*. Cambridge: Harvard University Press, 1924.

[———]. *Merrymount*. Boston: Merrymount Press, 1895.

———. *Notes on the Merrymount Press and Its Work*. Cambridge: Harvard University Press, 1934.

[———]. *On the Decorations of the Limited Edition of the Standard Prayer Book of MDCCCXCII*. New York: De Vinne Press, 1893.

———. *Printing Types: Their History, Forms, and Use: A Study in Survivals*. 2d ed. 2 vols. Cambridge: Harvard University Press, 1951.

———. *Some Aspects of Printing Old and New*. New Haven: William Edwin Rudge, 1941.

[———]. *To the Clergy and Laity of the Episcopal Church and to All Others Who are Interested in Ecclesiastical Printing*. Boston: Updike, 1894–1895.

[———]. *To the Trade*. Boston: Updike, 1893.

Updike: American Printer and His Merrymount Press. New York: American Institute of Graphic Arts, 1947.

Vallance, Aymer. *The Art of William Morris*. London: Bell, 1897.

———. *William Morris: His Art, His Writings, and His*

Public Life. London: Bell, 1897.

Vanderbilt, Kermit. *Charles Eliot Norton: Apostle of Culture in a Democracy*. Cambridge: Belknap Press of Harvard University Press, 1959.

Warde, Frederic. *Bruce Rogers: Designer of Books*. Cambridge: Harvard University Press, 1926.

Warren, Arthur. *The Charles Whittinghams Printers*. New York: Grolier Club, 1896.

Watkinson, Ray. *William Morris as Designer*. New York: Reinhold, 1967.

Watts, Stevens Lewis. *Henry Lewis Bullen and His Work*. Skyline Bend Farm, Virginia: Privateer Press, 1966.

_____. *Will Bradley & His Legacy to the Graphic Arts*. n.p.: Privateer Press, 1965.

Weitenkampf, Frank. *American Graphic Art*. New ed. rev. and enl. New York: Macmillan, 1924.

_____. *The Illustrated Book*. Cambridge: Harvard University Press, 1938.

_____. *Illustrated Books of the Past Four Centuries*. New York: New York Public Library, 1920.

Wells, James M. "Book Typography in the United States of America." In *Book Typography 1815-1965 in Europe and the United States*. Edited by Kenneth Day. London: Benn, 1966.

Whitaker, Charles H., ed. *B. G. Goodhue: Architect and Master of Many Arts*. New York: Press of the American Institute of Architects, 1925.

William Morris and the Art of the Book. New York: Pierpont Morgan Library, 1976.

William Morris Society. *A Handlist of the Public Addresses of William Morris to be Found in Generally Accessible Publications*. Dublin: William Morris Society, 1961.

_____. *The Typographical Adventure of William Morris*. London: William Morris Society, 1957.

Williamson, Audrey. *Artists and Writers in Revolt: The Pre-Raphaelites*. Newton Abbot: David & Charles, 1976.

Williamson, Hugh. *Methods of Book Design: The Practice of an Industrial Craft*. 2d ed. London: Oxford University Press, 1966.

Wilson, Adrian. *The Design of Books*. New York: Reinhold, 1967.

Winship, George Parker. *Daniel Berkeley Updike and the Merrymount Press of Boston, Massachusetts, 1860-1894-1941*. Rochester: Leo Hart, 1947.

Wroth, Lawrence C., ed. *A History of the Printed Book: Being the Third Number of the Dolphin*. New York: Limited Editions Club, 1938.

_____. *Typographic Heritage*. New York: Typophiles, 1949.

Ziff, Larzer. *The American 1890s*. New York: Viking, 1966.

ARTICLES IN PERIODICALS

Abbott, Leonard D. "Book Handicraft." *Chautauquan* XXX (November 1899): 142-148.

Adam, G. Mercer. [Letter to the Editor, dated January 26, 1884.] *Publishers Weekly* XXV (February 2, 1884): 151.

Adam, H. A. "Bradley's Influence on Printing." *Printer and Bookmaker* XXIV (June 1897): 142-143.

[Advertisement for American Type Founders Company]. *Bradley: His Book* I (May 1896): unpaged.

[Advertisement for the Golden Press]. *Bibelot* XIV (1908): unpaged.

[Advertisement for the Wayside Press]. *Bradley: His Book* III (January 1897): unpaged.

[Advertisement for Wayside Publications]. *Printing Art* I (April 1903): xiii.

"American Book Clubs," *American Book-Lore* I (June 1898): 15-16.

"American Bookmaking." *American Bookmaker* XI (July 1890): 2.

"Art Designing." *American Bookmaker* X (June 1890): 153.

B., G.E. "Concerning Recent Books and Bookmaking." *Knight Errant* I (January 1893): 123-126.

Babington, Percy L. "The First Book Decorated by Mr. Bruce Rogers." *Library* V (September 1924): 171.

Baker, Donald C. "The Private Presses and Their Influence on the Recent History of the Printed Book." *Occasional Notes* (Norlin Library, University of Colorado) No. 11 (May 1970): 1-3.

Battersly, Martin. "Art Nouveau." *Studio International* CLXXI (January 1966): 30-33.

Bay, J. Christian. "Scarce and Beautiful Imprints of Chicago." *Papers of the Bibliographical Society of America* XV (Second quarter 1921): 88-102.

Beisner, Robert L. "Commune in East Aurora." *American Heritage* XXII (February 1971): 72-77, 106-109.

Bennett, Paul A. "Mr. D. B. Updike—The Merrymount Press, Boston." *Linotype News* XIII (July 1935): 5.

Bergengren, Ralph. "Art and Craftsmanship in the Printing of Books: A Notable Example." *Outlook* XC (September 26, 1908): 203-209.

"'Big Six's' Booklet." *Printer and Bookmaker* XXIX (December 1899): 208.

Boas, George. "Silhouette of a Librarian." *New Colophon* I (April 1948): 151-159.

"Book Reviews" [of De Vinne's *Modern Methods of Book Composition*]. *Literary Collector* IX (March 1905): 101-106.

"Bookmaking, Good and Bad." *American Bookmaker* XII (January 1891): 4.

Bowdoin, W. G. "Private Presses—The Blue Sky Press." *New York Times Saturday Review* (August 1, 1903): 538.

Bowles, Joseph M. "The American 'Arts and Crafts.'" *Modern Art* V (Winter 1897): 17-20.

[_____]. "Echoes." *Modern Art* IV (Spring 1896): unpaged.

_____. "A German Printer's Criticism of Modern Art." *Modern Art* IV (Autumn 1896): 132-135.

_____. "Mr. Updike's Altar Book." *Modern Art* IV (Autumn 1896): 124-125.

_____. "Note." *Modern Art* I (Summer 1893): unpaged.

_____. "On the Early Work of Bruce Rogers." *Colophon* II (September 1932): unpaged.

_____. "Thoughts on Printing, Practical and Impractical." *Modern Art* II (Summer 1894): unpaged.

_____. "William Morris as a Printer: The Kelmscott Press." *Modern Art* II (Autumn 1894): unpaged.

[Bradley, Will H.]. "William Morris: Artist, Poet, Craftsman." *Bradley: His Book* II (November 1896): 7-11.

[_____]. "Some Book Reviews: A Few Poets." *Bradley: His Book* I (June 1896): 51-54.

_____. "Appropriateness in Typographic Decoration." *Graphic Arts* II (August 1911): 113-115.

Bragdon, Claude. "The Purple Cow Period: The 'Dinky Magazines' that Caught the Spirit of the 'Nineties." *Bookman* LXIX (July 1929): 475-478.

Bullen, A. H. "The Appledore Private Press." *Library* I (1889): 13-14, 51-55.

[Bullen, Henry Lewis]. "Discursions of a Retired Printer." *Inland Printer* XXXIX (June 1907): 353-359.

_____. "William Morris: Regenerator of the Typographic Art." *Inland Printer* LXIX (June 1922): 369-374.

Burgess, Gelett. "In Jenson Type." *Inland Printer* XVI (January 1896): 442.

[Cahoon, Herbert, ed.]. "News & Notes." *Papers of the Bibliographical Society of America* LIV (Second quarter 1960): 129-130.

Calkins, Ernest Elmo. "The Chap-Book," *Colophon* III (May 1932): unpaged.

"Carl H. Heintzemann." *American Printer* LXXIX (August 5, 1924): unpaged. No. 38 of Craftsman Exhibits.

Carrington, FitzRoy. "Private and Special Presses." *Book Buyer* XXIII (September-October 1901): 96-100, 215-218.

Chapman, Alfred K. "Thomas Bird Mosher." *Colby Library Quarterly* Series IV (February 1958): 229-244.

"Chicago Notes." *Inland Printer* XIV (December 1894): 278.

Cleland, Thomas Maitland. "Typographic Distinction." *Dolphin* IV (Winter 1941), 201-203.

"Closing of the Kelmscott Press." *New York Times Saturday Supplement* (December 26, 1896): 4.

"Closing of the Kelmscott Press." *New York Times Saturday Supplement* (December 18, 1897): 1.

"Copeland & Day Retire from the Publishing Business." *Publishers Weekly* LV (June 3, 1899): 920.

Cotton, Albert Louis. "The Kelmscott Press and the New Printing." *Contemporary Review* LXXIV (August 1898): 221-231.

"The Craftsman's Guild." *Publishers Weekly* LVIII (September 8, 1900): 486.

Crane, Walter. "Arts and Crafts Movement." *Encyclopaedia Britannica*, 11th ed., Vol. II: 700-701.

"Current Comment." *Engraver and Printer* VII (April 1895): 88-90.

"Current Illustrations." *Engraver and Printer* IV (May 1893): 13.

Cushing, J. S. "Notes on Morrisania." *Engraver and Printer* IX (March 1896): 150-152.

Dale. "Philadelphia Letter from our Regular Correspondent." *Engraver and Printer* VII (April 1895): 82-83.

Davis, Malcolm W. "Carl Purington Rollins." *Publishers Weekly* CXIX (June 6, 1931): 2707-2711.

[Day, Frederick Holland]. "Concerning Recent Books and Bookmaking." *Knight Errant* I (October 1892): 93-96.

[_____]. "William Morris." *Book Buyer* XII (November 1895): 545-549.

Day, Lewis F. "William Morris and His Decorative Art." *Littell's Living Age* CCXXXVIII (July 11, 1903): 102-109.

De Vinne, Theodore Low. "About Pages and Magazines." *Printing Art* I (April-May 1903): 27-31, 59-65.

_____. "A Book that Won the Grand Prize." *New York Times Saturday Review* (October 27, 1900): 736-737.

_____. "Masculine Printing." *American Bookmaker* XV (November 1892): 140-144.

_____. "The Printing of Books." *Outlook* (December 4, 1897): 805-809.

Dunlap, Joseph R. "Morris and the Book Arts Before the Kelmscott Press." *Victorian Poetry* XIII (Autumn-Winter 1975): 141-157.

Dunlop, William. "Product of a Mimic Press." *American Book-Lore* I (September 1898): 37-40.

Dwiggins, William A. "D. B. Updike and the Merrymount Press." *Fleuron* III (1924): 1-8.

Eckman, James. "The Inland Type Foundry, 1894-1911." *Printing and Graphic Arts* VIII (1960): 31-46.

[Editorial]. *American Bookmaker* IX (July 1889): 16-17.

[Editorial]. *Engraver and Printer* VI (Midsummer 1894): 18.

[Editorial Announcement]. *Butterfly Quarterly* No. 1 (Autumn 1907): 17.

"Editorial Comment." *American Bookmaker* XVII (December 1893): 165.

"Editorial Notes." *Engraver and Printer* III (July 1892): 23-24.

"Editorial Notes." *Engraver and Printer* III (March 1893): 87-88.

Edwards, George Wharton. "The Illustration of Books." *Outlook* (December 4, 1897): 817-822.

Ersites, T. H. "William Morris and the Kelmscott Press." *American Book Collector* X (November 1959): 19-25.

"Exhibition of the Gild of Arts and Crafts of New York." *Craftsman* II (May 1902): 99.

"Fall Announcements—Roberts Brothers." *Publishers Weekly* XL (September 26, 1891): 450-453.

Faxon, Frederick Winthrop. "Ephemeral Bibelots." *Bulletin of Bibliography* III (1903): 72-74, 92, 106-107, 124-126.

Fegan, Ethel S. "Modern Fine Printing Since the Kelmscott Press." *Library Association Record* XV (June 1913): 301-327.

"A Few Words about the Chicago Herald." *Inland Printer* IX (January 1892): 329-344.

"Finely Printed Bible Books." *New York Times Book Review* (October 10, 1896): 2.

Floud, Peter. "William Morris as an Artist: A New View" and "The Inconsistencies of William Morris." *Listener* (October 7, 1954): 562-564.

Franklin, Colin. "On the Binding of Kelmscott Press Books." *Journal of the William Morris Society* II (Summer 1970): 28-30.

French, George. "The Achievements of Bruce Rogers, Book Designer, Here and in England." *Inland Printer* LXXXVIII (November 1931); 59-63.

———. "The Pro and Con of Roycroftie." *American Printer* XXXIV (April 1902): 121-122.

———. "The Work of Private Presses." *Printing Art* II (December 1903): 117-119.

"From the 'Bibelot' Press." *Bookman* II (January 1896): 426.

Fulton, Deoch. "The Typophiles." *New Colophon* II (June 1949): 143-162.

Gandy, Lewis C. "Modern Commercial Typography." *Graphic Arts and Crafts Year Book* II (1908): 117-134.

"General Notes." *Engraver and Printer* II (April 1892): 86.

"George Wharton Edwards." *American Bookmaker* IV (May 1887): 137-138.

[Gilder, Jeannette L.]. [Morning with William Morris]. *Critic* XXIX (N.S. XXVI) (October 10, 1896): 214.

"A Glance at Roycroftie Methods and Principles." *International Printer* XXII (May 1902): 329-336.

Gomme, Laurence. "The 'Pirate of Portland'—Thomas Bird Mosher." *Maine Digest* II (Winter 1968): 90-93.

Goodhue, Bertram G. "The Final Flowering of Age-End Art." *Knight Errant* 1 [January 1893]: 106-112.

Goudy, Frederic W. "Printing as an Art." *Ars Typographica* I (Spring 1920): 39-40.

———. "William Morris: His Influence on American Printing." *Philobiblon* VII (1934): 185-191.

"The Grolier Club." *Publishers Weekly* XXV (March 22, 1884): 352.

Hamlin, A. D. F. "L'Art Nouveau, Its Origin and Development." *Craftsman* III (December 1902): 129-143.

Haraszti, Zoltan. "Mr. Updike and the Merrymount Press." *More Books* X (May 1935): 157-173.

Harding, R. Coupland. "Review of Type Designs." *Inland Printer* XVI (November 1895): 170-171.

———. "Review of Type Designs." *Inland Printer* XVI (January 1896): 409.

———. "Review of Type Specimens." *Inland Printer* XVII (April 1896): 68-71.

Harris, S. Dale. "Evaluating William Morris." *Book Club of California Quarterly News-Letter* XXXIII (Winter 1967): 3-10.

Hartt, Rollin Lynde. "Elbert Hubbard." *Critic* XXXV (N.S. XXXII) (November 1899): 1005-1008.

"The Henderson Memorial Collection of Shaw." *Yale University Library Gazette* XII (October 1937): 17-42.

Henry, Albert. "Classical Printing." *American Bookmaker* XIX (October 1894): 95.

Hiatt, Charles. "On Some Recent Designs by Will H. Bradley, of Chicago." *Studio* IV (1894): 166-168.

[Hubbard, Elbert]. "An Interesting Personality: Elbert Hubbard." *Cosmopolitan* XXXII (January 1902): 309-320.

Hunter, Dard. "Elbert Hubbard and 'A Message to Garcia.'" *New Colophon* I (January 1948): 27-35.

———. "The Lost Art of Making Books." *Miscellany* II (1915): 3-6.

———. "Peregrinations & Prospects." *Colophon* Part VII (September 1931): unpaged.

———. "The Story of Dard Hunter." *Ben Franklin Monthly* XXI (March 1923): 25-27, 59.

Hyder, Darrel. "Philadelphia Fine Printing 1789-1820." *Printing and Graphic Arts* IX (1961): 69-99.

I., H.I. "The Kelmscott Press—An Illustrated Interview with Mr. William Morris." *Bookselling* I (November 1895): 2-14.

Jackson, Holbrook. "The Aesthetics of Printing." *Gutenberg-Jahrbuch* XXV (1950): 395-396.

———. "The Nonage of Nineteenth Century Printing in England." *Fleuron* II (1924): 87-97.

———. "The Typography of William Morris." *American Book Collector* V (August–September 1934): 251-253.

———. "William Morris and the Arts and Crafts." *Book-Collector's Quarterly* XIV (April-June 1934): 1-10.

Johnson, Alfred Forbes. "Old-Face Types in the Victorian Age." *Monotype Recorder* XXX (September–December 1931): 5–14.

Johnson, Fridolf. "William Morris." *American Artist* XXXII (December 1968): 43–49.

Johnson, Henry Lewis. "Decorative Printing." *Graphic Arts and Crafts Year Book* I (1907): 325–331.

[_____]. [Editorial]. *Engraver and Printer* VI (Midsummer 1894): 18.

Johnston, Paul. "Frederic W. Goudy, American Typographer." *Fleuron* VII (1930): unpaged.

_____. "Modern Fine Book Printing in America." *American Printer* XC (March–April 1930): 35–39, 45–48.

Keane, Theodore J. "The Work of Ralph Fletcher Seymour." *Graphic Arts* V (December 1913): 361–372.

"The Kelmscott Press." *Modern Art* IV (April 1896): 36–39.

K[ennerley], M[itchell]. "Bibelot Issues." *Bookman* IV (January 1897): 467.

Koch, Robert. "Artistic Books, Periodicals and Posters in the 'Gay Nineties.'" *Art Quarterly* XXV (Winter 1962): 370–383.

_____. "Elbert Hubbard's Roycrofters as Artist-Craftsmen." *Winterthur Portfolio* III (1967): 67–82.

_____. "Will Bradley." *Art in America* L (Fall 1962): 78–83.

Koenig, Michael. "De Vinne and the De Vinne Press." *Library Quarterly* XLI (January 1970): 1–24.

Kraus, Joe Walker. "Messrs. Copeland & Day: Publishers to the 1890s." *Publishers Weekly* CXLI (March 21, 1942): 1168–1171.

_____. "The Publishing Activities of Way & Williams, Chicago 1895-98." *Papers of the Bibliographical Society of America* LXX (Second quarter, 1976): 221–260.

Larremore, Thomas A. "An American Typographic Tragedy: F. C. Bursch." *Papers of the Bibliographical Society of America* XLIII (First quarter, 1949): 1–38, 111–172.

"The Late William Morris." *Review of Reviews* XIV (December 1896): 732.

Lee, Francis Watts. "Regarding Recent Books and Bookmaking." *Knight Errant* I (April 1892): 31–32.

_____. "Some Thoughts upon Beauty in Typography Suggested by the Work of Mr. William Morris at the Kelmscott Press." *Knight Errant* I (July 1892): 53–63.

Lehmann-Haupt, Hellmut. "Five Centuries of Book Design: A Survey of Styles in the Columbia Library." *Columbia University Quarterly* XXIII (June 1931): 176–198.

Lemire, Eugene. "A Note on Morris's Western Outlet." *News from Anywhere* No. 10 (November 1968): 14–15.

Levison, Lois C. "A Maker of Books." *Quarto Club Papers* II (1927-1928): 3–20.

Lewis, Oscar. "The California School of Printing." *Colophon* Part 3 (September 1930): unpaged.

_____. "Fine Printing in the Far West." *Publishers Weekly* CIX (March 20, 1926): 1051–1055.

Life, Allan R. "Illustration and Morris' Ideal Book." *Victorian Poetry* XIII (Autumn–Winter 1975): 131–140.

"Literary and Trade Notes." *Publishers Weekly* XLV (February 17, 1894): 332–333.

"Literary Gossip." *Athenaeum* No. 3281 (September 13, 1890): 355.

"Literary Gossip." *Athenaeum* No. 3304 (February 21, 1891): 252.

"Literary Gossip." *Athenaeum* No. 3310 (April 4, 1891): 442.

Lockhart, Adelaide B. "The H. M. Marvin Bruce Rogers Collection." *Yale University Library Gazette* XXXV (October 1960): 53–60.

Mackay, A. F. "Better Books for 'The Trade.'" *Printing Art* II (November 1903): 81–88.

[McMurtrie, Douglas C.]. "Editorial Comment." *Ars Typographica* II (October 1925): 175–178.

McPharlin, Paul. "The Cranbrook Press." *Dolphin* No. 4 (Spring 1941): 268–278.

_____. "Crawhall's Chap-Book Chaplets, 1883." *Publishers Weekly* CXLII (November 7, 1942): 1965–1970.

McQuilken, A. H. "Will H. Bradley and His Work." *Inland Printer* XIV (February 1895): 430–433.

"A Maker of Beautiful Books." *Literary Miscellany* II (Autumn, 1909): 57–58.

Marillier, H. C. "The Vale Press and the Modern Revival of Printing." *Pall Mall Magazine* XXII (October 1900): 179–190.

Melcher, Frederic G. "An Evening with Updike." *Printing and Graphic Arts* VI (February 1958): 33–35.

Mencken, Henry Louis. "On Breaking into Type." *Colophon* Part I (February 1930): unpaged.

Menzies, William G. "The Present Value of the Publications of the Kelmscott Press." *Connoisseur* XII (1905): 42–44.

Mills, T. L. "William Morris and the Kelmscott Press." *Inland Printer* XVIII (December 1896): 299–301.

"Modern Typography." *Times Literary Supplement Printing Number* (October 13, 1927): 3–10.

Moran, James. "Stanley Morison: 1889-1967." *Monotype Recorder* XLIII (Autumn 1968): 1–32.

"More News from Nowhere." *Times Literary Supplement* LXVI (March 16, 1961): 214.

Morey, Charles R. "Mediaeval Art and America." *Journal of the Warburg and Courtauld Institutes* VII (January–June 1944): 1–6.

"Morris's 'Story of the Glittering Plain.'" *Critic* XIX

(N.S. XVI) (November 29, 1891): 298.

Nash, Ray. "Notes on the Riverside Press and D. B. Updike." *Gutenberg-Jahrbuch* XXXV (1960): 329-333.

"A New Era in English Printing." *Inland Printer* X (March 1893): 518.

"A New Publishing Firm: Copeland & Day." *Publishers Weekly* XLIV (December 2, 1893): 927.

Newdigate, Bernard H. "Book Production Notes: Mr. Bruce Rogers and His Printed Books." *London Mercury* III (April 1921): 649-650.

["Note"]. *Critic* XX (N.S. XVII) (March 19, 1892): 168.

["Note"]. *Printing World* I (February 25, 1891): 59

["Note"]. *Critic* XVIII (N.S. XV) (February 28, 1891): 117.

Orcutt, William Dana. "American Low-Cost Volumes." *Times Literary Supplement Printing Number* (October 13, 1927): 56-62.

———. "Frederick Holland Day." *Publishers Weekly* CXXV (January 6, 1934): 51-54.

"Original Initial Designs by F. W. Goudy, Chicago." *Inland Printer* XVII (April 1896): 92; (May 1896): 204; (June 1896): 313.

"The Passing of the Bibelot." *American Book-Lore* I (June 1898): 8-11.

"Passing of the Freak Magazine." *Printer and Bookmaker* XXV (January 1898): 280.

Paul, C. Kegan. "The Production and Life of Books." *Fortnightly Review* XXXIX (April 1, 1883): 485-499.

[Pennell, Elizabeth Robins]. "The Kelmscott Chaucer." *Nation* LXIII (September 3, 1896): 173-174.

[———]. "N. N." "The Kelmscott Press." *Nation* LVI (March 16, 1893): 196-197.

———. "Some Memories of William Morris." *Magazine of Art* (February 1920): 124-127.

———. "William Ernest Henley: Lover of the Art of Bookmaking." *Colophon* Part V (March 1931): unpaged.

[———]. "N.N." "William Morris and the Arts and Crafts in London." *Nation* LXIX (October 26, 1899): 313-315.

Phelps, Soule. "Rollins at Montague." *Print* II (May-June 1941): 44-46.

"The Poet, William Morris." *British Printer* IV (November-December 1891): 48.

Pollard, Alfred W. "Private Presses and Their Influence on the Art of Printing." *Ars Typographica* I (Autumn 1934): 36-42.

———. "Reminiscences of an Amateur Book-Builder." *Colophon* Part 4 (December 1930): unpaged.

———. "The Work of Bruce Rogers, Printer." *Transactions of the Bibliographical Society* XIV (1919): 9-22.

Priestman, Mable Tuke. "History of the Arts and Crafts Movement in America." *House Beautiful* XX (October 1906): 15-16, (November 1906): 14-16.

"Progressive Type Making." *Typographic Advertiser* XLI (October 1896): 10.

Rae, Frank B., Jr. "Setters of Types." *Impressions Quarterly* III (March 1902): unpaged.

Randall, David A. "Bruce Rogers' First Decorated Book." *Papers of the Bibliographical Society of America* LV (First quarter 1961): 10-42.

———. "Waverley in America." *Colophon* N.S. I (Summer 1935): 39-55.

Ransom, Will. "Collectors' Presses." *Book-Collector's Packet* II (June 1938): 5-7.

"Recent Books of Fiction." *Dial* XII (December 1891): 275.

"Recent Fiction." *Nation* LIII (December 17, 1891): 470-472.

"Recent Type Designs." *Inland Printer* XIV (March 1895): 574.

[Review of *American Book Clubs* by A. Growoll]. *Nation* LXVI (March 3, 1898): 173.

Richardson, Charles F. "Kelmscott Press Work and Other Recent Printing." *Bookman* IV (November 1896): 216-217.

Ridler, Vivian. "Artistic Printing: A Search for Principles." *Alphabet and Image* No. 6 (January 1948): 4-17.

Rigby, J. Scarratt, "Remarks on Morris Work and Its Influence on British Decorative Arts of To-Day." *Art Workers' Quarterly* I (January-April 1902): 2-5, 61-64.

Rollins, Carl Purington. "The Compleat Collector." *Saturday Review of Literature* XI (September 29, 1934): 151.

———. "The Golden Age of American Printing." *New Colophon* II (September 1949): 299-303.

———. "Modern 'Special' Types." *Printing Art* I (March 1903): 13-18.

———. "Morris's Typographical Adventure." *Printing and Graphic Arts* VI (June 1958): 29-32.

———. "Since Gutenberg: Notes Commemorating Three Notable Anniversaries: Part II, 1800-1940." *Print* I (September 1940): 42-60.

———. "Theodore Low De Vinne." *Signature* N.S. (1950): 3-21.

"The Roycroft Printing Shop." *Printer and Bookmaker* XXV (November 1897): 152.

"The Roycrofters of East Aurora." *American Bulletin* No. 4 (August 1910): 1.

"Rubricated Book Pages." *Printing Art* II (February 1904): 173-180.

Schmutzler, Robert. "Blake and Art Nouveau." *Architectural Review* CXVIII (August 1955): 90-97.

———. "The English Origins of Art Nouveau." *Architectural Review* CXVII (February 1955): 108-116.

Schwarz, Philip John. "Will Ransom: The Early Years." *Journal of Library History* III (April 1968): 138-155.

"The Sense of Order." *Times Literary Supplement*

XLVII (March 20, 1948): 168.

S[hand], J[ames]. "De Vinne." *Typography* V (Spring 1938): 30.

Sharp, William. "William Morris: The Man and His Work." *Atlantic Monthly* LXXVIII (December 1896): 768-781.

Sherman, Frederic Fairchild. "Private and Special Presses in England." *Book Buyer* XXIII (1901): 21-25.

Siberell, Lloyd Emerson. "Chillicothe's Dard Hunter." *Book Collector's Packet* II (July 1938): 1-3.

Sills, R. Malcolm. "W. J. Linton at Yale—The Appledore Private Press." *Yale University Library Gazette* XII (January 1938): 43-52.

Singleton, Frederick T. "Will Bradley: Printer." *Printer and Bookmaker* XXVI (June 1898): 184-186.

———. "Will Bradley: Turn of the Century Renovator of American Typography and Decorative Art." *American Printer* CIII (August 1936): 13-17.

"Small, Maynard & Co. Acquire Copeland & Day's List." *Publishers Weekly* LVI (July 15, 1899): 125.

"Some Recent Publications." *Publishers Weekly* XL (November 7, 1891): 686.

Spatt, Hartley S. "William Morris and the Uses of the Past." *Victorian Poetry* XIII (Autumn–Winter, 1975): 1-9.

"Specimens from the Merrymount Press." *Inland Printer* XVII (May 1896): 188.

Standard, Paul. "D. B. Updike: The Merrymount Press." *Penrose Annual* XXXVIII (1936): 17-22.

———. "The Libraries Men Live By. I. A Printer's Library." *Dolphin* IV (Fall 1940): 41-47.

Steinhardt, Maxwell. "An Appreciation of Mosher." *Quarto Club Papers* I (1926-1927): 45-54.

Stevens, Edward F. "The Kelmscott Influence in Maine." *Colby Library Quarterly* Series I (March 1944): 92-95.

Stevens, Thomas Wood. "On Some American Book-Makers." *Bibliographical Society of Chicago Year-Book* II (1900-1901): 25-31.

Stillwell, Margaret Bingham. "The Heritage of the Modern Printer." *Bulletin of the New York Public Library* XX (October 1916): 737-750.

"Stone & Kimball of Cambridge, Mass. and Chicago, Ill.." *Publishers Weekly* LXIV (September 9, 1893): 311.

Sturgis, Russell. "The Art of William Morris." *Architectural Record* VII (April–June, 1898): 441-461.

[———]. "The Art of William Morris." *Nation* LXVI (February 10, 1898): 111-112.

———. "The Ornamentation of Books." *Independent* L (December 15, 1898): 1737-1739.

Swift, Lindsay. "The Value of Precedent in Printing." *Printing Art* I (April 1903): 32-34.

Symons, A. J. A. "An Unacknowledged Movement in Fine Printing: The Typography of the Eighteen-Nineties." *Fleuron* VII (1930): 83-119.

Tanselle, G. Thomas. "Legler's American Book-Lore." *Gutenberg-Jahrbuch* XLIV (1969): 331-334.

Thompson, Susan Otis. "A 'Golden Age' in American Printing." *Columbia Library Columns* XXII (February 1973): 22-33.

"Trade News and Notes." *Printing World* I (October 25, 1891): 322.

[Turnure, Arthur B.]. "Book Titles." *Art Age* I (October 1883): 17-18.

[———]. "A Cluny for Bookmakers." *Art Age* I (January 1884): 57-58.

[———]. "Decline of the Limited Edition." *Art Age* IV (December 1886): 77.

[———]. "Future American Bookmaking." *Art Age* I (April 1884): 97-98.

[———]. "Its Printing." *Art Age* III (January 1886): 95.

[———]. "Limited Editions." *Art Age* I (May 1883): 9-10.

[———]. "Preface." *Art Age* I (April 1883): 1-2.

Twose, George M. R. "William Morris: His Work and His Life." *Dial* XXV (November 16, 1898): 343-346.

Underwood, John Curtis. [Review of *War Is Kind*]. *Bookman* IX (July 1899): 466-467.

Updike, Daniel Berkeley. "The De Vinne Press." *Literary Review* (January 20, 1923): 405-406.

———. "Thomas Maitland Cleland." *Fleuron* VII (1930): 133-142.

"The Use of Decorative Initials." *Printing Art* I (May 1903): 75-76.

Valentine, K. B. "Motifs from Nature in the Design Work and Prose Romances of William Morris, 1876-1896." *Victorian Poetry* XIII (Autumn–Winter 1975): 83-89.

"Victorian Virtuosi." *Heidelberg News* XVI (December 1968): 1-6.

"W. Irving Way." *Inland Printer* XVII (April 1896): 67.

[Warde, Beatrice]. "Fine Printing: Mr. Bruce Rogers and the 'Monotype' Machine." *Monotype Recorder* XXII (January–February 1924): 7-10.

[———]. "'I Am a Communicator.'" *Monotype Recorder* XLIV (Autumn 1970): 1-60.

[———]. "Paul Beaujon." [Review of *The Nonesuch Century*] *Signature* No. 3 (July 1936): 48.

Way, W. Irving. "Arts and Crafts Essays." *Inland Printer* XII (December 1893): 205-206.

———. "Bibliophilism in Chicago." *Book-Lovers Almanac* I (1893): unpaged.

———. "Book-Cover and Title-Page Designing." *Inland Printer* XII (January 1894): 291-293 (February 1894): 369-371.

[———], "Irving." "Books, Authors, and Kindred Subjects." *Inland Printer* IX (July 1892): 871-872.

[———], "Irving." "Books, Authors, and Kindred Subjects." *Inland Printer* XIII (July 1894): 331-333.

[_____], "Irving." "Books, Authors, and Kindred Subjects." *Inland Printer* XIV (January 1895): 345-346.

[_____], "Irving." "Books, Authors, and Kindred Subjects." *Inland Printer* XIV (March 1895): 547-549.

_____. "Eugene Field—Francis Wilson—R. M. Field." *Inland Printer* IX (April 1892): 581-584.

_____. "The Riverside Press and Mr. Bruce Rogers." *Inland Printer* XXVI (November 1900): 264-267.

_____. "A Visit to William Morris." *Modern Art* IV (July 1, 1896): 78-81.

_____. "William Morris and the Kelmscott Press." *Inland Printer* XI (June 1893): 213-215; (July 1893): 301-303.

"Weekly Record." *Publishers Weekly* XL (October 24, 1891): 627.

Weiss, Harry B. "The Miniature Books of William Lewis Washburn." *Book Collector's Packet* III (September 1938): 20-22.

Wells, Carolyn. "What a Lark!" *Colophon* Part 8 (December 1931): unpaged.

Wells, James M., ed. "Letters from Bruce Rogers to Henry Watson Kent." *Printing and Graphic Arts* III (February, May, September 1955): 1-15, 38-49, 61-78, and IV (February, May, September 1956): 19-26, 46-49, 64-81.

Whetton, H. "American *Versus* British Printing." *Penrose Annual* II (1896): 105-108.

"William Morris." *Inland Printer* XVIII (November 1896): 157.

"William Morris and His Work." *American Architect and Building News* LIV (October 24, 1896): 29.

"William Morris's Influence on Good Book-Making." *Publishers Weekly* L (November 14, 1896): 830-832.

"William S. Hadaway." *Bradley: His Book* II (January 1897): 90-92.

Winship, George Parker. "Recollections of a Private Printer." *Colophon* N.S. III (Spring, 1938): 210-224.

Winslow, W. Henry. "William Morris the Artist." *New England Magazine* N.S. XVI (April 1897): 161-177.

Woods, L. H. "Prospects of Printing as a Fine Art: From an Englishman's Point of View." *American Bookmaker* XVII (November 1893): 139-140.

MANUSCRIPTS

Bullen, Henry Lewis. Letter to John Henry Nash, March 21, 1930. Typographic Library Manuscripts Collection, Columbia University Libraries.

_____. Letter to John Henry Nash, April 2, 1930. Typographic Library Manuscripts Collection, Columbia University Libraries.

Dunlap, Joseph R. "The Road to Kelmscott." D.L.S. dissertation, School of Library Service, Columbia University, 1972.

Gilliss, Walter. Letter to Henry Lewis Bullen, September 10, 1921. Typographic Library Manuscripts Collection, Columbia University Libraries.

Jones, Thomas S., Jr. Letter to Hellmut Lehmann-Haupt, January 29, 1931. Xerox copy in Book Arts Press Specimens, Columbia University Libraries.

Kraus, Joe Walker. "A History of Copeland & Day (1839-1899); With a Bibliographical Checklist of Their Publications." M.A.L.S. thesis, University of Illinois, 1941.

Lamb, J. & R., Ecclesiastical Art Workers. Letter to Roberts Brothers, November 13, 1891. Roberts Brothers Manuscripts Collection, Columbia University Libraries.

Mosher, Thomas Bird. Letter to Edmund Clarence Stedman, April 13, 1893. Stedman Manuscripts Collection, Columbia University Libraries.

_____. Letter to Edmund Clarence Stedman, January 21, 1894. Stedman Manuscripts Collection, Columbia University Libraries.

_____. Letter to Edmund Clarence Stedman, April 22, 1895. Stedman Manuscripts Collection, Columbia University Libraries.

_____. Letter to Edmund Clarence Stedman, September 17, 1895. Stedman Manuscripts Collection, Columbia University Libraries.

Nash, John Henry. Letter to Henry Lewis Bullen, March 28, 1930. Typographic Library Manuscripts Collection, Columbia University Libraries.

Ransom, Will. Letter to Porter Garnett, April 4, 1923. Laboratory Press Manuscripts Collection, Columbia University Libraries.

Rogers, Bruce, "The Firt Q[uarter] C[entury]." Manuscript, undated, Victor H. Borsodi Collection, New York City.

_____. Letter to Henry Lewis Bullen, October 7, 1910. Typographic Library Manuscripts Collection, Columbia University Libraries.

_____. Letter to Henry Lewis Bullen, November 4, 1916. Typographic Library Manuscripts Collection, Columbia University Libraries.

_____. Letter to Henry Lewis Bullen, March 28, 1919. Typographic Library Manuscripts Collection, Columbia University Libraries.

Weinstein, Frederic D. "Walter Crane and the American Book Arts, 1880-1915." D.L.S. dissertation, School of Library Service, Columbia University, 1970.

INDEX

254

Credits

Books owned by Columbia University Libraries: Plates 1, 2, 3, 4, 6, 7, 8, 9, 10, 14, 15, 16, 18, 19, 20, 21, 27, 29, 30, 31, 32, 33, 34, 35, 38, 39, 40, 41, 43, 44, 52, 53, 55, 65, 66, 67, 68, 69, 70, 71, 72, 73, 78, 79, 80, 81, 83, 84, 89, 95, 107, 108, 109

Books owned by Susan O. Thompson: Plates 12, 17, 26, 36, 42, 46, 47, 49, 57, 58, 59, 61, 62, 63, 64, 74, 75, 76, 77, 85, 86, 87, 88, 90, 91, 92, 93, 94, 96, 98, 99, 100, 101, 102, 103, 104, 106, 110

Books owned by Joseph R. Dunlap: Plates 13, 22, 23, 24, 25, 28, 45, 48, 50, 51, 54, 56, 60, 105.

Book owned by City College, City University of New York, Library: Plate 5

Book owned by Thomas L. Sloan: Plate 11

Book owned by Princeton University Library: Plate 37

Book owned by Eleanor McDowell Thompson: Plate 82

Book owned by Robert Judson Clark: Plate 97

Book owned by Sandra Markham: Plate 111

Photographs by Philip Grushkin: Plates 1, 4, 9, 12, 13, 15, 16, 17, 18, 19, 20, 21, 22, 23, 26, 27, 28, 29, 30, 33, 34, 35, 36, 38, 39, 40, 41, 42, 43, 44, 45, 46, 47, 48, 49, 52, 54, 55, 56, 57, 58, 59, 60, 61, 62, 63, 64, 65, 66, 67, 68, 69, 70, 71, 72, 73, 74, 75, 76, 77, 78, 79, 80, 81, 84, 85, 87, 88, 89, 90, 91, 93, 95, 96, 98, 99, 100, 101, 102, 104, 106, 107, 109, 110, 111

Photographs by Columbia University Photographic Services: Plates 2, 3, 5, 6, 7, 10, 14, 24, 25, 31, 32, 50, 51, 53, 83, 86, 92, 103, 105, 108

Photographs by Princeton Art Museum: Plates 8, 11, 37, 82, 94, 97